# INUYAROKU SS

## maison de ayakashi

# 3

Welcome to Maison de Ayakashi.
The exclusive Secret Service of
this Mansion guarantees
your mental and physical
safety by providing
superior escorts.

# Contents



inuboku secret service

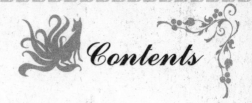

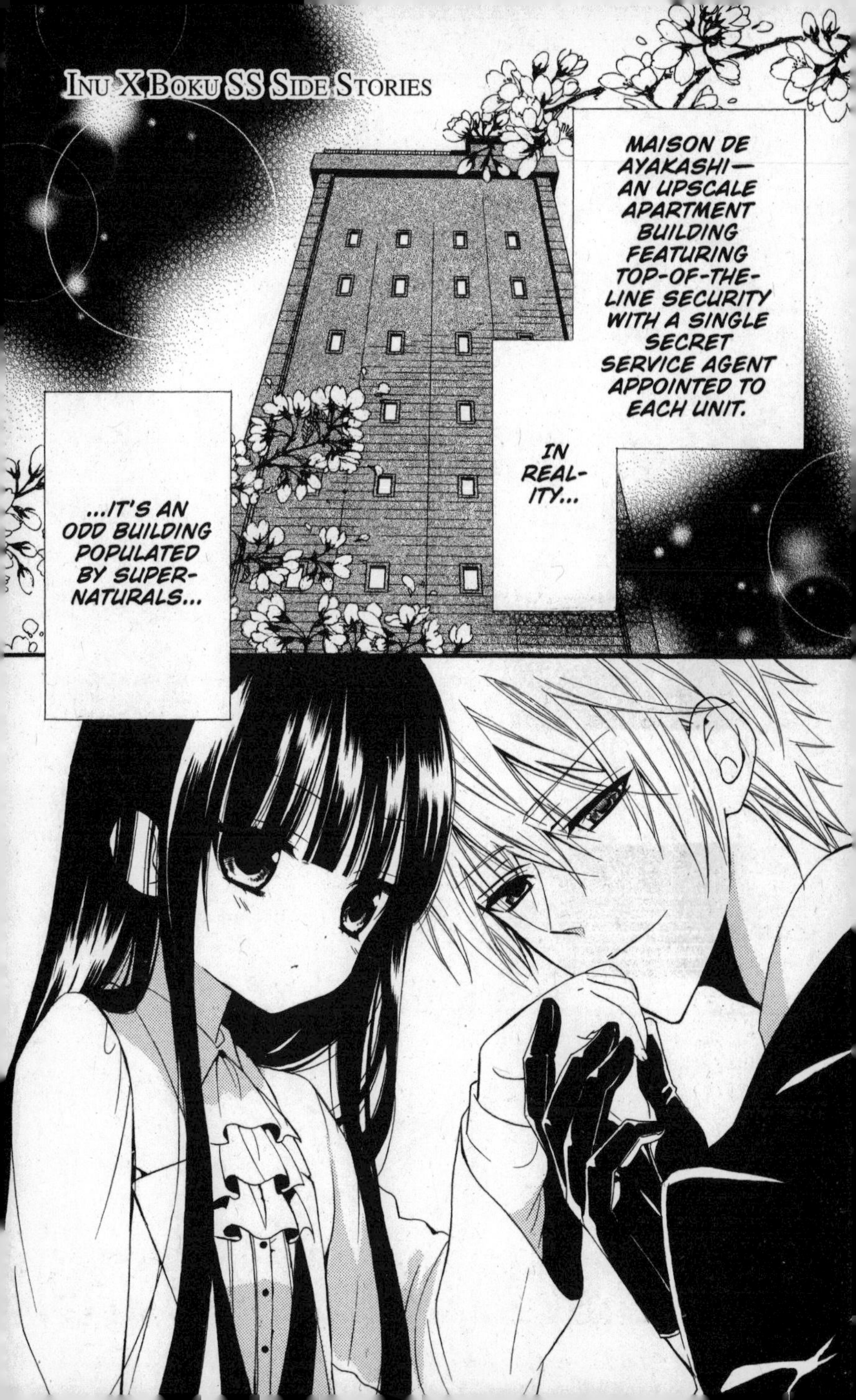
MAISON DE AYAKASHI— AN UPSCALE APARTMENT BUILDING FEATURING TOP-OF-THE-LINE SECURITY WITH A SINGLE SECRET SERVICE AGENT APPOINTED TO EACH UNIT.
IN REAL-ITY...
...IT'S AN ODD BUILDING POPULATED BY SUPER-NATURALS...

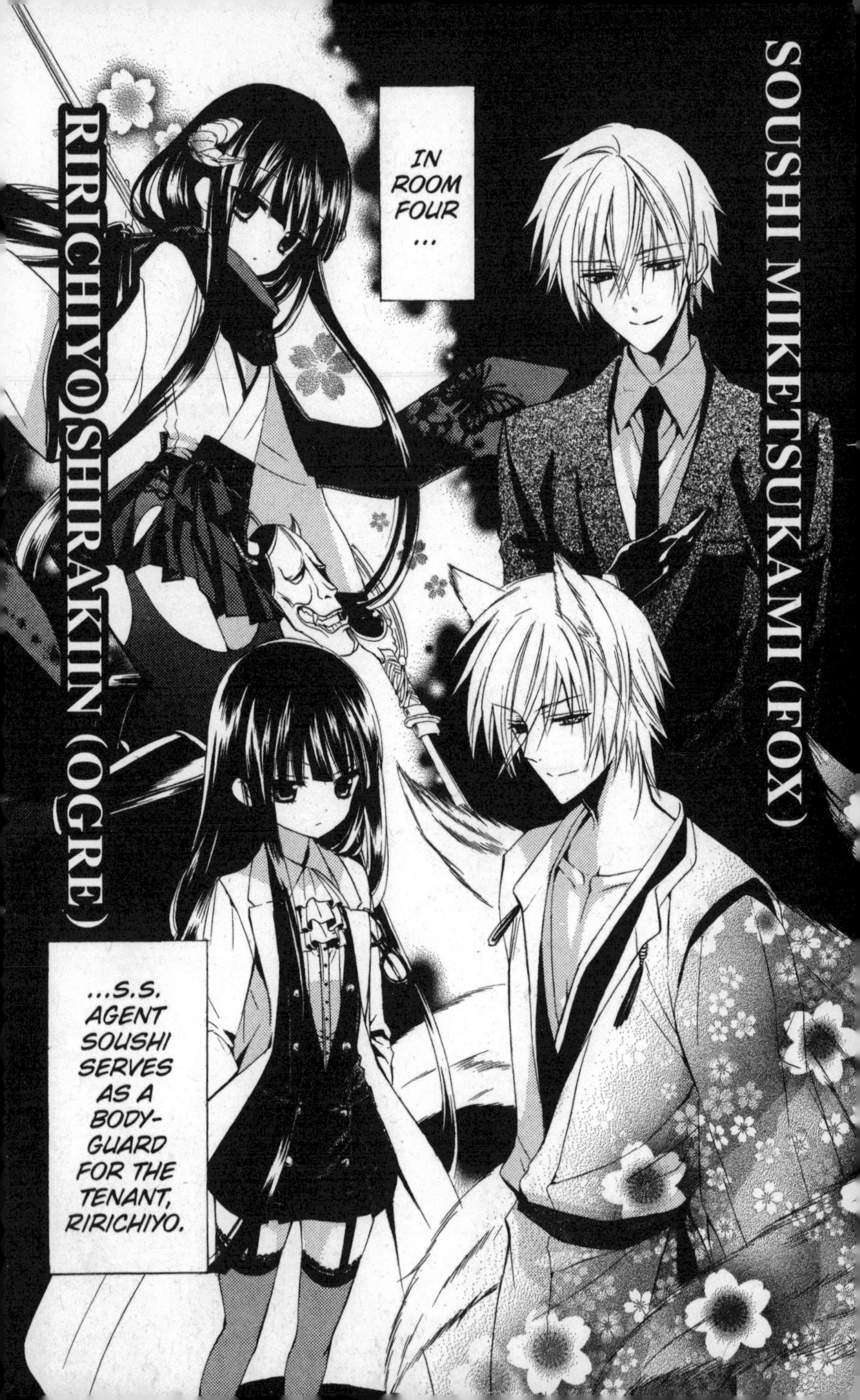
SOUSHI MIKETSUKAMI (FOX)
IN ROOM FOUR ...
RIRICHIYO SHIRAKIIN (OGRE)
...S.S. AGENT SOUSHI SERVES AS A BODY-GUARD FOR THE TENANT, RIRICHIYO.

# RIRICHIYO AND SOUSHI

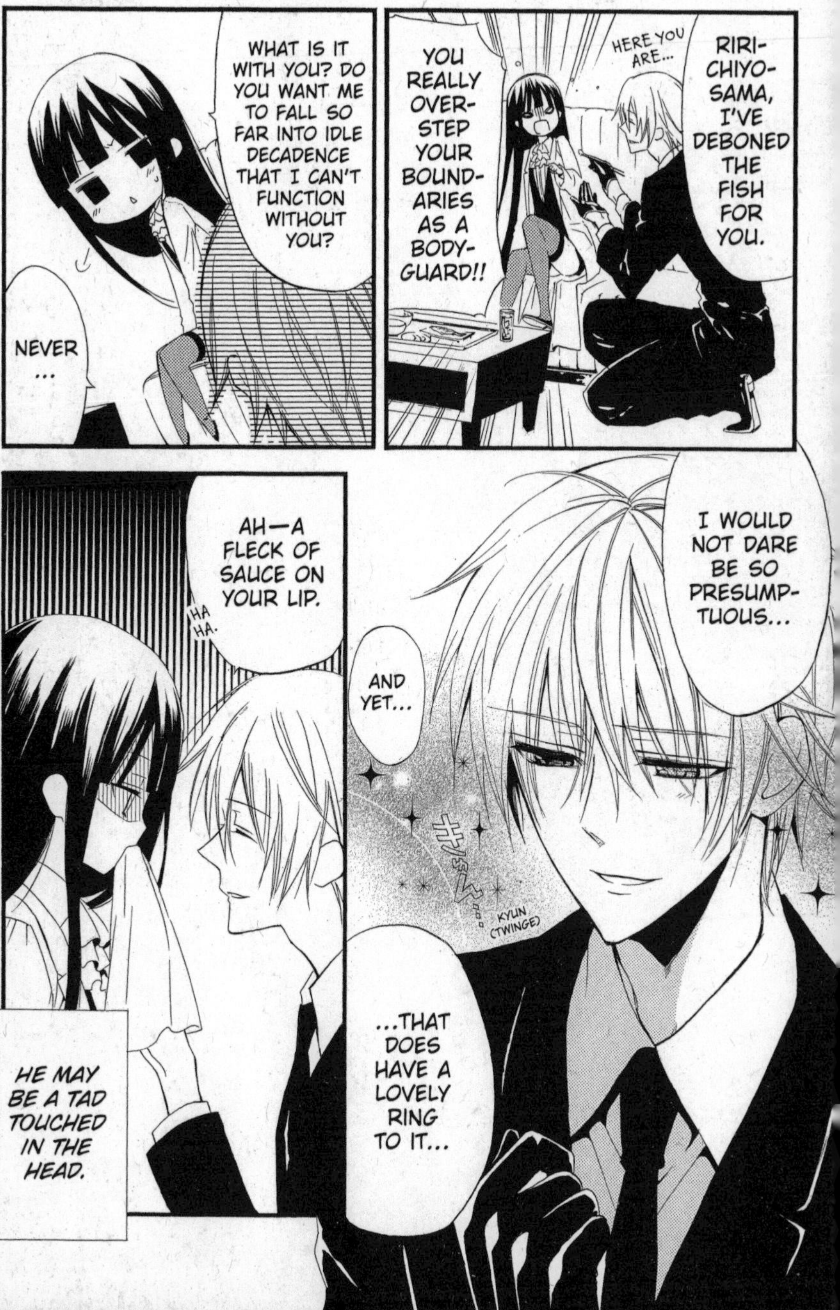
RIRI-CHIYO-SAMA, I'VE DEBONED THE FISH FOR YOU.
HERE YOU ARE...
YOU REALLY OVER-STEP YOUR BOUND-ARIES AS A BODY-GUARD!!
WHAT IS IT WITH YOU? DO YOU WANT ME TO FALL SO FAR INTO IDLE DECADENCE THAT I CAN'T FUNCTION WITHOUT YOU?
NEVER...
I WOULD NOT DARE BE SO PRESUMP-TUOUS...
AND YET...
KYUN (TWINGE)
...THAT DOES HAVE A LOVELY RING TO IT...
AH—A FLECK OF SAUCE ON YOUR LIP.
HA HA.
HE MAY BE A TAD TOUCHED IN THE HEAD.

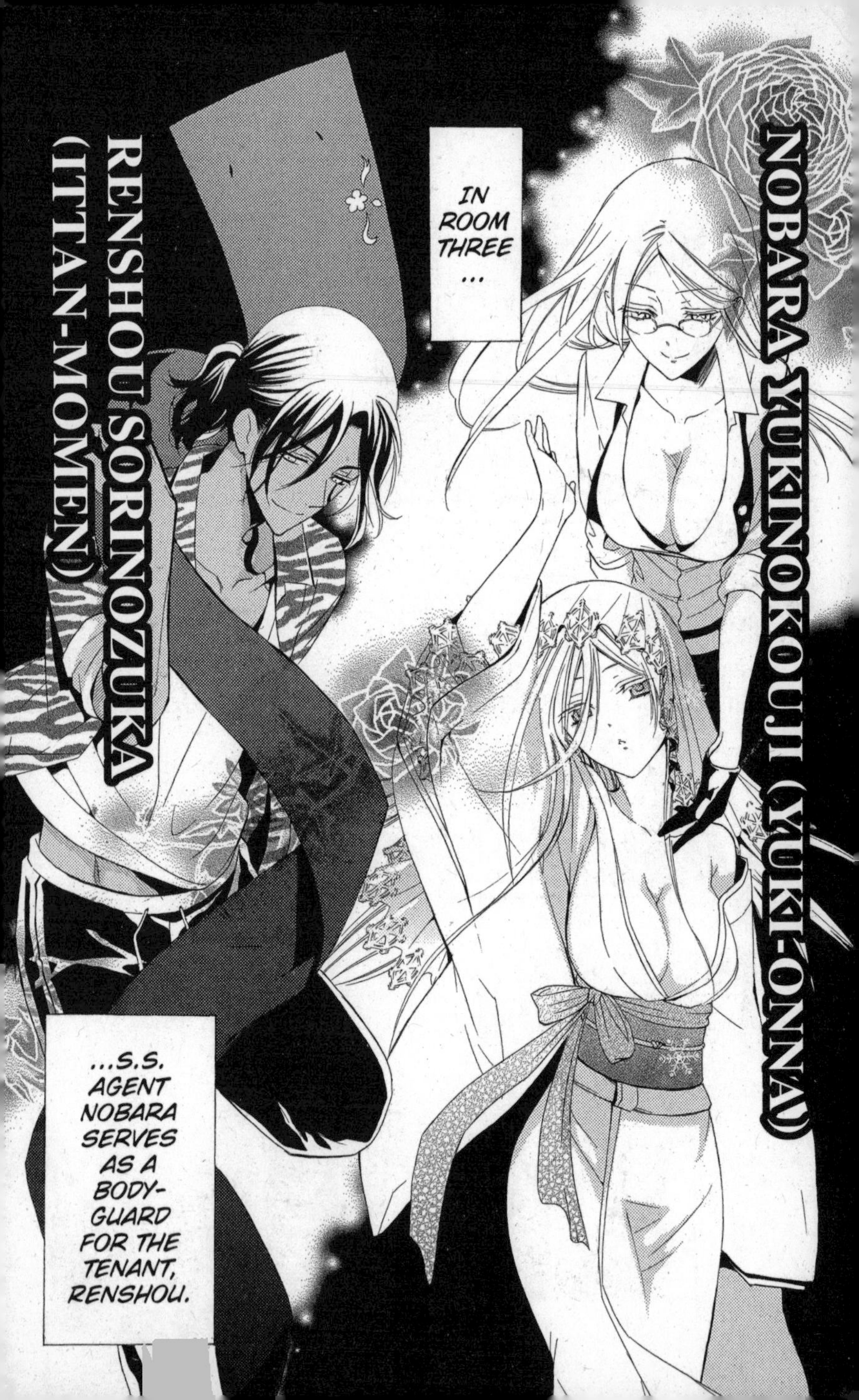
NOBARA YUKINOKOUJI (YUKI-ONNA)
IN ROOM THREE ...
RENSHOU SORINOZUKA (ITTAN-MOMEN)
...S.S. AGENT NOBARA SERVES AS A BODY-GUARD FOR THE TENANT, RENSHOU.

# NOBARA AND RENSHOU

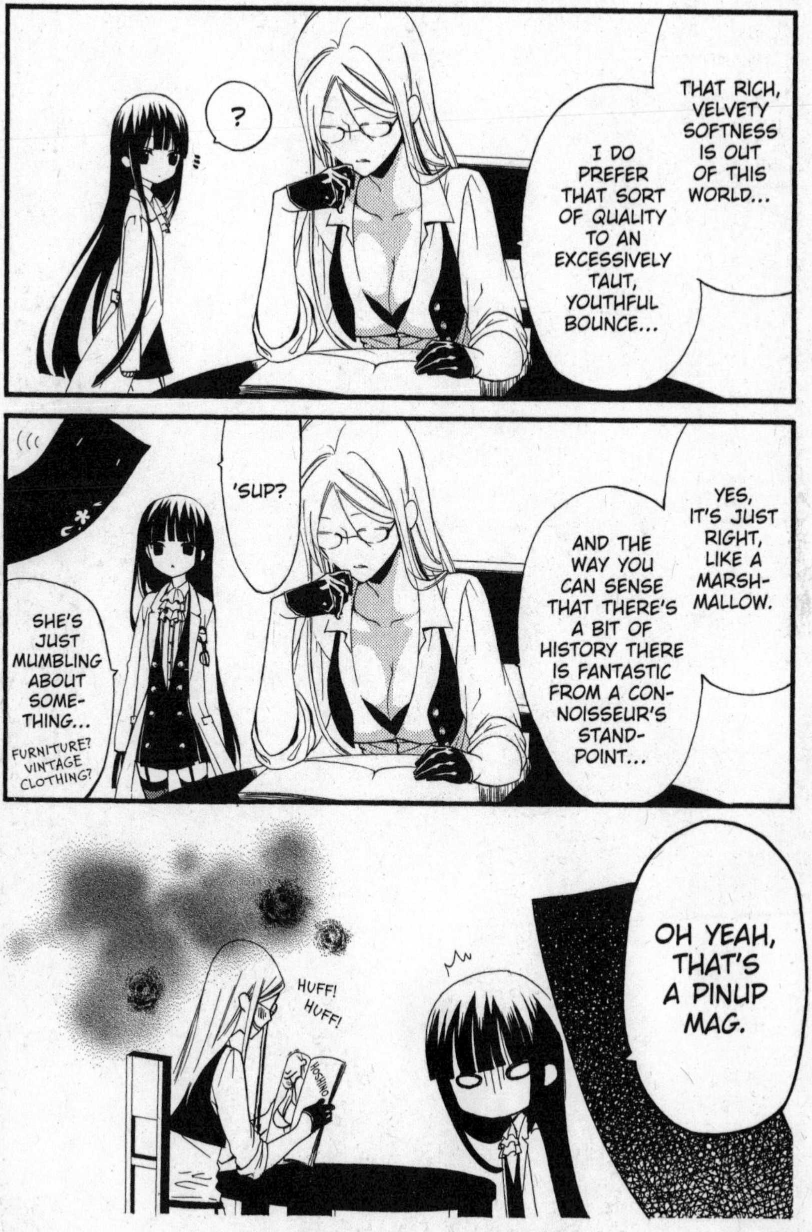
THAT RICH, VELVETY SOFTNESS IS OUT OF THIS WORLD...
I DO PREFER THAT SORT OF QUALITY TO AN EXCESSIVELY TAUT, YOUTHFUL BOUNCE...
?
YES, IT'S JUST RIGHT, LIKE A MARSH-MALLOW.
AND THE WAY YOU CAN SENSE THAT THERE'S A BIT OF HISTORY THERE IS FANTASTIC FROM A CON-NOISSEUR'S STAND-POINT...
'SUP?
SHE'S JUST MUMBLING ABOUT SOME-THING...
FURNITURE? VINTAGE CLOTHING?
OH YEAH, THAT'S A PINUP MAG.
HUFF! HUFF!
HOSHINO

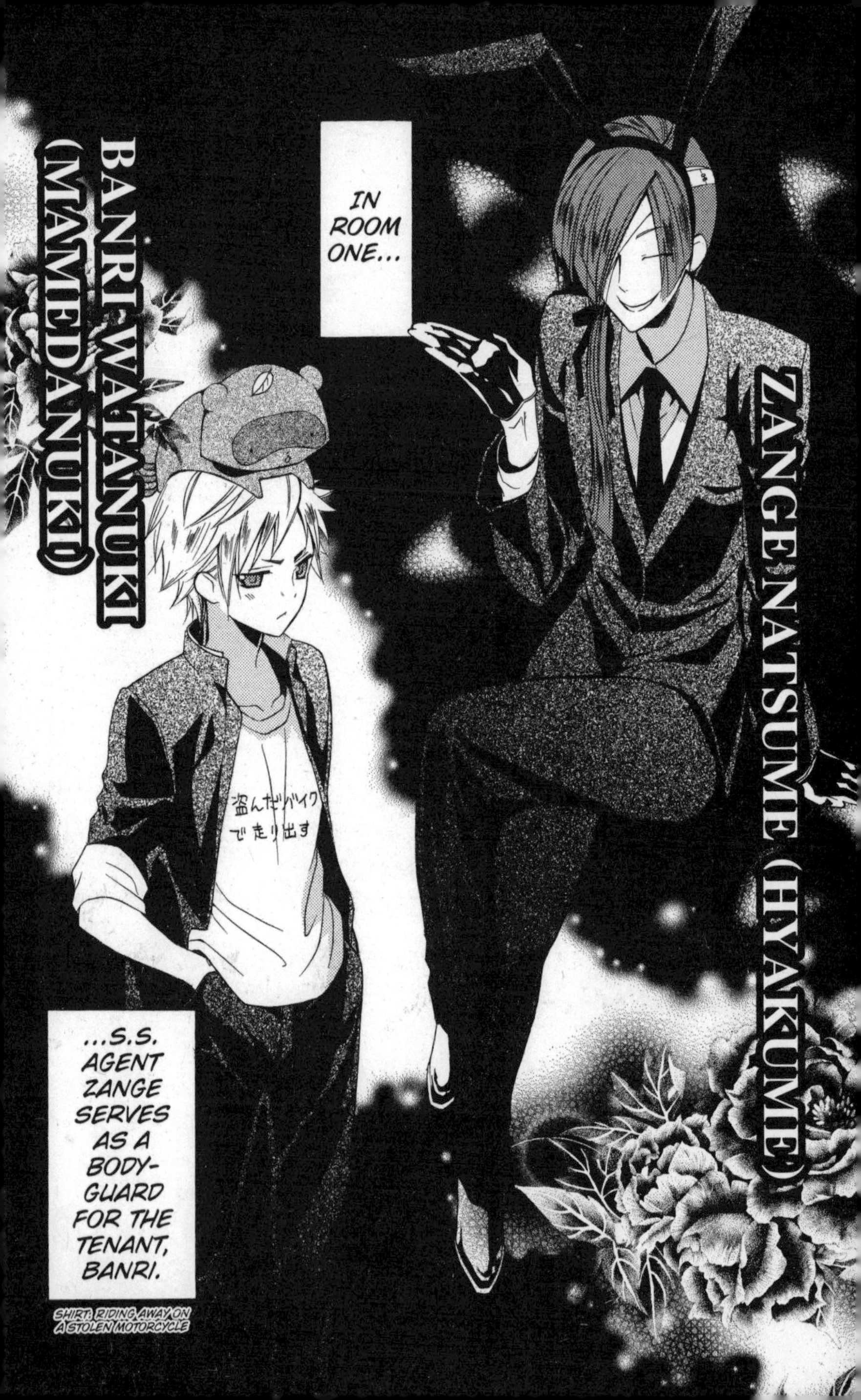
IN ROOM ONE...
ZANGE NATSUME (HYAKUME)
BANRI WATANUKI (MAMEDANUKI)
盗んだバイクで走り出す
...S.S. AGENT ZANGE SERVES AS A BODY-GUARD FOR THE TENANT, BANRI.
SHIRT: RIDING AWAY ON A STOLEN MOTORCYCLE

# ZANGE AND BANRI

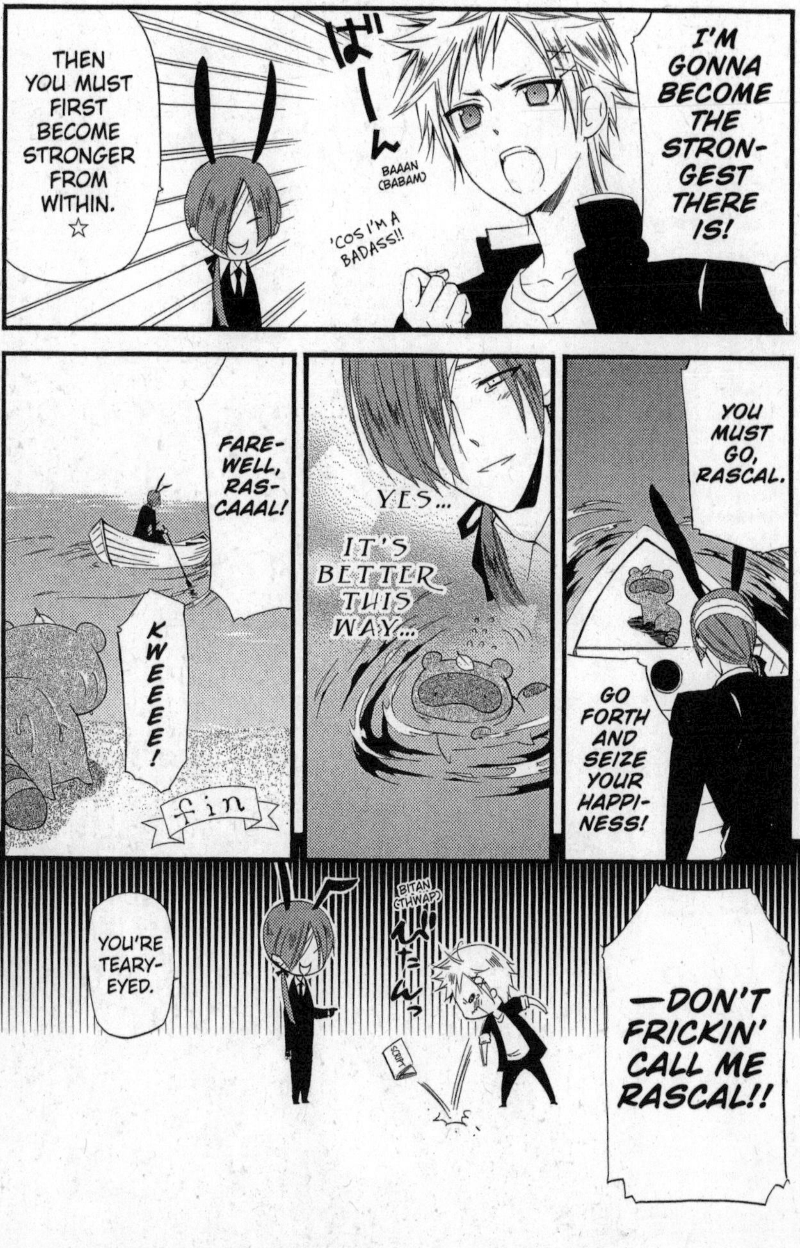
I'M GONNA BECOME THE STRON-GEST THERE IS!
ばーん
BAAAN (BABAM)
'COS I'M A BADASS!!
THEN YOU MUST FIRST BECOME STRONGER FROM WITHIN. ☆
YOU MUST GO, RASCAL.
GO FORTH AND SEIZE YOUR HAPPI-NESS!
YES...
IT'S BETTER THIS WAY...
FARE-WELL, RAS-CAAAL!
KWEEEEE!
fin
—DON'T FRICKIN' CALL ME RASCAL!!
びたんっ
BITAN (THWAP)
SCRIPT
YOU'RE TEARY-EYED.

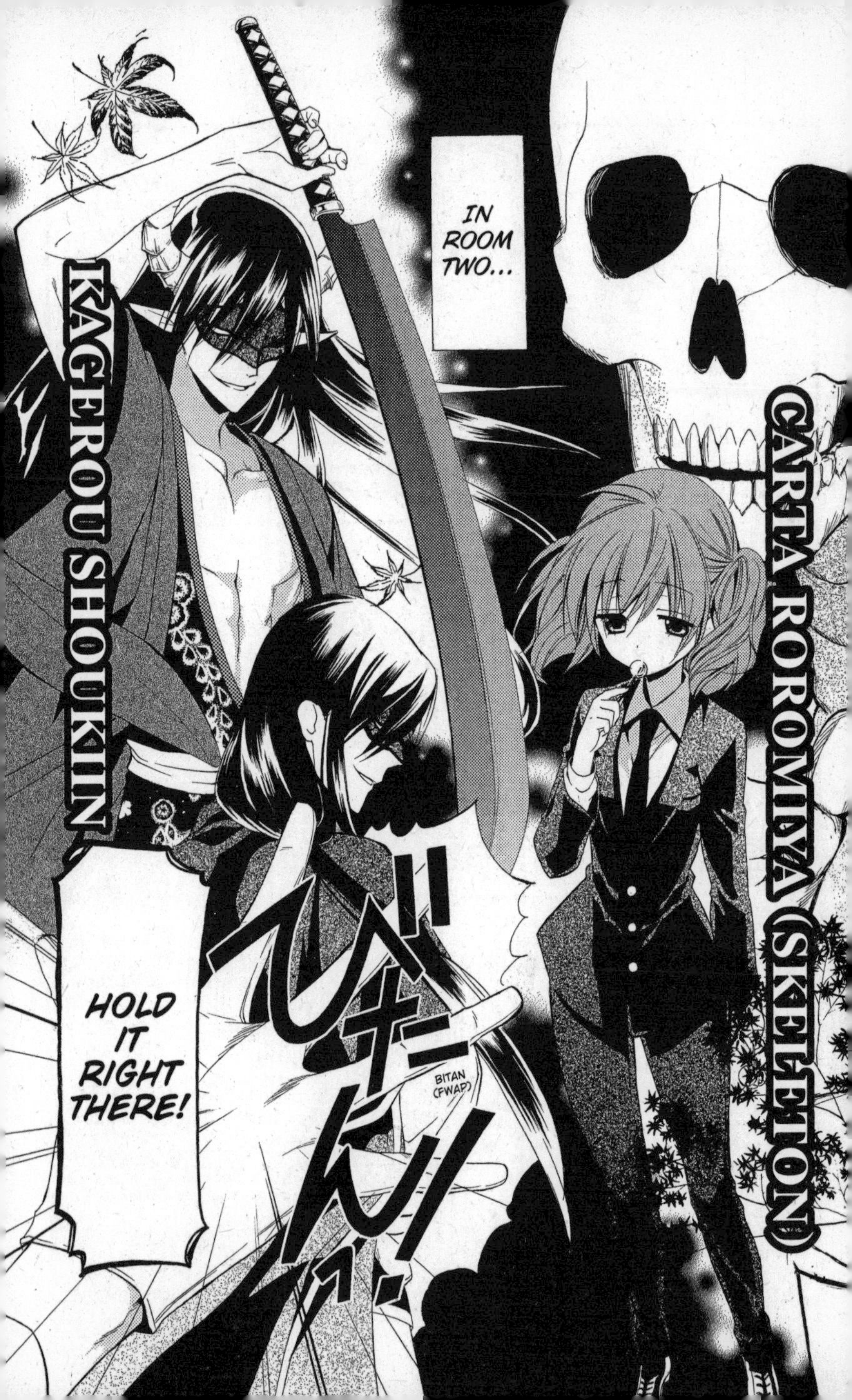
IN ROOM TWO...
CARTA ROROMIYA (SKELETON)
KAGEROU SHOUKIN
BITAN (FWAP)
HOLD IT RIGHT THERE!

# CARTA AND KAGEROU

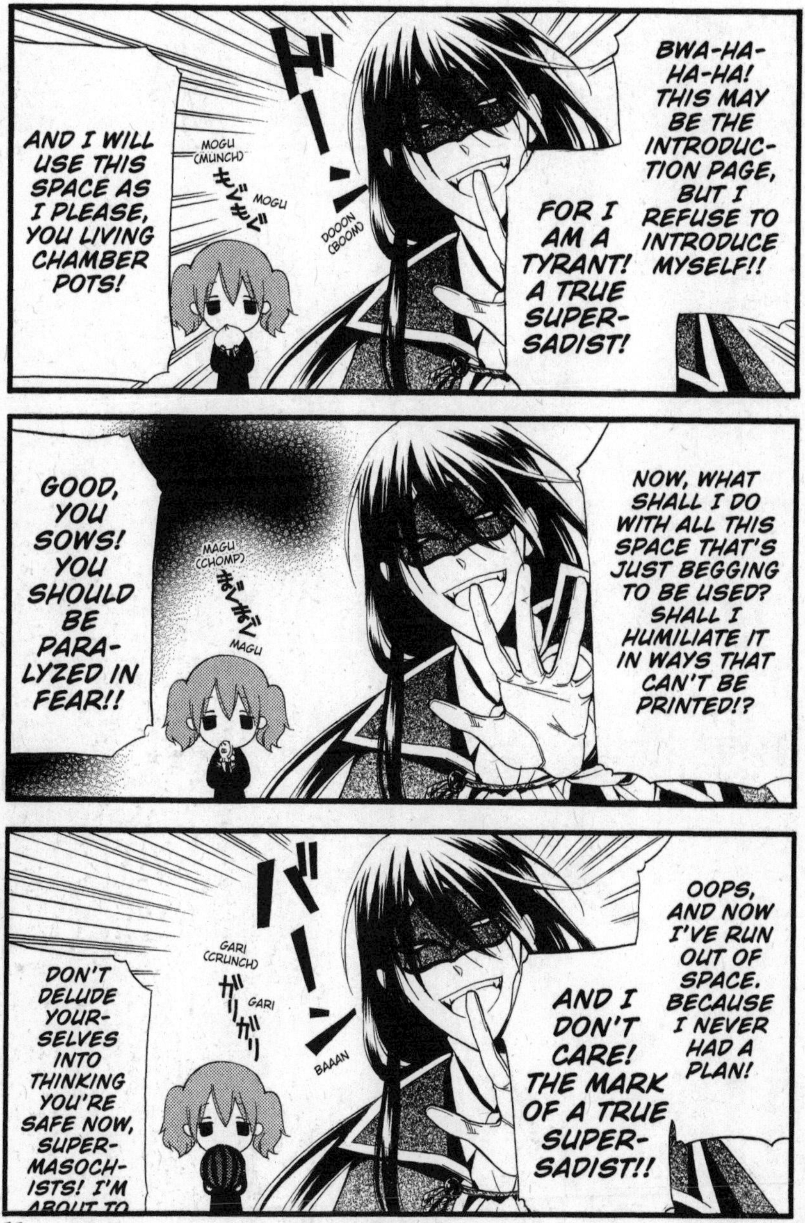
BWA-HA-HA-HA! THIS MAY BE THE INTRODUCTION PAGE, BUT I REFUSE TO INTRODUCE MYSELF!!
FOR I AM A TYRANT! A TRUE SUPER-SADIST!
DOOON (BOOM)
MOGU (MUNCH) MOGU
もぐもぐ
AND I WILL USE THIS SPACE AS I PLEASE, YOU LIVING CHAMBER POTS!
NOW, WHAT SHALL I DO WITH ALL THIS SPACE THAT'S JUST BEGGING TO BE USED? SHALL I HUMILIATE IT IN WAYS THAT CAN'T BE PRINTED!?
MAGU (CHOMP) MAGU
まぐまぐ
GOOD, YOU SOWS! YOU SHOULD BE PARALYZED IN FEAR!!
OOPS, AND NOW I'VE RUN OUT OF SPACE. BECAUSE I NEVER HAD A PLAN!
AND I DON'T CARE! THE MARK OF A TRUE SUPER-SADIST!!
BAAAN
GARI (CRUNCH) GARI
がりがり
DON'T DELUDE YOURSELVES INTO THINKING YOU'RE SAFE NOW, SUPER-MASOCHISTS! I'M ABOUT TO

AND SO, POPULATED BY SUCH CHARACTERS, "INU X BOKU SS" IS......

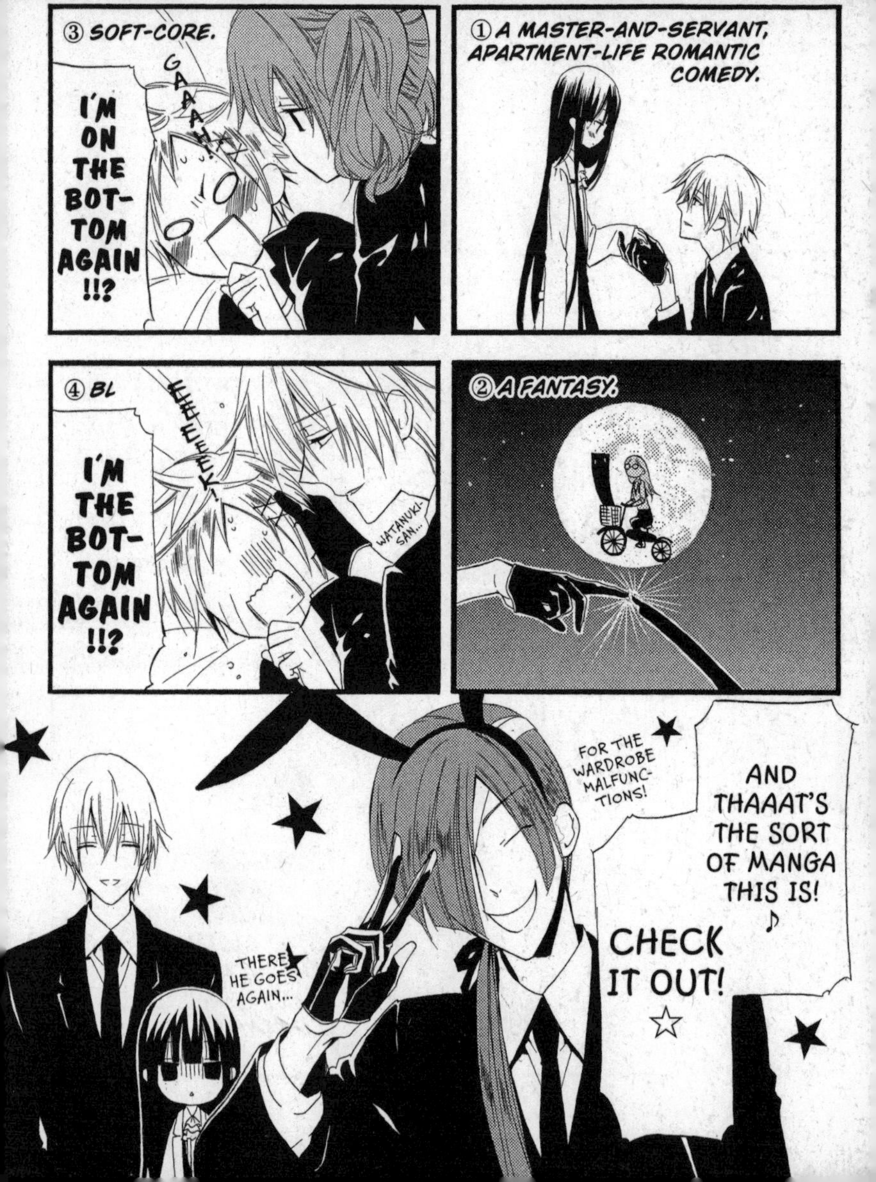
① A MASTER-AND-SERVANT, APARTMENT-LIFE ROMANTIC COMEDY.
③ SOFT-CORE.
GAAAH!
I'M ON THE BOT-TOM AGAIN!!?
② A FANTASY.
④ BL
EEEEEK!
I'M THE BOT-TOM AGAIN!!?
WATANUKI-SAN...
AND THAAAT'S THE SORT OF MANGA THIS IS! ♪
FOR THE WARDROBE MALFUNC-TIONS!
CHECK IT OUT! ☆
THERE HE GOES AGAIN...

# INU×BOKU SS

maison de ayakashi

Welcome to Maison de Ayakashi.
The exclusive Secret Service of
this Mansion guarantees
your mental and physical
safety by providing
superior escorts.

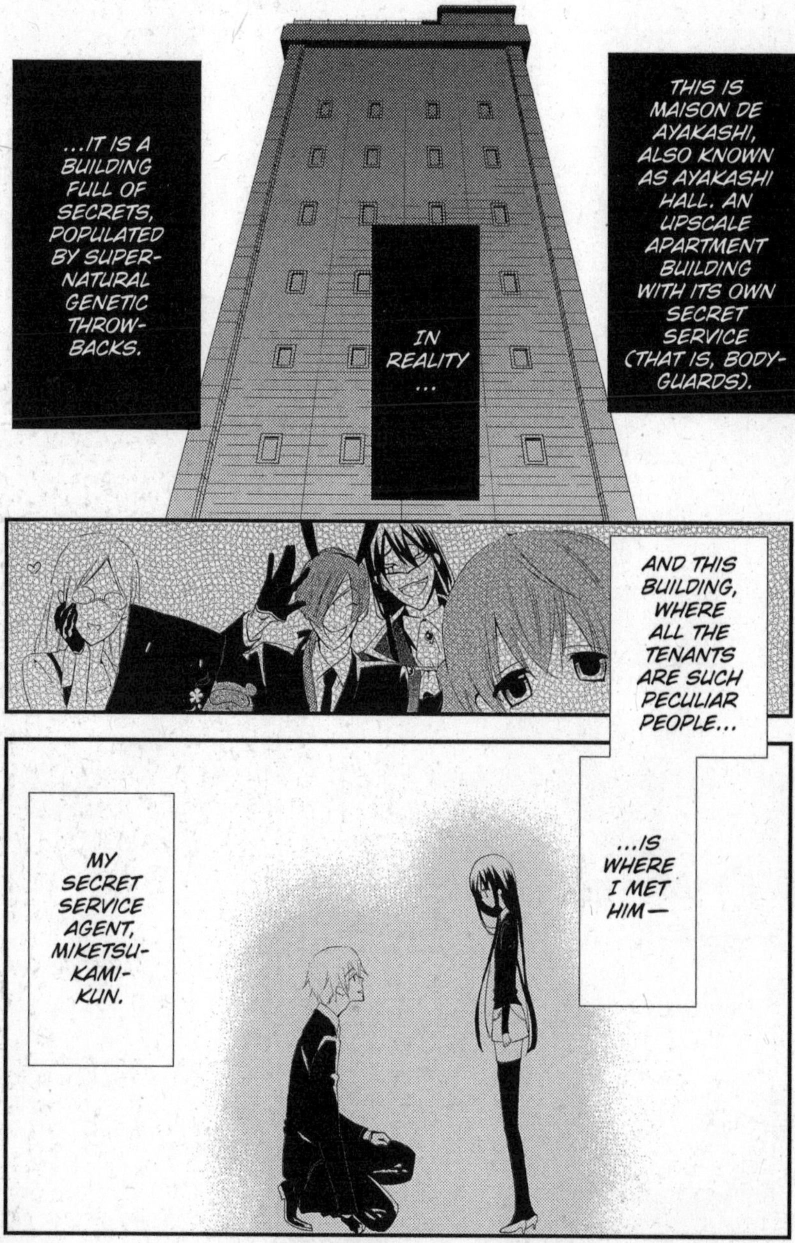
THIS IS MAISON DE AYAKASHI, ALSO KNOWN AS AYAKASHI HALL. AN UPSCALE APARTMENT BUILDING WITH ITS OWN SECRET SERVICE (THAT IS, BODY-GUARDS).
IN REALITY...
...IT IS A BUILDING FULL OF SECRETS, POPULATED BY SUPER-NATURAL GENETIC THROW-BACKS.
AND THIS BUILDING, WHERE ALL THE TENANTS ARE SUCH PECULIAR PEOPLE...
...IS WHERE I MET HIM—
MY SECRET SERVICE AGENT, MIKETSU-KAMI-KUN.

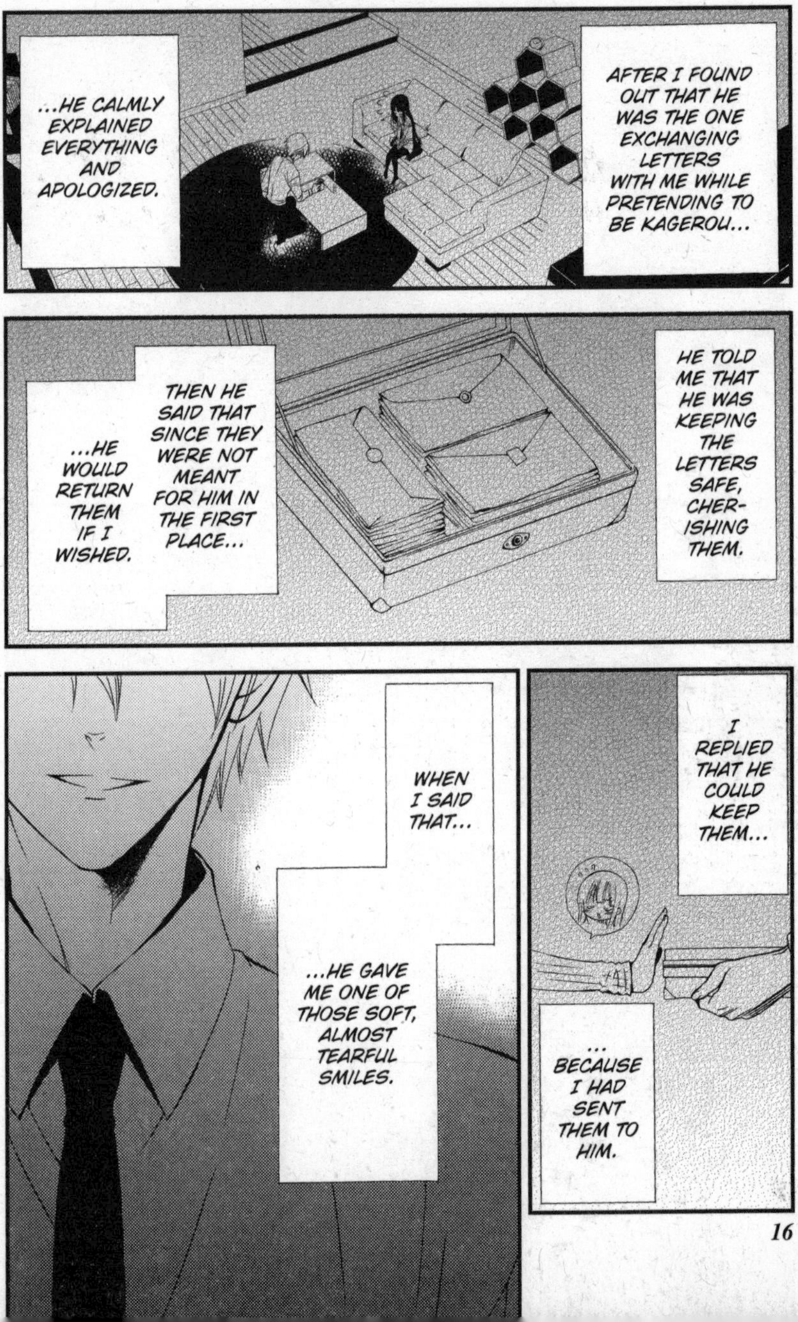
AFTER I FOUND OUT THAT HE WAS THE ONE EXCHANGING LETTERS WITH ME WHILE PRETENDING TO BE KAGEROU...
...HE CALMLY EXPLAINED EVERYTHING AND APOLOGIZED.
HE TOLD ME THAT HE WAS KEEPING THE LETTERS SAFE, CHER-ISHING THEM.
THEN HE SAID THAT SINCE THEY WERE NOT MEANT FOR HIM IN THE FIRST PLACE...
...HE WOULD RETURN THEM IF I WISHED.
I REPLIED THAT HE COULD KEEP THEM...
...BECAUSE I HAD SENT THEM TO HIM.
WHEN I SAID THAT...
...HE GAVE ME ONE OF THOSE SOFT, ALMOST TEARFUL SMILES.

# Chapter 9: What We Are to Him

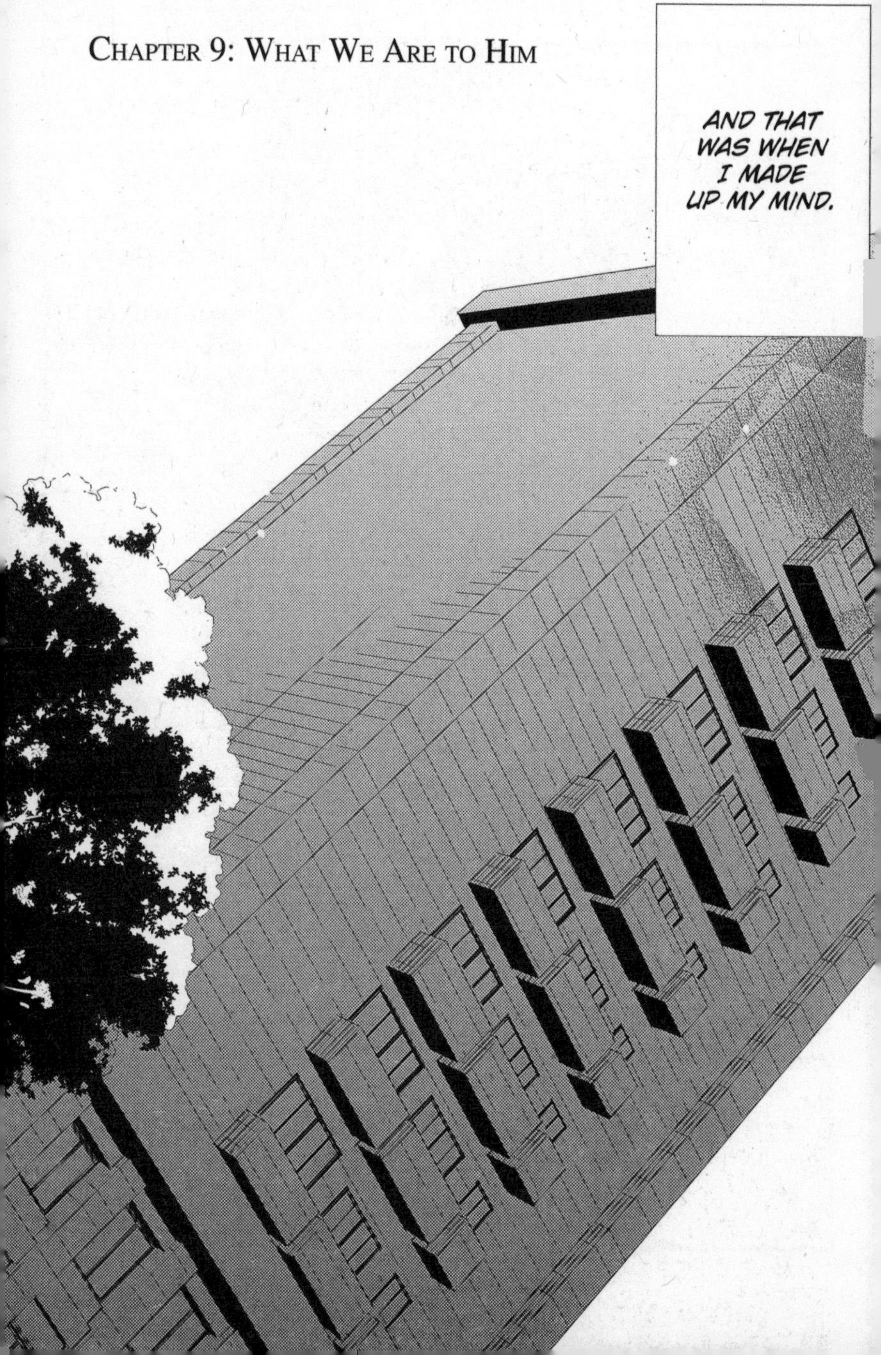
AND THAT WAS WHEN I MADE UP MY MIND.

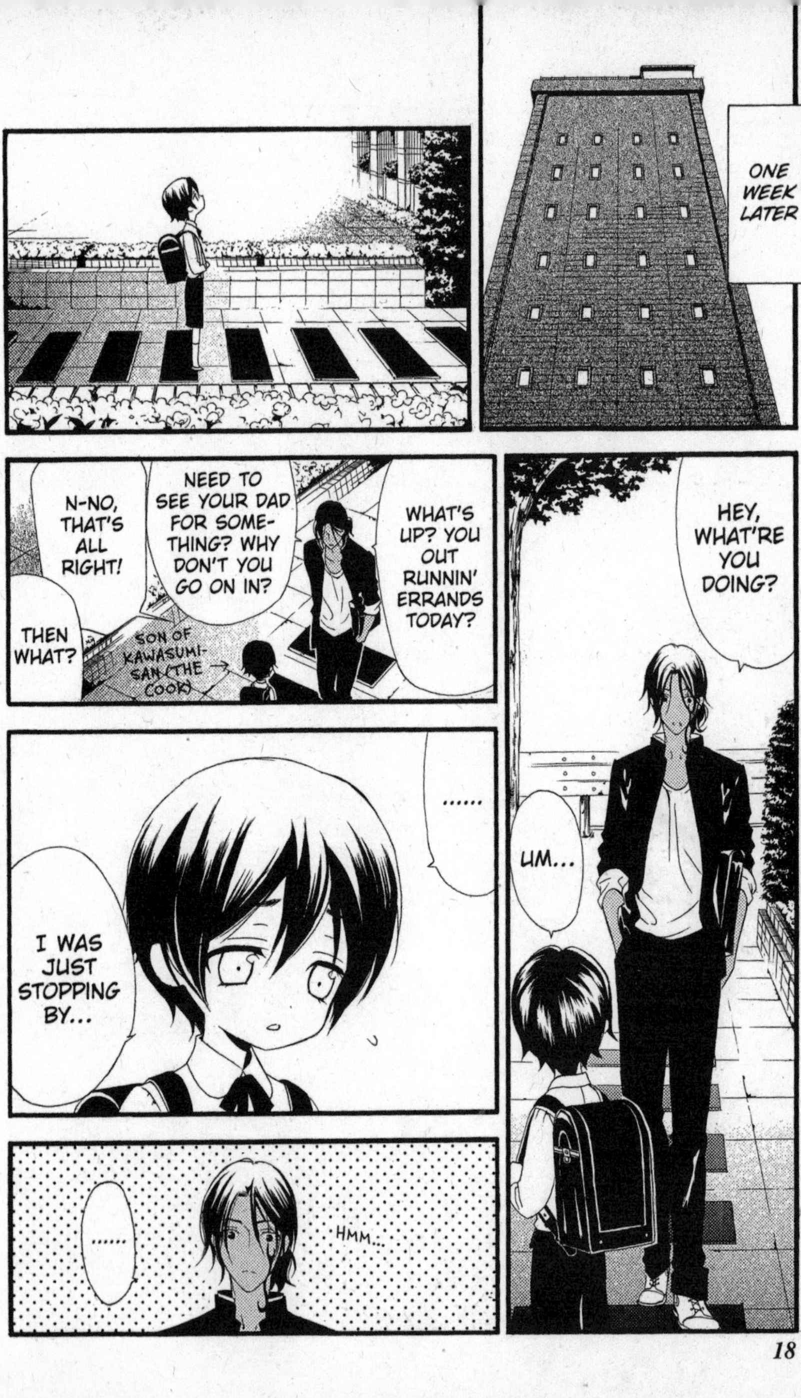
ONE WEEK LATER
HEY, WHAT'RE YOU DOING?
UM...
WHAT'S UP? YOU OUT RUNNIN' ERRANDS TODAY?
NEED TO SEE YOUR DAD FOR SOME-THING? WHY DON'T YOU GO ON IN?
N-NO, THAT'S ALL RIGHT!
THEN WHAT?
SON OF KAWASUMI-SAN (THE COOK)
......
I WAS JUST STOPPING BY...
HMM..
......

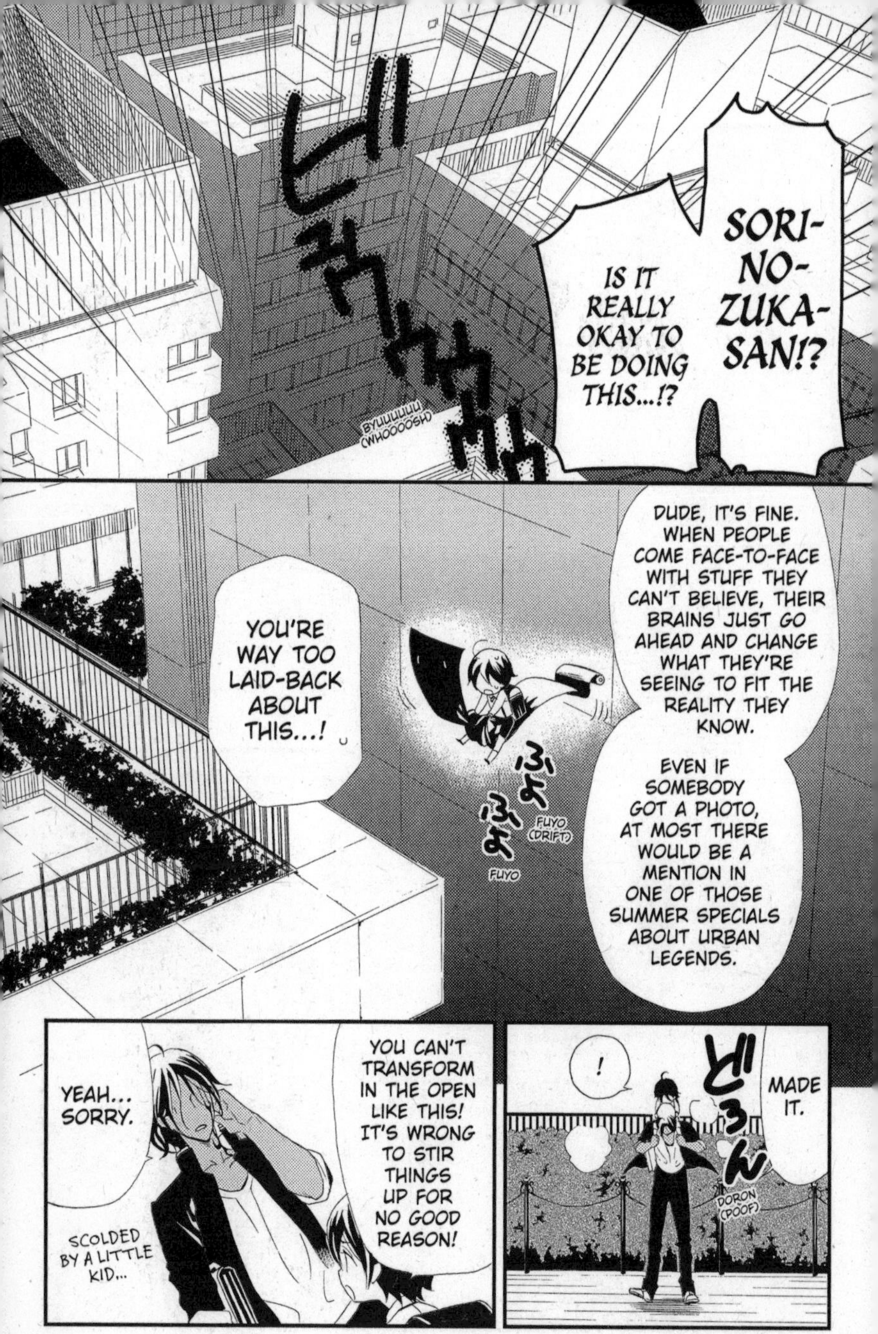
SORI-NO-ZUKA-SAN!?
IS IT REALLY OKAY TO BE DOING THIS...!?
BYUUUUUUN (WHOOOOSH)
DUDE, IT'S FINE. WHEN PEOPLE COME FACE-TO-FACE WITH STUFF THEY CAN'T BELIEVE, THEIR BRAINS JUST GO AHEAD AND CHANGE WHAT THEY'RE SEEING TO FIT THE REALITY THEY KNOW.
EVEN IF SOMEBODY GOT A PHOTO, AT MOST THERE WOULD BE A MENTION IN ONE OF THOSE SUMMER SPECIALS ABOUT URBAN LEGENDS.
ふよ
FUYO (DRIFT)
ふよ
FUYO
YOU'RE WAY TOO LAID-BACK ABOUT THIS...!
MADE IT.
どろん
DORON (POOF)
!
YOU CAN'T TRANSFORM IN THE OPEN LIKE THIS! IT'S WRONG TO STIR THINGS UP FOR NO GOOD REASON!
YEAH... SORRY.
SCOLDED BY A LITTLE KID...

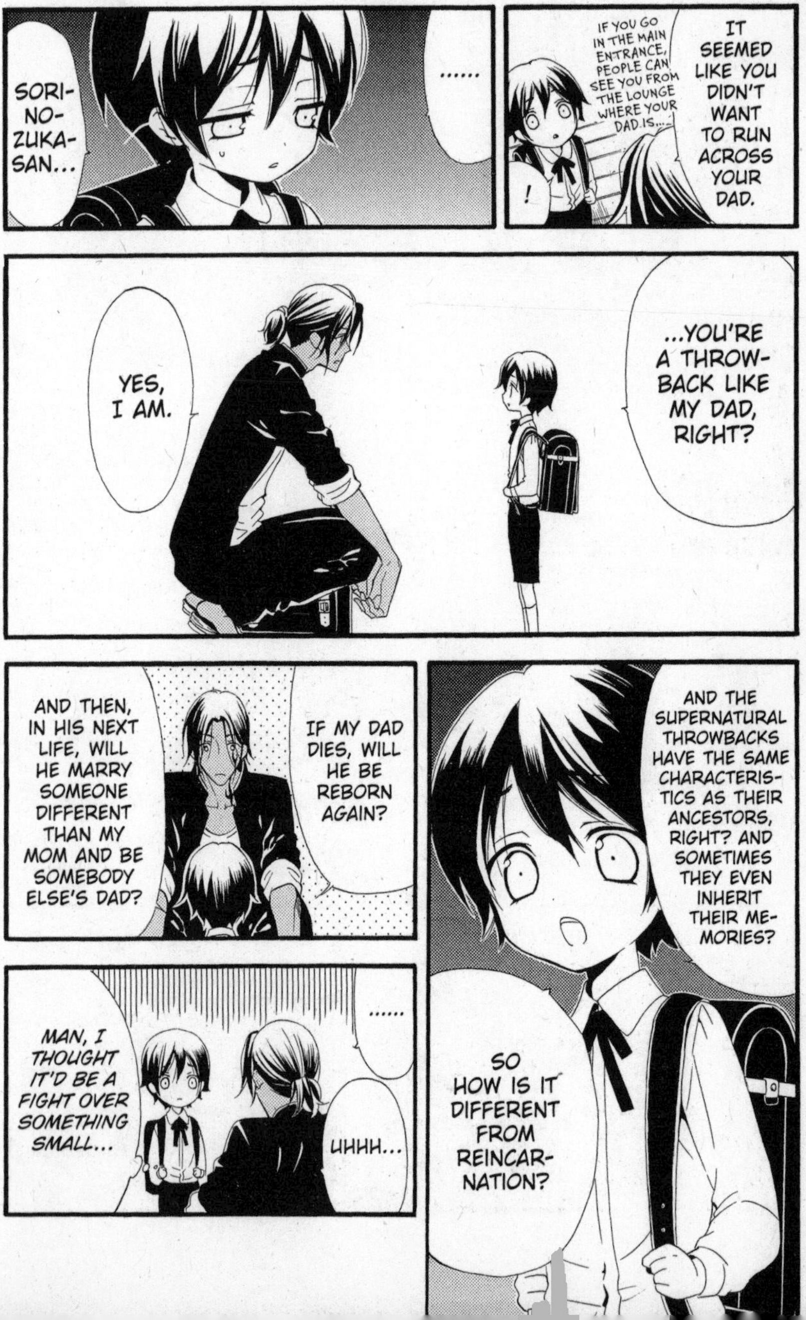
IT SEEMED LIKE YOU DIDN'T WANT TO RUN ACROSS YOUR DAD.
IF YOU GO IN THE MAIN ENTRANCE, PEOPLE CAN SEE YOU FROM THE LOUNGE WHERE YOUR DAD IS...
!
......
SORI-NO-ZUKA-SAN...
...YOU'RE A THROW-BACK LIKE MY DAD, RIGHT?
YES, I AM.
AND THE SUPERNATURAL THROWBACKS HAVE THE SAME CHARACTERIS-TICS AS THEIR ANCESTORS, RIGHT? AND SOMETIMES THEY EVEN INHERIT THEIR ME-MORIES?
SO HOW IS IT DIFFERENT FROM REINCAR-NATION?
IF MY DAD DIES, WILL HE BE REBORN AGAIN?
AND THEN, IN HIS NEXT LIFE, WILL HE MARRY SOMEONE DIFFERENT THAN MY MOM AND BE SOMEBODY ELSE'S DAD?
......
UHHH...
MAN, I THOUGHT IT'D BE A FIGHT OVER SOMETHING SMALL...

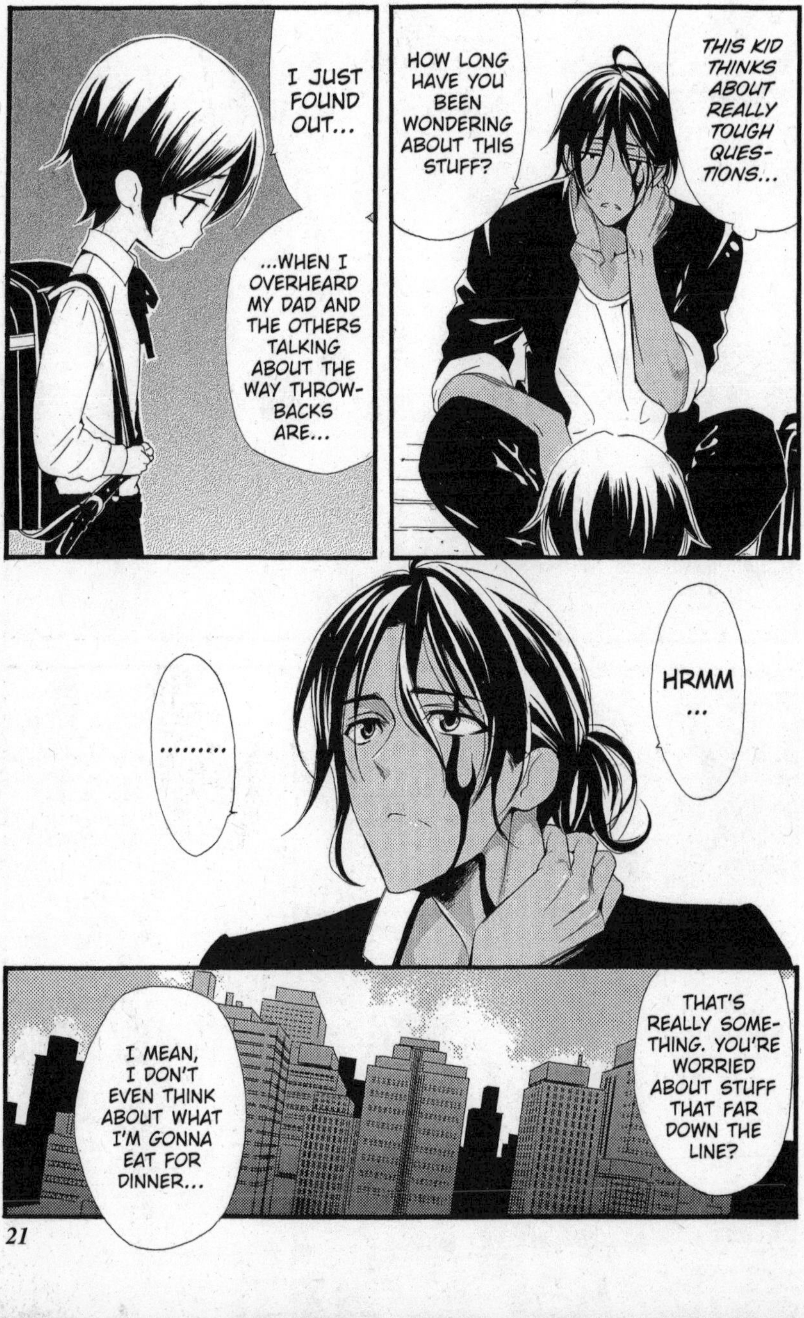
THIS KID THINKS ABOUT REALLY TOUGH QUES-TIONS...
HOW LONG HAVE YOU BEEN WONDERING ABOUT THIS STUFF?
I JUST FOUND OUT...
...WHEN I OVERHEARD MY DAD AND THE OTHERS TALKING ABOUT THE WAY THROW-BACKS ARE...
HRMM ...
.........
THAT'S REALLY SOME-THING. YOU'RE WORRIED ABOUT STUFF THAT FAR DOWN THE LINE?
I MEAN, I DON'T EVEN THINK ABOUT WHAT I'M GONNA EAT FOR DINNER...

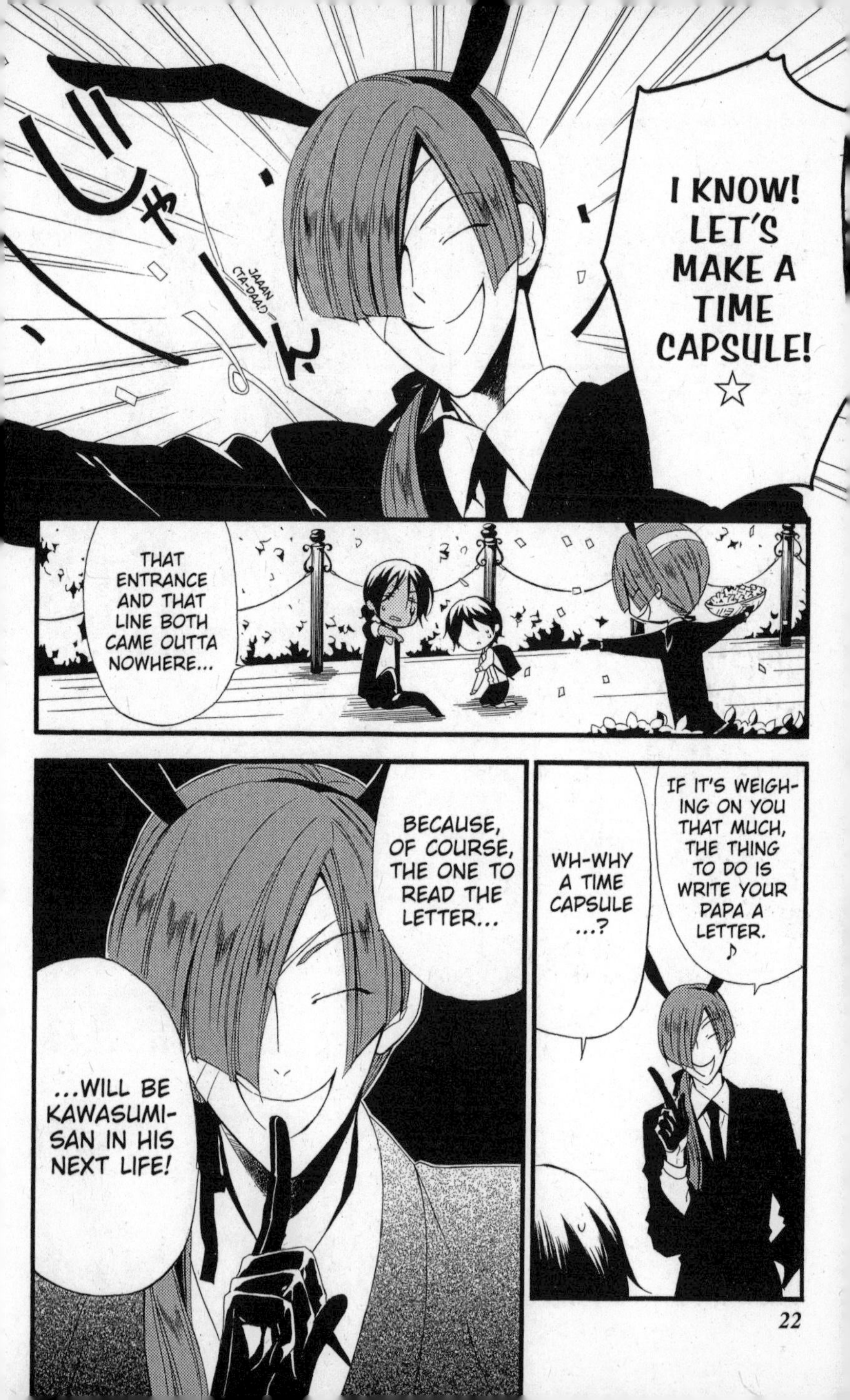
I KNOW! LET'S MAKE A TIME CAPSULE! ☆
じゃーん
JAAAN (TA-DAA!)
THAT ENTRANCE AND THAT LINE BOTH CAME OUTTA NOWHERE...
IF IT'S WEIGH-ING ON YOU THAT MUCH, THE THING TO DO IS WRITE YOUR PAPA A LETTER. ♪
WH-WHY A TIME CAPSULE ...?
BECAUSE, OF COURSE, THE ONE TO READ THE LETTER...
...WILL BE KAWASUMI-SAN IN HIS NEXT LIFE!

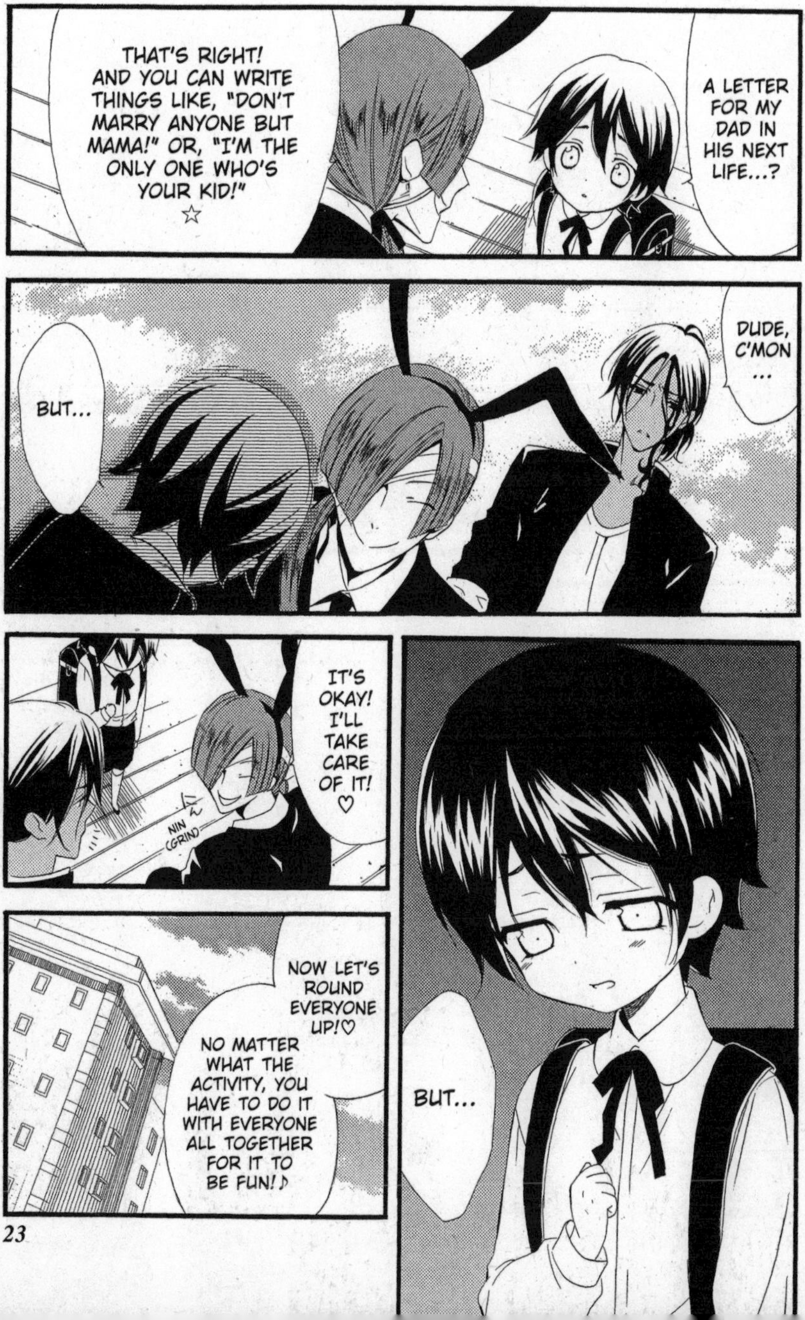
A LETTER FOR MY DAD IN HIS NEXT LIFE...?
THAT'S RIGHT! AND YOU CAN WRITE THINGS LIKE, "DON'T MARRY ANYONE BUT MAMA!" OR, "I'M THE ONLY ONE WHO'S YOUR KID!" ☆
DUDE, C'MON...
BUT...
BUT...
IT'S OKAY! I'LL TAKE CARE OF IT! ♡
NIN (GRIN)
NOW LET'S ROUND EVERYONE UP!♡
NO MATTER WHAT THE ACTIVITY, YOU HAVE TO DO IT WITH EVERYONE ALL TOGETHER FOR IT TO BE FUN!♪

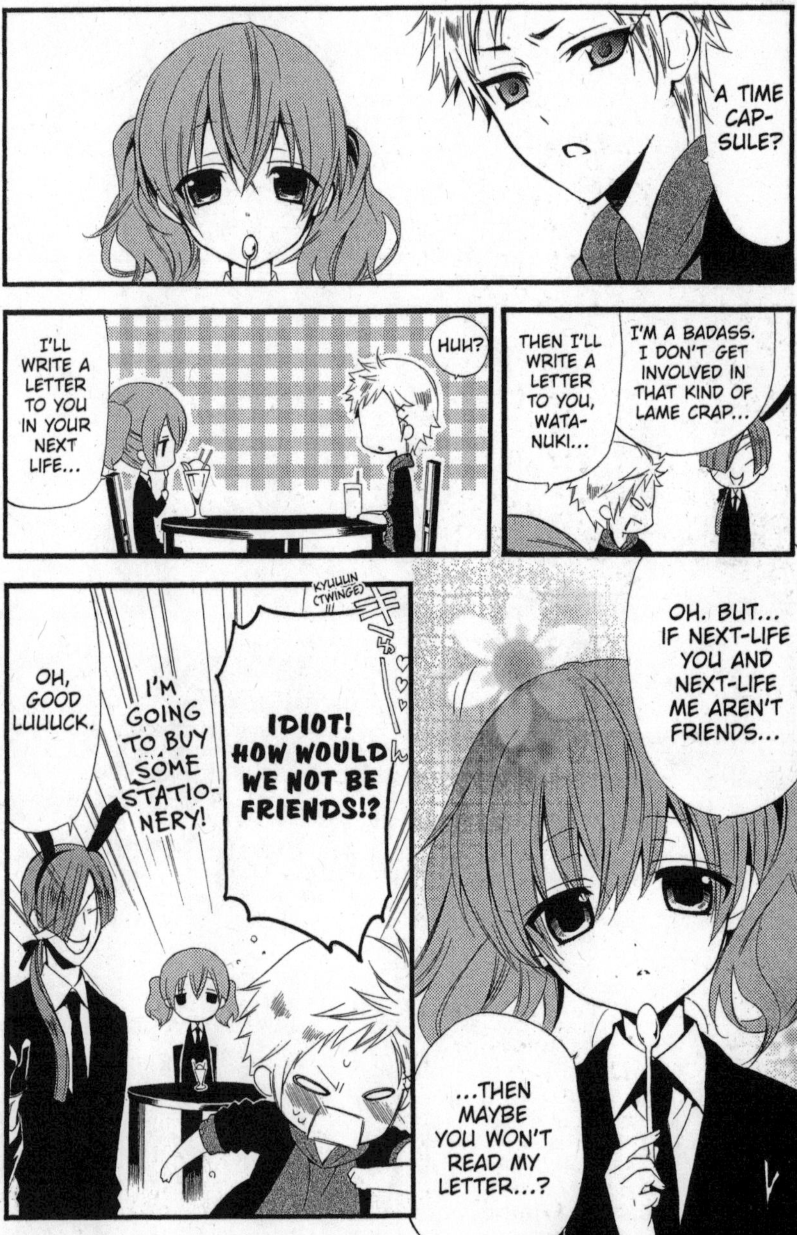
A TIME CAPSULE?
I'M A BADASS. I DON'T GET INVOLVED IN THAT KIND OF LAME CRAP...
THEN I'LL WRITE A LETTER TO YOU, WATANUKI...
HUH?
I'LL WRITE A LETTER TO YOU IN YOUR NEXT LIFE...
OH. BUT... IF NEXT-LIFE YOU AND NEXT-LIFE ME AREN'T FRIENDS...
...THEN MAYBE YOU WON'T READ MY LETTER...?
KYUUUN (TWINGE)
IDIOT! HOW WOULD WE NOT BE FRIENDS!?
I'M GOING TO BUY SOME STATIONERY!
OH, GOOD LUUUCK.

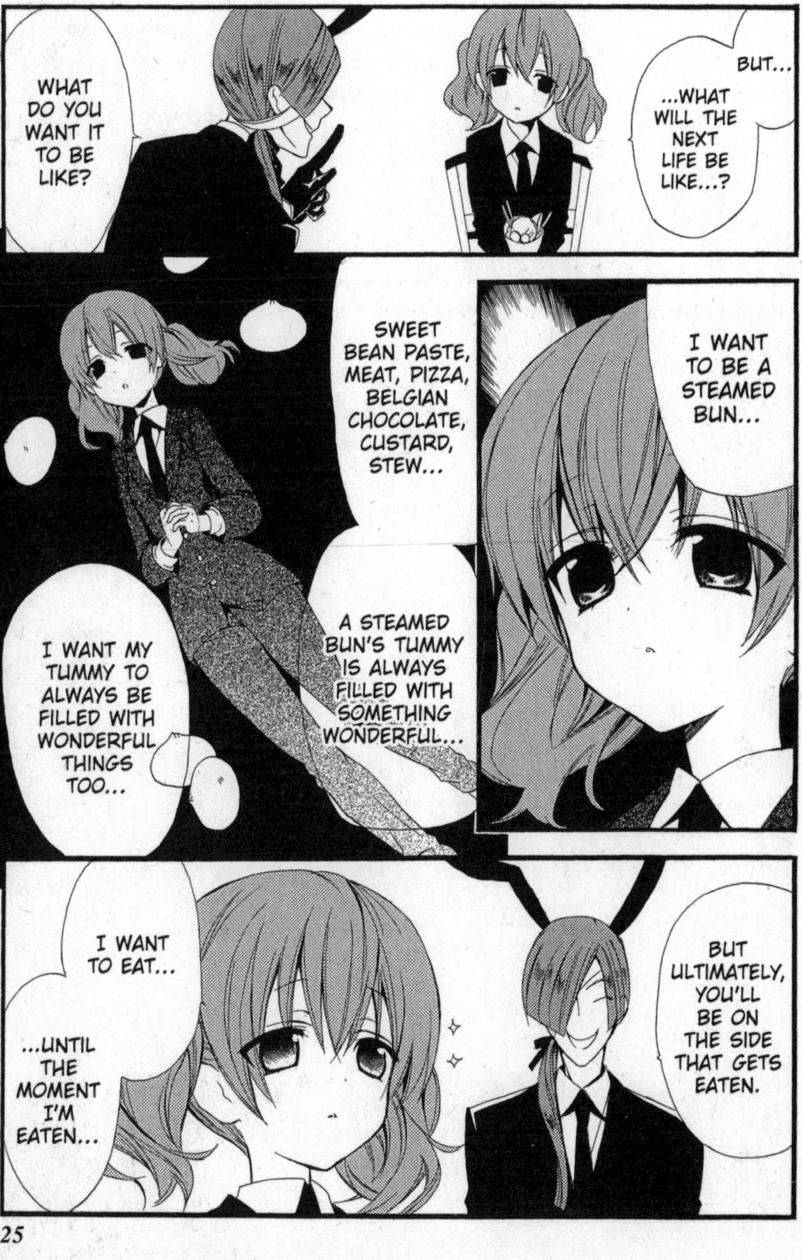
BUT...
...WHAT WILL THE NEXT LIFE BE LIKE...?
WHAT DO YOU WANT IT TO BE LIKE?
I WANT TO BE A STEAMED BUN...
SWEET BEAN PASTE, MEAT, PIZZA, BELGIAN CHOCOLATE, CUSTARD, STEW...
A STEAMED BUN'S TUMMY IS ALWAYS FILLED WITH SOMETHING WONDERFUL...
I WANT MY TUMMY TO ALWAYS BE FILLED WITH WONDERFUL THINGS TOO...
I WANT TO EAT...
...UNTIL THE MOMENT I'M EATEN...
BUT ULTIMATELY, YOU'LL BE ON THE SIDE THAT GETS EATEN.

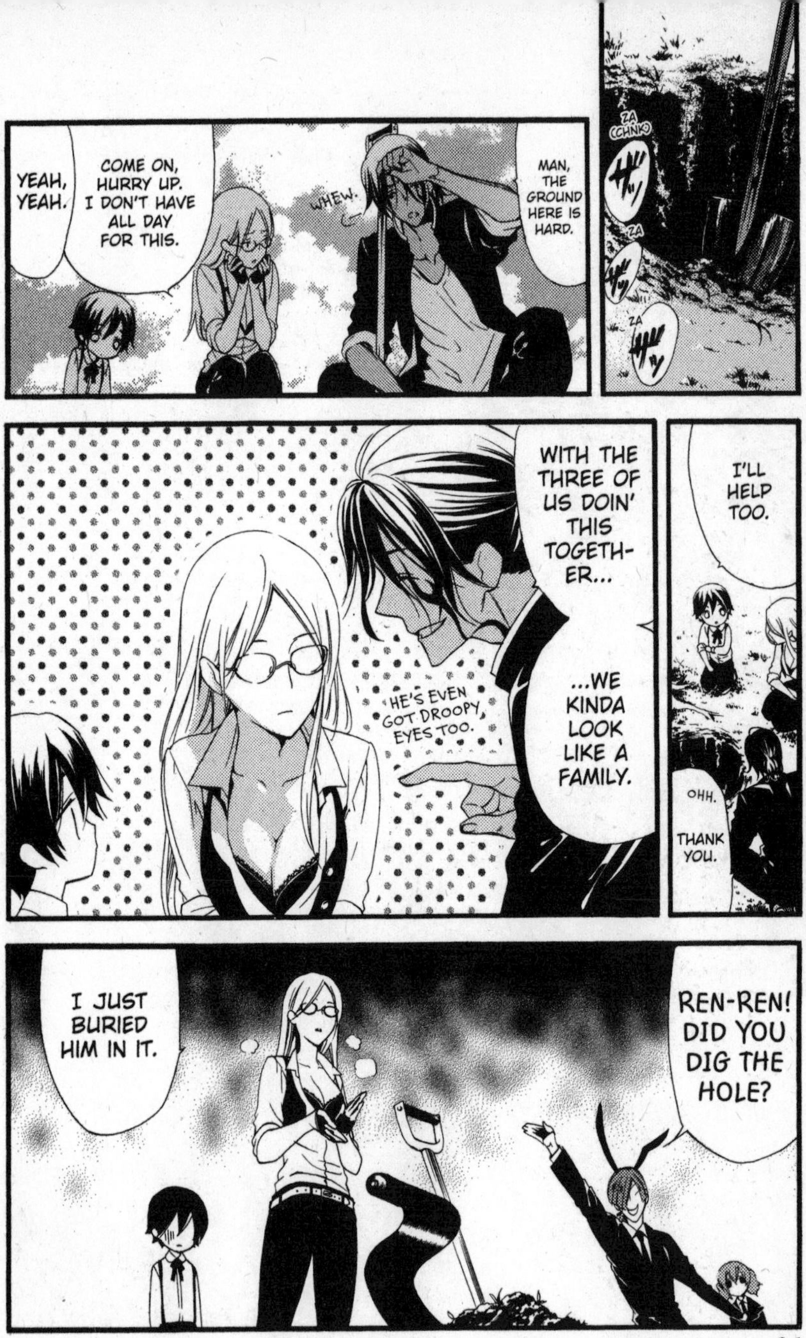
ZA (CHNK)
ZA
ZA
MAN, THE GROUND HERE IS HARD.
WHEW.
COME ON, HURRY UP. I DON'T HAVE ALL DAY FOR THIS.
YEAH, YEAH.
I'LL HELP TOO.
OHH.
THANK YOU.
WITH THE THREE OF US DOIN' THIS TOGETH-ER...
...WE KINDA LOOK LIKE A FAMILY.
HE'S EVEN GOT DROOPY EYES TOO.
REN-REN! DID YOU DIG THE HOLE?
I JUST BURIED HIM IN IT.

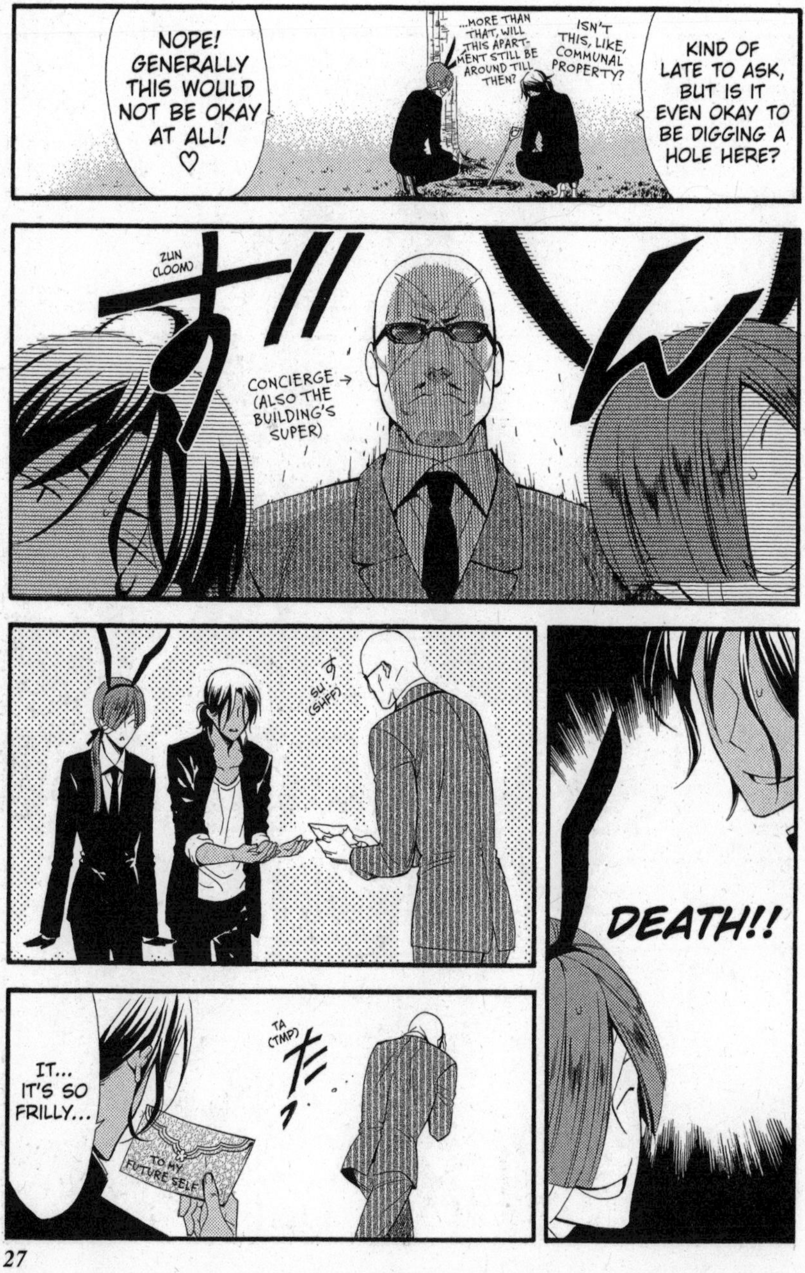

KIND OF LATE TO ASK, BUT IS IT EVEN OKAY TO BE DIGGING A HOLE HERE?
ISN'T THIS, LIKE, COMMUNAL PROPERTY?
...MORE THAN THAT, WILL THIS APARTMENT STILL BE AROUND TILL THEN?
NOPE! GENERALLY THIS WOULD NOT BE OKAY AT ALL! ♡
ZUN (LOOM)
CONCIERGE → (ALSO THE BUILDING'S SUPER)
DEATH!!
SU (SHFF)
TA (TMP)
IT... IT'S SO FRILLY...
TO MY FUTURE SELF

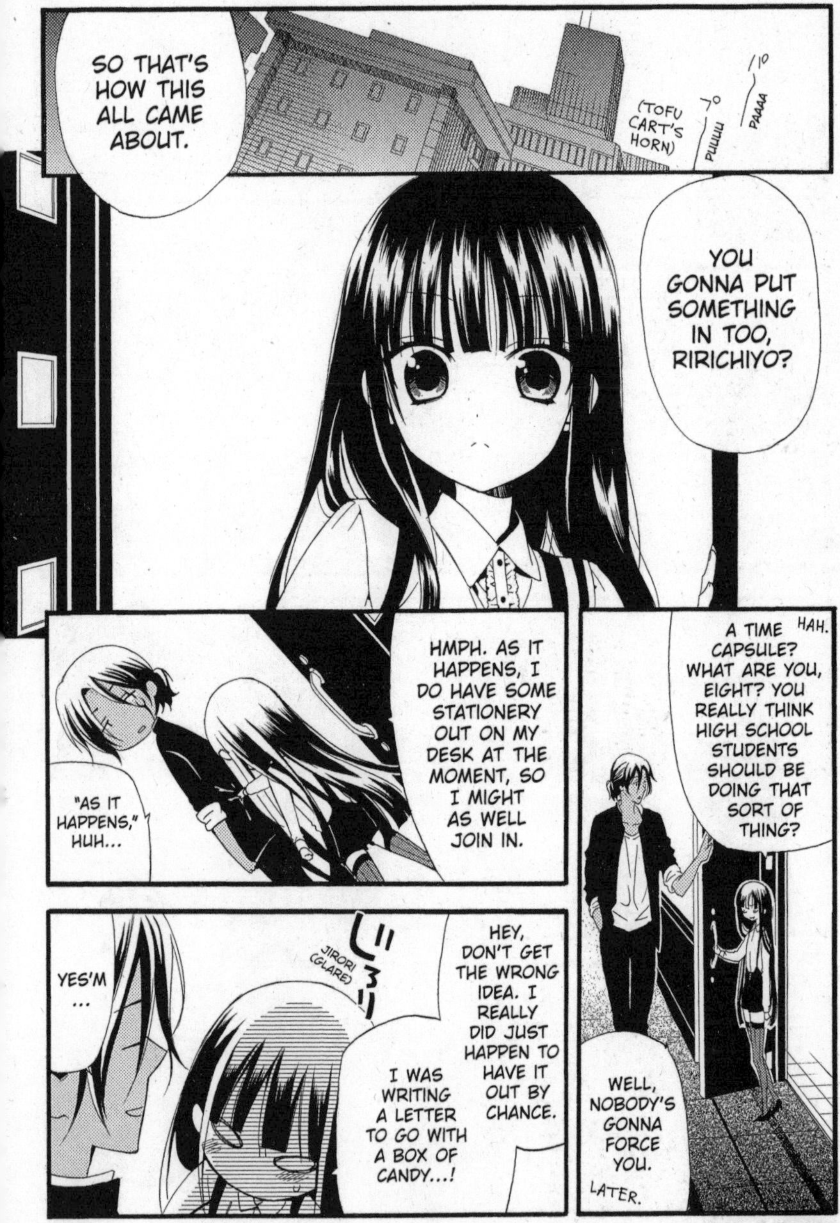
PAAAA
PUUUU
(TOFU CART'S HORN)
SO THAT'S HOW THIS ALL CAME ABOUT.
YOU GONNA PUT SOMETHING IN TOO, RIRICHIYO?
HAH.
A TIME CAPSULE? WHAT ARE YOU, EIGHT? YOU REALLY THINK HIGH SCHOOL STUDENTS SHOULD BE DOING THAT SORT OF THING?
WELL, NOBODY'S GONNA FORCE YOU.
LATER.
HMPH. AS IT HAPPENS, I DO HAVE SOME STATIONERY OUT ON MY DESK AT THE MOMENT, SO I MIGHT AS WELL JOIN IN.
"AS IT HAPPENS," HUH...
JIRORI (GLARE)
HEY, DON'T GET THE WRONG IDEA. I REALLY DID JUST HAPPEN TO HAVE IT OUT BY CHANCE.
I WAS WRITING A LETTER TO GO WITH A BOX OF CANDY...!
YES'M ...

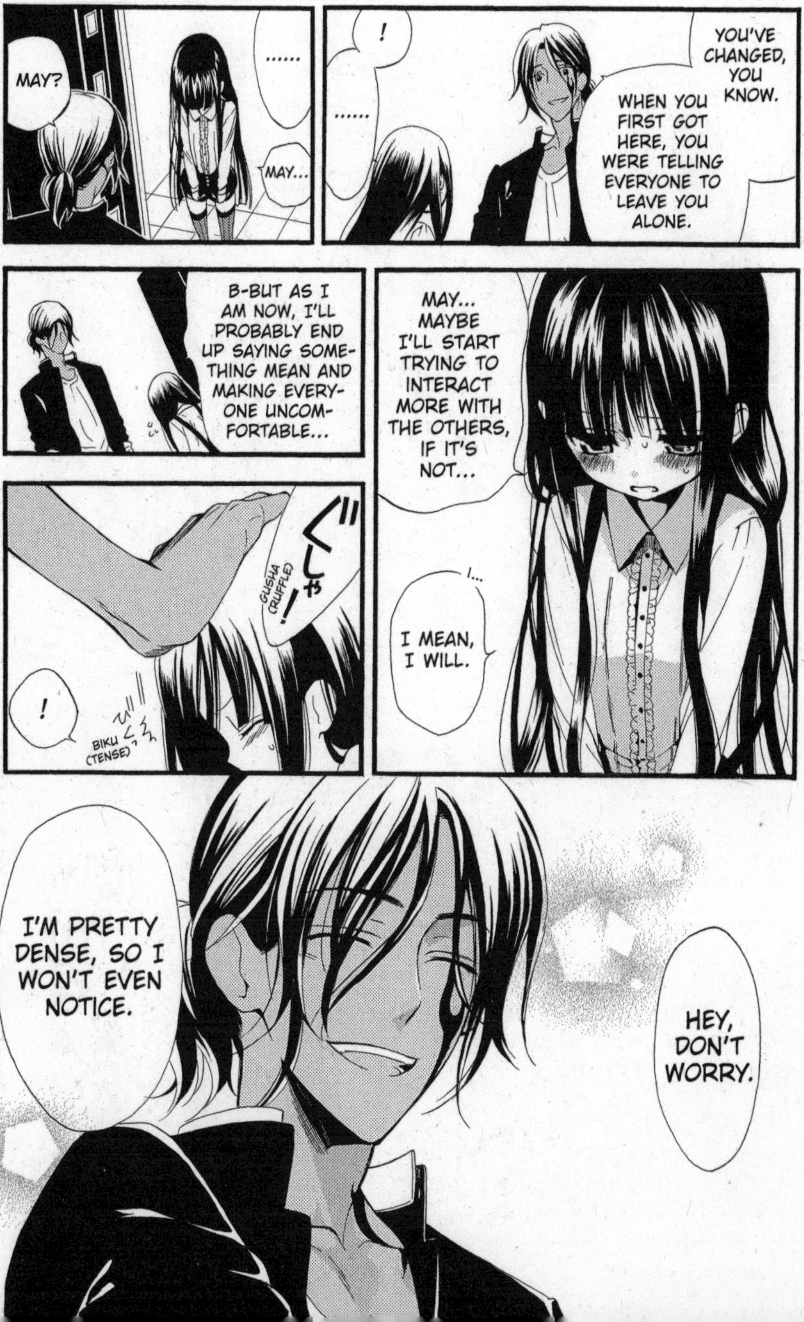
YOU'VE CHANGED, YOU KNOW.
WHEN YOU FIRST GOT HERE, YOU WERE TELLING EVERYONE TO LEAVE YOU ALONE.
!
......
......
MAY...
MAY?
MAY... MAYBE I'LL START TRYING TO INTERACT MORE WITH THE OTHERS, IF IT'S NOT...
I...
I MEAN, I WILL.
B-BUT AS I AM NOW, I'LL PROBABLY END UP SAYING SOME-THING MEAN AND MAKING EVERY-ONE UNCOM-FORTABLE...
GUSHA (RUFFLE)
!
BIKU (TENSE)
HEY, DON'T WORRY.
I'M PRETTY DENSE, SO I WON'T EVEN NOTICE.

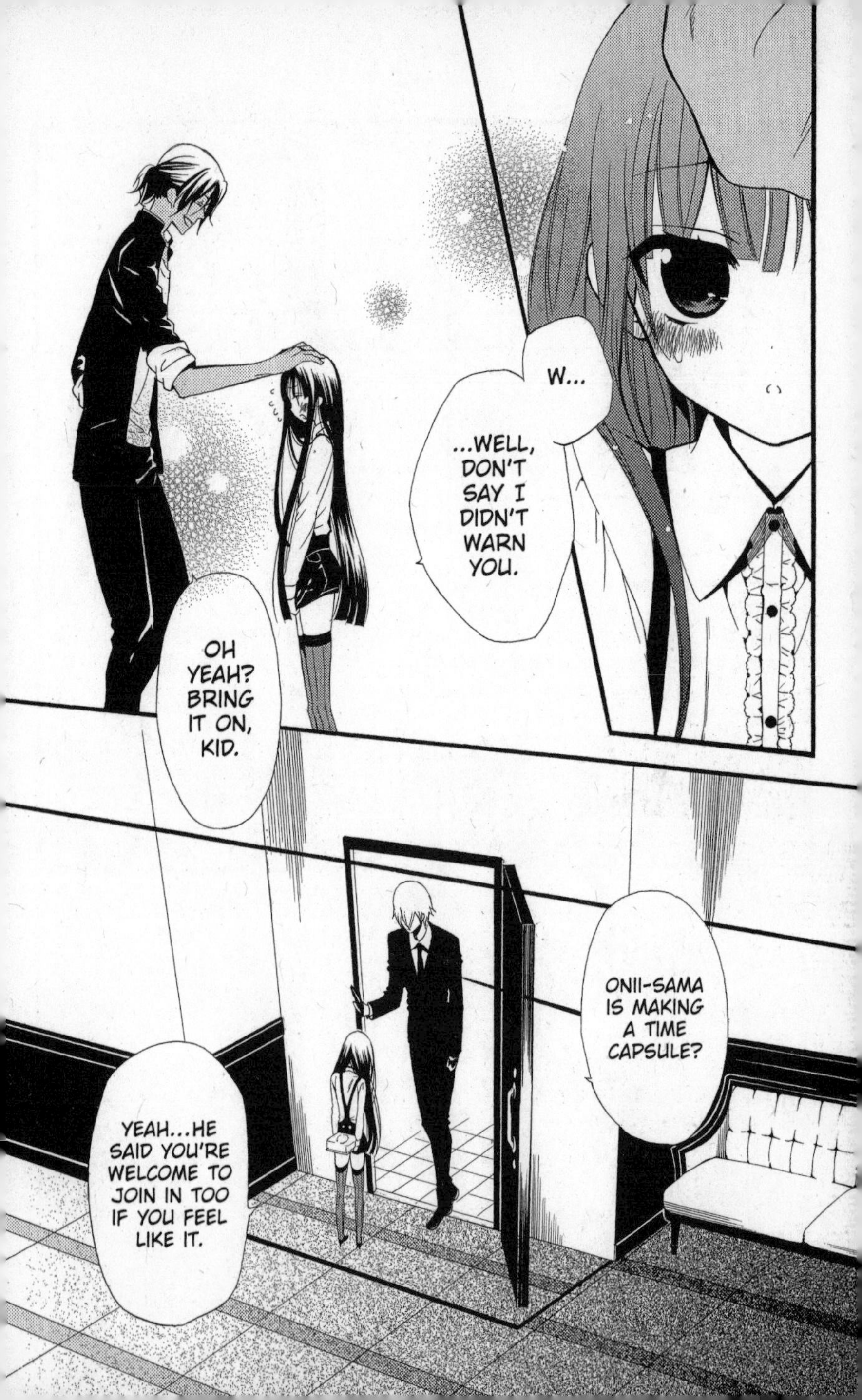
W...
...WELL, DON'T SAY I DIDN'T WARN YOU.
OH YEAH? BRING IT ON, KID.
ONII-SAMA IS MAKING A TIME CAPSULE?
YEAH...HE SAID YOU'RE WELCOME TO JOIN IN TOO IF YOU FEEL LIKE IT.

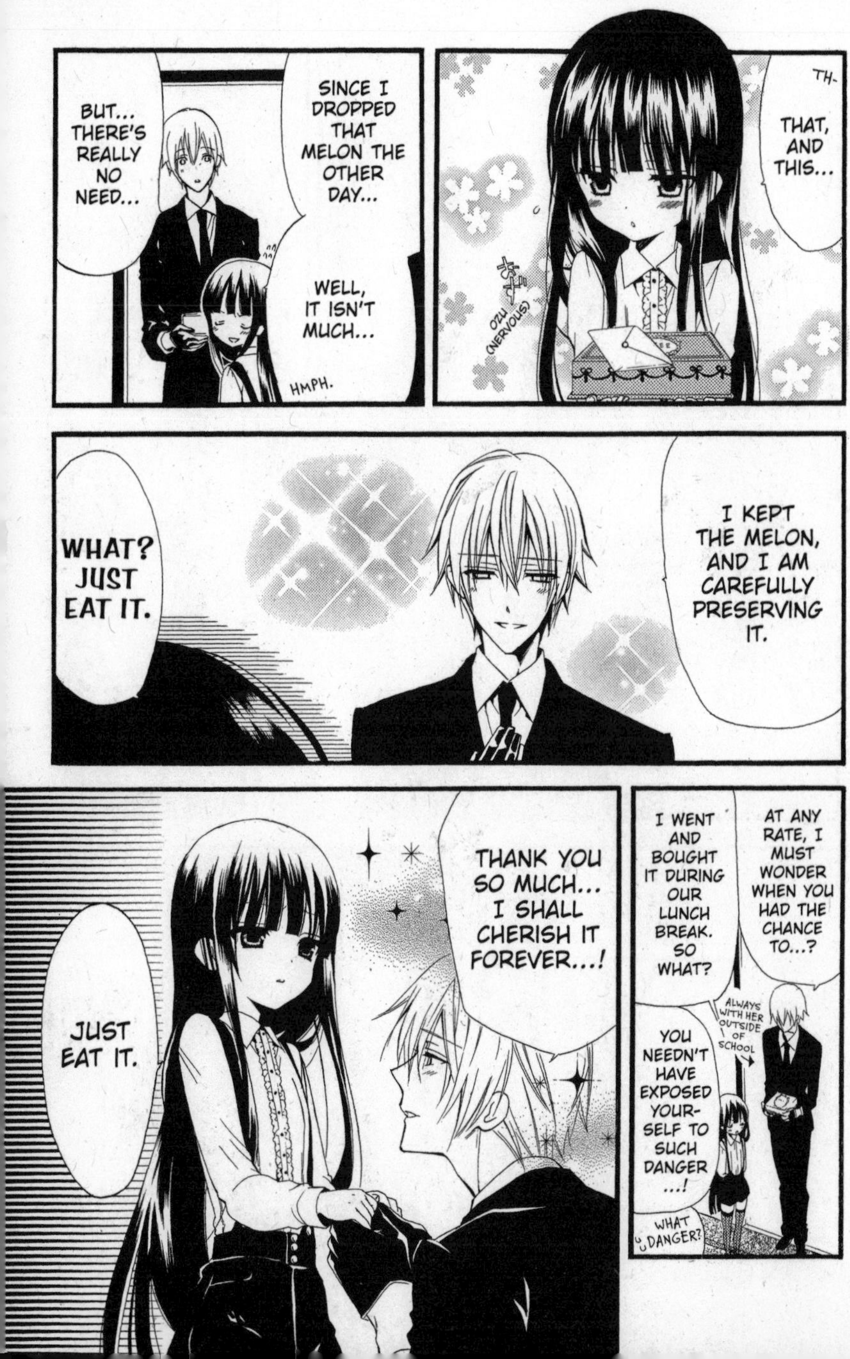
TH-
THAT, AND THIS...
OZU (NERVOUS)
SINCE I DROPPED THAT MELON THE OTHER DAY...
WELL, IT ISN'T MUCH...
BUT... THERE'S REALLY NO NEED...
HMPH.
I KEPT THE MELON, AND I AM CAREFULLY PRESERVING IT.
WHAT? JUST EAT IT.
AT ANY RATE, I MUST WONDER WHEN YOU HAD THE CHANCE TO...?
I WENT AND BOUGHT IT DURING OUR LUNCH BREAK. SO WHAT?
ALWAYS WITH HER OUTSIDE OF SCHOOL
YOU NEEDN'T HAVE EXPOSED YOURSELF TO SUCH DANGER...!
WHAT DANGER?
THANK YOU SO MUCH... I SHALL CHERISH IT FOREVER...!
JUST EAT IT.

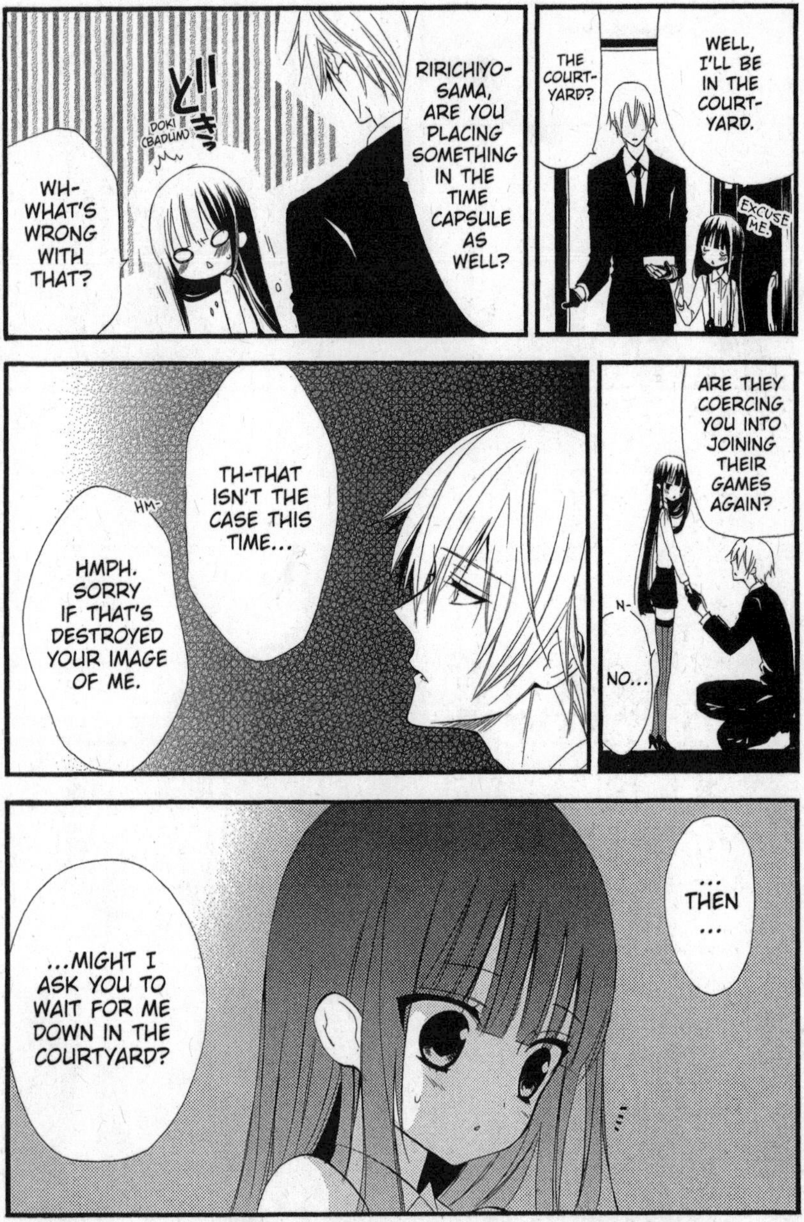
WELL, I'LL BE IN THE COURTYARD.
THE COURTYARD?
EXCUSE ME.
RIRICHIYO-SAMA, ARE YOU PLACING SOMETHING IN THE TIME CAPSULE AS WELL?
DOKI (BADUM)
WH-WHAT'S WRONG WITH THAT?
ARE THEY COERCING YOU INTO JOINING THEIR GAMES AGAIN?
N-
NO...
TH-THAT ISN'T THE CASE THIS TIME...
HM-
HMPH. SORRY IF THAT'S DESTROYED YOUR IMAGE OF ME.
...THEN...
...MIGHT I ASK YOU TO WAIT FOR ME DOWN IN THE COURTYARD?

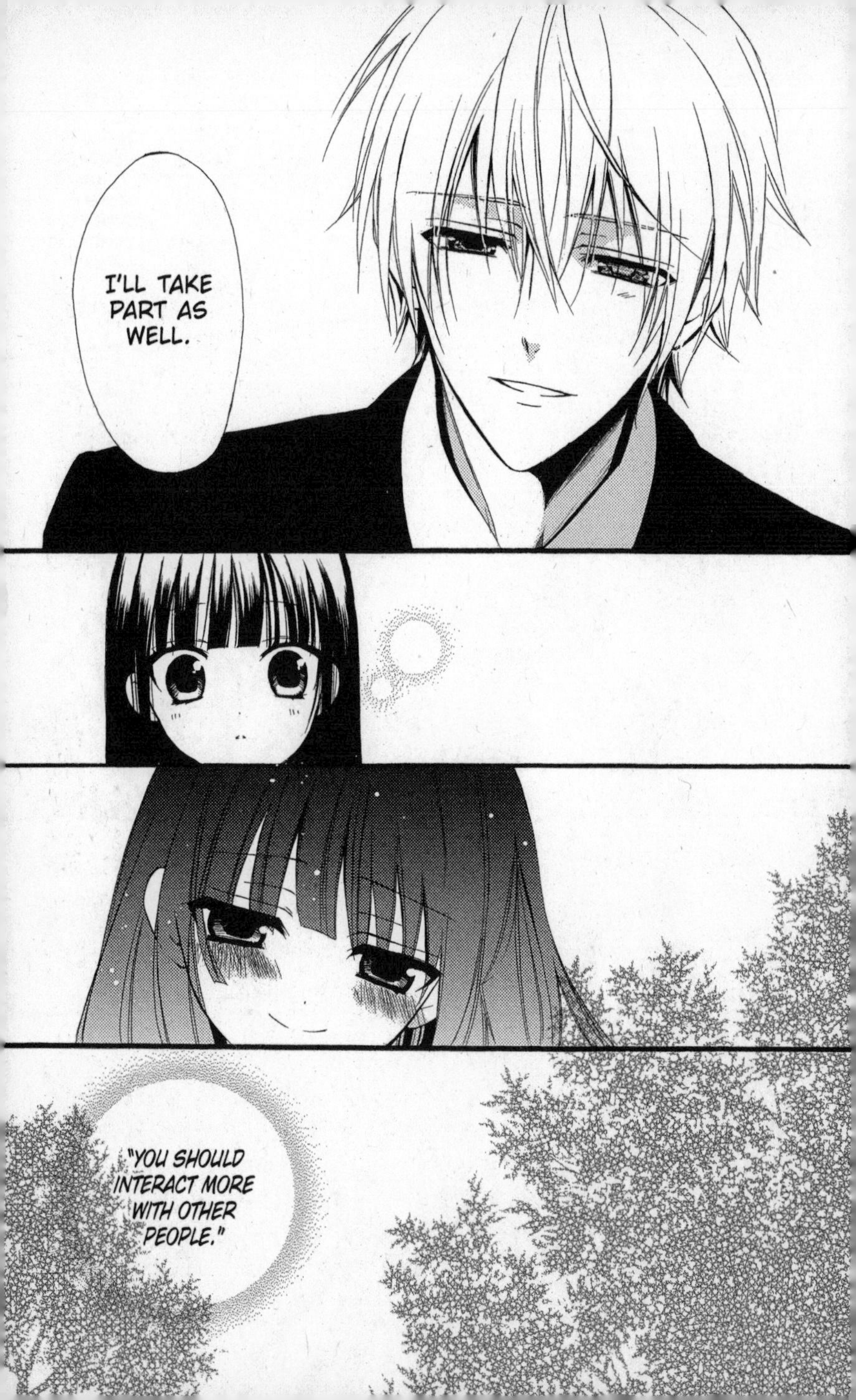
I'LL TAKE PART AS WELL.
"YOU SHOULD INTERACT MORE WITH OTHER PEOPLE."

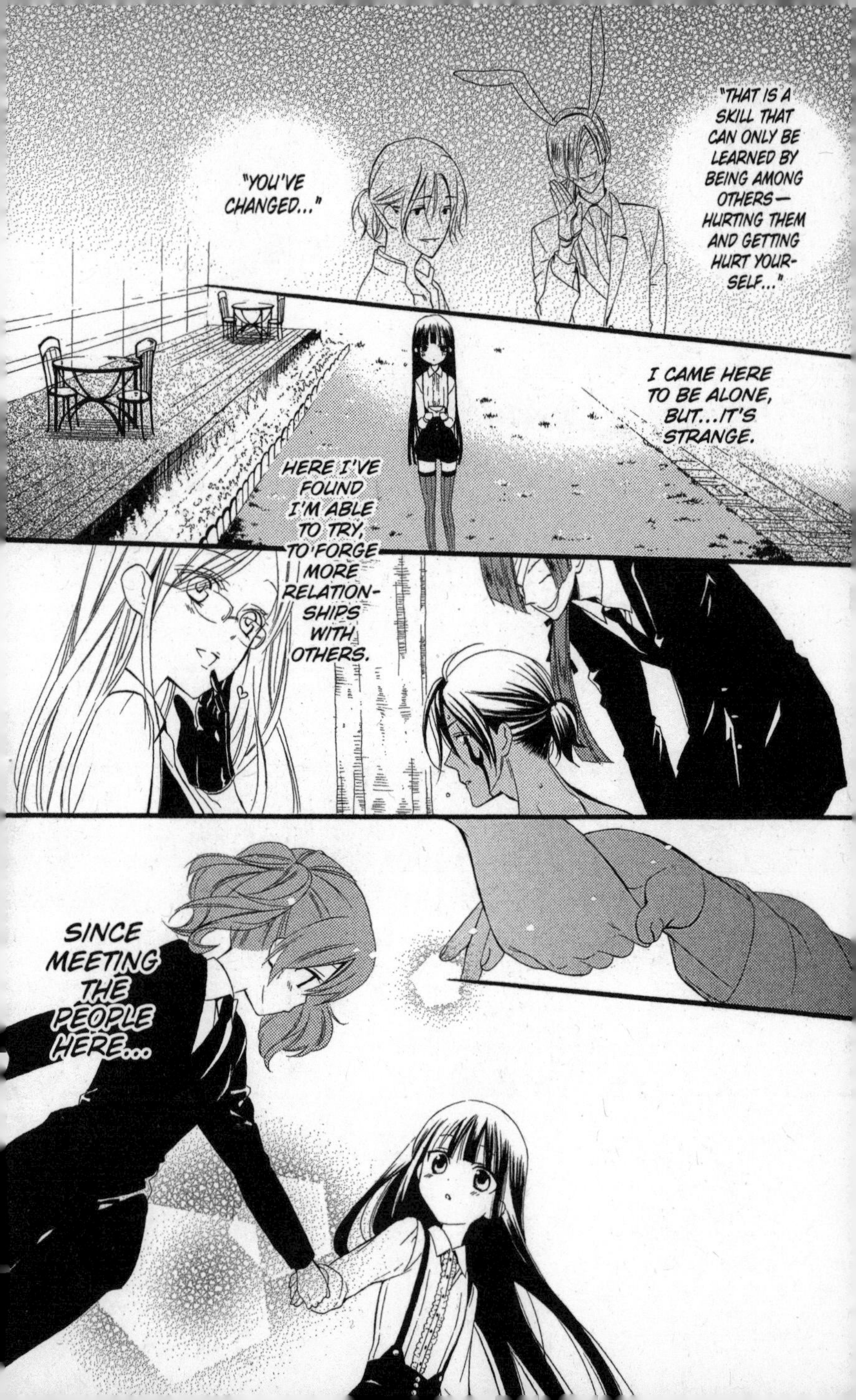
"THAT IS A SKILL THAT CAN ONLY BE LEARNED BY BEING AMONG OTHERS—HURTING THEM AND GETTING HURT YOURSELF..."
"YOU'VE CHANGED..."
I CAME HERE TO BE ALONE, BUT...IT'S STRANGE.
HERE I'VE FOUND I'M ABLE TO TRY, TO FORGE MORE RELATIONSHIPS WITH OTHERS.
SINCE MEETING THE PEOPLE HERE...

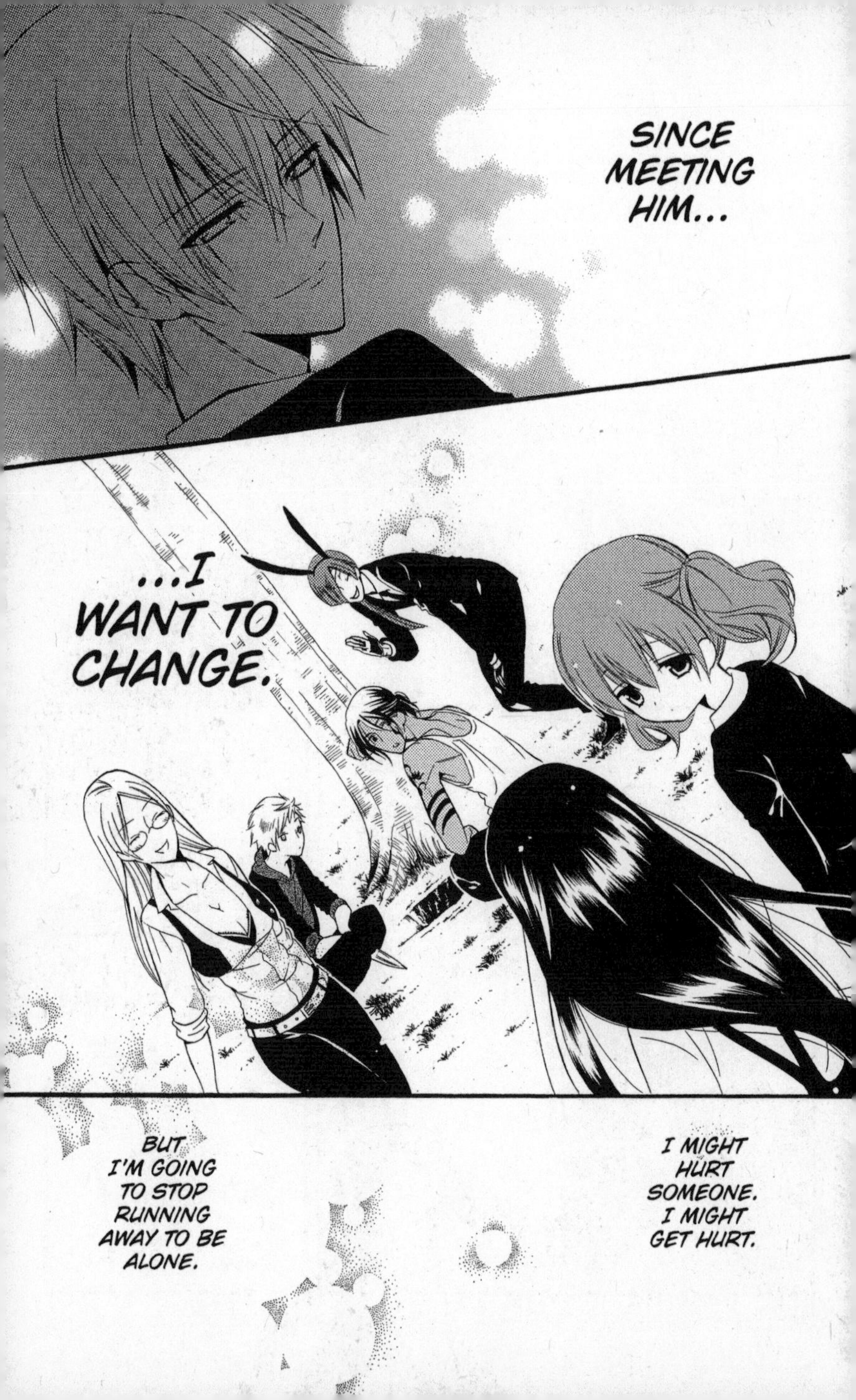
SINCE MEETING HIM...
...I WANT TO CHANGE.
I MIGHT HURT SOMEONE. I MIGHT GET HURT.
BUT I'M GOING TO STOP RUNNING AWAY TO BE ALONE.

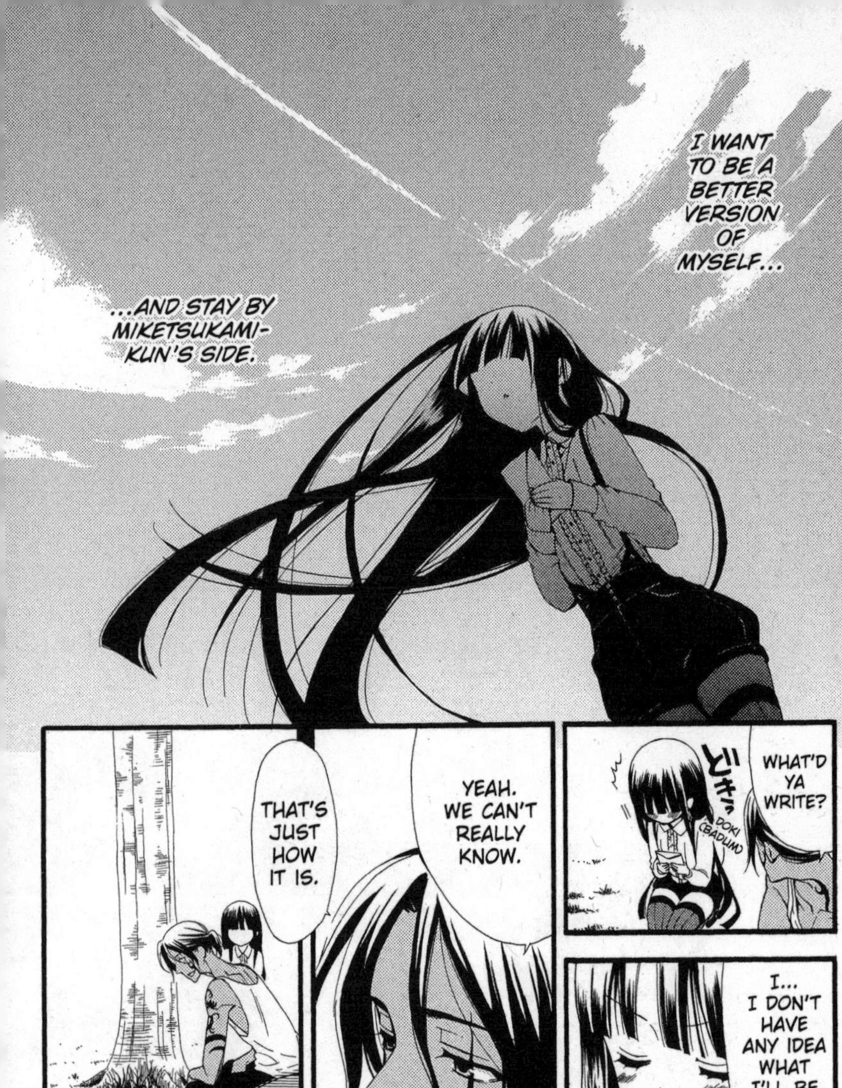
I WANT TO BE A BETTER VERSION OF MYSELF...
...AND STAY BY MIKETSUKAMI-KUN'S SIDE.
WHAT'D YA WRITE?
どきっ
DOKI (BADUM)
I... I DON'T HAVE ANY IDEA WHAT I'LL BE LIKE IN MY NEXT LIFE.
SO I JUST WROTE DOWN SOME OF MY CURRENT GOALS.
YEAH. WE CAN'T REALLY KNOW.
THAT'S JUST HOW IT IS.

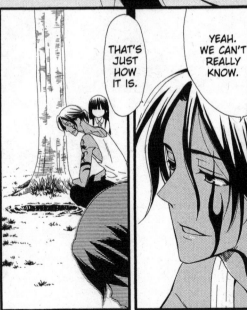

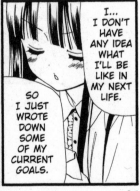

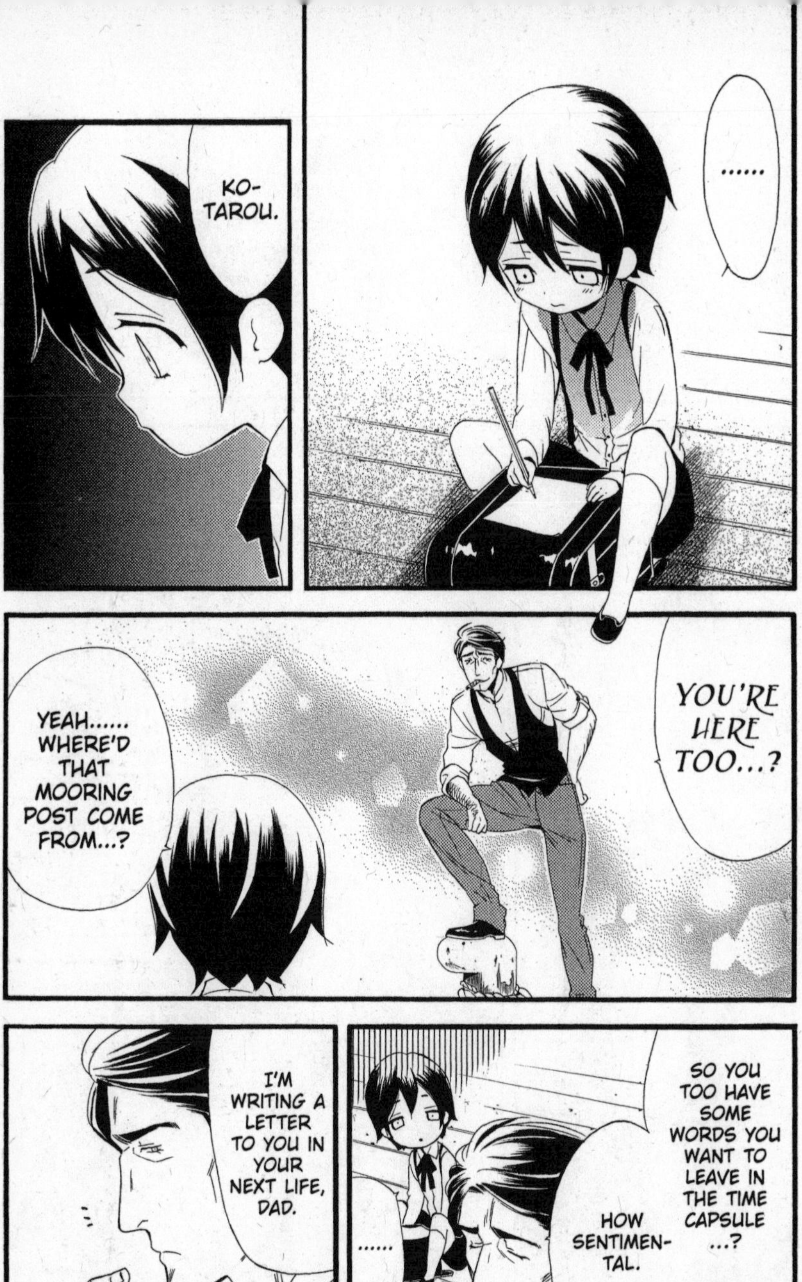
......
KO-TAROU.
YOU'RE HERE TOO...?
YEAH...... WHERE'D THAT MOORING POST COME FROM...?
SO YOU TOO HAVE SOME WORDS YOU WANT TO LEAVE IN THE TIME CAPSULE ...?
HOW SENTIMENTAL.
......
I'M WRITING A LETTER TO YOU IN YOUR NEXT LIFE, DAD.

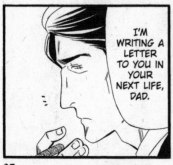

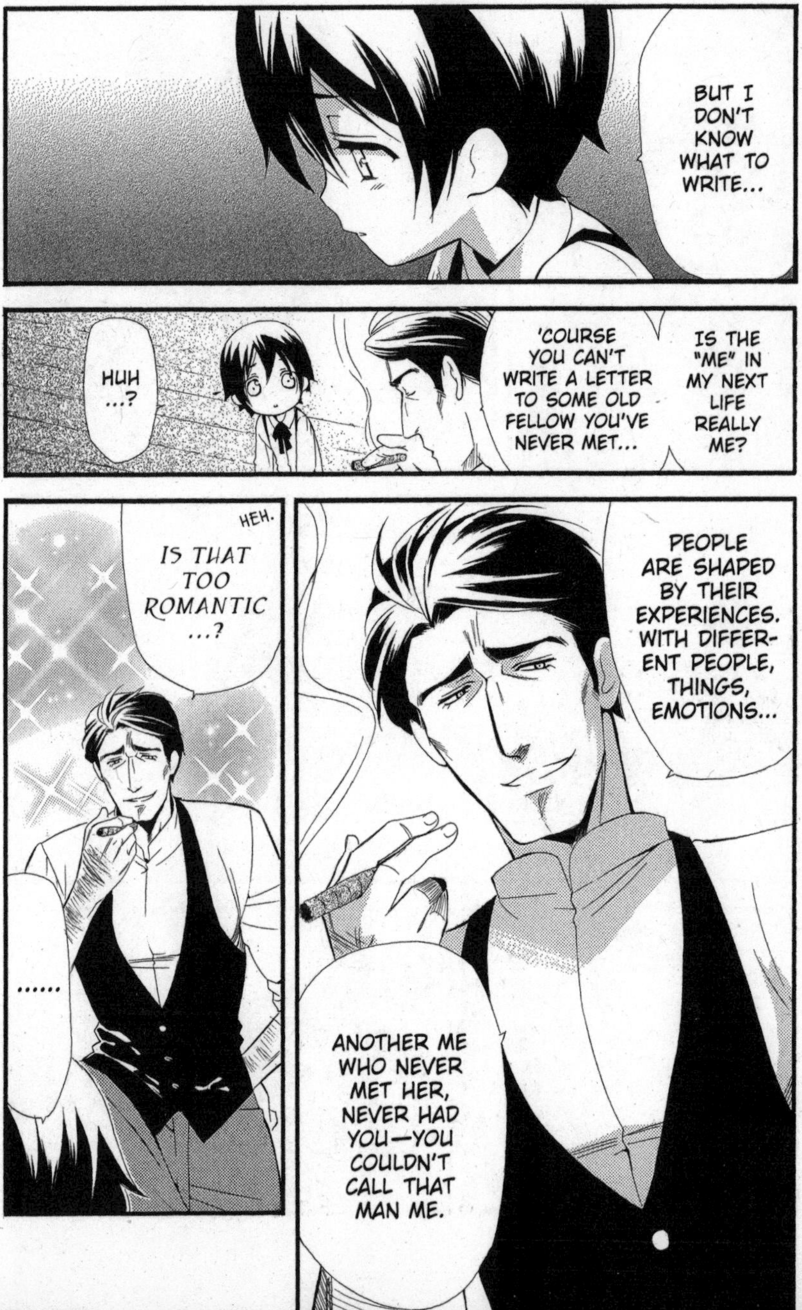
BUT I DON'T KNOW WHAT TO WRITE...
IS THE "ME" IN MY NEXT LIFE REALLY ME?
'COURSE YOU CAN'T WRITE A LETTER TO SOME OLD FELLOW YOU'VE NEVER MET...
HUH ...?
PEOPLE ARE SHAPED BY THEIR EXPERIENCES. WITH DIFFER-ENT PEOPLE, THINGS, EMOTIONS...
ANOTHER ME WHO NEVER MET HER, NEVER HAD YOU—YOU COULDN'T CALL THAT MAN ME.
HEH.
IS THAT TOO ROMANTIC ...?
......

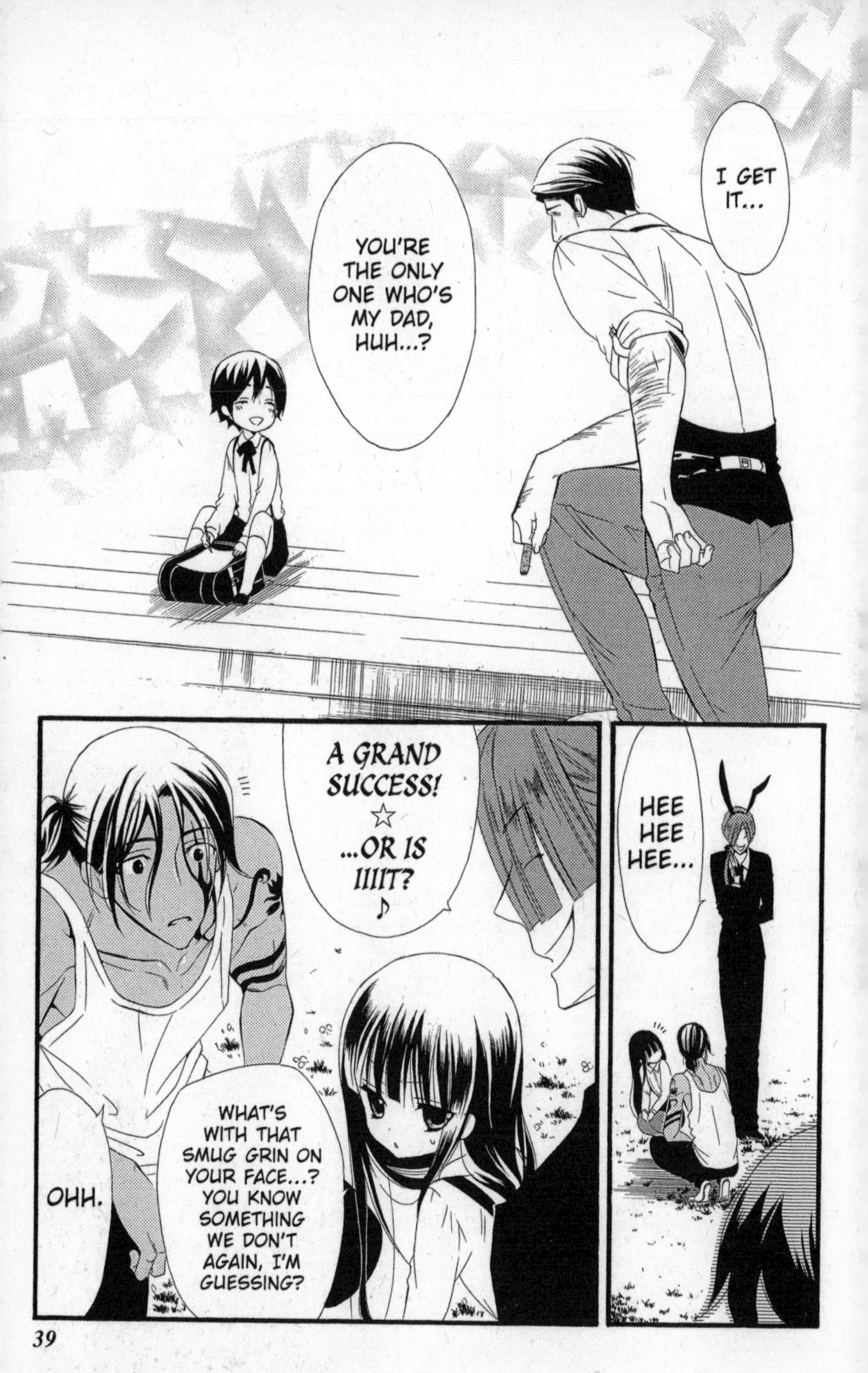
I GET IT...
YOU'RE THE ONLY ONE WHO'S MY DAD, HUH...?
HEE HEE HEE...
A GRAND SUCCESS! ☆ ...OR IS IIIIT? ♪
WHAT'S WITH THAT SMUG GRIN ON YOUR FACE...? YOU KNOW SOMETHING WE DON'T AGAIN, I'M GUESSING?
OHH.

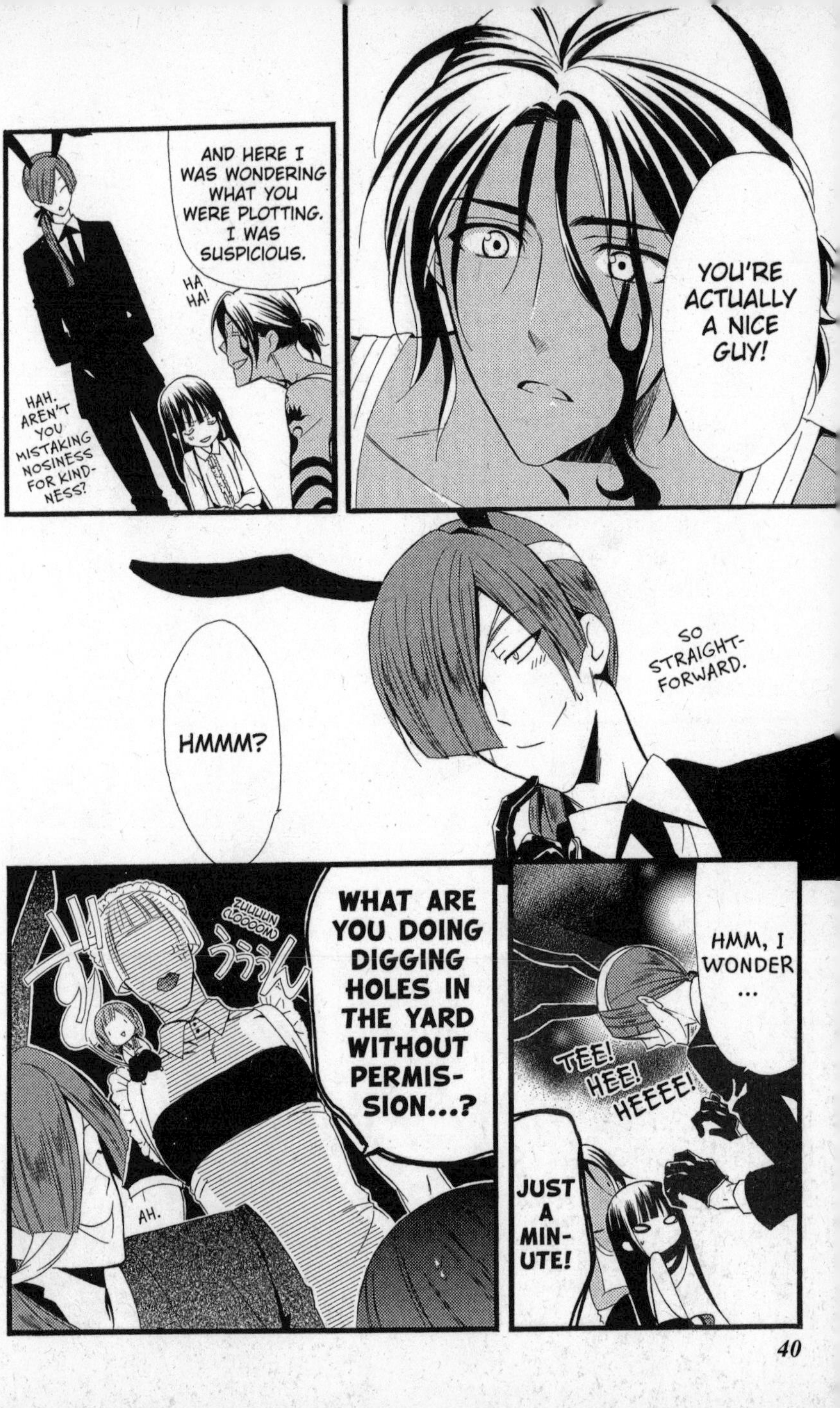
YOU'RE ACTUALLY A NICE GUY!
AND HERE I WAS WONDERING WHAT YOU WERE PLOTTING. I WAS SUSPICIOUS.
HA HA!
HAH. AREN'T YOU MISTAKING NOSINESS FOR KIND-NESS?
SO STRAIGHT-FORWARD.
HMMM?
HMM, I WONDER ...
TEE! HEE! HEEEE!
JUST A MIN-UTE!
WHAT ARE YOU DOING DIGGING HOLES IN THE YARD WITHOUT PERMIS-SION...?
ZUUUUN (LOOOOM)
うううん
AH.

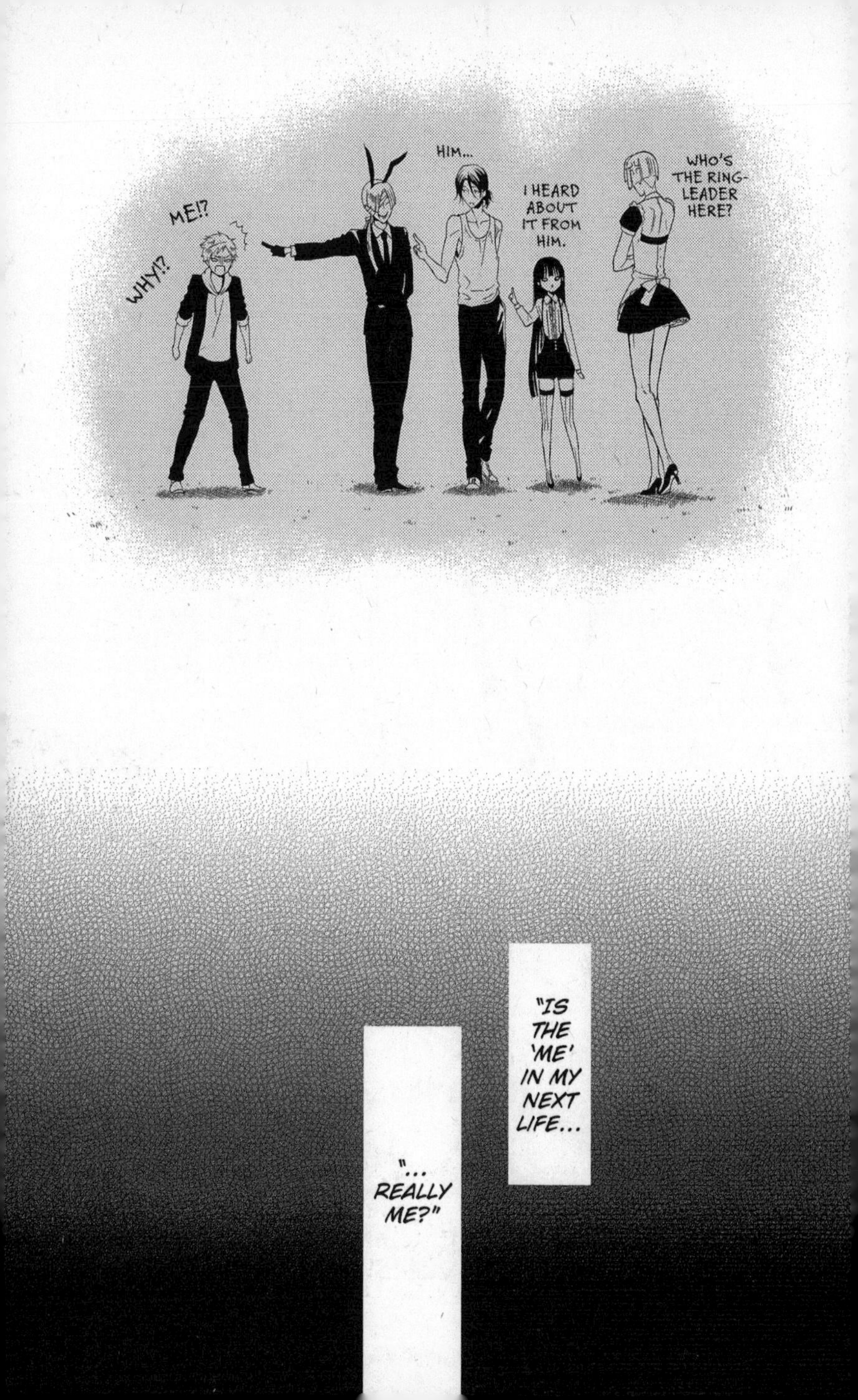
WHO'S THE RING-LEADER HERE?
I HEARD ABOUT IT FROM HIM.
HIM...
ME!?
WHY!?
"IS THE 'ME' IN MY NEXT LIFE...
"... REALLY ME?"

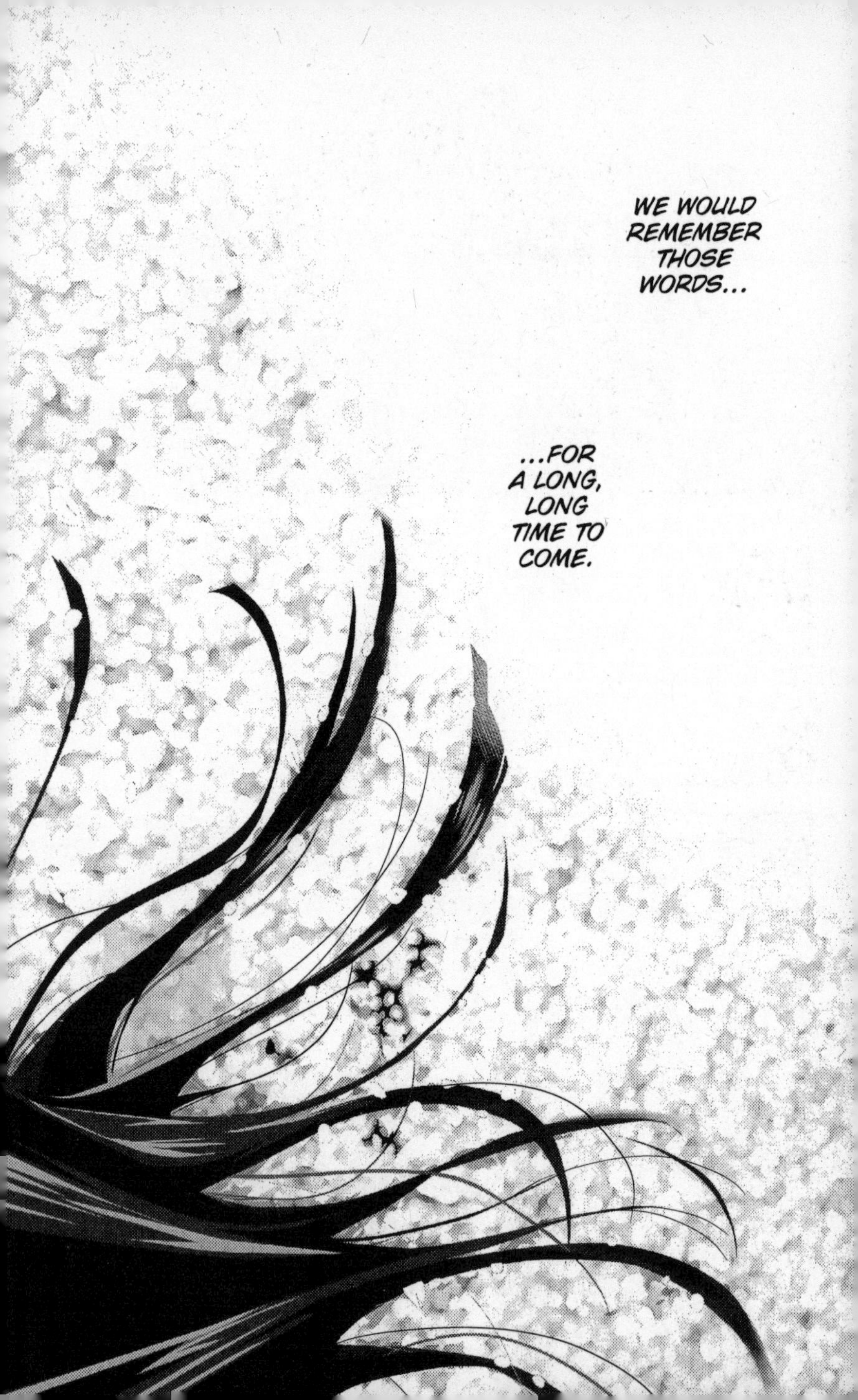
WE WOULD REMEMBER THOSE WORDS...
...FOR A LONG, LONG TIME TO COME.

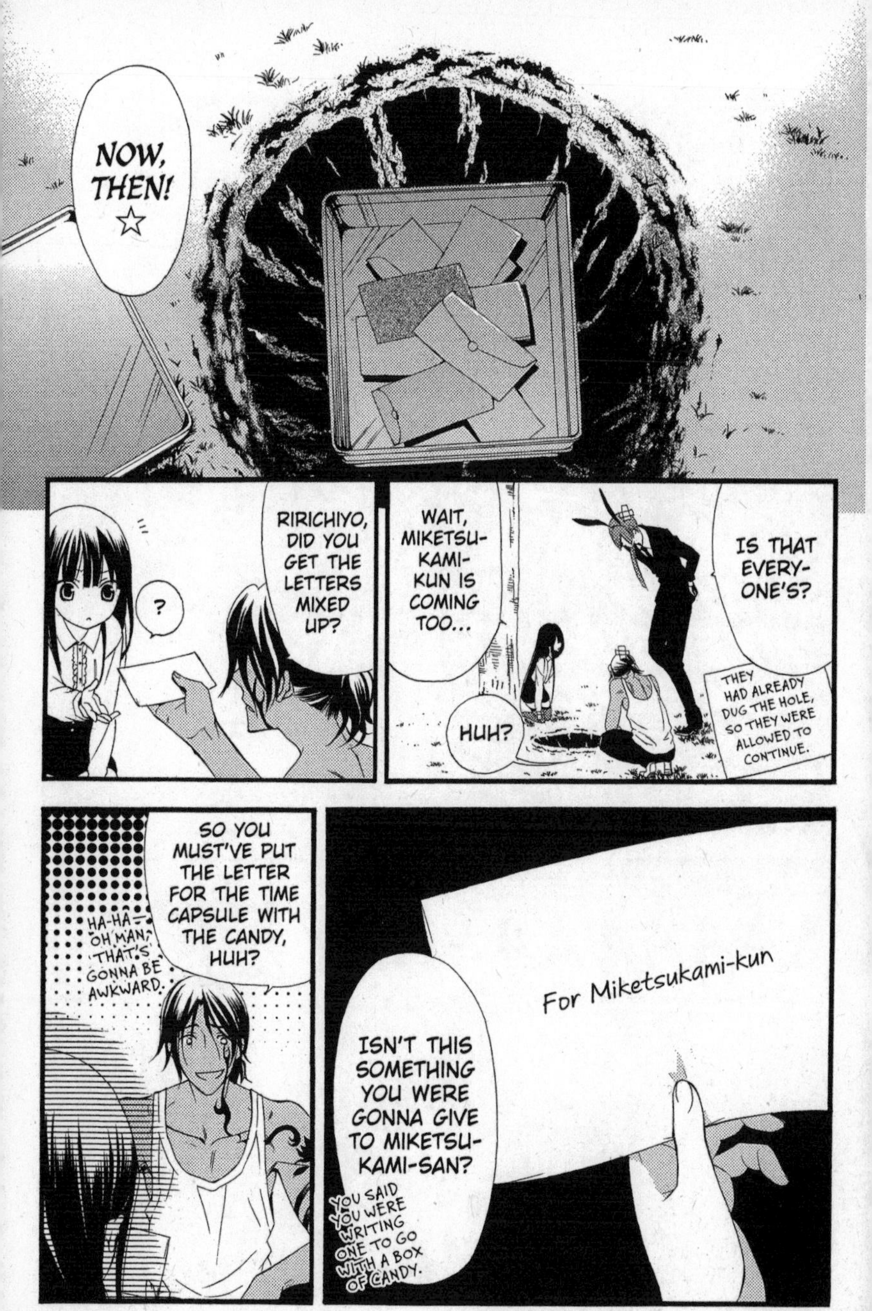
NOW, THEN! ☆
IS THAT EVERY-ONE'S?
THEY HAD ALREADY DUG THE HOLE, SO THEY WERE ALLOWED TO CONTINUE.
WAIT, MIKETSU-KAMI-KUN IS COMING TOO...
HUH?
RIRICHIYO, DID YOU GET THE LETTERS MIXED UP?
?
For Miketsukami-kun
ISN'T THIS SOMETHING YOU WERE GONNA GIVE TO MIKETSU-KAMI-SAN?
YOU SAID YOU WERE WRITING ONE TO GO WITH A BOX OF CANDY.
SO YOU MUST'VE PUT THE LETTER FOR THE TIME CAPSULE WITH THE CANDY, HUH?
HA-HA— OH MAN, THAT'S GONNA BE AWKWARD.

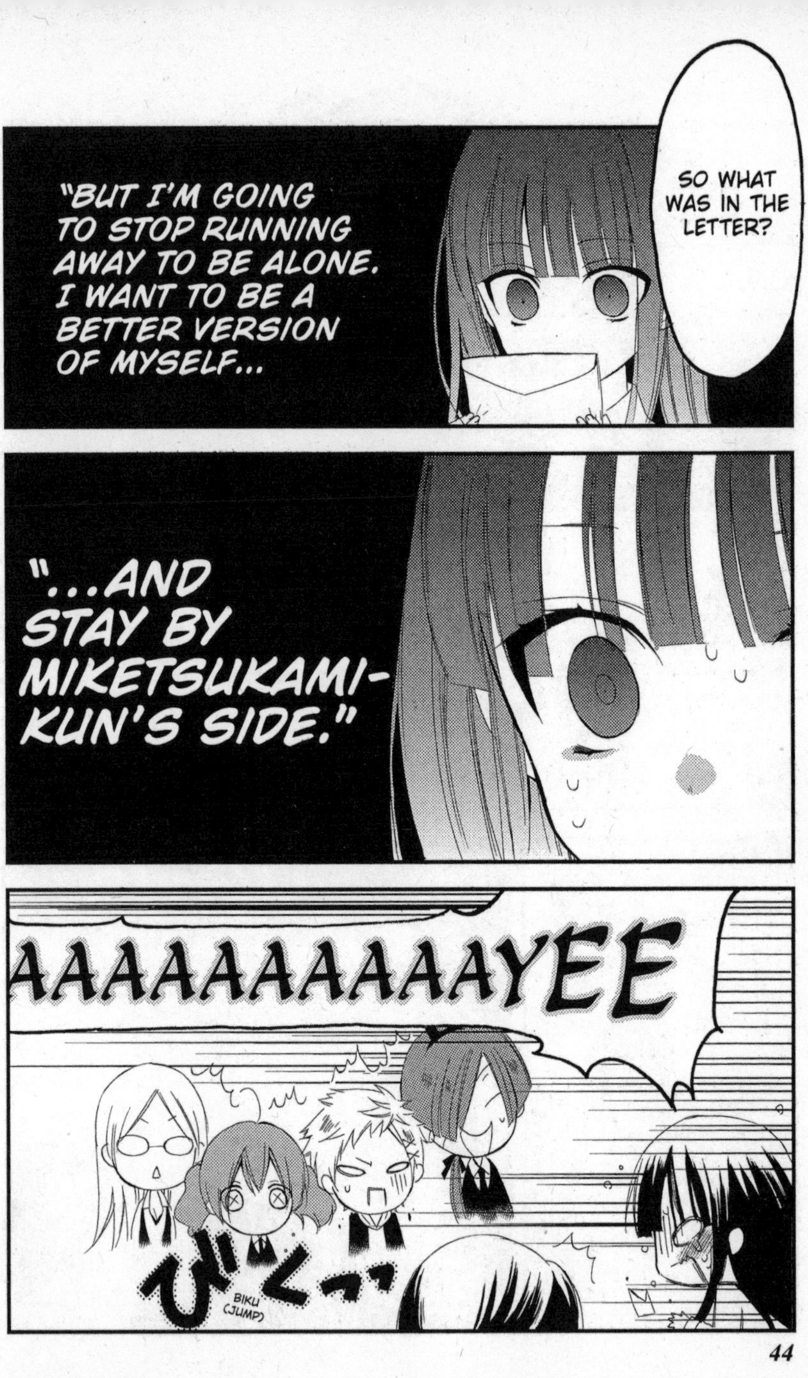
SO WHAT WAS IN THE LETTER?
"BUT I'M GOING TO STOP RUNNING AWAY TO BE ALONE. I WANT TO BE A BETTER VERSION OF MYSELF...
"...AND STAY BY MIKETSUKAMI-KUN'S SIDE."
AAAAAAAAAAAYEE
びくっ
BIKU (JUMP)

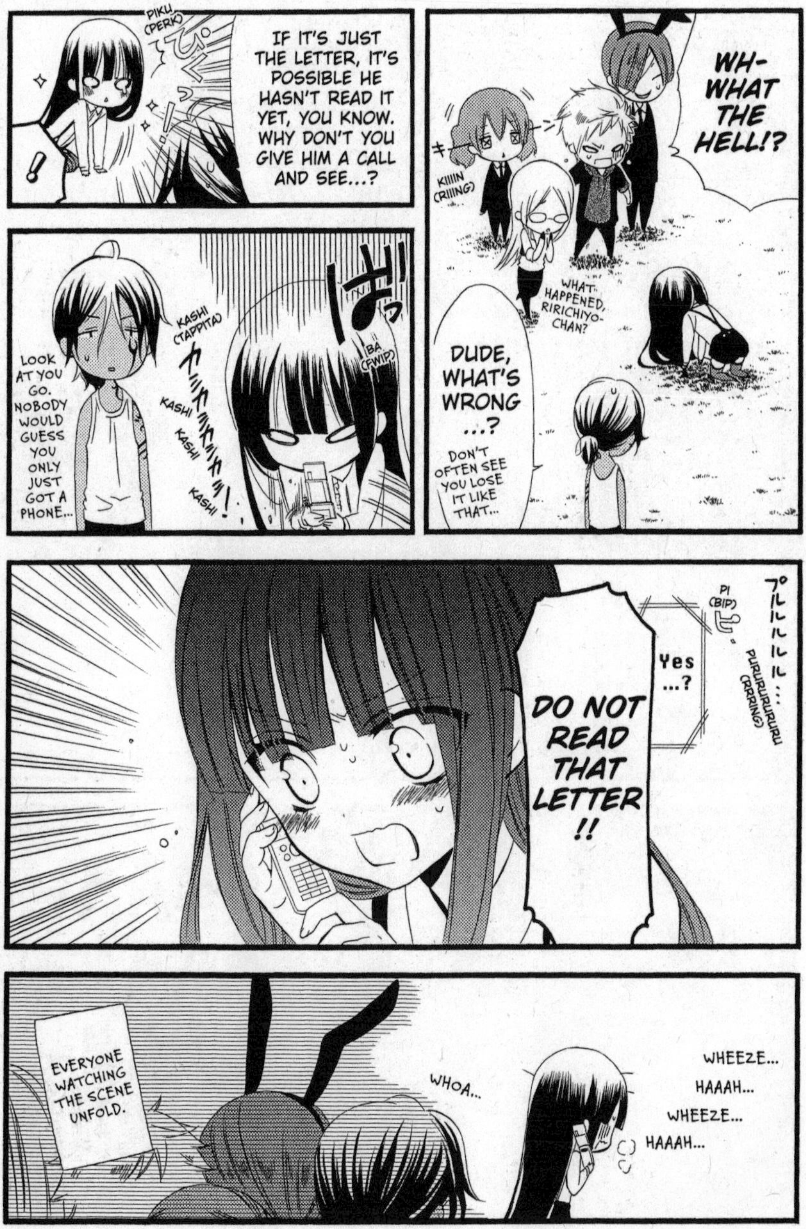
WH-WHAT THE HELL!?
KIIIN (RIIING)
WHAT HAPPENED, RIRICHIYO-CHAN?
DUDE, WHAT'S WRONG ...?
DON'T OFTEN SEE YOU LOSE IT LIKE THAT...
IF IT'S JUST THE LETTER, IT'S POSSIBLE HE HASN'T READ IT YET, YOU KNOW. WHY DON'T YOU GIVE HIM A CALL AND SEE...?
PIKU (PERK)
BA (FWIP)
KASHI (TAPPITA)
KASHI
KASHI
KASHI
LOOK AT YOU GO. NOBODY WOULD GUESS YOU ONLY JUST GOT A PHONE...
プルルル…
PURURURURU (RRRING)
ピ
PI (BIP)
Yes ...?
DO NOT READ THAT LETTER !!
WHEEZE...
HAAAH...
WHEEZE...
HAAAH...
WHOA...
EVERYONE WATCHING THE SCENE UNFOLD.

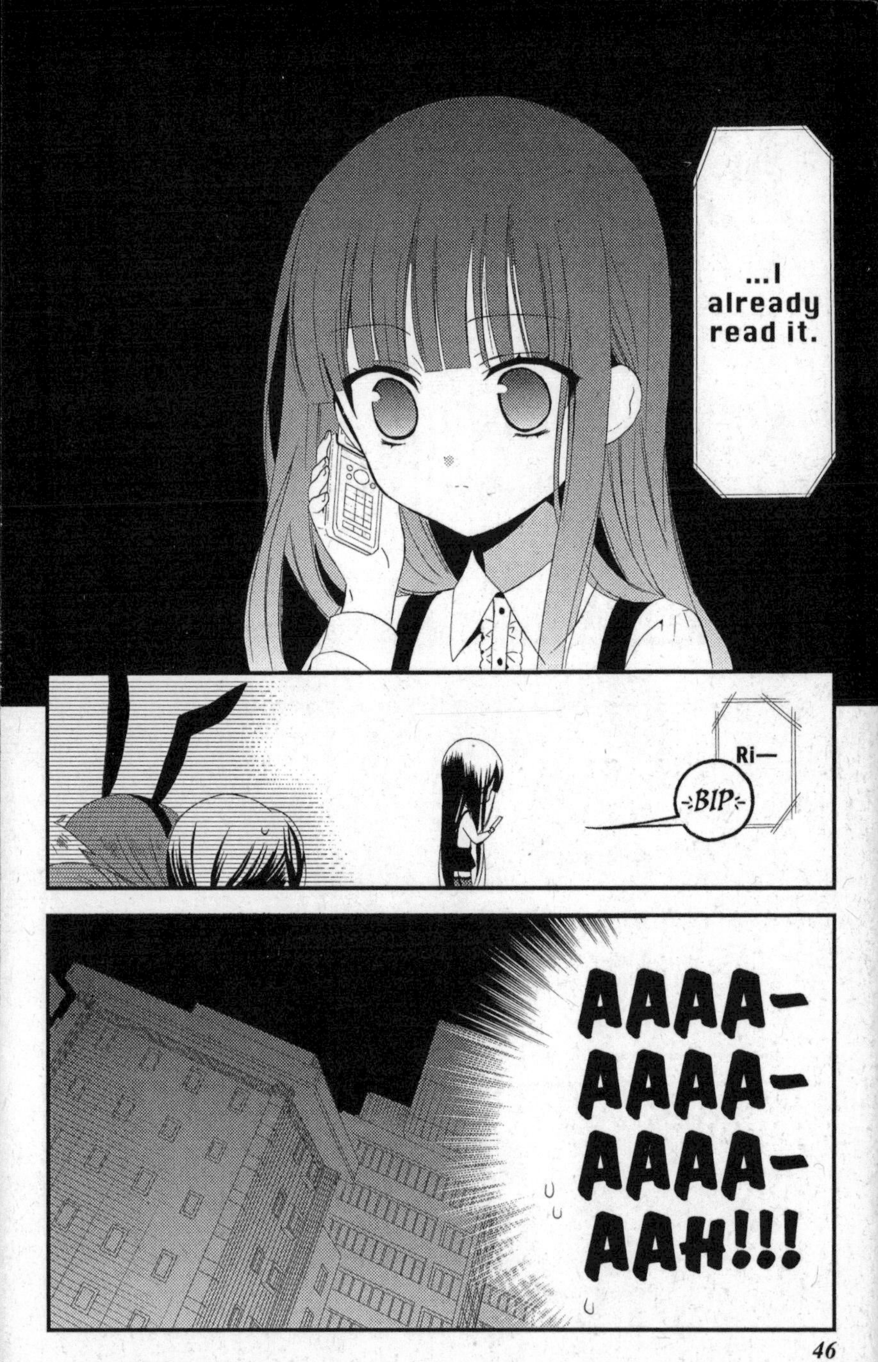
...I already read it.
Ri—
BIP
AAAA-AAAA-AAAA-AAH!!!

# INU×BOKU SS

maison de ayakashi

Welcome to Maison de Ayakashi.
The exclusive Secret Service of
this Mansion guarantees
your mental and physical
safety by providing
superior escorts.

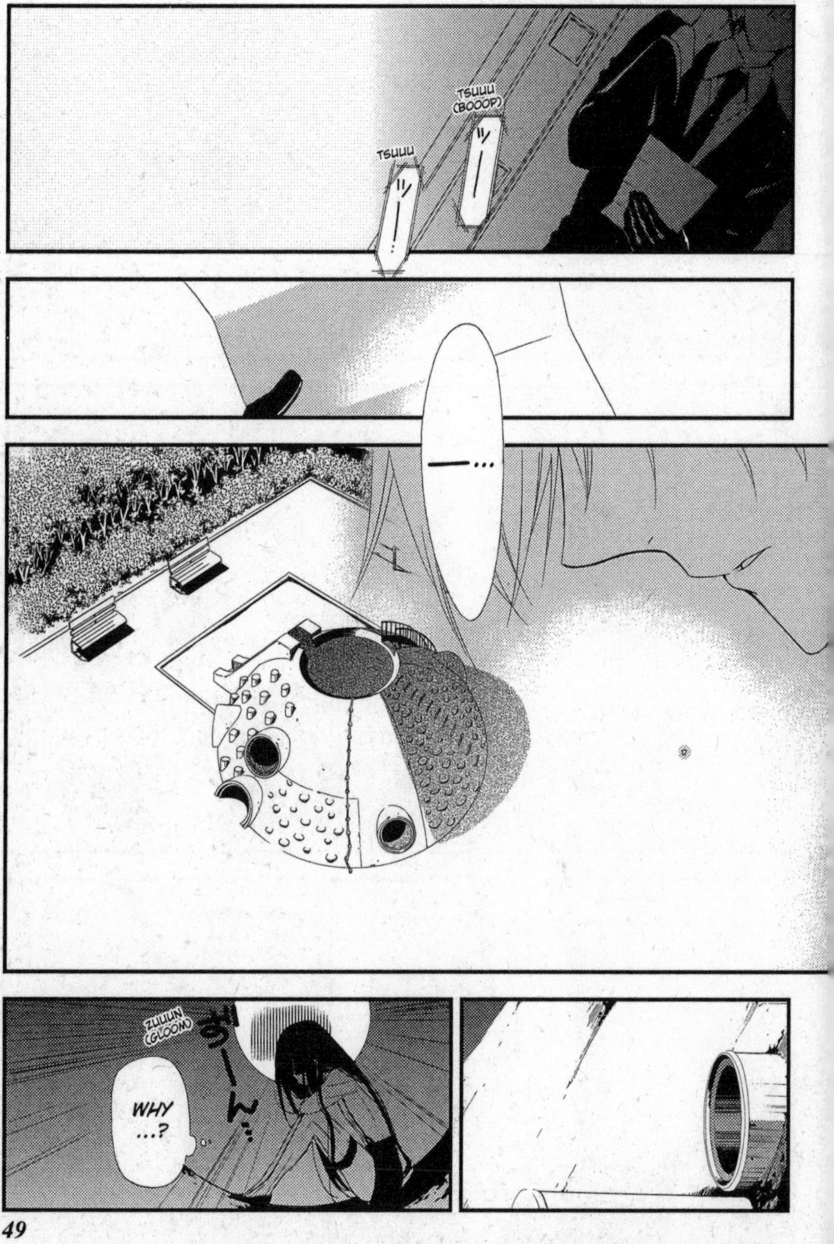
TSUUU (BOOOP)
TSUUU
——...
ZUUUN (GLOOM)
WHY ...?

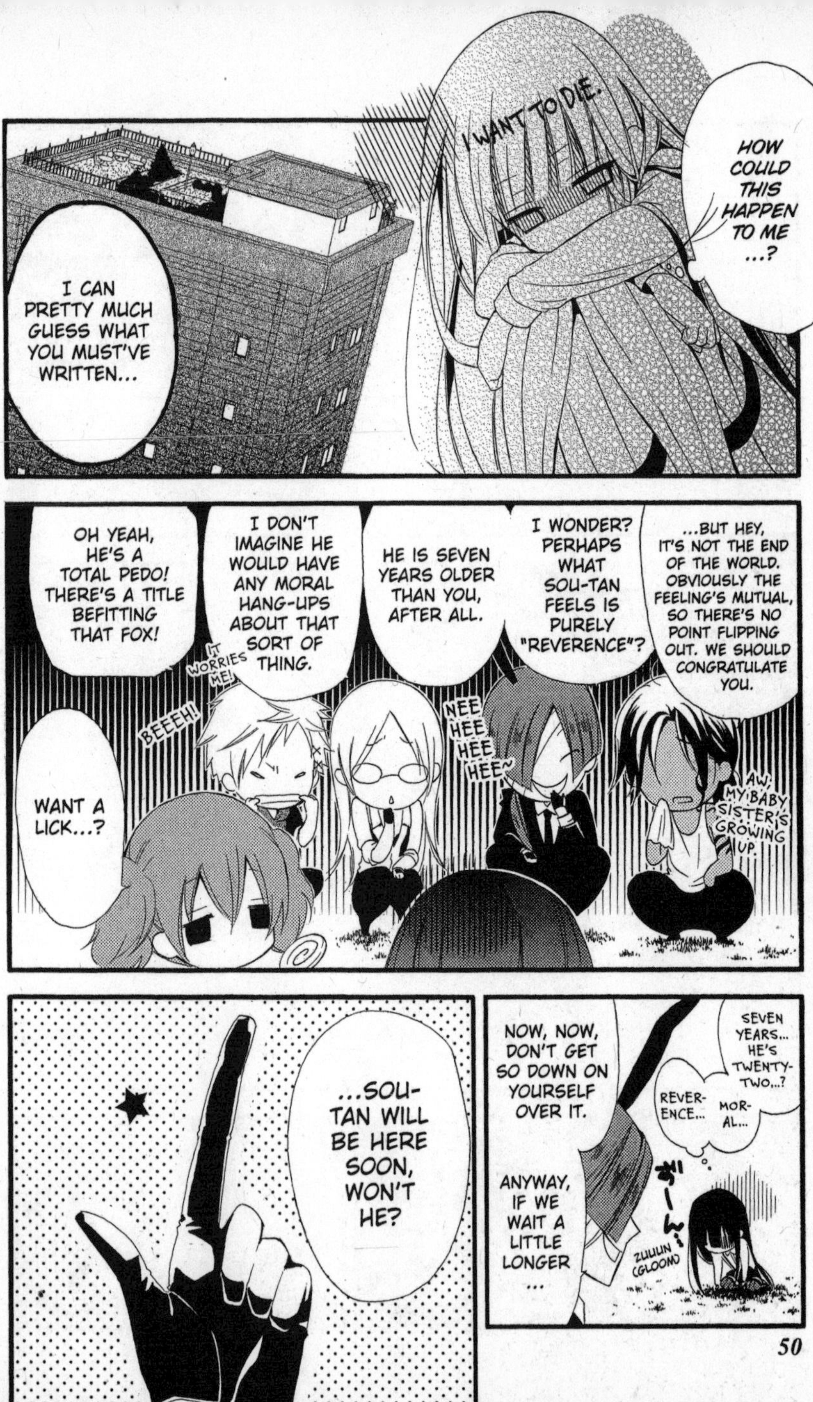
HOW COULD THIS HAPPEN TO ME ...?
I WANT TO DIE.
I CAN PRETTY MUCH GUESS WHAT YOU MUST'VE WRITTEN...
...BUT HEY, IT'S NOT THE END OF THE WORLD. OBVIOUSLY THE FEELING'S MUTUAL, SO THERE'S NO POINT FLIPPING OUT. WE SHOULD CONGRATULATE YOU.
I WONDER? PERHAPS WHAT SOU-TAN FEELS IS PURELY "REVERENCE"?
HE IS SEVEN YEARS OLDER THAN YOU, AFTER ALL.
I DON'T IMAGINE HE WOULD HAVE ANY MORAL HANG-UPS ABOUT THAT SORT OF THING.
OH YEAH, HE'S A TOTAL PEDO! THERE'S A TITLE BEFITTING THAT FOX!
AW, MY BABY SISTER'S GROWING UP.
NEE HEE HEE HEE~
IT WORRIES ME!
BEEEH!
WANT A LICK...?
NOW, NOW, DON'T GET SO DOWN ON YOURSELF OVER IT.
SEVEN YEARS... HE'S TWENTY-TWO...?
MORAL...
REVERENCE...
ZUUUN (GLOOM)
ANYWAY, IF WE WAIT A LITTLE LONGER ...
...SOU-TAN WILL BE HERE SOON, WON'T HE?

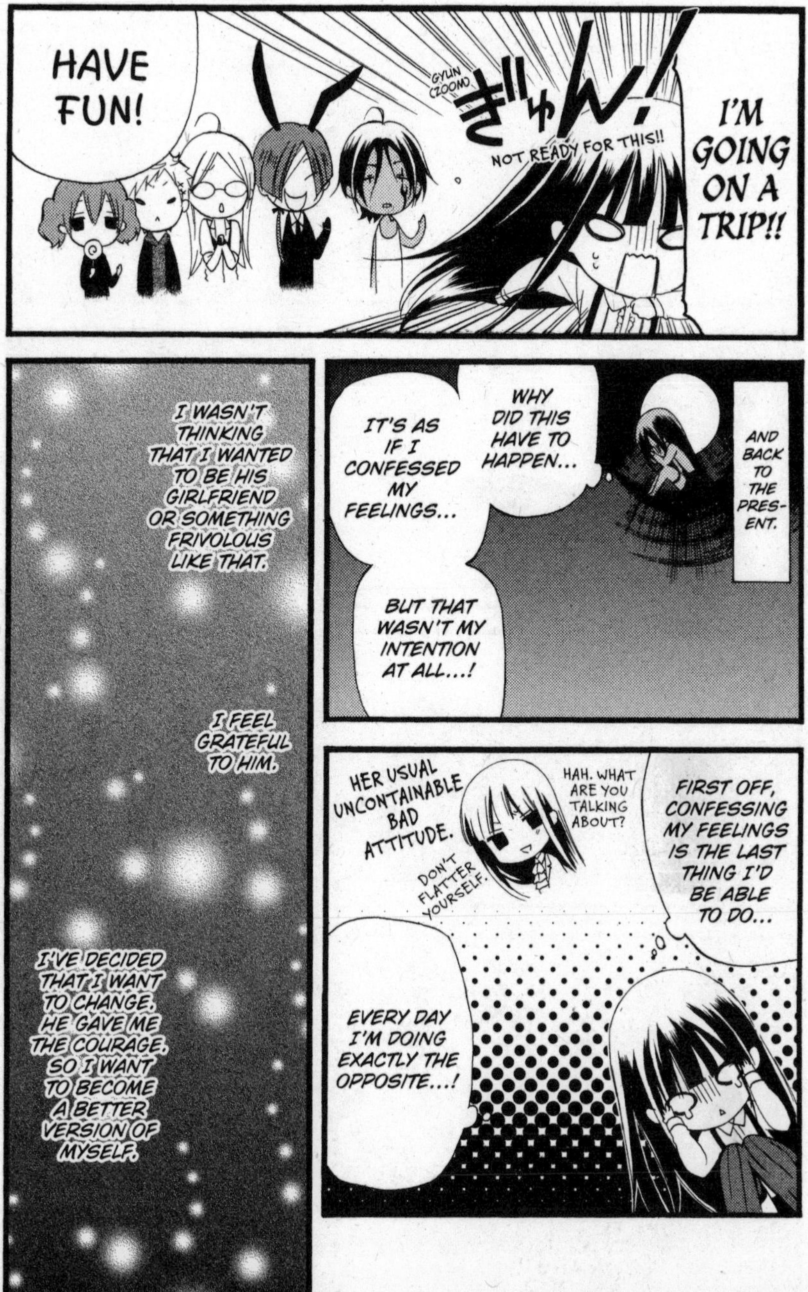
I'M GOING ON A TRIP!!
GYUN (ZOOM)
ぎゅん!
NOT READY FOR THIS!!
HAVE FUN!
AND BACK TO THE PRESENT.
WHY DID THIS HAVE TO HAPPEN...
IT'S AS IF I CONFESSED MY FEELINGS...
BUT THAT WASN'T MY INTENTION AT ALL...!
FIRST OFF, CONFESSING MY FEELINGS IS THE LAST THING I'D BE ABLE TO DO...
HAH. WHAT ARE YOU TALKING ABOUT?
HER USUAL UNCONTAINABLE BAD ATTITUDE.
DON'T FLATTER YOURSELF.
EVERY DAY I'M DOING EXACTLY THE OPPOSITE...!
I WASN'T THINKING THAT I WANTED TO BE HIS GIRLFRIEND OR SOMETHING FRIVOLOUS LIKE THAT.
I FEEL GRATEFUL TO HIM.
I'VE DECIDED THAT I WANT TO CHANGE. HE GAVE ME THE COURAGE. SO I WANT TO BECOME A BETTER VERSION OF MYSELF.

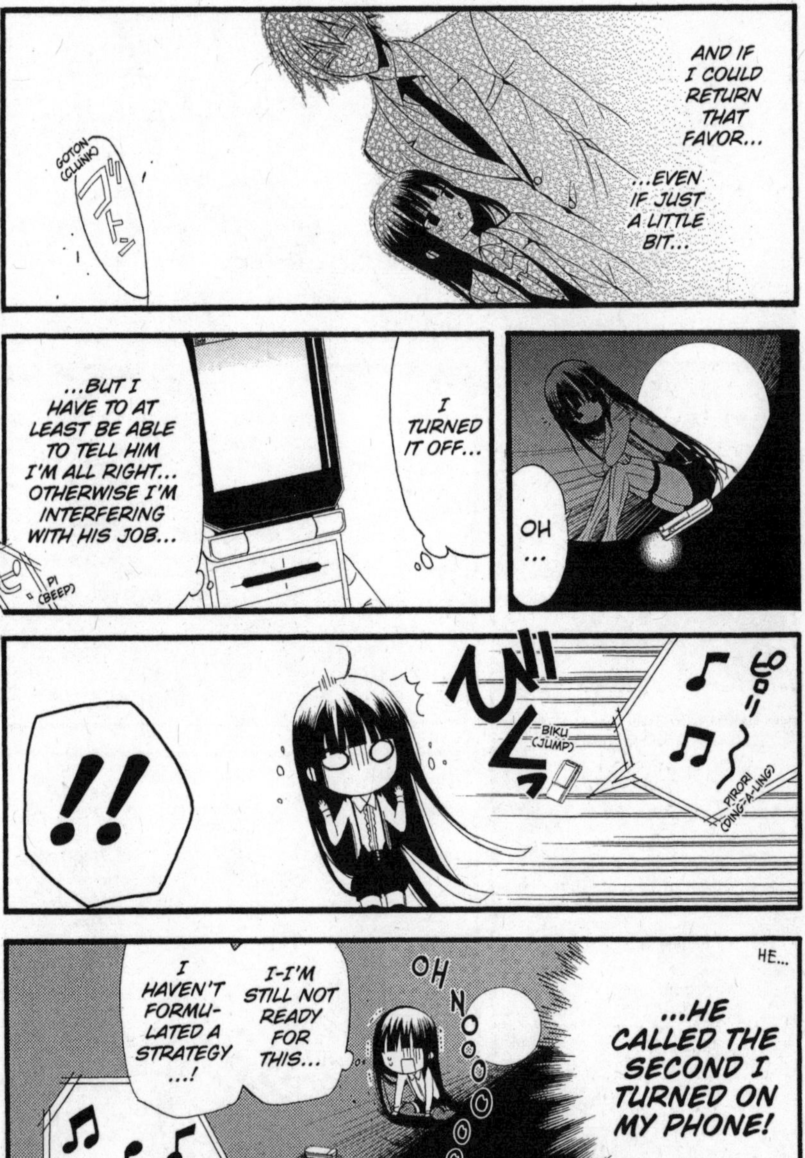
AND IF I COULD RETURN THAT FAVOR...
...EVEN IF JUST A LITTLE BIT...
GOTON (CLUNK)
OH ...
I TURNED IT OFF...
...BUT I HAVE TO AT LEAST BE ABLE TO TELL HIM I'M ALL RIGHT... OTHERWISE I'M INTERFERING WITH HIS JOB...
PI (BEEP)
PIRORI (DING-A-LING)
BIKU (JUMP)
!!
HE...
...HE CALLED THE SECOND I TURNED ON MY PHONE!
OH NOOOOOOO
I-I'M STILL NOT READY FOR THIS...
I HAVEN'T FORMULATED A STRATEGY ...!

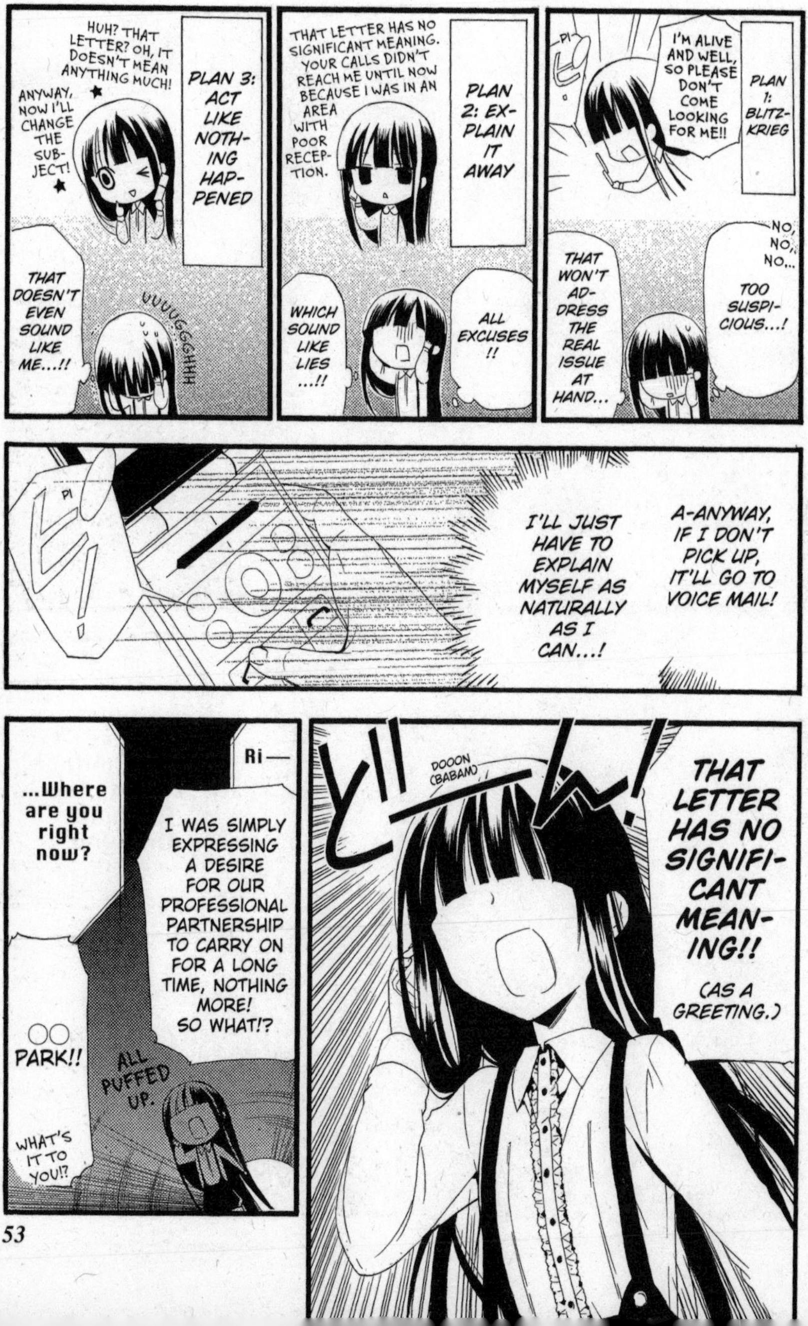
PLAN 1: BLITZKRIEG
I'M ALIVE AND WELL, SO PLEASE DON'T COME LOOKING FOR ME!!
PI
NO, NO, NO... TOO SUSPICIOUS...!
THAT WON'T ADDRESS THE REAL ISSUE AT HAND...
PLAN 2: EXPLAIN IT AWAY
THAT LETTER HAS NO SIGNIFICANT MEANING. YOUR CALLS DIDN'T REACH ME UNTIL NOW BECAUSE I WAS IN AN AREA WITH POOR RECEPTION.
ALL EXCUSES!!
WHICH SOUND LIKE LIES...!!
PLAN 3: ACT LIKE NOTHING HAPPENED
HUH? THAT LETTER? OH, IT DOESN'T MEAN ANYTHING MUCH!
ANYWAY, NOW I'LL CHANGE THE SUBJECT!
THAT DOESN'T EVEN SOUND LIKE ME...!!
UUUUGGGHHH
A-ANYWAY, IF I DON'T PICK UP, IT'LL GO TO VOICE MAIL!
I'LL JUST HAVE TO EXPLAIN MYSELF AS NATURALLY AS I CAN...!
PI
THAT LETTER HAS NO SIGNIFICANT MEANING!!
DOOON (BABAM)
(AS A GREETING.)
Ri—
...Where are you right now?
I WAS SIMPLY EXPRESSING A DESIRE FOR OUR PROFESSIONAL PARTNERSHIP TO CARRY ON FOR A LONG TIME, NOTHING MORE! SO WHAT!?
○○ PARK!!
ALL PUFFED UP.
WHAT'S IT TO YOU!?

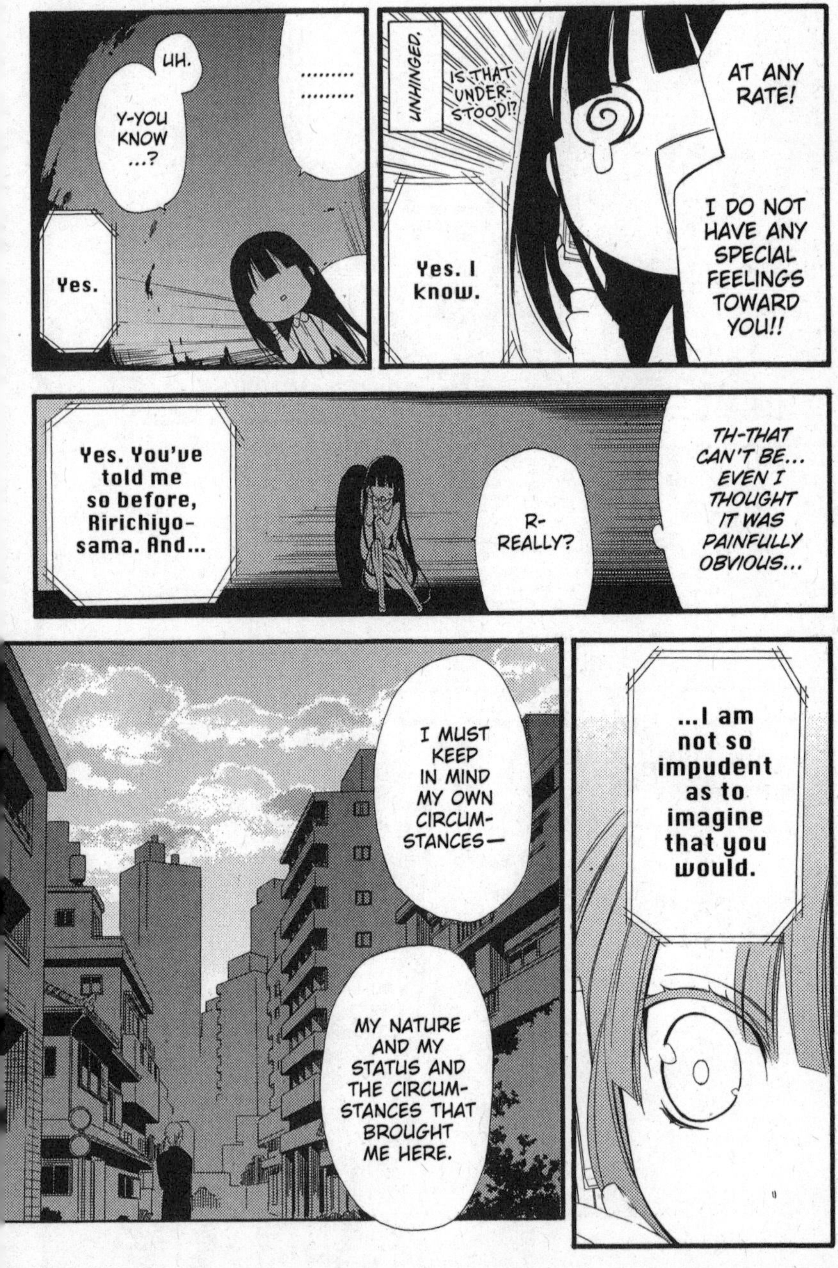
AT ANY RATE!
I DO NOT HAVE ANY SPECIAL FEELINGS TOWARD YOU!!
IS THAT UNDERSTOOD!?
UNHINGED,
Yes. I know.
.........
.........
UH.
Y-YOU KNOW ...?
Yes.
TH-THAT CAN'T BE... EVEN I THOUGHT IT WAS PAINFULLY OBVIOUS...
R-REALLY?
Yes. You've told me so before, Ririchiyo-sama. And...
...I am not so impudent as to imagine that you would.
I MUST KEEP IN MIND MY OWN CIRCUMSTANCES—
MY NATURE AND MY STATUS AND THE CIRCUMSTANCES THAT BROUGHT ME HERE.

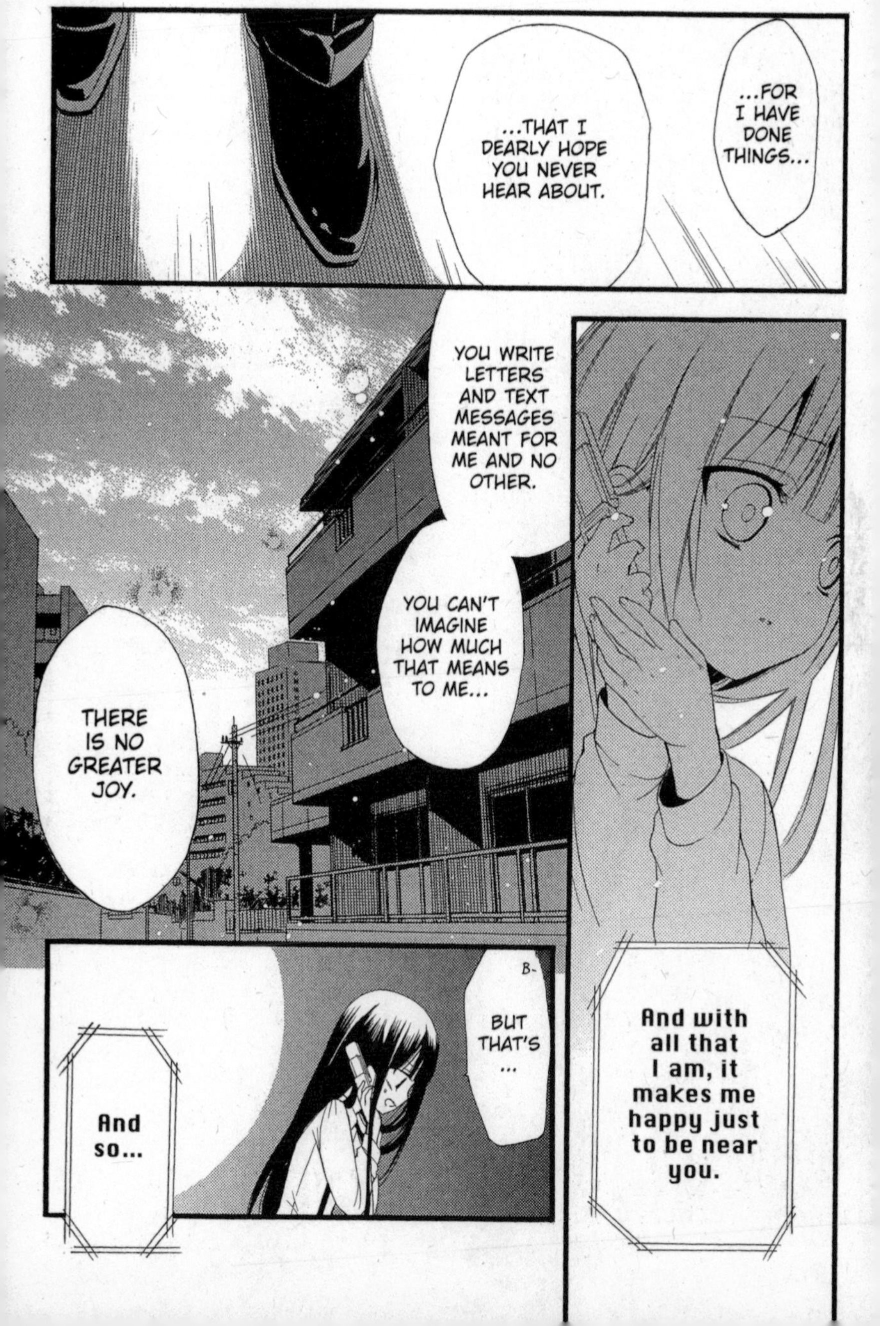
...FOR I HAVE DONE THINGS...
...THAT I DEARLY HOPE YOU NEVER HEAR ABOUT.
And with all that I am, it makes me happy just to be near you.
YOU WRITE LETTERS AND TEXT MESSAGES MEANT FOR ME AND NO OTHER.
YOU CAN'T IMAGINE HOW MUCH THAT MEANS TO ME...
THERE IS NO GREATER JOY.
B- BUT THAT'S ...
And so...

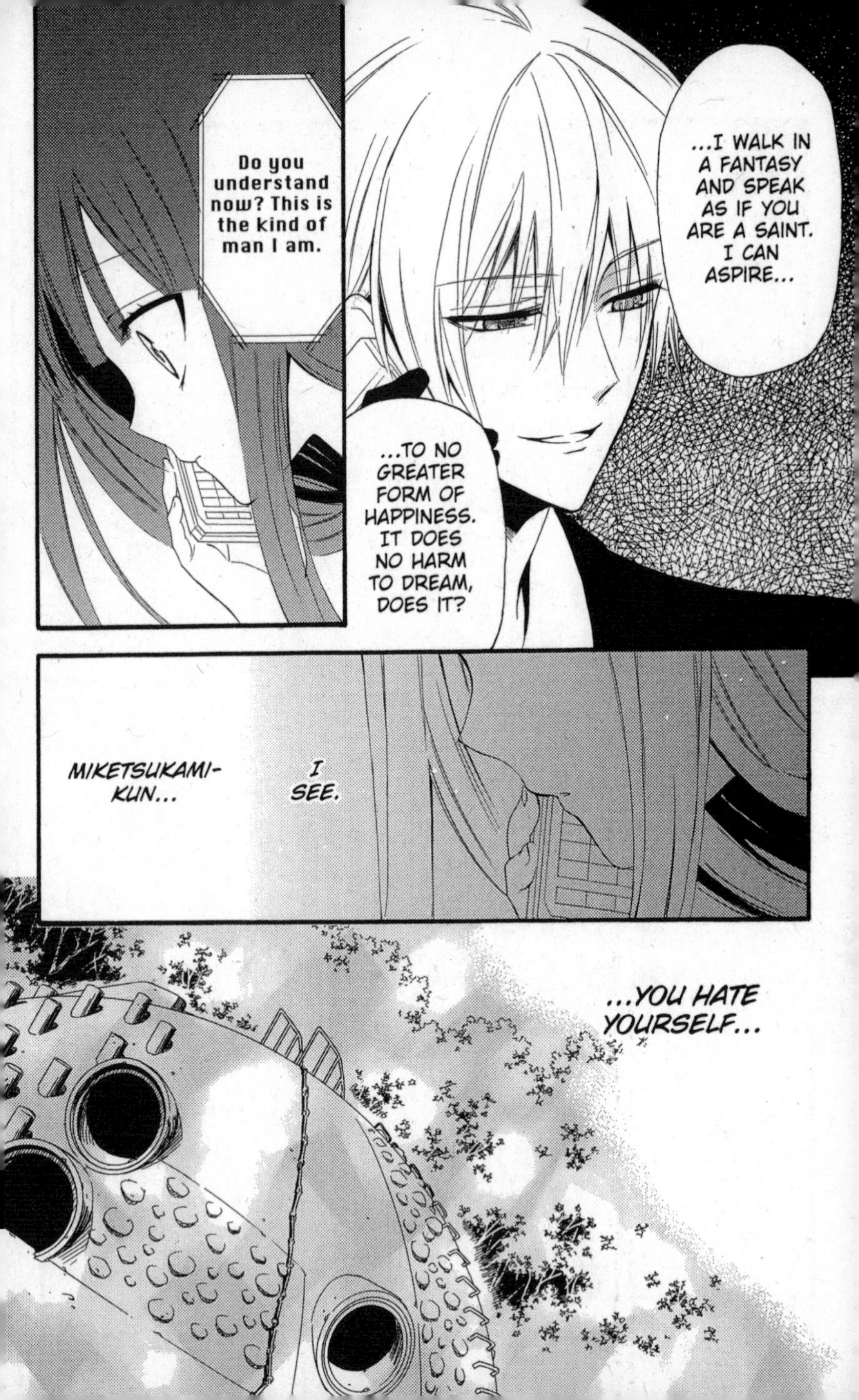
...I WALK IN A FANTASY AND SPEAK AS IF YOU ARE A SAINT. I CAN ASPIRE...
...TO NO GREATER FORM OF HAPPINESS. IT DOES NO HARM TO DREAM, DOES IT?
Do you understand now? This is the kind of man I am.
I SEE.
MIKETSUKAMI-KUN...
...YOU HATE YOURSELF...

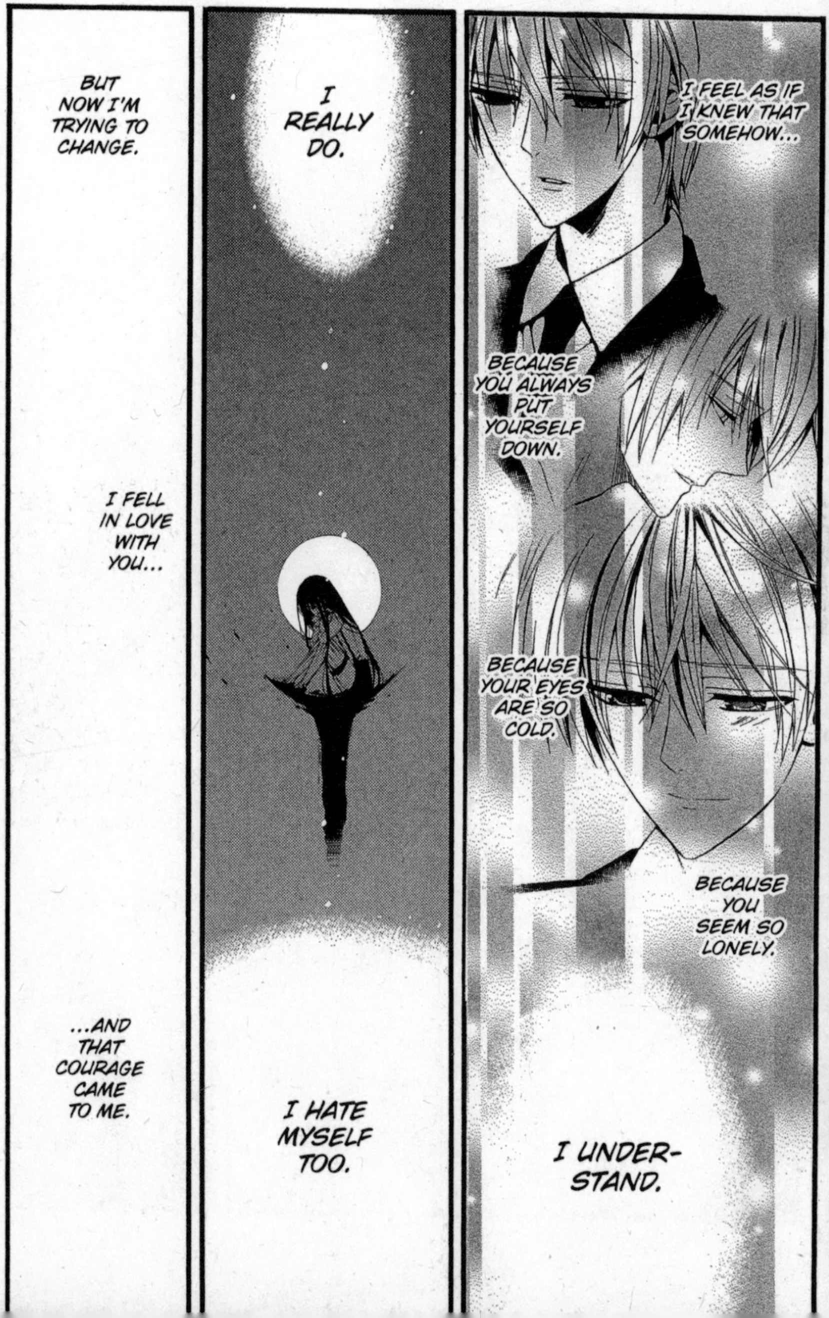
I FEEL AS IF I KNEW THAT SOMEHOW...
BECAUSE YOU ALWAYS PUT YOURSELF DOWN.
BECAUSE YOUR EYES ARE SO COLD.
BECAUSE YOU SEEM SO LONELY.
I UNDER-STAND.
I REALLY DO.
I HATE MYSELF TOO.
BUT NOW I'M TRYING TO CHANGE.
I FELL IN LOVE WITH YOU...
...AND THAT COURAGE CAME TO ME.

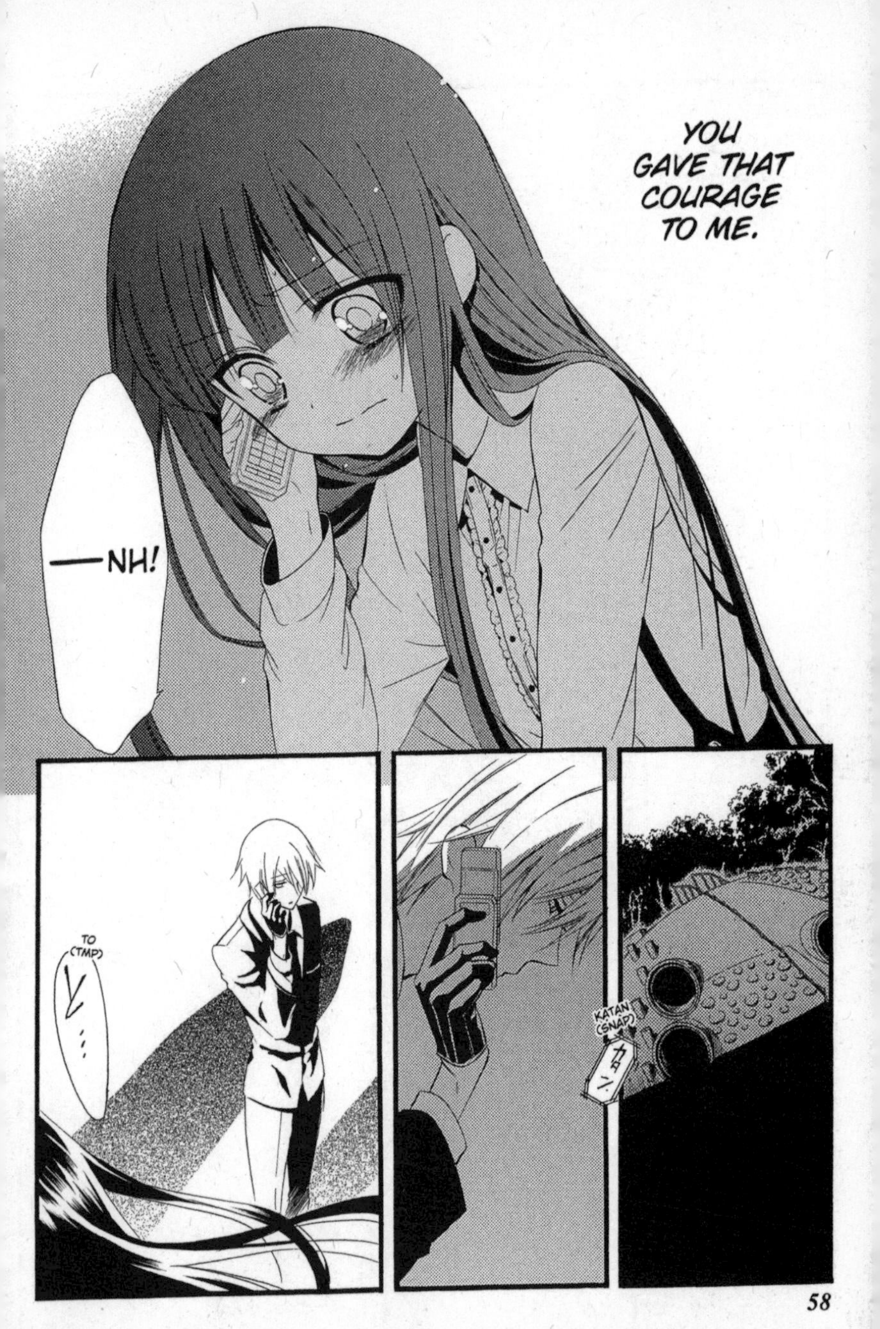
YOU GAVE THAT COURAGE TO ME.
—NH!
KATAN (SNAP)
TO (TMP)

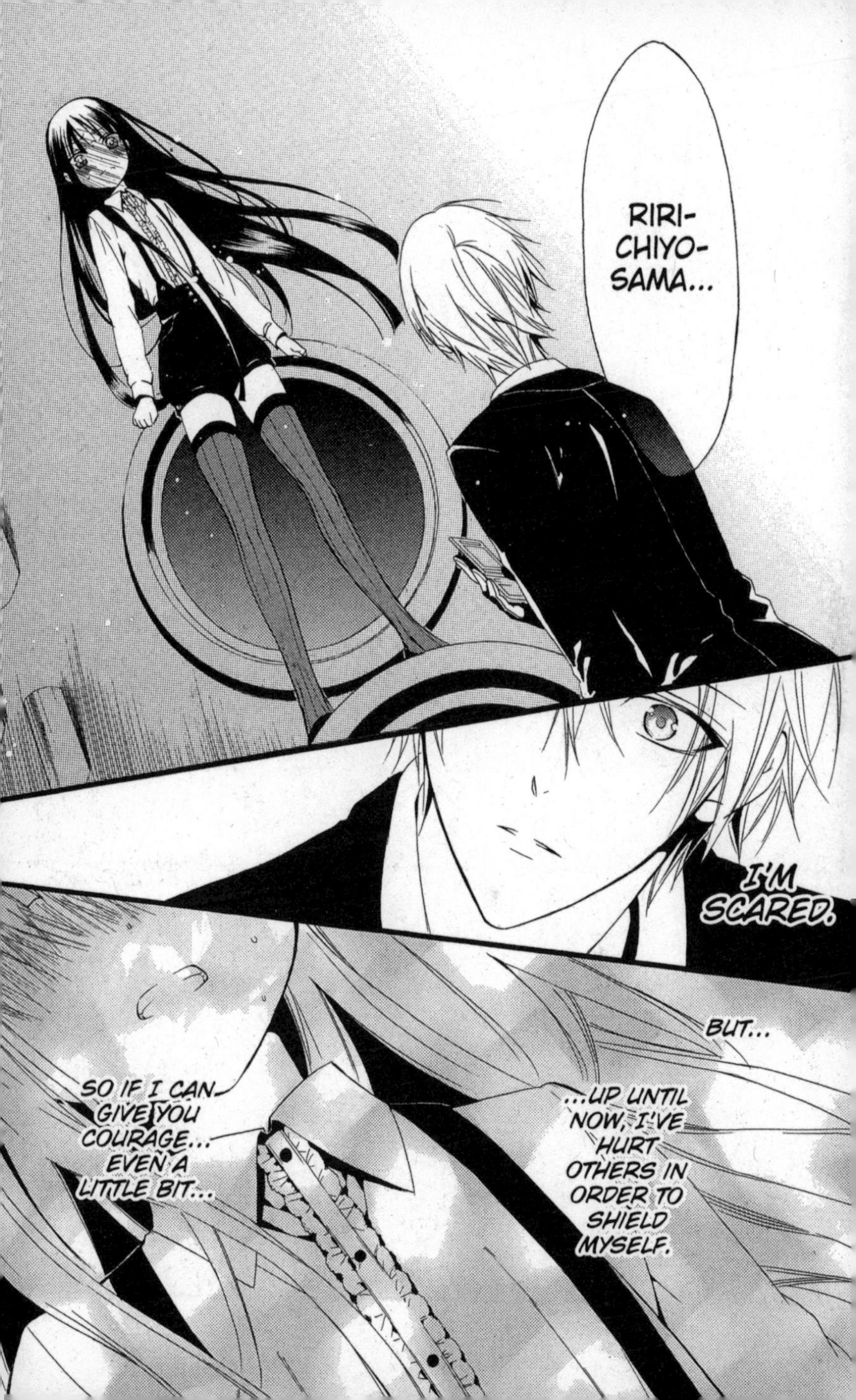
RIRI-CHIYO-SAMA...
I'M SCARED.
BUT...
...UP UNTIL NOW, I'VE HURT OTHERS IN ORDER TO SHIELD MYSELF.
SO IF I CAN GIVE YOU COURAGE... EVEN A LITTLE BIT...

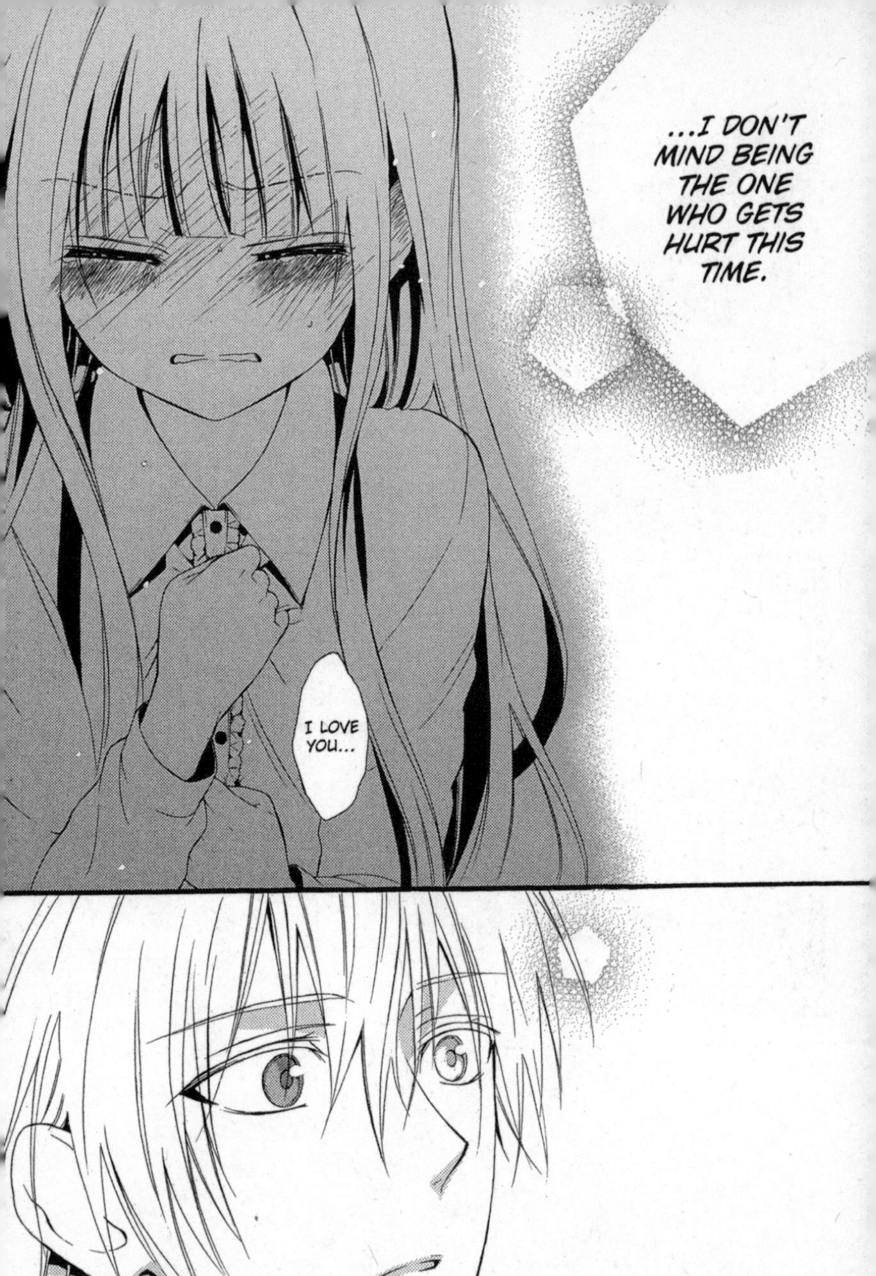
...I DON'T MIND BEING THE ONE WHO GETS HURT THIS TIME.
I LOVE YOU...

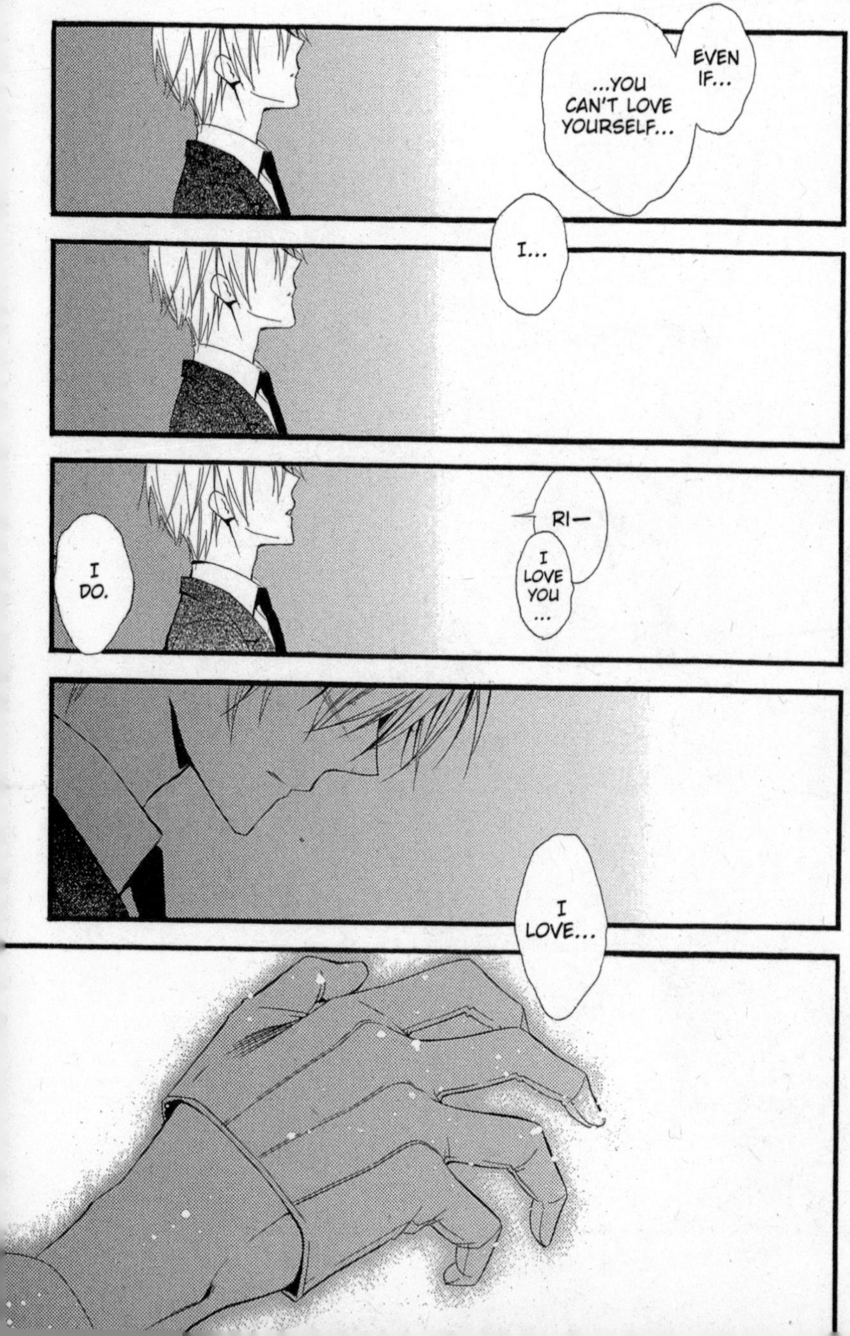
EVEN IF...
...YOU CAN'T LOVE YOURSELF...
I...
RI—
I LOVE YOU ...
I DO.
I LOVE...

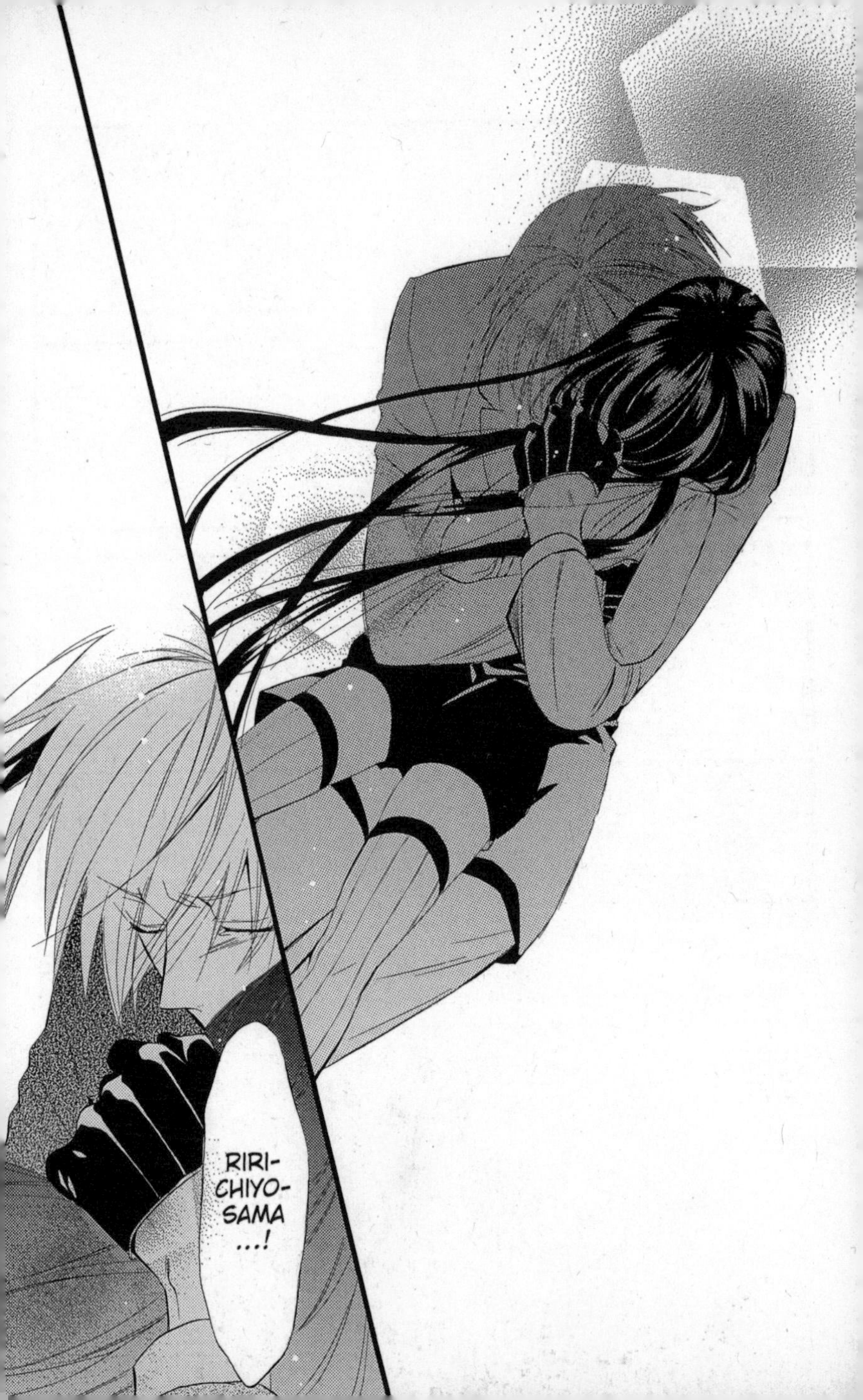
RIRI-
CHIYO-
SAMA
...!

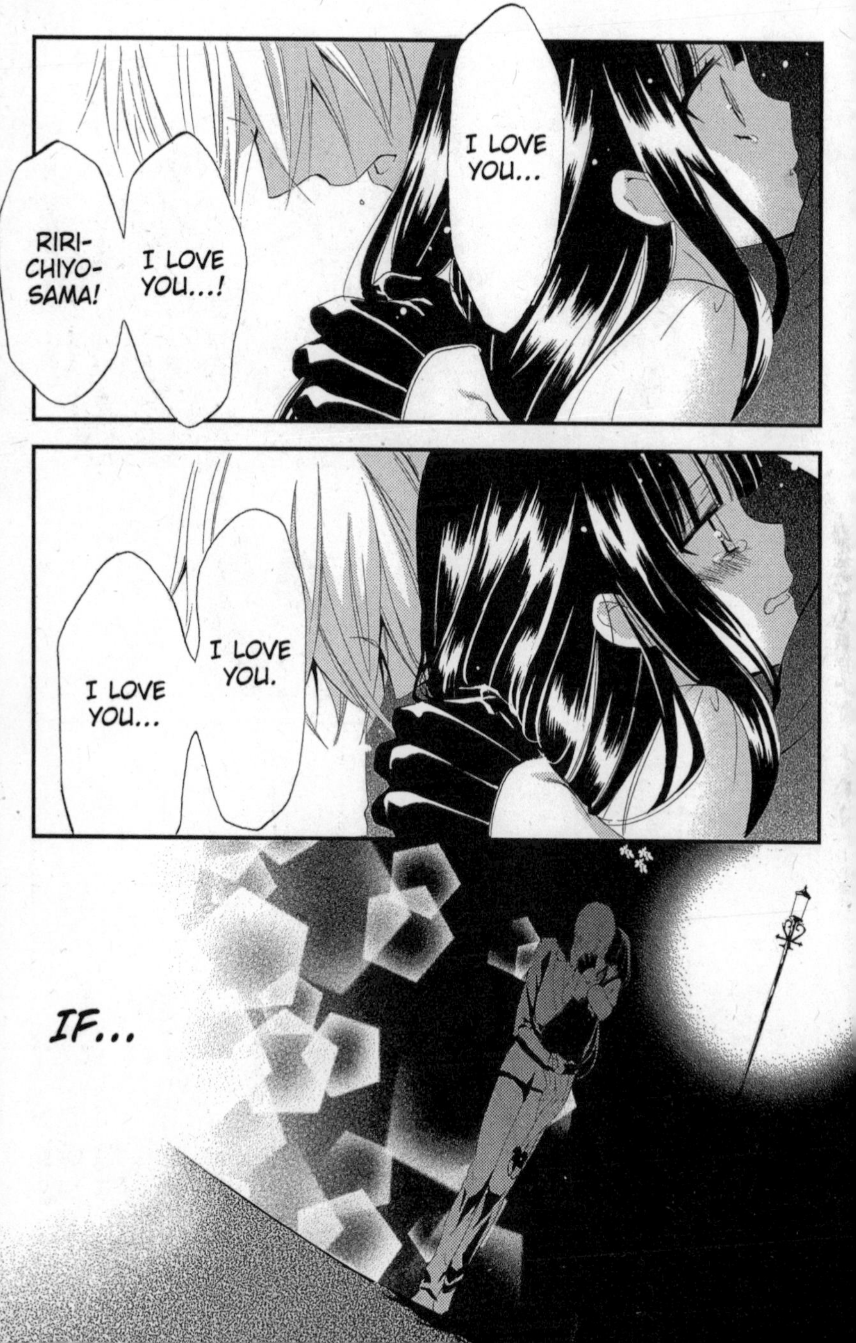
I LOVE YOU...
I LOVE YOU...!
RIRI-CHIYO-SAMA!
I LOVE YOU.
I LOVE YOU...
IF...

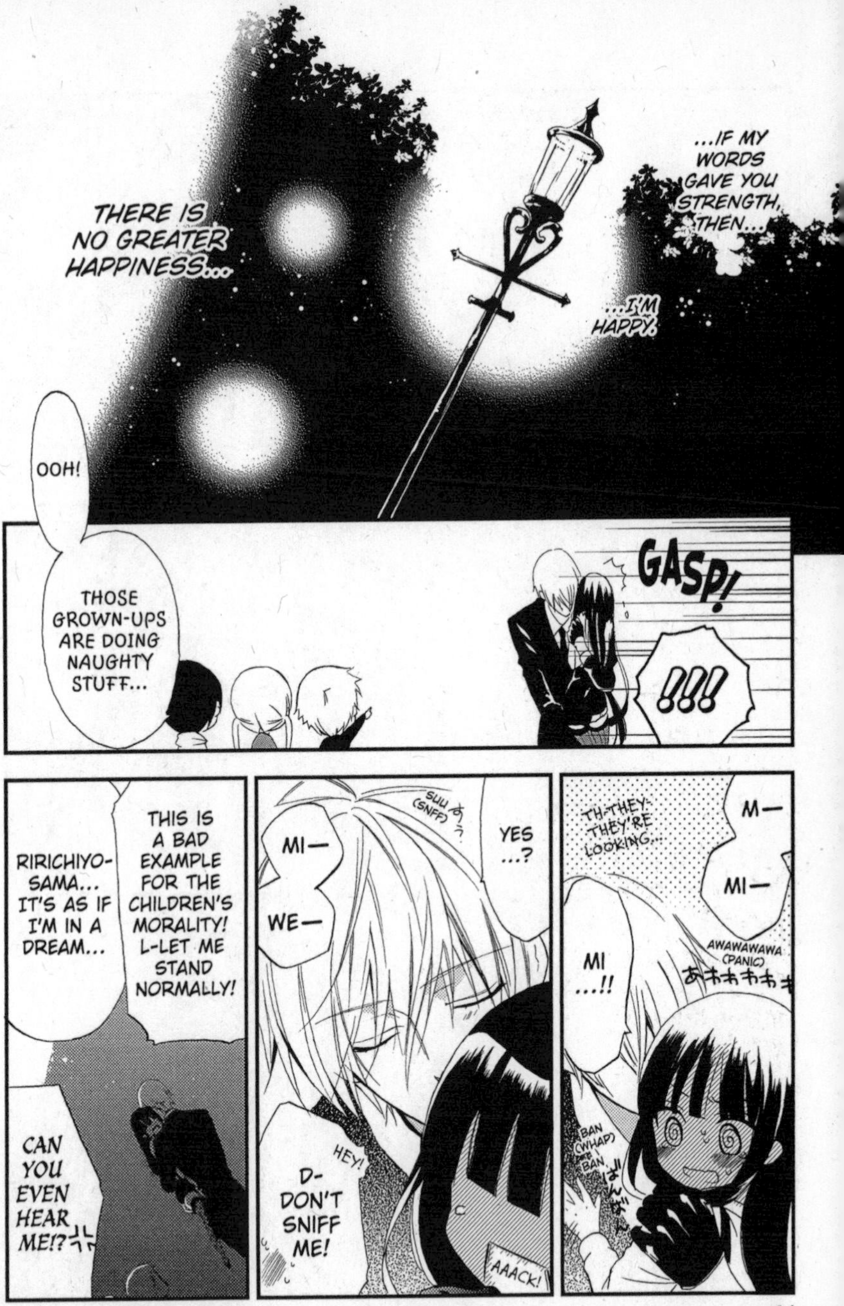
...IF MY WORDS GAVE YOU STRENGTH, THEN...
...I'M HAPPY.
THERE IS NO GREATER HAPPINESS...
GASP!
!!!
OOH!
THOSE GROWN-UPS ARE DOING NAUGHTY STUFF...
M—
MI—
TH-THEY THEY'RE LOOKING...
AWAWAWAWA (PANIC)
あわわわわ
MI ...!!
BAN (WHAP) BAN
ばんばん
AAACK!
SUU (SNIFF)
すぅ
YES ...?
MI—
WE—
HEY!
D-DON'T SNIFF ME!
THIS IS A BAD EXAMPLE FOR THE CHILDREN'S MORALITY! L-LET ME STAND NORMALLY!
RIRICHIYO-SAMA... IT'S AS IF I'M IN A DREAM...
CAN YOU EVEN HEAR ME!?

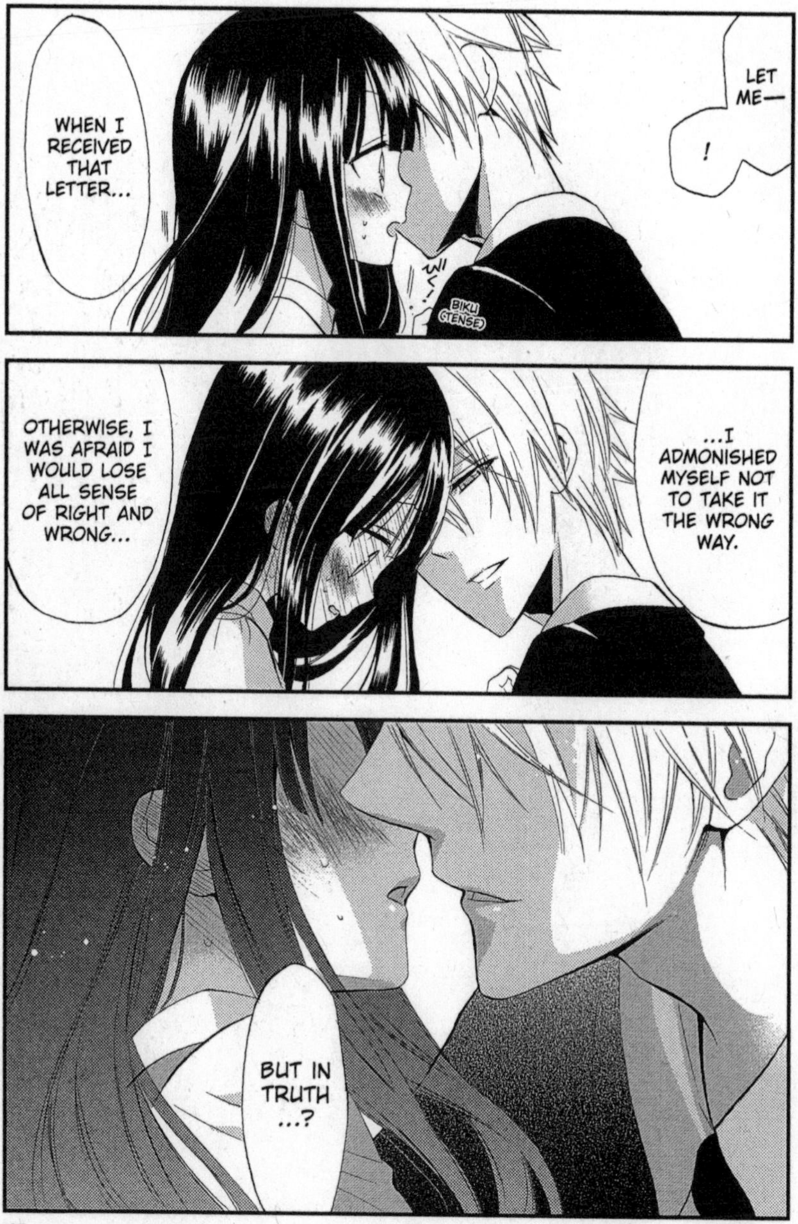
LET ME—
!
WHEN I RECEIVED THAT LETTER...
BIKU (TENSE)
...I ADMONISHED MYSELF NOT TO TAKE IT THE WRONG WAY.
OTHERWISE, I WAS AFRAID I WOULD LOSE ALL SENSE OF RIGHT AND WRONG...
BUT IN TRUTH ...?

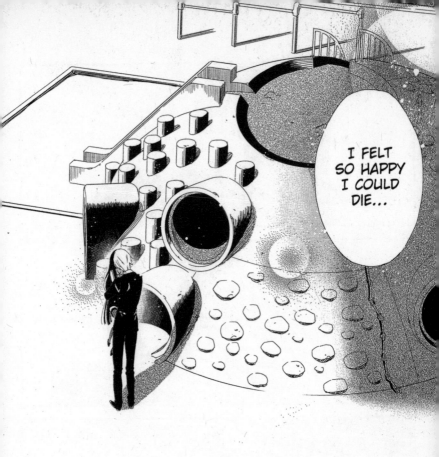

I FELT SO HAPPY I COULD DIE...

CHAPTER 10:
THE DAY WE CAME TOGETHER / THREE MONTHS LATER

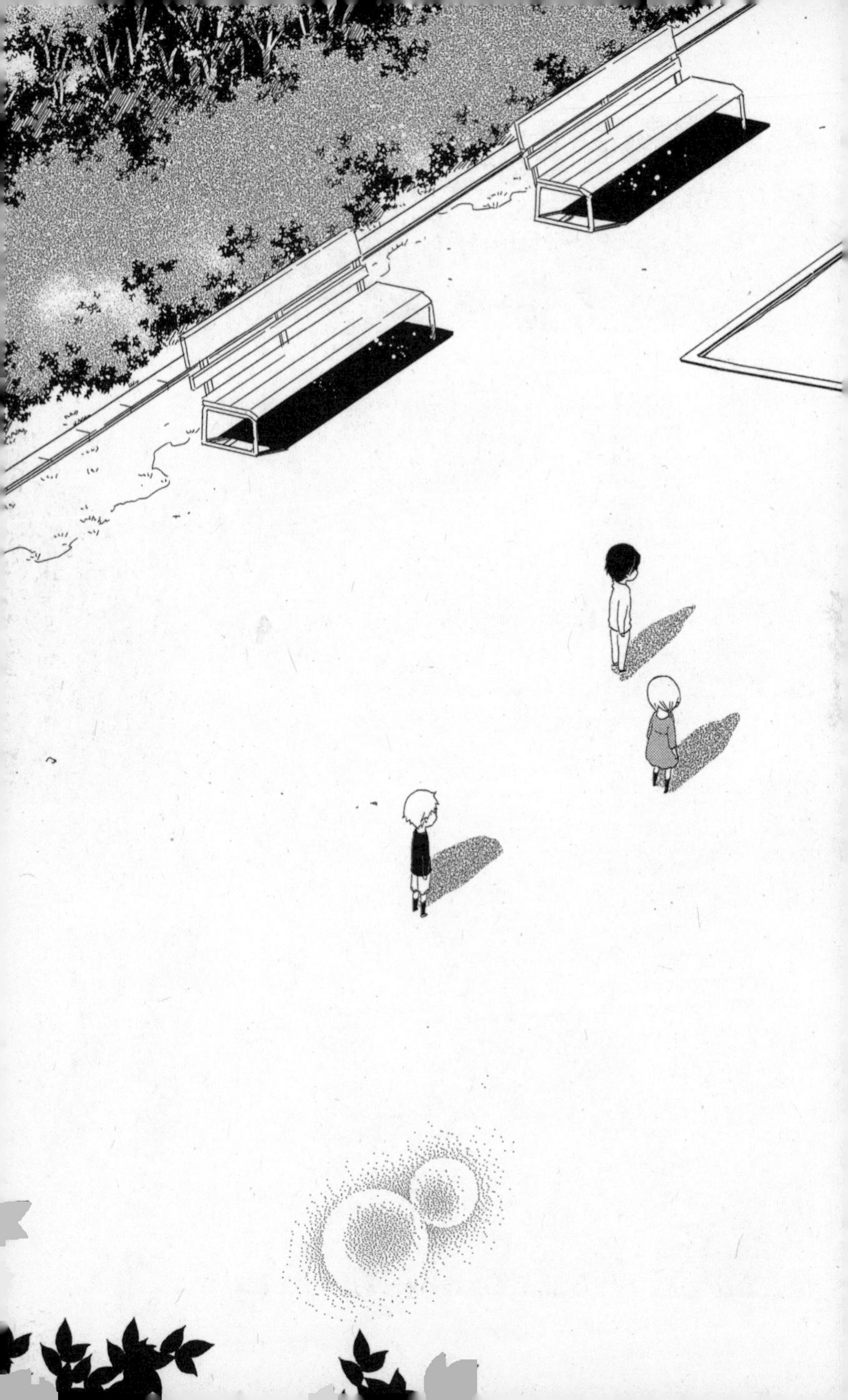

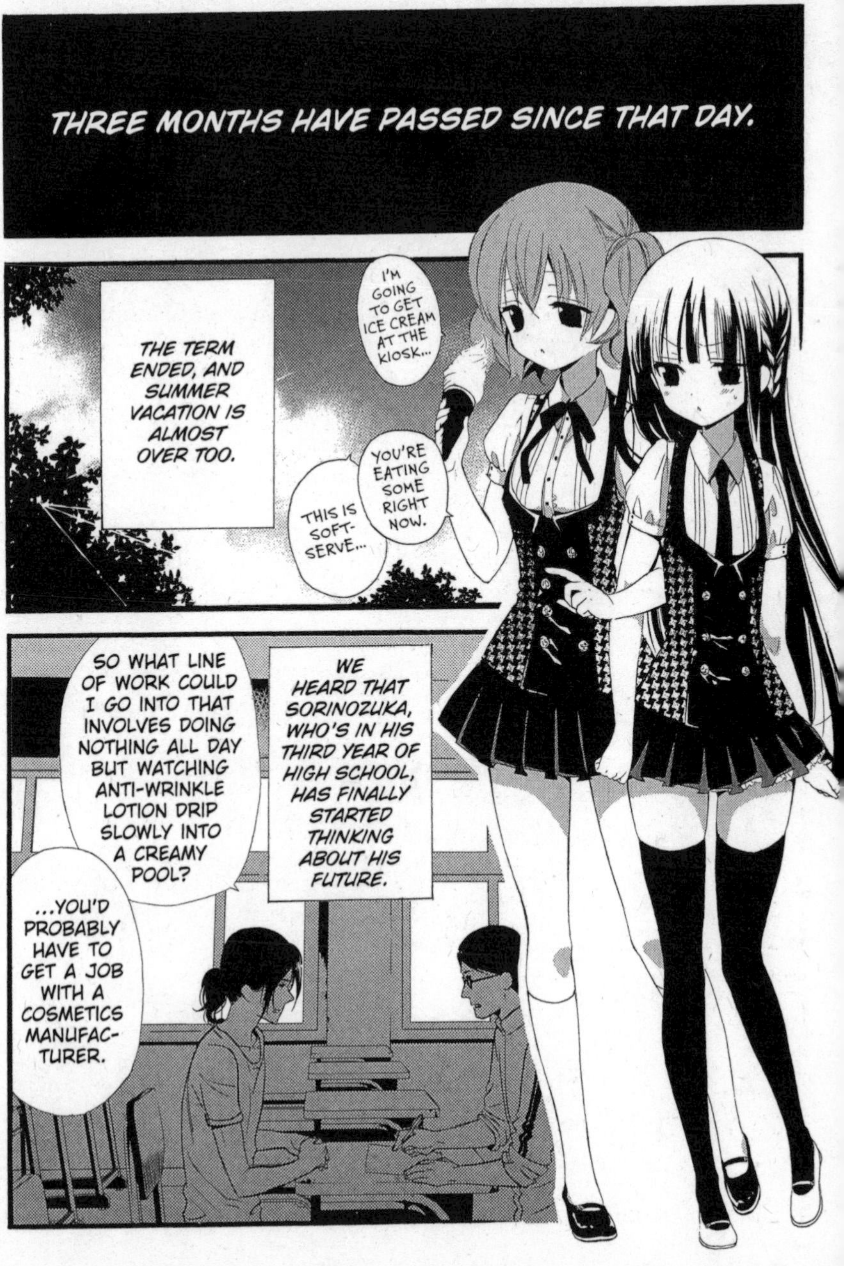
THREE MONTHS HAVE PASSED SINCE THAT DAY.
I'M GOING TO GET ICE CREAM AT THE KIOSK...
YOU'RE EATING SOME RIGHT NOW.
THIS IS SOFT-SERVE...
THE TERM ENDED, AND SUMMER VACATION IS ALMOST OVER TOO.
WE HEARD THAT SORINOZUKA, WHO'S IN HIS THIRD YEAR OF HIGH SCHOOL, HAS FINALLY STARTED THINKING ABOUT HIS FUTURE.
SO WHAT LINE OF WORK COULD I GO INTO THAT INVOLVES DOING NOTHING ALL DAY BUT WATCHING ANTI-WRINKLE LOTION DRIP SLOWLY INTO A CREAMY POOL?
...YOU'D PROBABLY HAVE TO GET A JOB WITH A COSMETICS MANUFAC-TURER.

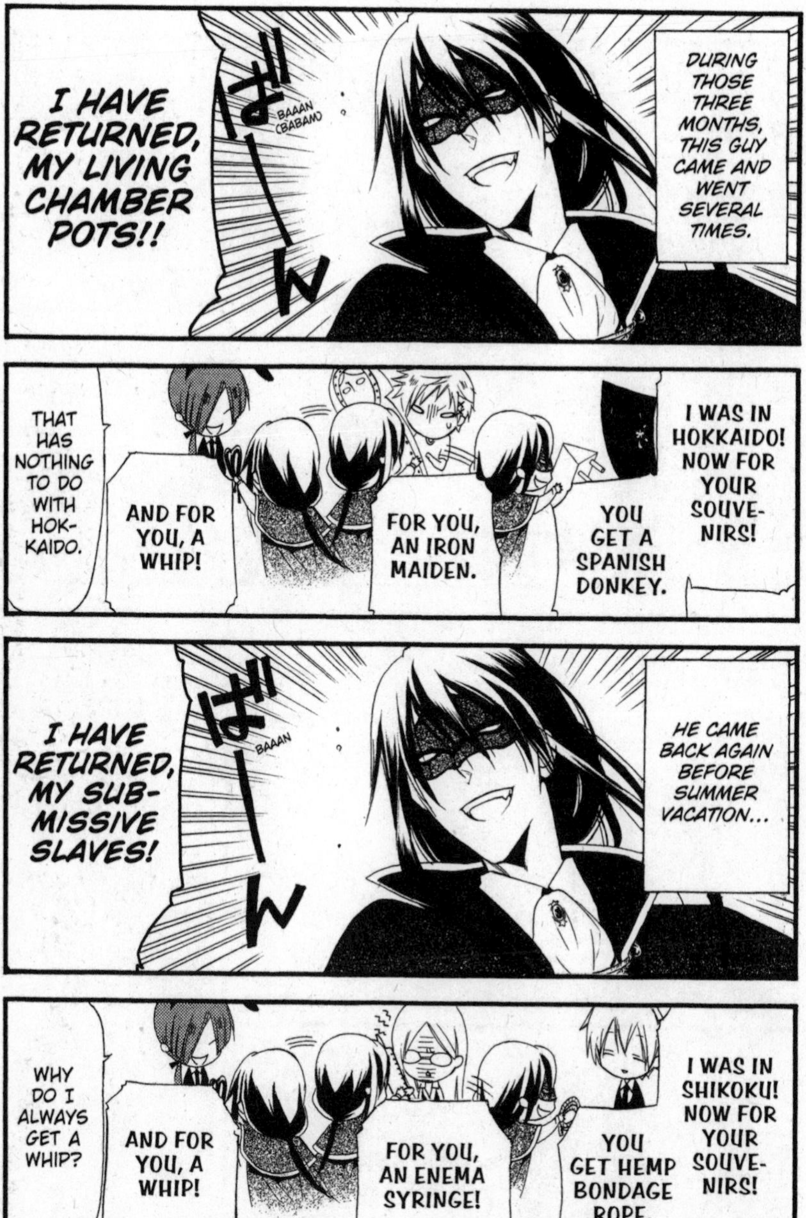
DURING THOSE THREE MONTHS, THIS GUY CAME AND WENT SEVERAL TIMES.
BAAAN (BABAM)
I HAVE RETURNED, MY LIVING CHAMBER POTS!!
I WAS IN HOKKAIDO! NOW FOR YOUR SOUVENIRS!
YOU GET A SPANISH DONKEY.
FOR YOU, AN IRON MAIDEN.
AND FOR YOU, A WHIP!
THAT HAS NOTHING TO DO WITH HOKKAIDO.
HE CAME BACK AGAIN BEFORE SUMMER VACATION...
BAAAN
I HAVE RETURNED, MY SUBMISSIVE SLAVES!
I WAS IN SHIKOKU! NOW FOR YOUR SOUVENIRS!
YOU GET HEMP BONDAGE ROPE.
FOR YOU, AN ENEMA SYRINGE!
AND FOR YOU, A WHIP!
WHY DO I ALWAYS GET A WHIP?

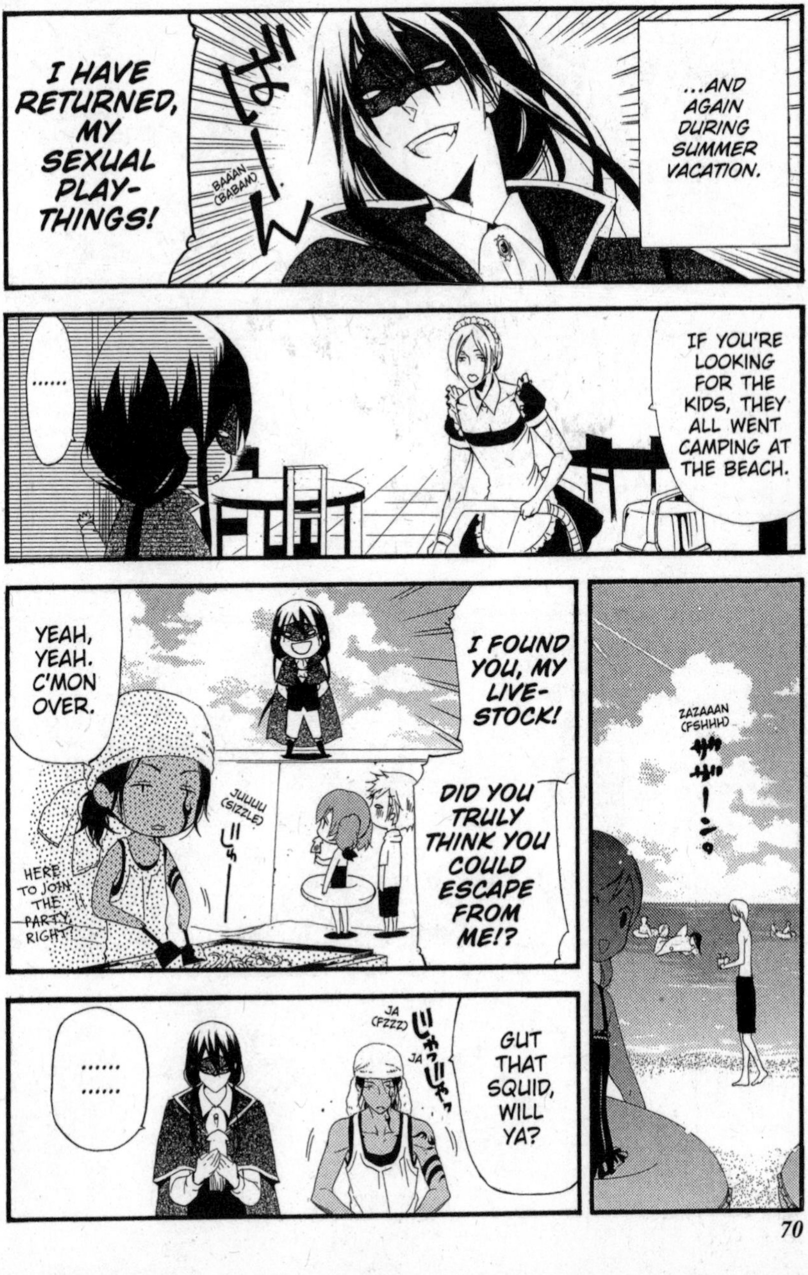

...AND AGAIN DURING SUMMER VACATION.
BAAAN (BABAM)
I HAVE RETURNED, MY SEXUAL PLAY-THINGS!
IF YOU'RE LOOKING FOR THE KIDS, THEY ALL WENT CAMPING AT THE BEACH.
......
ZAZAAAN (FSHHH)
I FOUND YOU, MY LIVE-STOCK!
DID YOU TRULY THINK YOU COULD ESCAPE FROM ME!?
JUUUU (SIZZLE)
YEAH, YEAH. C'MON OVER.
HERE TO JOIN THE PARTY, RIGHT?
GUT THAT SQUID, WILL YA?
JA (FZZZ) JA
......
......

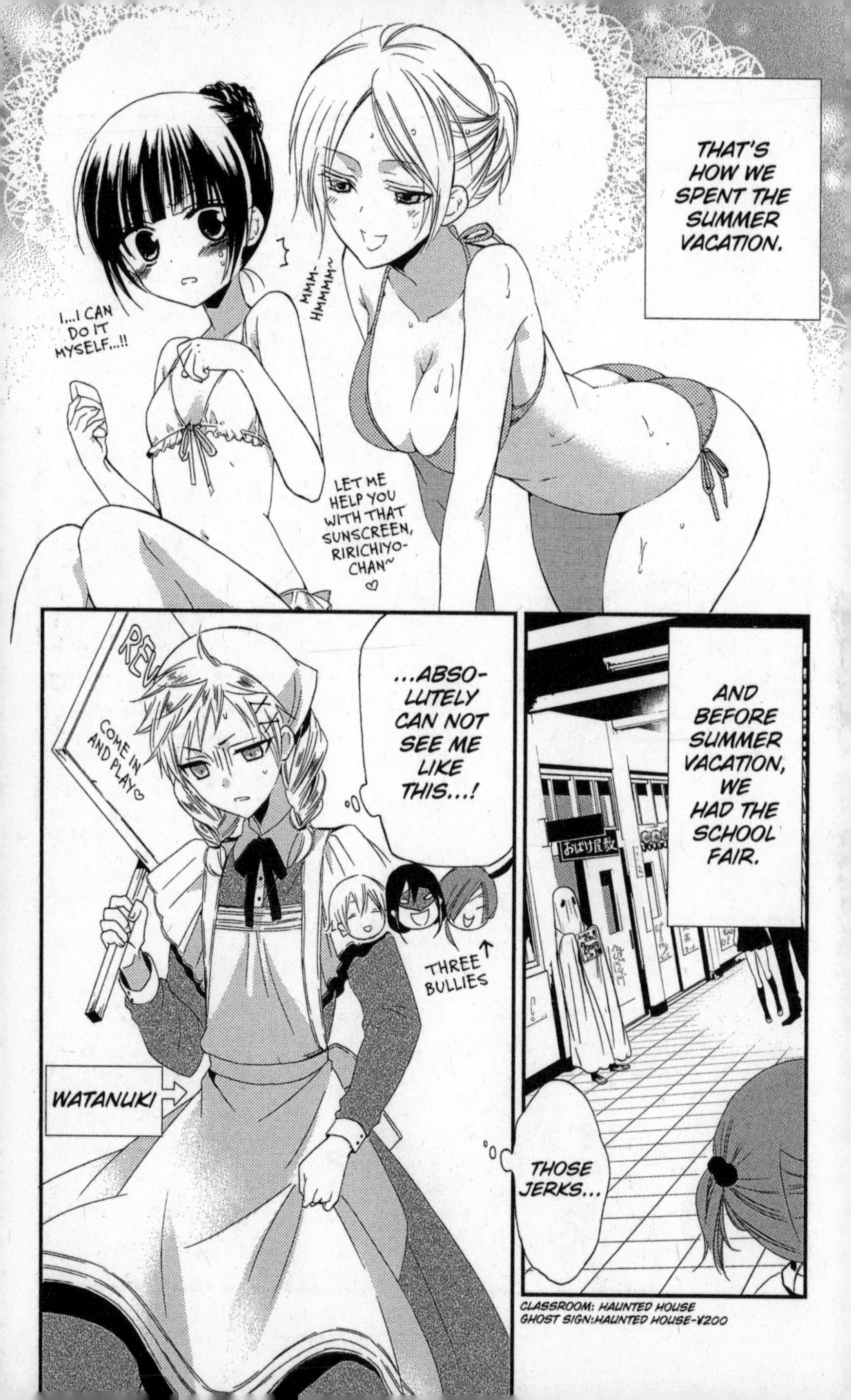
THAT'S HOW WE SPENT THE SUMMER VACATION.
MMM-HMMMM~
LET ME HELP YOU WITH THAT SUNSCREEN, RIRICHIYO-CHAN~ ♡
I...I CAN DO IT MYSELF...!!
AND BEFORE SUMMER VACATION, WE HAD THE SCHOOL FAIR.
おばけ屋敷
THOSE JERKS...
...ABSOLUTELY CAN NOT SEE ME LIKE THIS...!
COME IN AND PLAY♡
THREE BULLIES
WATANUKI

CLASSROOM: HAUNTED HOUSE
GHOST SIGN: HAUNTED HOUSE-¥200

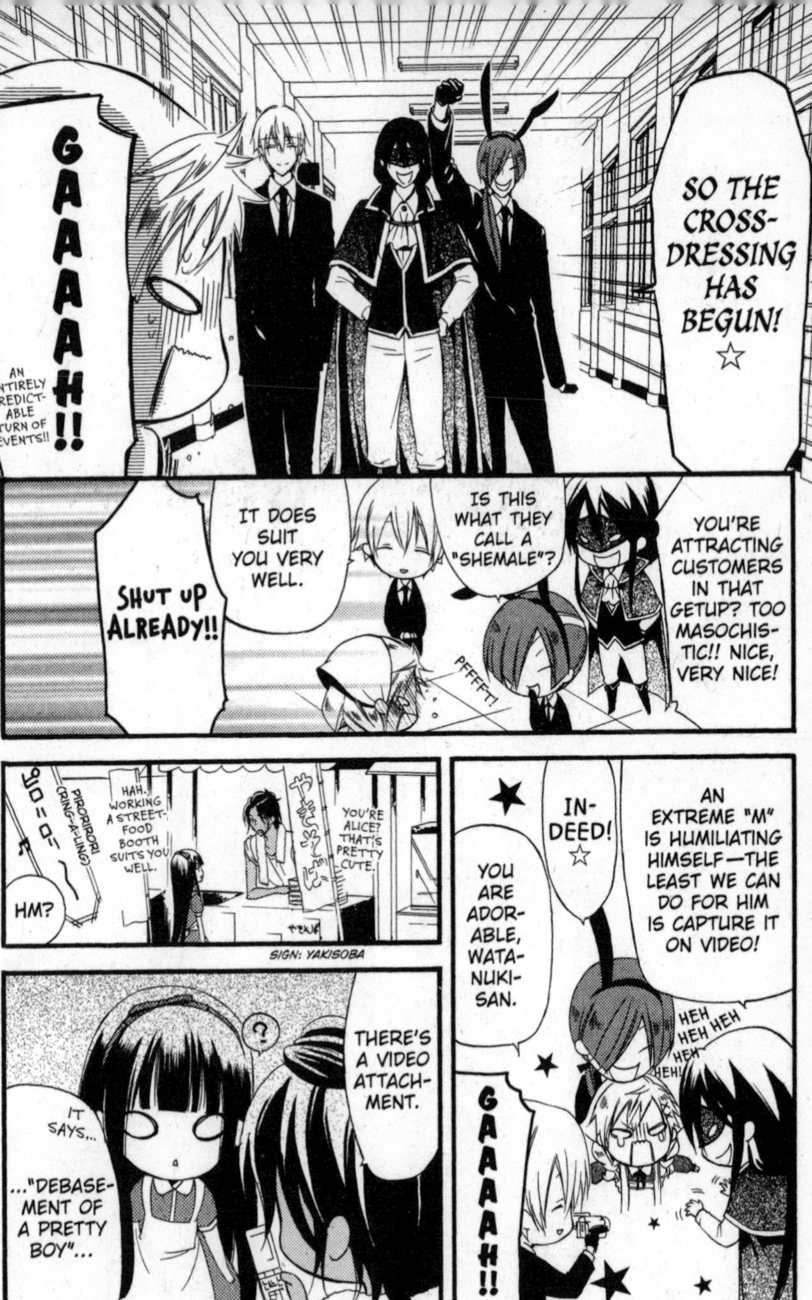
SO THE CROSS-DRESSING HAS BEGUN! ☆
GAAAAAH!!
AN ENTIRELY PREDICTABLE TURN OF EVENTS!!
YOU'RE ATTRACTING CUSTOMERS IN THAT GETUP? TOO MASOCHISTIC!! NICE, VERY NICE!
PFFFFT!
IS THIS WHAT THEY CALL A "SHEMALE"?
IT DOES SUIT YOU VERY WELL.
SHUT UP ALREADY!!
AN EXTREME "M" IS HUMILIATING HIMSELF—THE LEAST WE CAN DO FOR HIM IS CAPTURE IT ON VIDEO!
IN-DEED! ☆
YOU ARE ADORABLE, WATANUKI-SAN.
HEH HEH HEH HEH HEH!
GAAAAAH!!
PERVERTS!!
YOU'RE ALICE? THAT'S PRETTY CUTE.
HAH. WORKING A STREET-FOOD BOOTH SUITS YOU WELL.
PIRORIRORI (RING-A-LING)
HM?
SIGN: YAKISOBA
THERE'S A VIDEO ATTACHMENT.
?
IT SAYS...
..."DEBASEMENT OF A PRETTY BOY"...

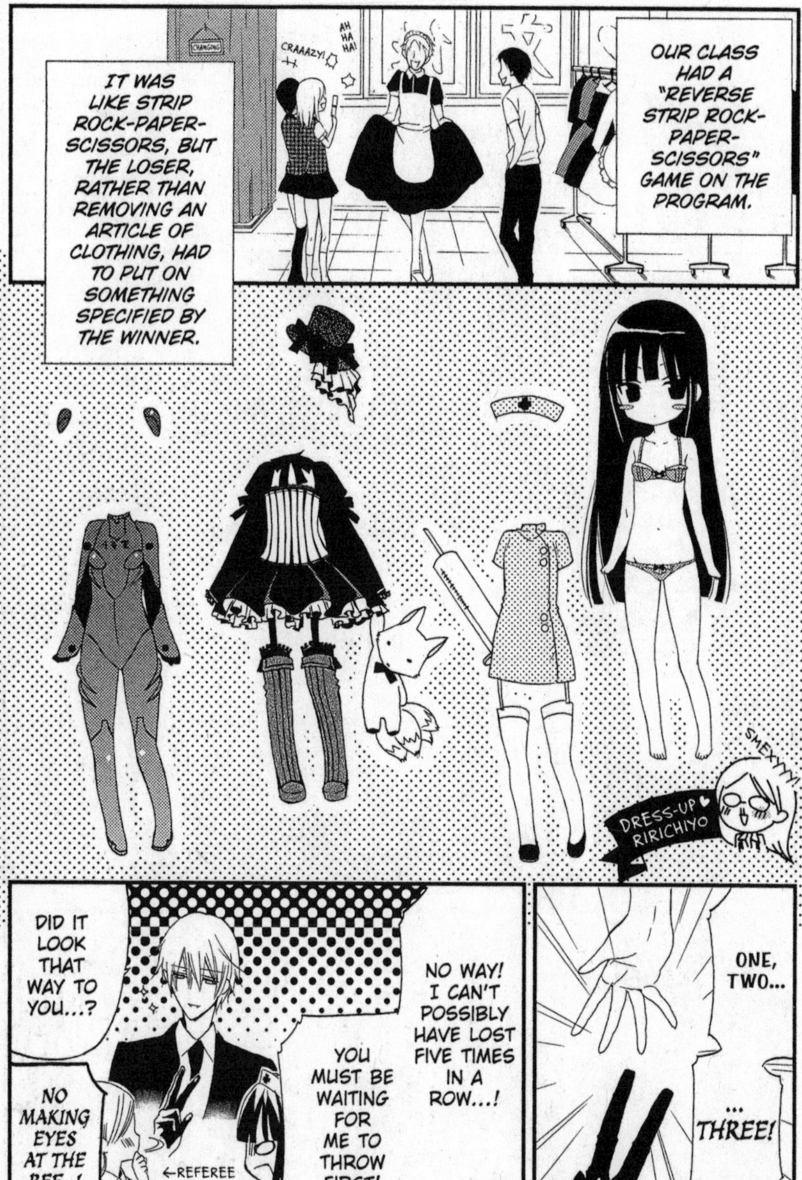
OUR CLASS HAD A "REVERSE STRIP ROCK-PAPER-SCISSORS" GAME ON THE PROGRAM.
AH HA HA!
CRAAAZY!
CHANGING
IT WAS LIKE STRIP ROCK-PAPER-SCISSORS, BUT THE LOSER, RATHER THAN REMOVING AN ARTICLE OF CLOTHING, HAD TO PUT ON SOMETHING SPECIFIED BY THE WINNER.
SMEXYYY!
DRESS-UP♥ RIRICHIYO
ONE, TWO...
...THREE!
NO WAY! I CAN'T POSSIBLY HAVE LOST FIVE TIMES IN A ROW...!
YOU MUST BE WAITING FOR ME TO THROW FIRST!
DID IT LOOK THAT WAY TO YOU...?
NO MAKING EYES AT THE REF...!
←REFEREE

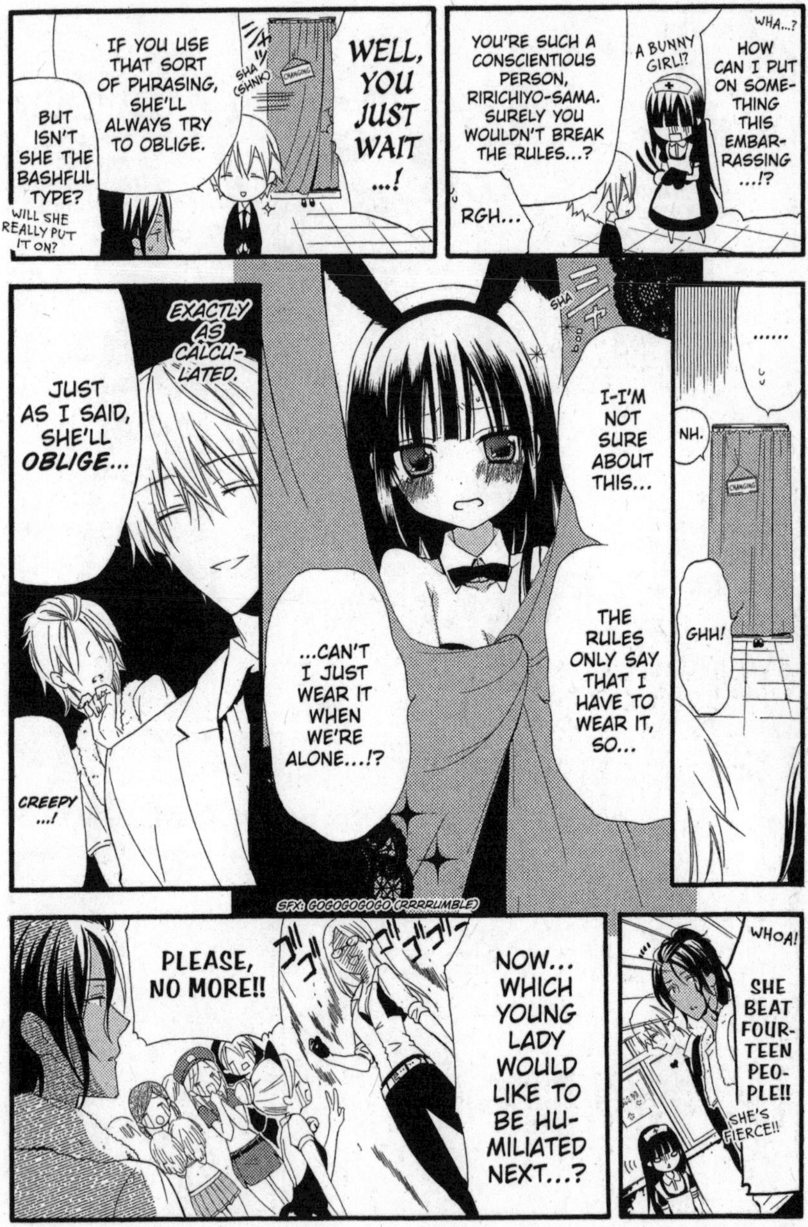
WHA...?
HOW CAN I PUT ON SOMETHING THIS EMBARRASSING...!?
A BUNNY GIRL!?
YOU'RE SUCH A CONSCIENTIOUS PERSON, RIRICHIYO-SAMA. SURELY YOU WOULDN'T BREAK THE RULES...?
RGH...
WELL, YOU JUST WAIT...!
SHA (SHNK)
CHANGING
IF YOU USE THAT SORT OF PHRASING, SHE'LL ALWAYS TRY TO OBLIGE.
BUT ISN'T SHE THE BASHFUL TYPE?
WILL SHE REALLY PUT IT ON?
......
NH.
CHANGING
GHH!
SHA
I-I'M NOT SURE ABOUT THIS...
THE RULES ONLY SAY THAT I HAVE TO WEAR IT, SO...
...CAN'T I JUST WEAR IT WHEN WE'RE ALONE...!?
EXACTLY AS CALCULATED.
JUST AS I SAID, SHE'LL OBLIGE...
CREEPY...!
SFX: GOGOGOGOGO (RRRRUMBLE)
WHOA!
SHE BEAT FOURTEEN PEOPLE!!
SHE'S FIERCE!!
NOW... WHICH YOUNG LADY WOULD LIKE TO BE HUMILIATED NEXT...?
PLEASE, NO MORE!!

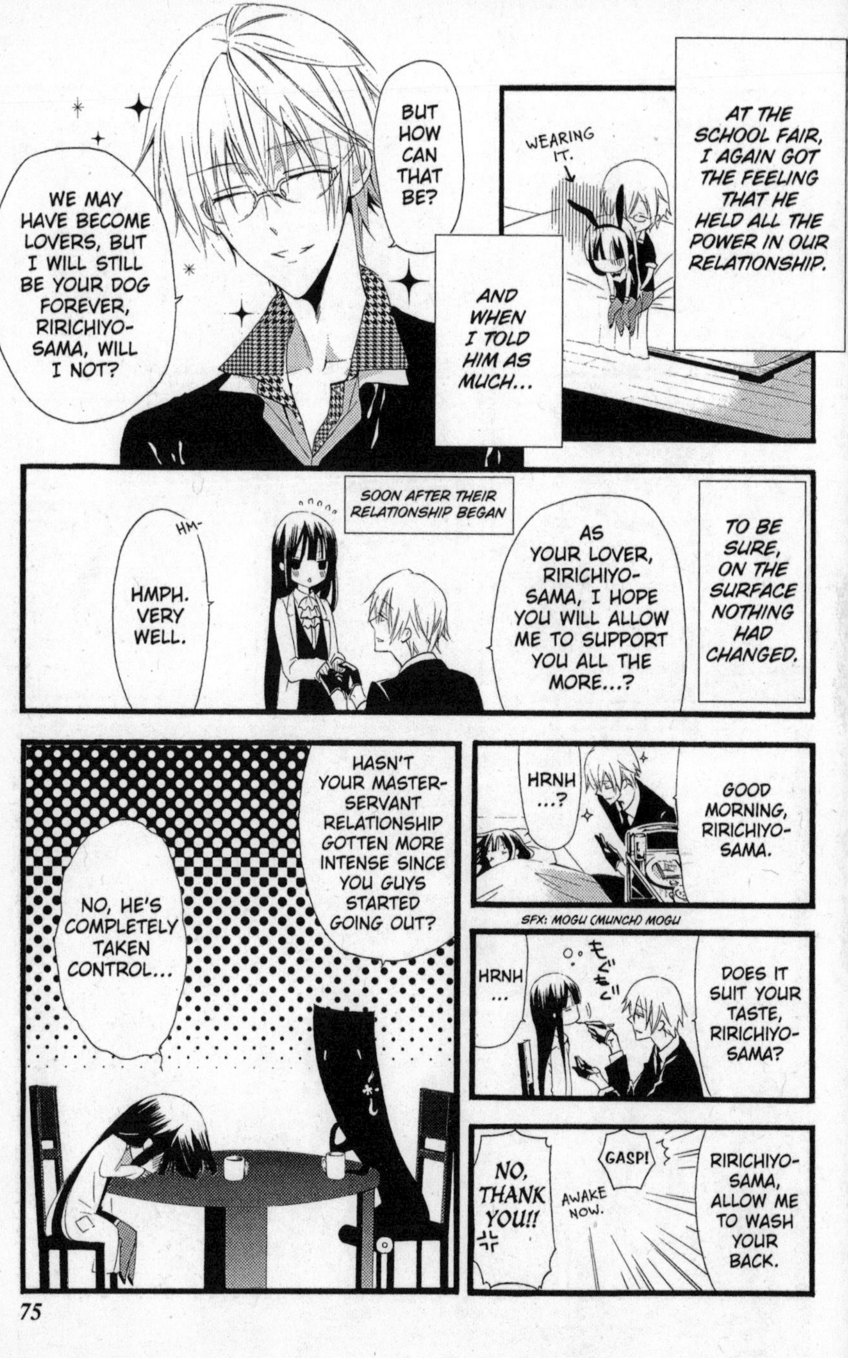
AT THE SCHOOL FAIR, I AGAIN GOT THE FEELING THAT HE HELD ALL THE POWER IN OUR RELATIONSHIP.
WEARING IT.
AND WHEN I TOLD HIM AS MUCH...
BUT HOW CAN THAT BE?
WE MAY HAVE BECOME LOVERS, BUT I WILL STILL BE YOUR DOG FOREVER, RIRICHIYO-SAMA, WILL I NOT?
TO BE SURE, ON THE SURFACE NOTHING HAD CHANGED.
SOON AFTER THEIR RELATIONSHIP BEGAN
AS YOUR LOVER, RIRICHIYO-SAMA, I HOPE YOU WILL ALLOW ME TO SUPPORT YOU ALL THE MORE...?
HM-
HMPH. VERY WELL.
GOOD MORNING, RIRICHIYO-SAMA.
HRNH ...?
SFX: MOGU (MUNCH) MOGU
DOES IT SUIT YOUR TASTE, RIRICHIYO-SAMA?
HRNH ...
RIRICHIYO-SAMA, ALLOW ME TO WASH YOUR BACK.
GASP!
AWAKE NOW.
NO, THANK YOU!!
HASN'T YOUR MASTER-SERVANT RELATIONSHIP GOTTEN MORE INTENSE SINCE YOU GUYS STARTED GOING OUT?
NO, HE'S COMPLETELY TAKEN CONTROL...

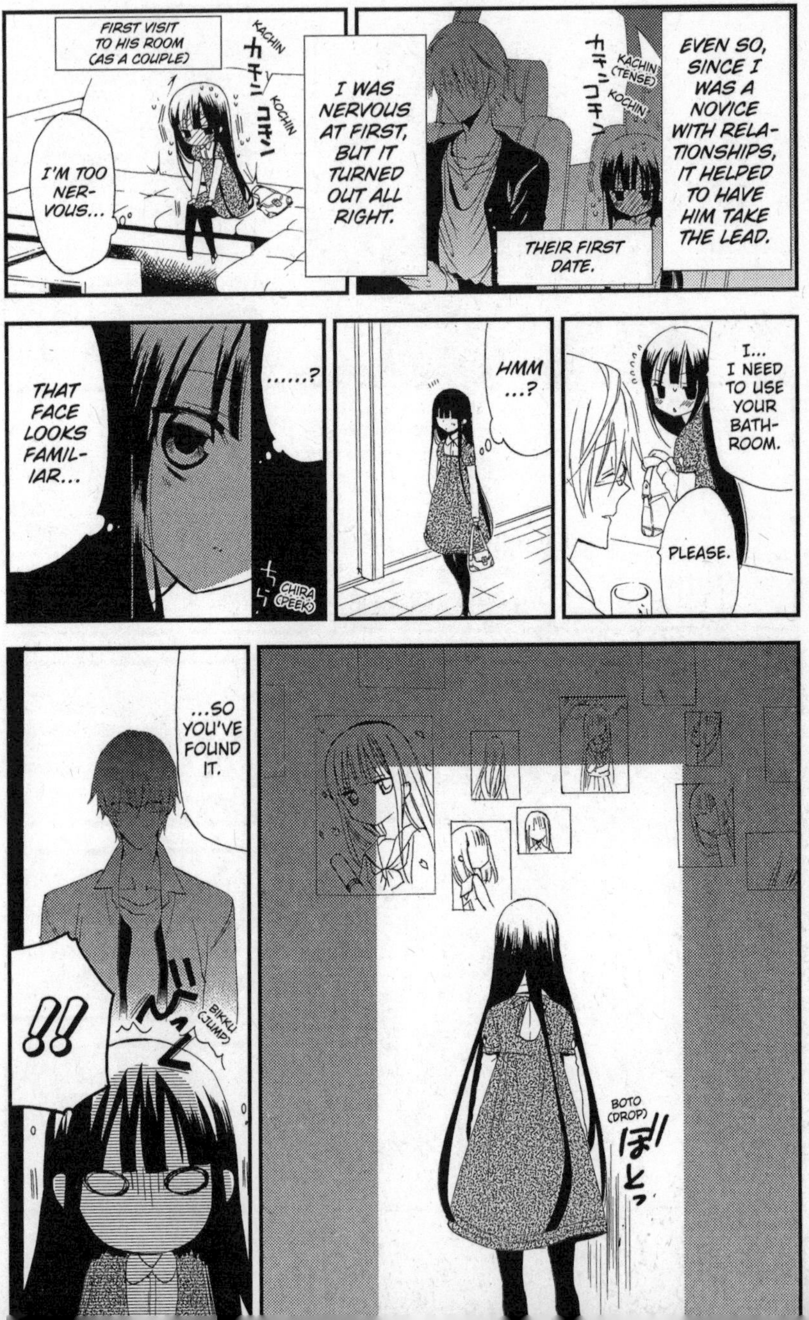
EVEN SO, SINCE I WAS A NOVICE WITH RELATIONSHIPS, IT HELPED TO HAVE HIM TAKE THE LEAD.
KACHIN (TENSE)
KOCHIN
THEIR FIRST DATE.
I WAS NERVOUS AT FIRST, BUT IT TURNED OUT ALL RIGHT.
FIRST VISIT TO HIS ROOM (AS A COUPLE)
KACHIN
KOCHIN
I'M TOO NERVOUS...
I... I NEED TO USE YOUR BATHROOM.
PLEASE.
HMM...?
......?
THAT FACE LOOKS FAMILIAR...
CHIRA (PEEK)
BOTO (DROP)
...SO YOU'VE FOUND IT.
BIKKU (JUMP)
!!

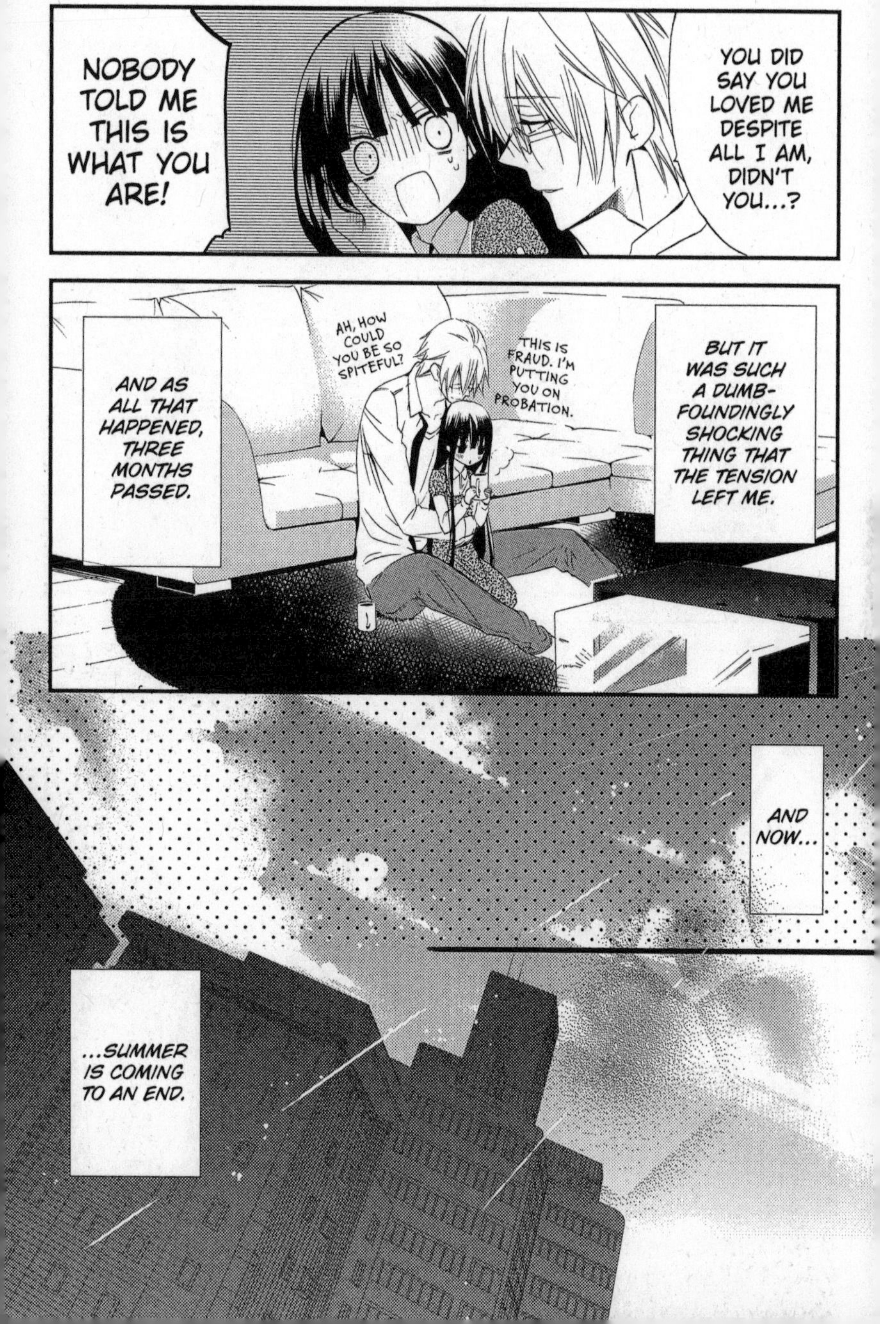
YOU DID SAY YOU LOVED ME DESPITE ALL I AM, DIDN'T YOU...?
NOBODY TOLD ME THIS IS WHAT YOU ARE!
BUT IT WAS SUCH A DUMB-FOUNDINGLY SHOCKING THING THAT THE TENSION LEFT ME.
THIS IS FRAUD. I'M PUTTING YOU ON PROBATION.
AH, HOW COULD YOU BE SO SPITEFUL?
AND AS ALL THAT HAPPENED, THREE MONTHS PASSED.
AND NOW...
...SUMMER IS COMING TO AN END.

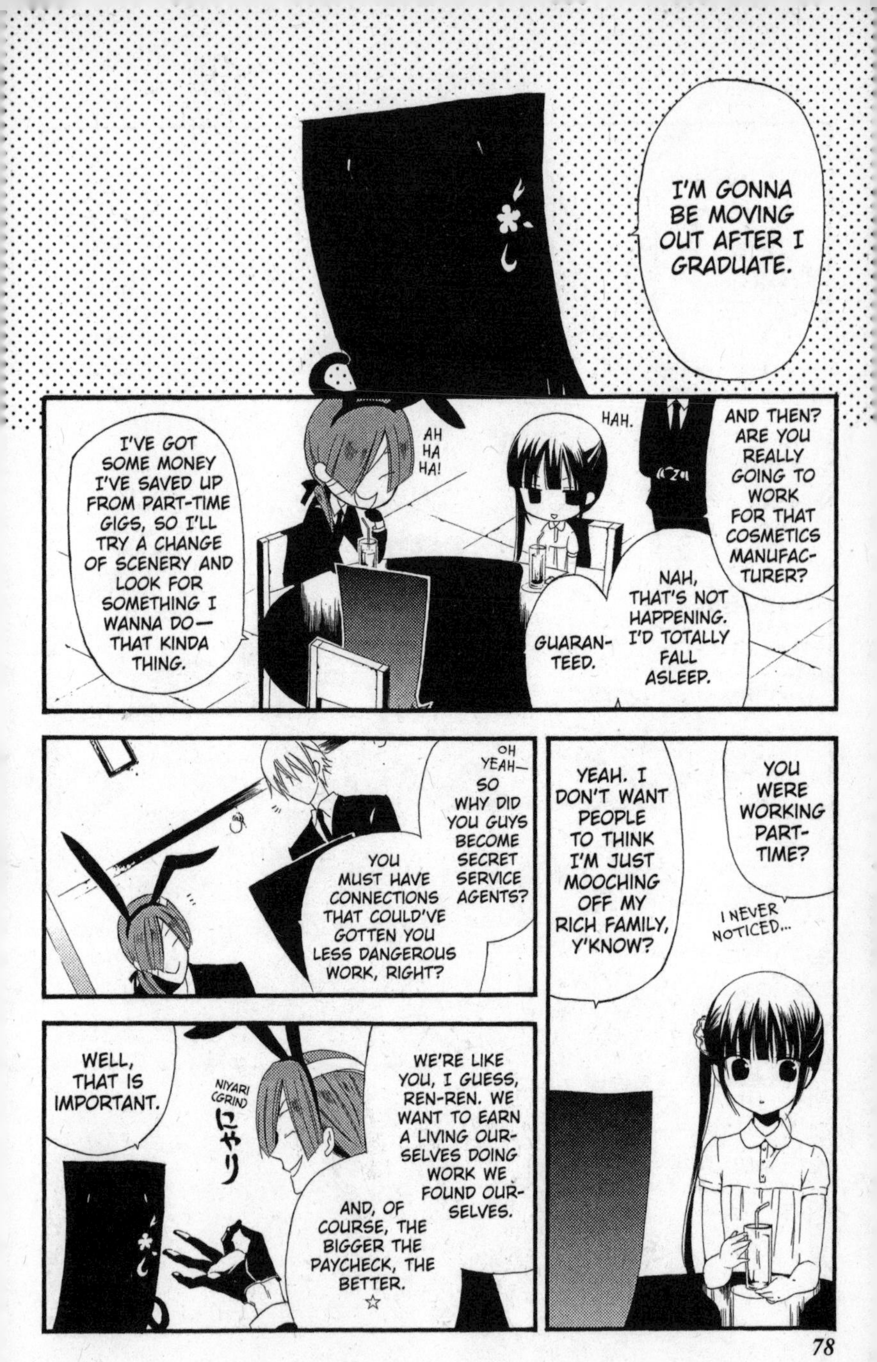
I'M GONNA BE MOVING OUT AFTER I GRADUATE.
AND THEN? ARE YOU REALLY GOING TO WORK FOR THAT COSMETICS MANUFACTURER?
HAH.
NAH, THAT'S NOT HAPPENING. I'D TOTALLY FALL ASLEEP.
GUARANTEED.
AH HA HA!
I'VE GOT SOME MONEY I'VE SAVED UP FROM PART-TIME GIGS, SO I'LL TRY A CHANGE OF SCENERY AND LOOK FOR SOMETHING I WANNA DO—THAT KINDA THING.
YOU WERE WORKING PART-TIME?
I NEVER NOTICED...
YEAH. I DON'T WANT PEOPLE TO THINK I'M JUST MOOCHING OFF MY RICH FAMILY, Y'KNOW?
OH YEAH— SO WHY DID YOU GUYS BECOME SECRET SERVICE AGENTS?
YOU MUST HAVE CONNECTIONS THAT COULD'VE GOTTEN YOU LESS DANGEROUS WORK, RIGHT?
WE'RE LIKE YOU, I GUESS, REN-REN. WE WANT TO EARN A LIVING OURSELVES DOING WORK WE FOUND OURSELVES.
AND, OF COURSE, THE BIGGER THE PAYCHECK, THE BETTER. ☆
NIYARI (GRIN)
にやり
WELL, THAT IS IMPORTANT.

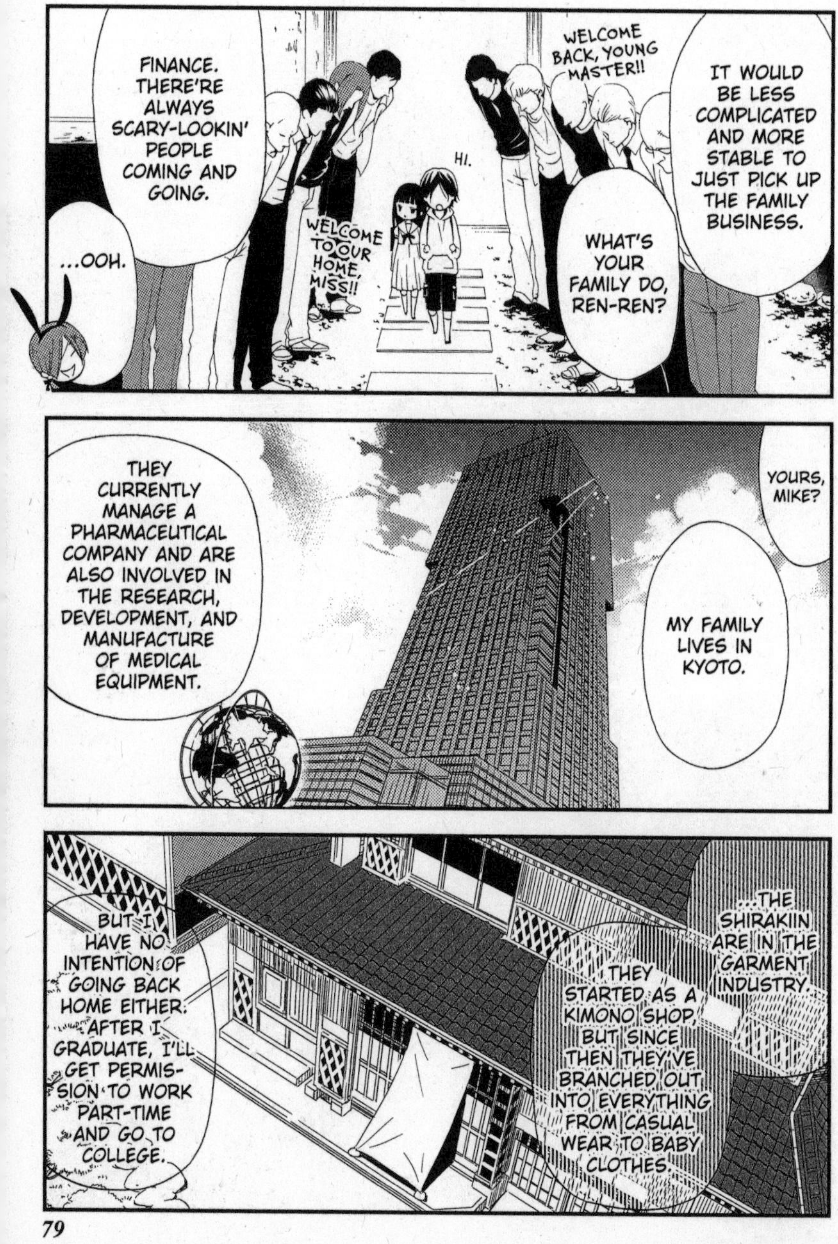
IT WOULD BE LESS COMPLICATED AND MORE STABLE TO JUST PICK UP THE FAMILY BUSINESS.
WELCOME BACK, YOUNG MASTER!!
WHAT'S YOUR FAMILY DO, REN-REN?
HI.
WELCOME TO OUR HOME, MISS!!
FINANCE. THERE'RE ALWAYS SCARY-LOOKIN' PEOPLE COMING AND GOING.
...OOH.
YOURS, MIKE?
MY FAMILY LIVES IN KYOTO.
THEY CURRENTLY MANAGE A PHARMACEUTICAL COMPANY AND ARE ALSO INVOLVED IN THE RESEARCH, DEVELOPMENT, AND MANUFACTURE OF MEDICAL EQUIPMENT.
...THE SHIRAKIIN ARE IN THE GARMENT INDUSTRY.
THEY STARTED AS A KIMONO SHOP, BUT SINCE THEN THEY'VE BRANCHED OUT INTO EVERYTHING FROM CASUAL WEAR TO BABY CLOTHES.
BUT I HAVE NO INTENTION OF GOING BACK HOME EITHER. AFTER I GRADUATE, I'LL GET PERMISSION TO WORK PART-TIME AND GO TO COLLEGE.

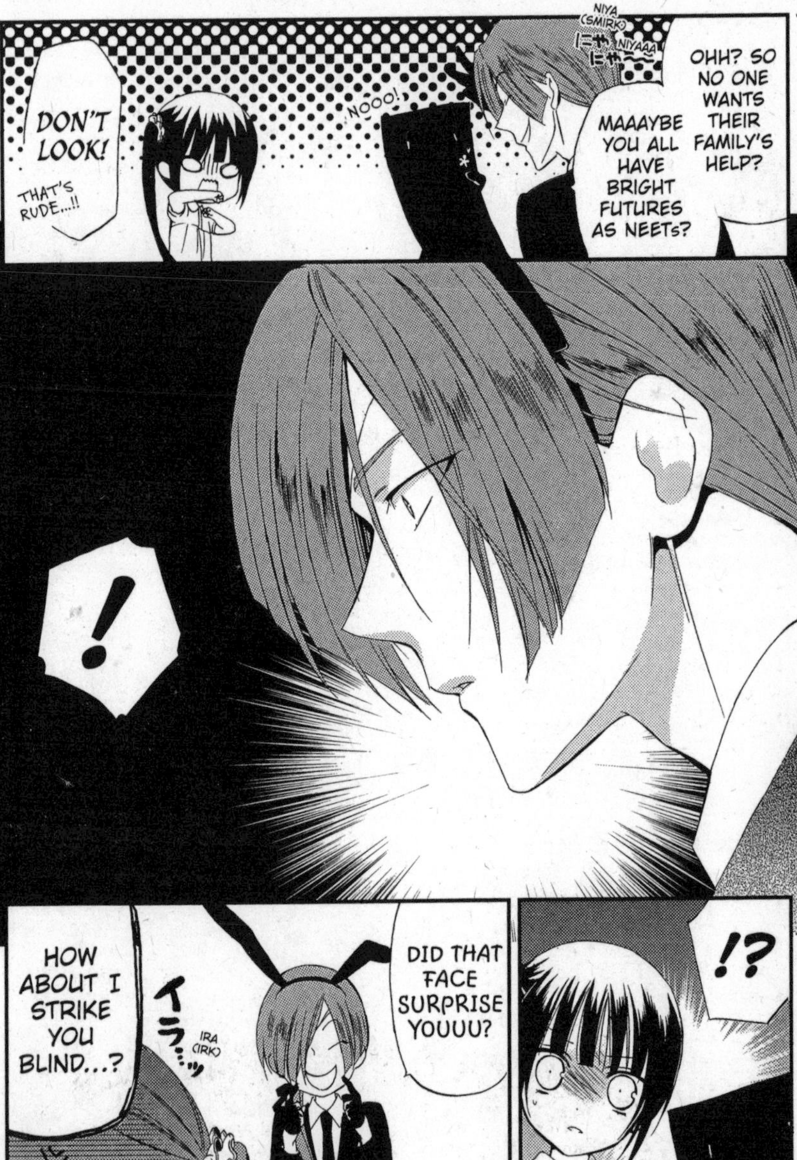
NIYA (SMIRK)
NIYAAA
OHH? SO NO ONE WANTS THEIR FAMILY'S HELP?
MAAAYBE YOU ALL HAVE BRIGHT FUTURES AS NEETs?
NOOO!
DON'T LOOK!
THAT'S RUDE...!!
!
!?
DID THAT FACE SURPRISE YOUUU?
イラ…ッ
IRA (IRK)
HOW ABOUT I STRIKE YOU BLIND...?

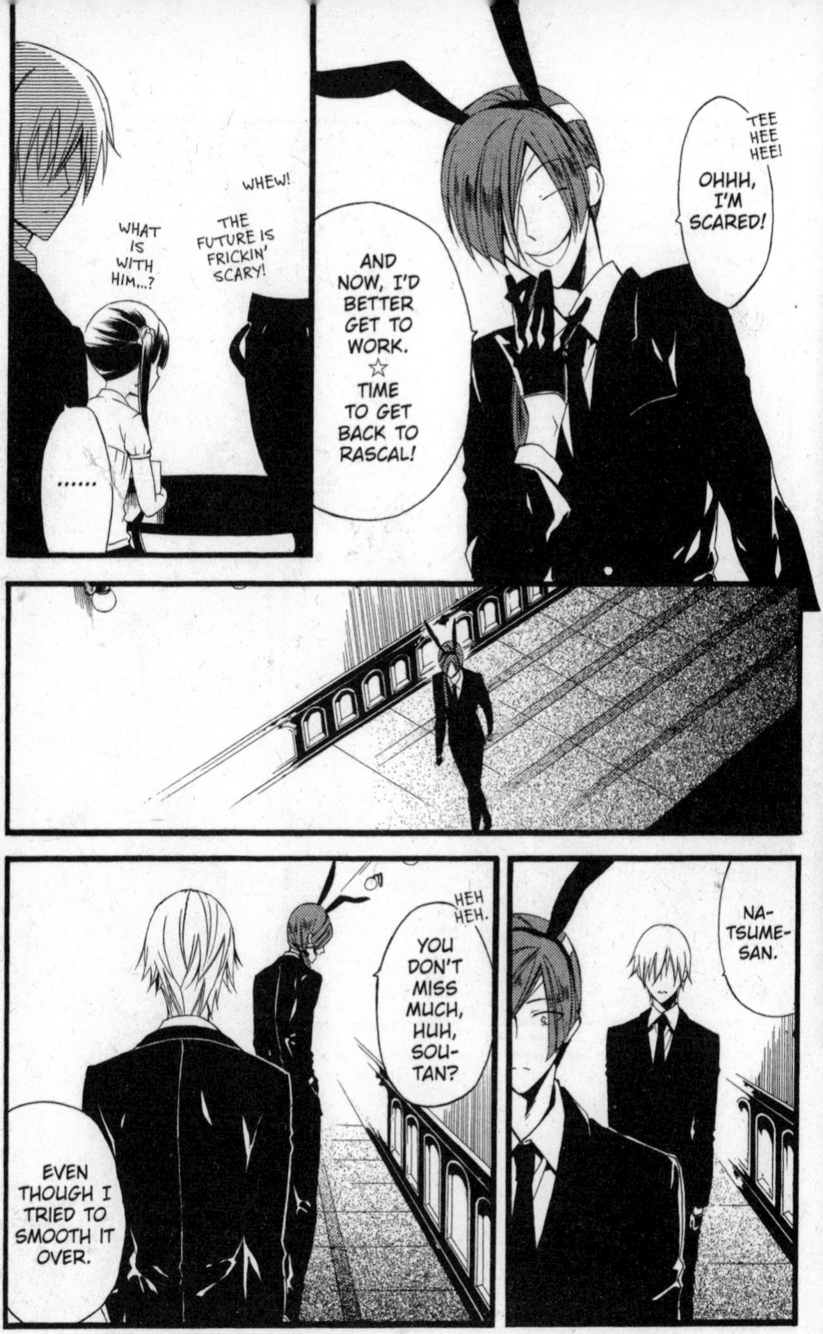
TEE HEE HEE!
OHHH, I'M SCARED!
AND NOW, I'D BETTER GET TO WORK. ☆ TIME TO GET BACK TO RASCAL!
WHEW!
THE FUTURE IS FRICKIN' SCARY!
WHAT IS WITH HIM...?
......
NA-TSUME-SAN.
HEH HEH.
YOU DON'T MISS MUCH, HUH, SOU-TAN?
EVEN THOUGH I TRIED TO SMOOTH IT OVER.

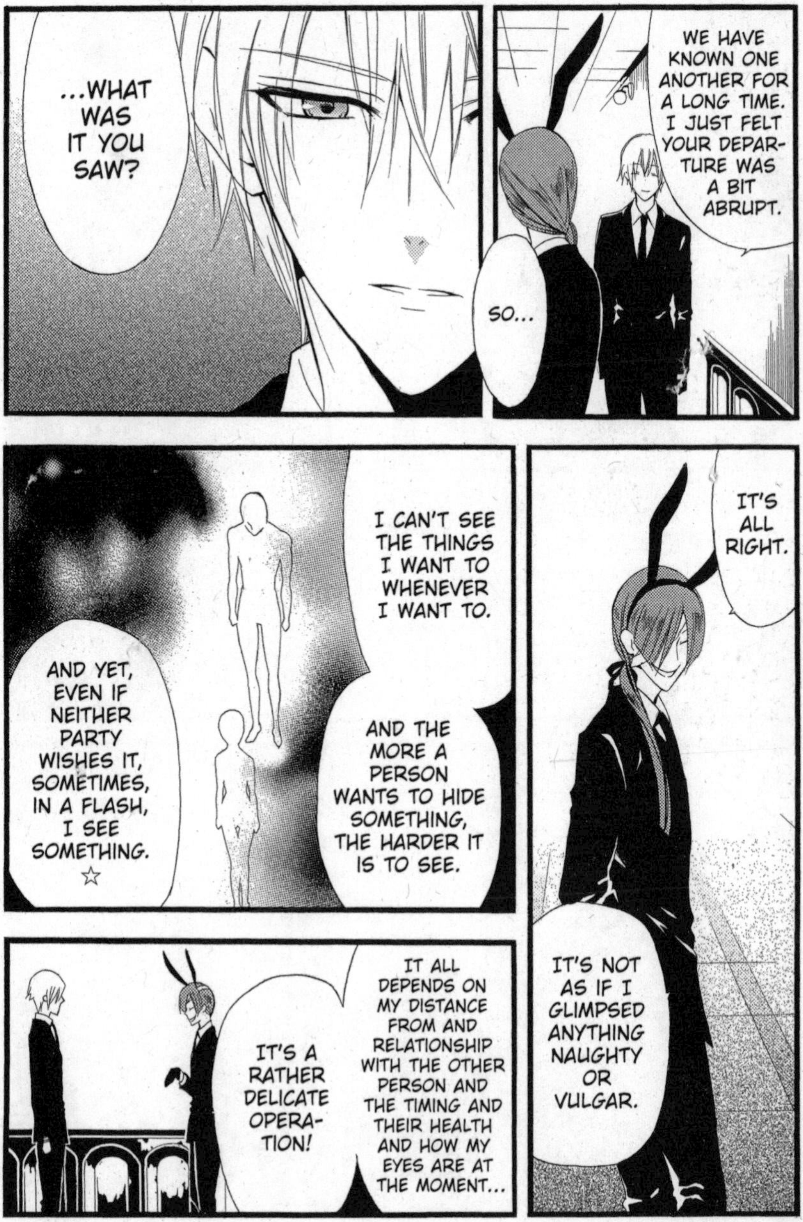
WE HAVE KNOWN ONE ANOTHER FOR A LONG TIME. I JUST FELT YOUR DEPARTURE WAS A BIT ABRUPT.
SO...
...WHAT WAS IT YOU SAW?
IT'S ALL RIGHT.
IT'S NOT AS IF I GLIMPSED ANYTHING NAUGHTY OR VULGAR.
I CAN'T SEE THE THINGS I WANT TO WHENEVER I WANT TO.
AND THE MORE A PERSON WANTS TO HIDE SOMETHING, THE HARDER IT IS TO SEE.
AND YET, EVEN IF NEITHER PARTY WISHES IT, SOMETIMES, IN A FLASH, I SEE SOMETHING. ☆
IT ALL DEPENDS ON MY DISTANCE FROM AND RELATIONSHIP WITH THE OTHER PERSON AND THE TIMING AND THEIR HEALTH AND HOW MY EYES ARE AT THE MOMENT...
IT'S A RATHER DELICATE OPERATION!

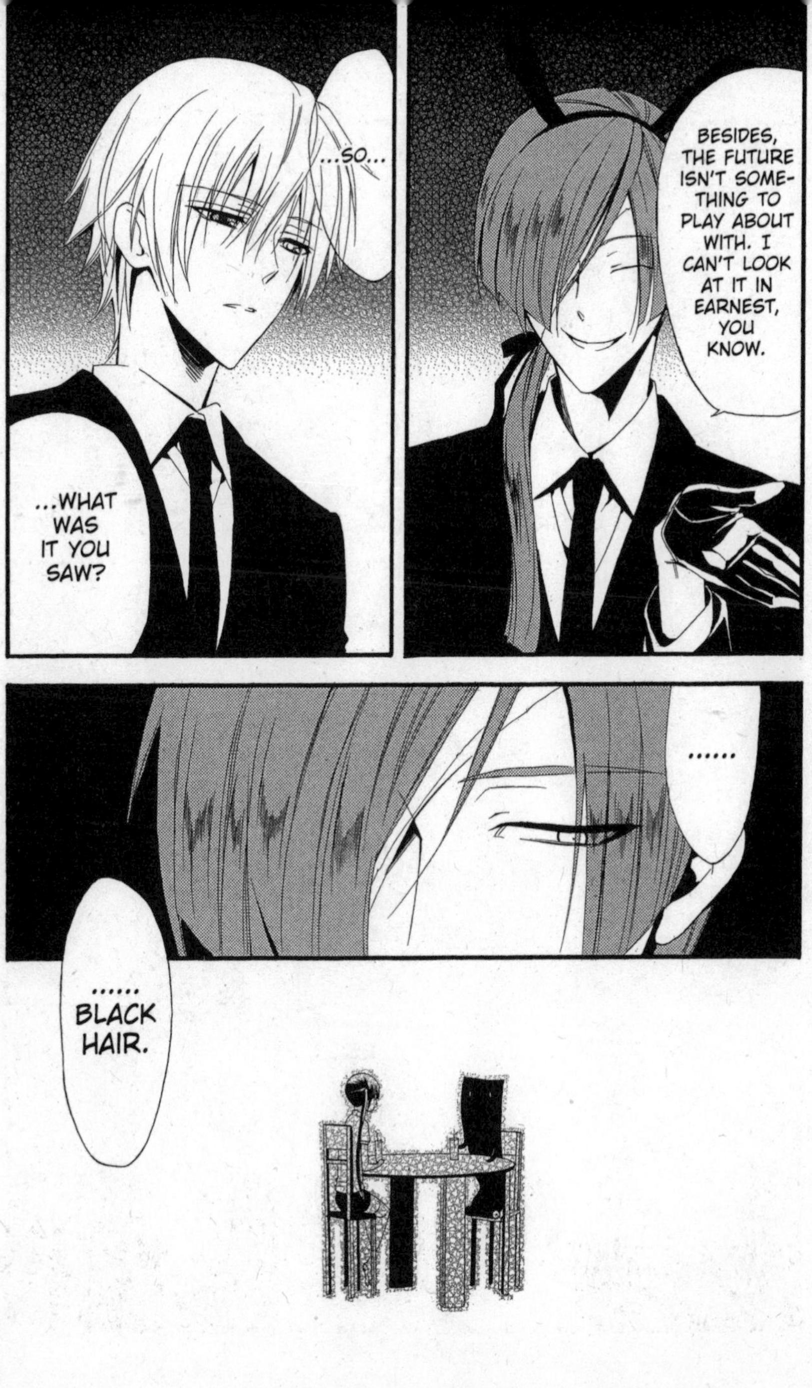
BESIDES, THE FUTURE ISN'T SOME-THING TO PLAY ABOUT WITH. I CAN'T LOOK AT IT IN EARNEST, YOU KNOW.
...SO...
...WHAT WAS IT YOU SAW?
......
...... BLACK HAIR.

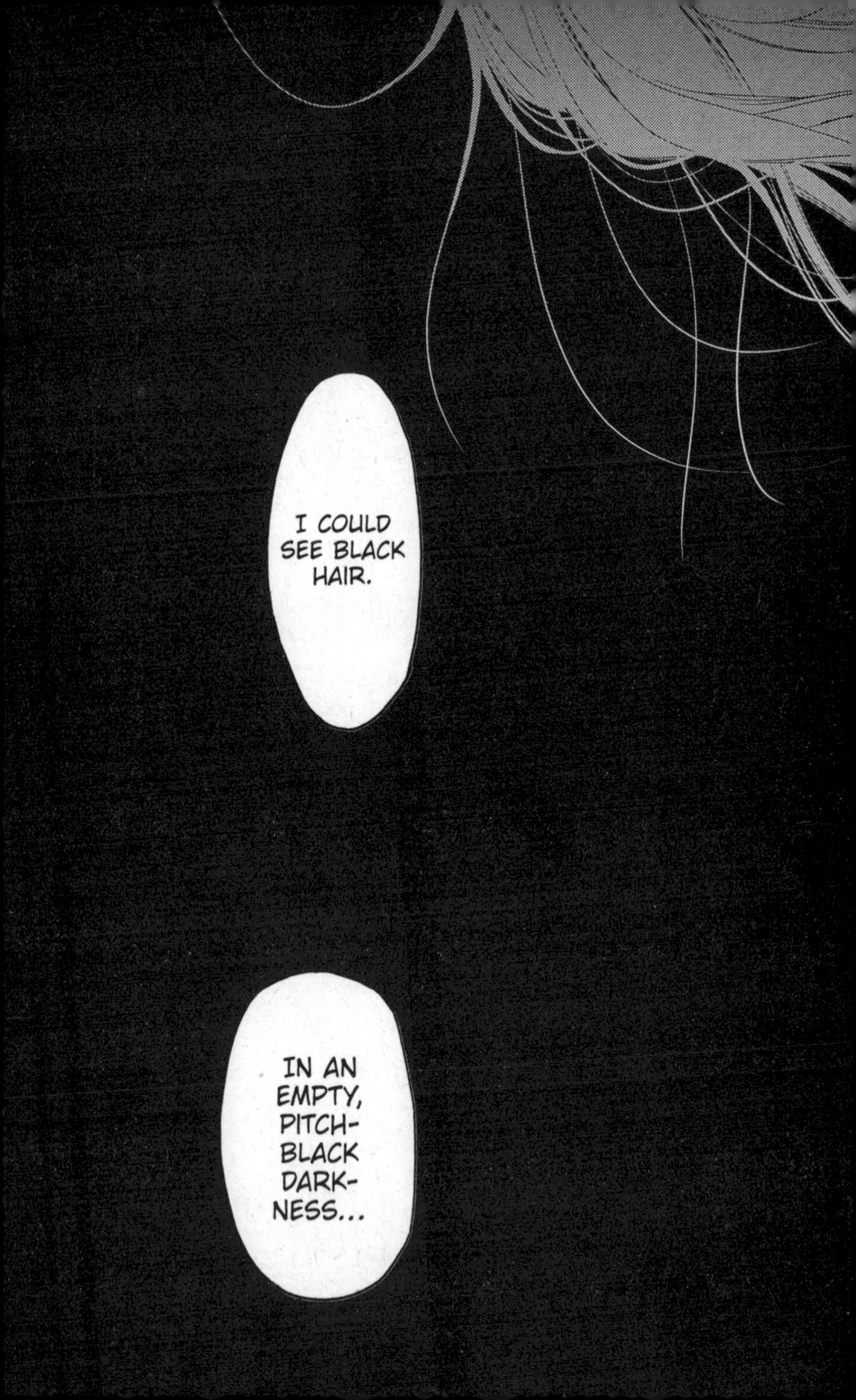
I COULD SEE BLACK HAIR.
IN AN EMPTY, PITCH-BLACK DARK-NESS...

INU×BOKU SS

maison de ayakashi

Welcome to Maison de Ayakashi.
The exclusive Secret Service of
this Mansion guarantees
your mental and physical
safety by providing
superior escorts.

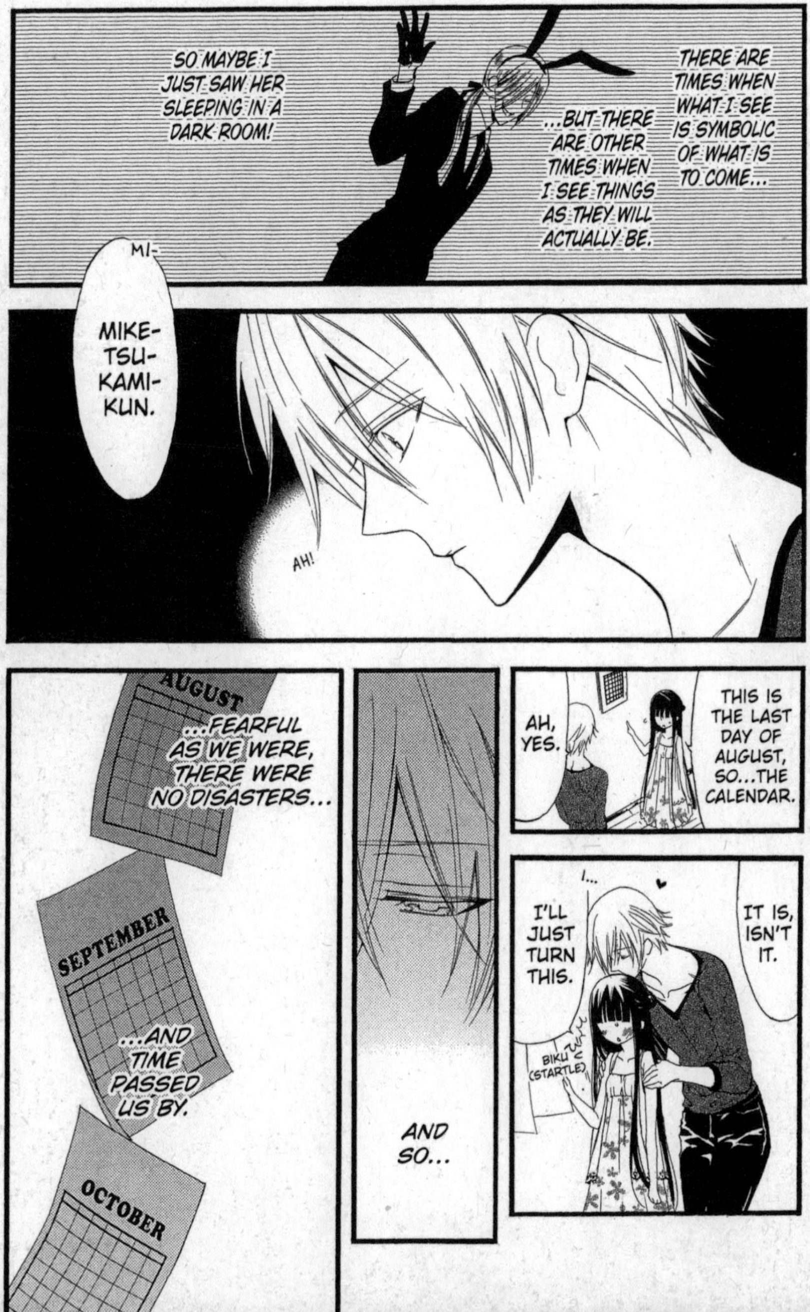
THERE ARE TIMES WHEN WHAT I SEE IS SYMBOLIC OF WHAT IS TO COME...
...BUT THERE ARE OTHER TIMES WHEN I SEE THINGS AS THEY WILL ACTUALLY BE.
SO MAYBE I JUST SAW HER SLEEPING IN A DARK ROOM!
MI-
MIKE-TSUKAMI-KUN.
AH!
THIS IS THE LAST DAY OF AUGUST, SO...THE CALENDAR.
AH, YES.
IT IS, ISN'T IT.
I...
I'LL JUST TURN THIS.
BIKU (STARTLE)
AND SO...
AUGUST
...FEARFUL AS WE WERE, THERE WERE NO DISASTERS...
SEPTEMBER
...AND TIME PASSED US BY.
OCTOBER

# CHAPTER 11:
## THE SEASON TURNS

# THE MYSTERIOUS COMMANDS

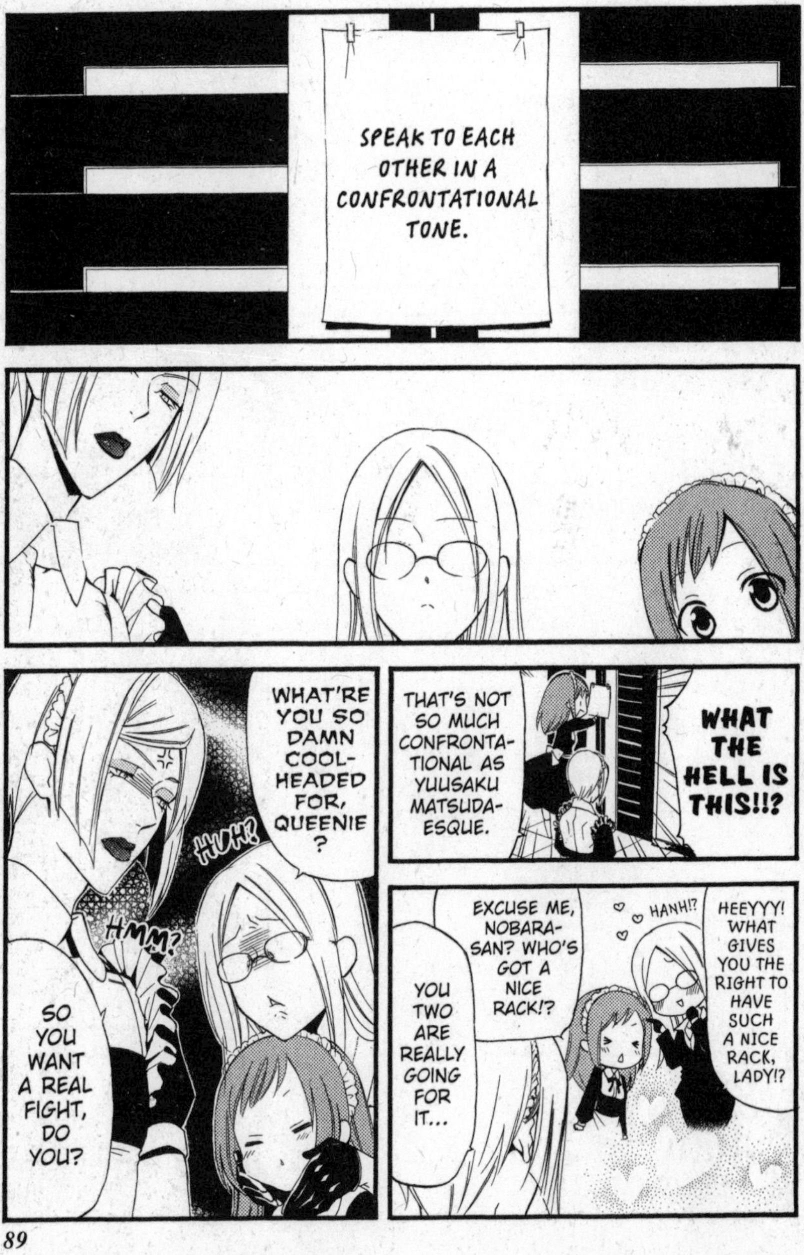
SPEAK TO EACH OTHER IN A CONFRONTATIONAL TONE.
WHAT THE HELL IS THIS!!?
THAT'S NOT SO MUCH CONFRONTA-TIONAL AS YUUSAKU MATSUDA-ESQUE.
HEEYYY! WHAT GIVES YOU THE RIGHT TO HAVE SUCH A NICE RACK, LADY!?
HANH!?
EXCUSE ME, NOBARA-SAN? WHO'S GOT A NICE RACK!?
YOU TWO ARE REALLY GOING FOR IT...
WHAT'RE YOU SO DAMN COOL-HEADED FOR, QUEENIE?
HUH?
HMM?
SO YOU WANT A REAL FIGHT, DO YOU?

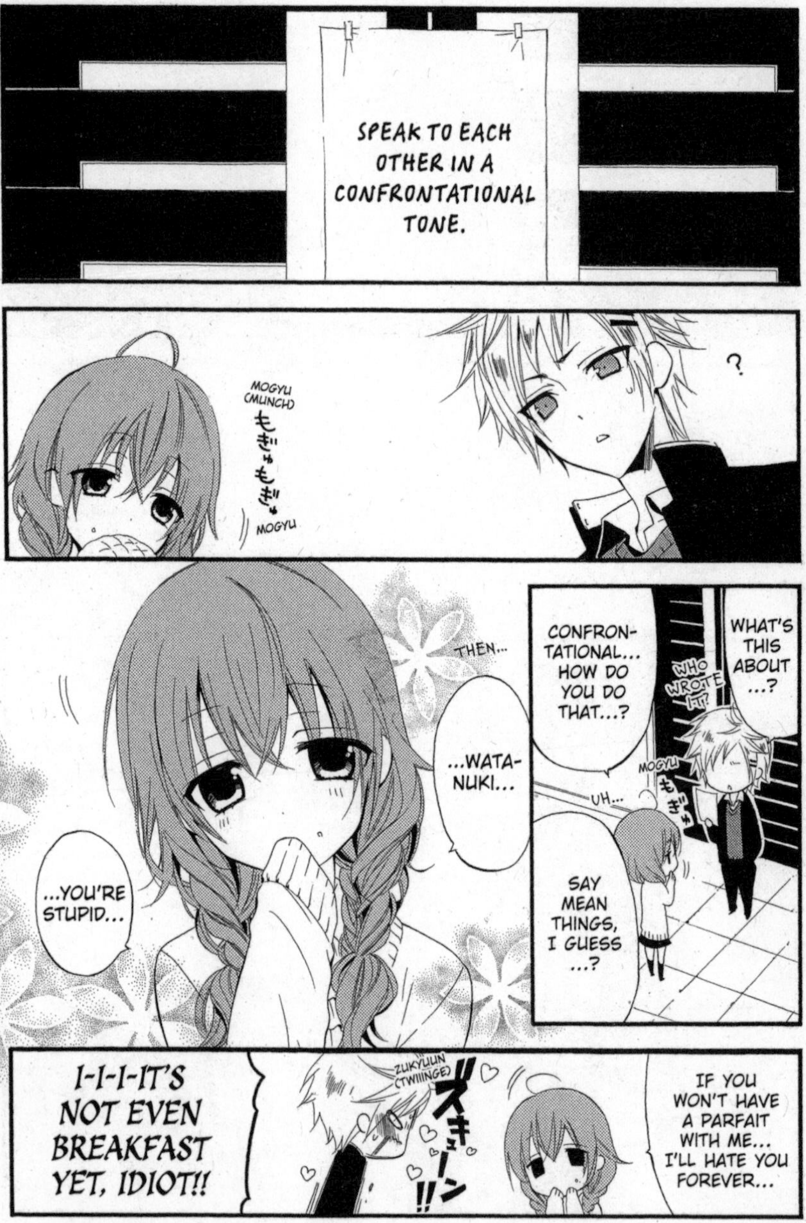
SPEAK TO EACH OTHER IN A CONFRONTATIONAL TONE.
?
MOGYU (MUNCH)
もぎゅもぎゅ
MOGYU
WHAT'S THIS ABOUT ...?
WHO WROTE IT?
CONFRONTATIONAL... HOW DO YOU DO THAT...?
MOGYU
もぎゅ
UH...
SAY MEAN THINGS, I GUESS ...?
THEN...
...WATANUKI...
...YOU'RE STUPID...
IF YOU WON'T HAVE A PARFAIT WITH ME... I'LL HATE YOU FOREVER...
ZUKYUUN (TWIIINGE)
ズキューン!!
I-I-I-IT'S NOT EVEN BREAKFAST YET, IDIOT!!

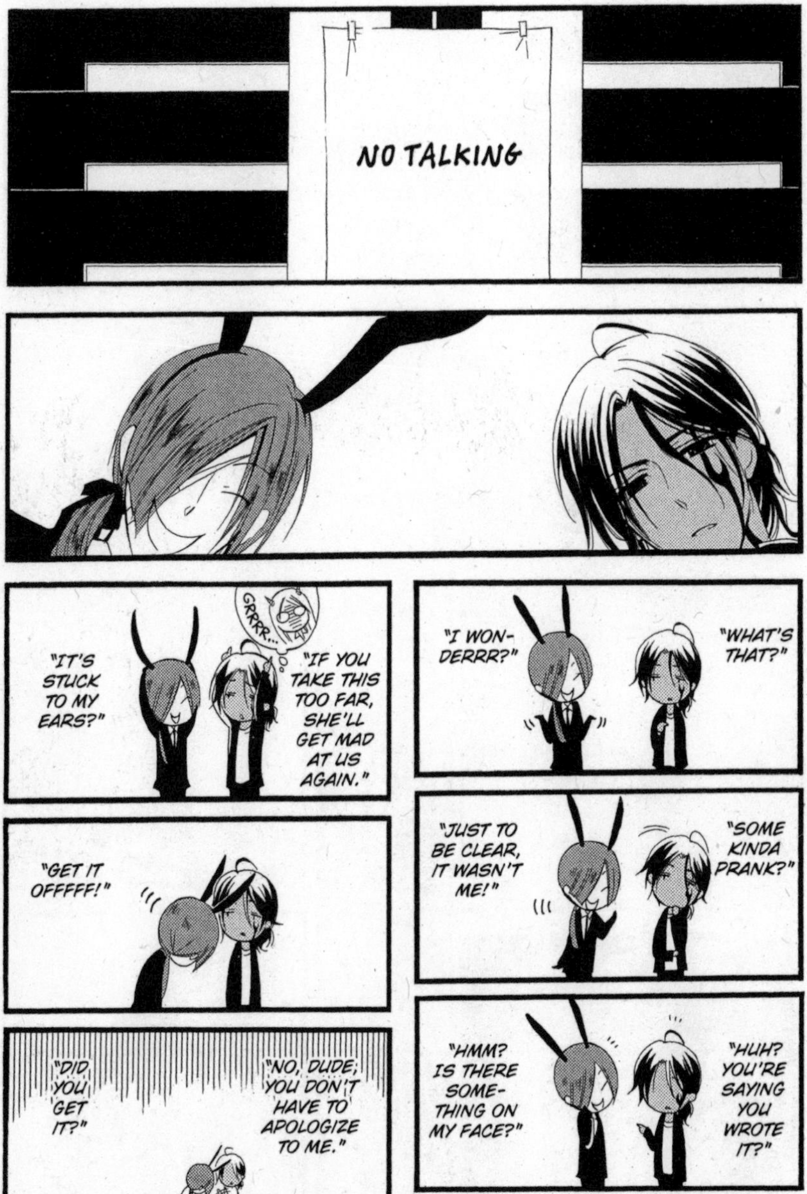
NO TALKING
"WHAT'S THAT?"
"I WON-DERRR?"
"SOME KINDA PRANK?"
"JUST TO BE CLEAR, IT WASN'T ME!"
"HUH? YOU'RE SAYING YOU WROTE IT?"
"HMM? IS THERE SOME-THING ON MY FACE?"
GRRRR...
"IF YOU TAKE THIS TOO FAR, SHE'LL GET MAD AT US AGAIN."
"IT'S STUCK TO MY EARS?"
"GET IT OFFFFF!"
"NO, DUDE; YOU DON'T HAVE TO APOLOGIZE TO ME."
"DID YOU GET IT?"

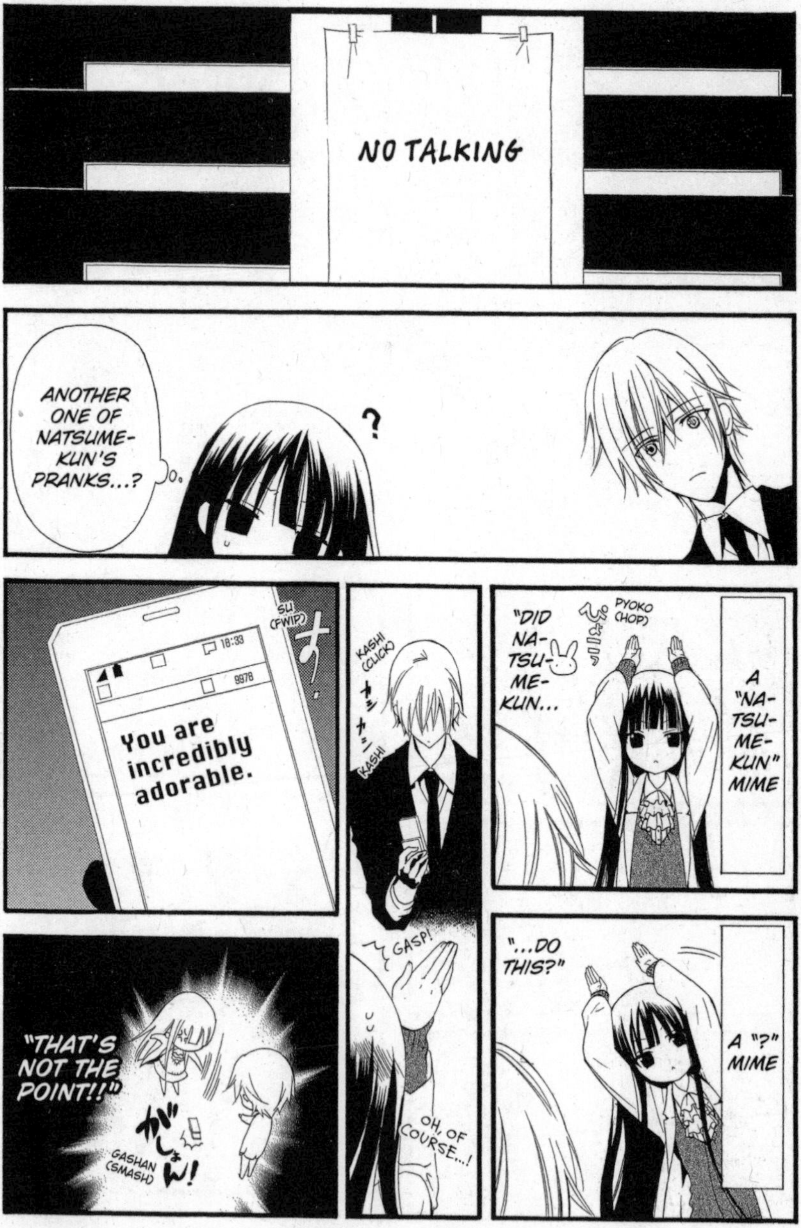
NO TALKING
?
ANOTHER ONE OF NATSUME-KUN'S PRANKS...?
A "NATSUME-KUN" MIME
PYOKO (HOP)
"DID NATSUME-KUN...
A "?" MIME
"...DO THIS?"
KASHI (CLICK)
KASHI
GASP!
OH, OF COURSE...!
SU (FWIP)
18:33
9978
You are incredibly adorable.
"THAT'S NOT THE POINT!!"
GASHAN (SMASH)

# STUDY GROUP

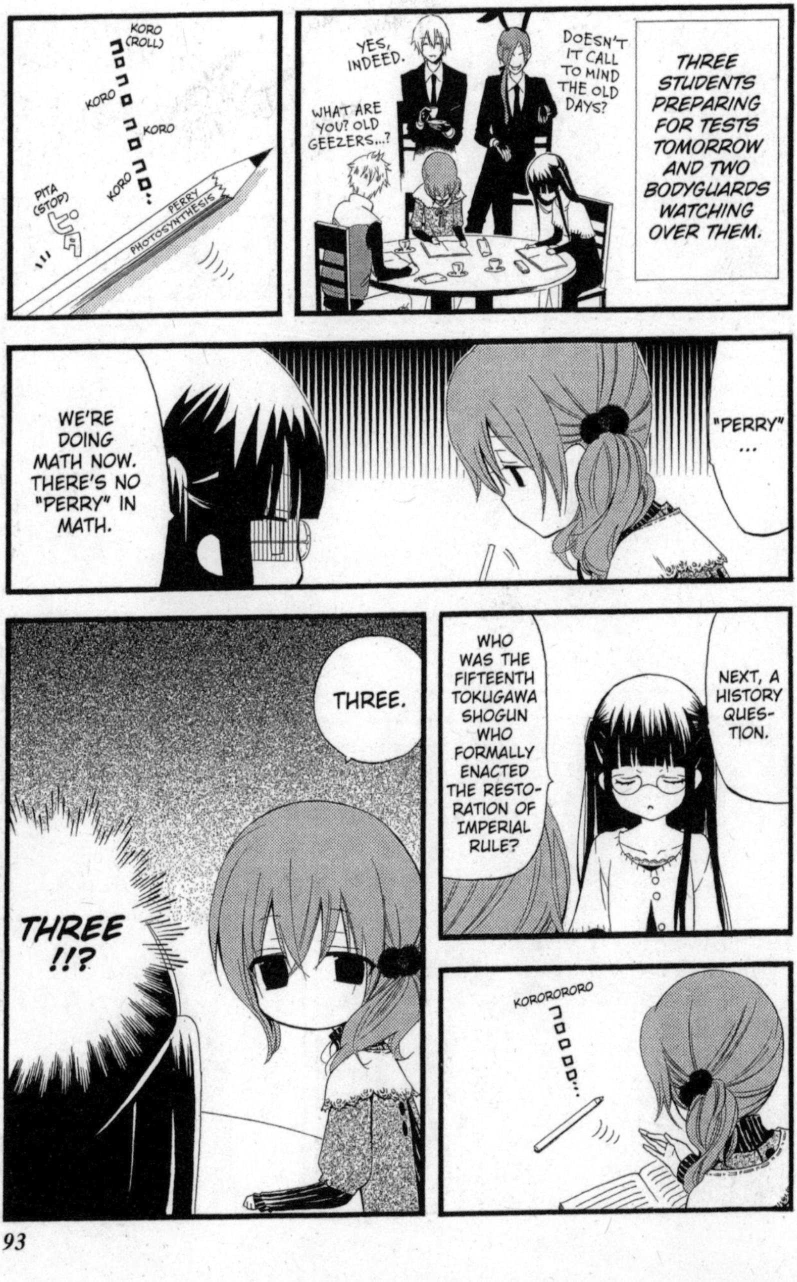

THREE STUDENTS PREPARING FOR TESTS TOMORROW AND TWO BODYGUARDS WATCHING OVER THEM.
DOESN'T IT CALL TO MIND THE OLD DAYS?
YES, INDEED.
WHAT ARE YOU? OLD GEEZERS...?
KORO (ROLL)
KORO
KORO
KORO
PERRY
PHOTOSYNTHESIS
PITA (STOP)
"PERRY" ...
WE'RE DOING MATH NOW. THERE'S NO "PERRY" IN MATH.
NEXT, A HISTORY QUES-TION.
WHO WAS THE FIFTEENTH TOKUGAWA SHOGUN WHO FORMALLY ENACTED THE RESTO-RATION OF IMPERIAL RULE?
KORORORORO
THREE.
THREE !!?

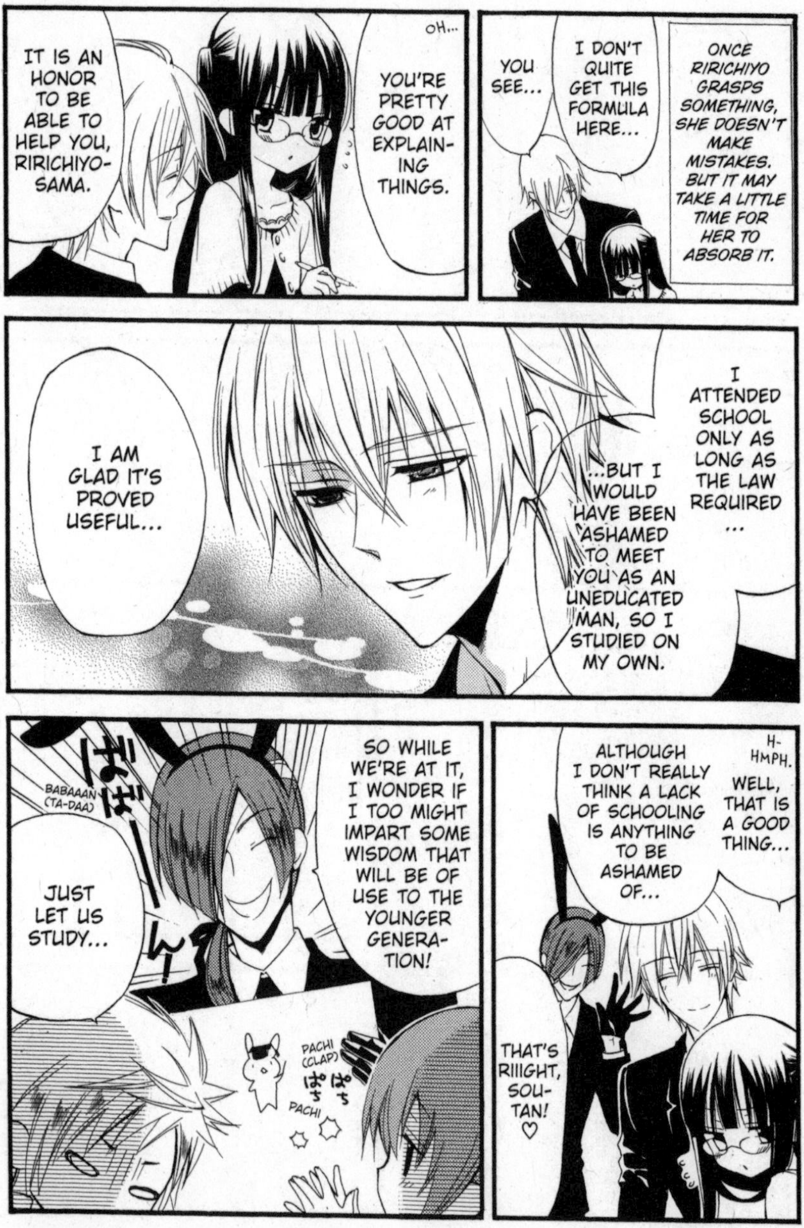
ONCE RIRICHIYO GRASPS SOMETHING, SHE DOESN'T MAKE MISTAKES. BUT IT MAY TAKE A LITTLE TIME FOR HER TO ABSORB IT.
I DON'T QUITE GET THIS FORMULA HERE...
YOU SEE...
OH...
YOU'RE PRETTY GOOD AT EXPLAIN-ING THINGS.
IT IS AN HONOR TO BE ABLE TO HELP YOU, RIRICHIYO-SAMA.
I ATTENDED SCHOOL ONLY AS LONG AS THE LAW REQUIRED...
...BUT I WOULD HAVE BEEN ASHAMED TO MEET YOU AS AN UNEDUCATED MAN, SO I STUDIED ON MY OWN.
I AM GLAD IT'S PROVED USEFUL...
H-HMPH. WELL, THAT IS A GOOD THING...
ALTHOUGH I DON'T REALLY THINK A LACK OF SCHOOLING IS ANYTHING TO BE ASHAMED OF...
THAT'S RIIIGHT, SOU-TAN! ♡
SO WHILE WE'RE AT IT, I WONDER IF I TOO MIGHT IMPART SOME WISDOM THAT WILL BE OF USE TO THE YOUNGER GENERA-TION!
ばばーーん!
BABAAAN (TA-DAA)
PACHI (CLAP)
ぱちぱち
PACHI
JUST LET US STUDY...

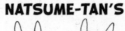

## TRIVIA CORNER ★

SOME TRIVIA THAT, IF YOU BELIEVE IT, WILL CERTAINLY COME IN HANDY SOMEDAY... ☆

WE WANT TO KNOW THINGS THAT WILL HELP US ON THE TESTS TOMORROW, NOT "SOME-DAY"...

---

FIRST, HAVE A PRAYING MANTIS READY. ☆

YOU CAN'T JUST SUMMON UP A PRAYING MANTIS OUT OF NOWHERE!!

---

BLRB! BLRBLE!

FILL A CONTAINER WITH WATER, AND DUNK THE PRAYING MANTIS IN THE WATER. ☆

WHAT!? DON'T DO THAT!!

ISN'T THAT ANIMAL CRUELTY!!?

---

IT DIES!!

WHAT DO YOU SUPPOSE HAPPENS THENNN?

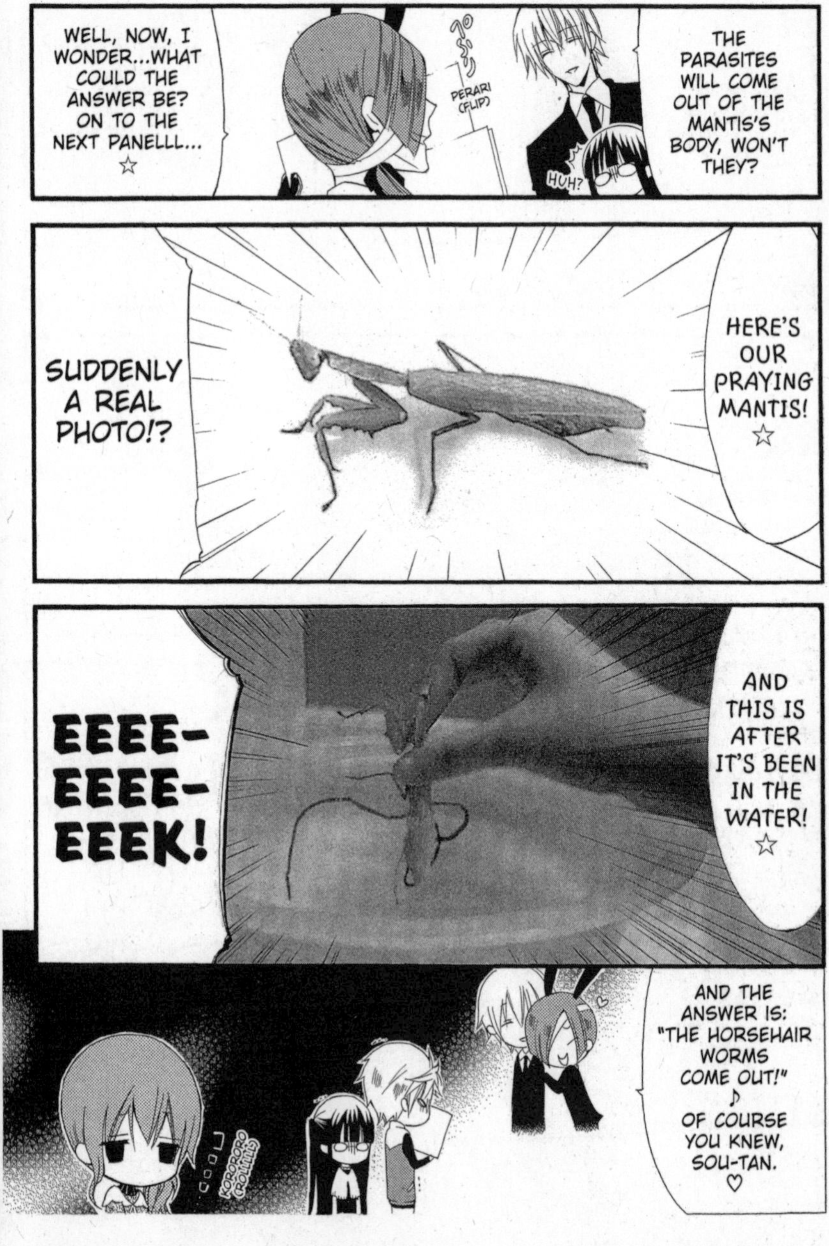
THE PARASITES WILL COME OUT OF THE MANTIS'S BODY, WON'T THEY?
HUH?
PERARI (FLIP)
WELL, NOW, I WONDER...WHAT COULD THE ANSWER BE? ON TO THE NEXT PANELLL... ☆
HERE'S OUR PRAYING MANTIS! ☆
SUDDENLY A REAL PHOTO!?
AND THIS IS AFTER IT'S BEEN IN THE WATER! ☆
EEEE-EEEE-EEEK!
AND THE ANSWER IS: "THE HORSEHAIR WORMS COME OUT!" ♪ OF COURSE YOU KNEW, SOU-TAN. ♡
KORORORO (ROLLLL)

# CARTA AND RIRICHIYO

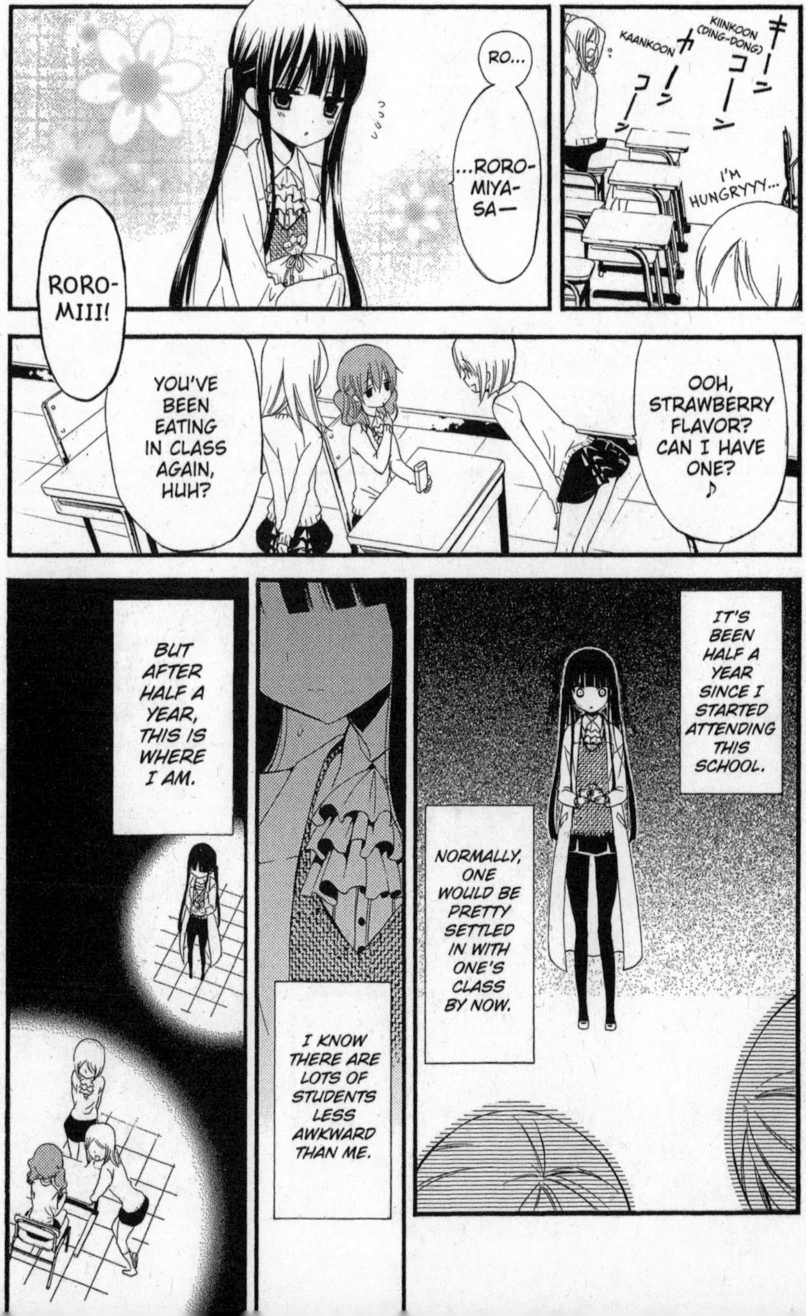
KIINKOON (DING-DONG)
キーンコーン
KAANKOON
カーンコーン
I'M HUNGRYYY...
RO...
...ROROMIYA-SA—
ROROMIII!
OOH, STRAWBERRY FLAVOR? CAN I HAVE ONE? ♪
YOU'VE BEEN EATING IN CLASS AGAIN, HUH?
IT'S BEEN HALF A YEAR SINCE I STARTED ATTENDING THIS SCHOOL.
NORMALLY, ONE WOULD BE PRETTY SETTLED IN WITH ONE'S CLASS BY NOW.
I KNOW THERE ARE LOTS OF STUDENTS LESS AWKWARD THAN ME.
BUT AFTER HALF A YEAR, THIS IS WHERE I AM.

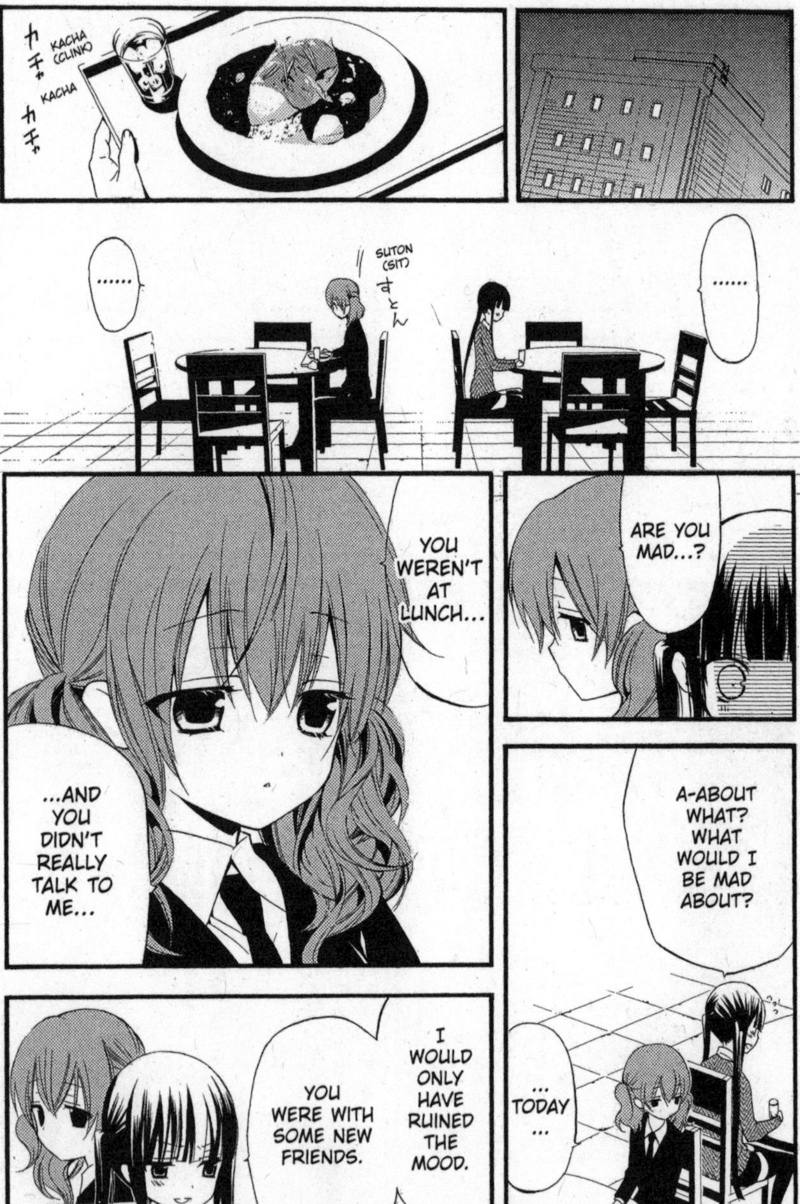
KACHA (CLINK)
カチャ
KACHA
カチャ
......
SUTON (SIT)
すとん
......
ARE YOU MAD...?
A-ABOUT WHAT? WHAT WOULD I BE MAD ABOUT?
... TODAY ...
YOU WEREN'T AT LUNCH...
...AND YOU DIDN'T REALLY TALK TO ME...
I WOULD ONLY HAVE RUINED THE MOOD.
YOU WERE WITH SOME NEW FRIENDS.

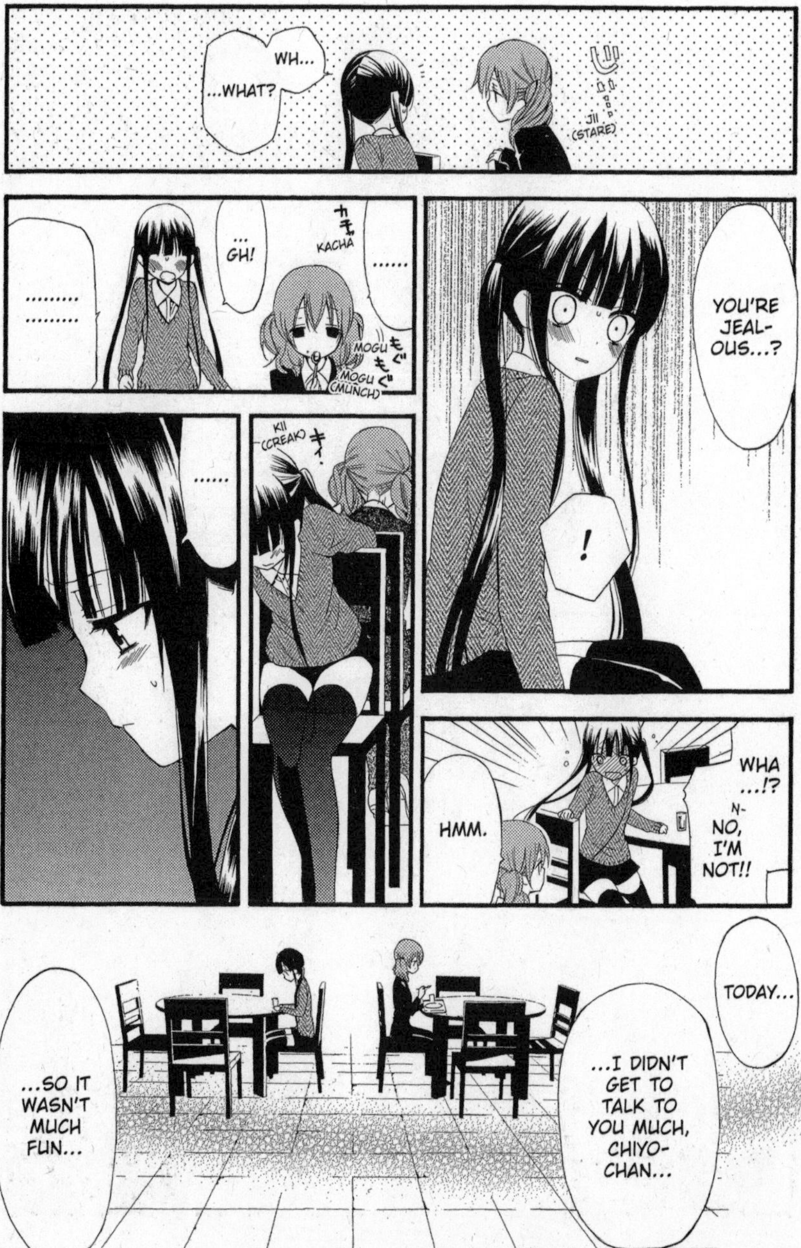
JII (STARE)
WH...
...WHAT?
YOU'RE JEAL-OUS...?
!
......
KACHA
...GH!
MOGU MOGU (MUNCH)
.........
.........
WHA ...!?
N-NO, I'M NOT!!
HMM.
KII (CREAK)
......
TODAY...
...I DIDN'T GET TO TALK TO YOU MUCH, CHIYO-CHAN...
...SO IT WASN'T MUCH FUN...

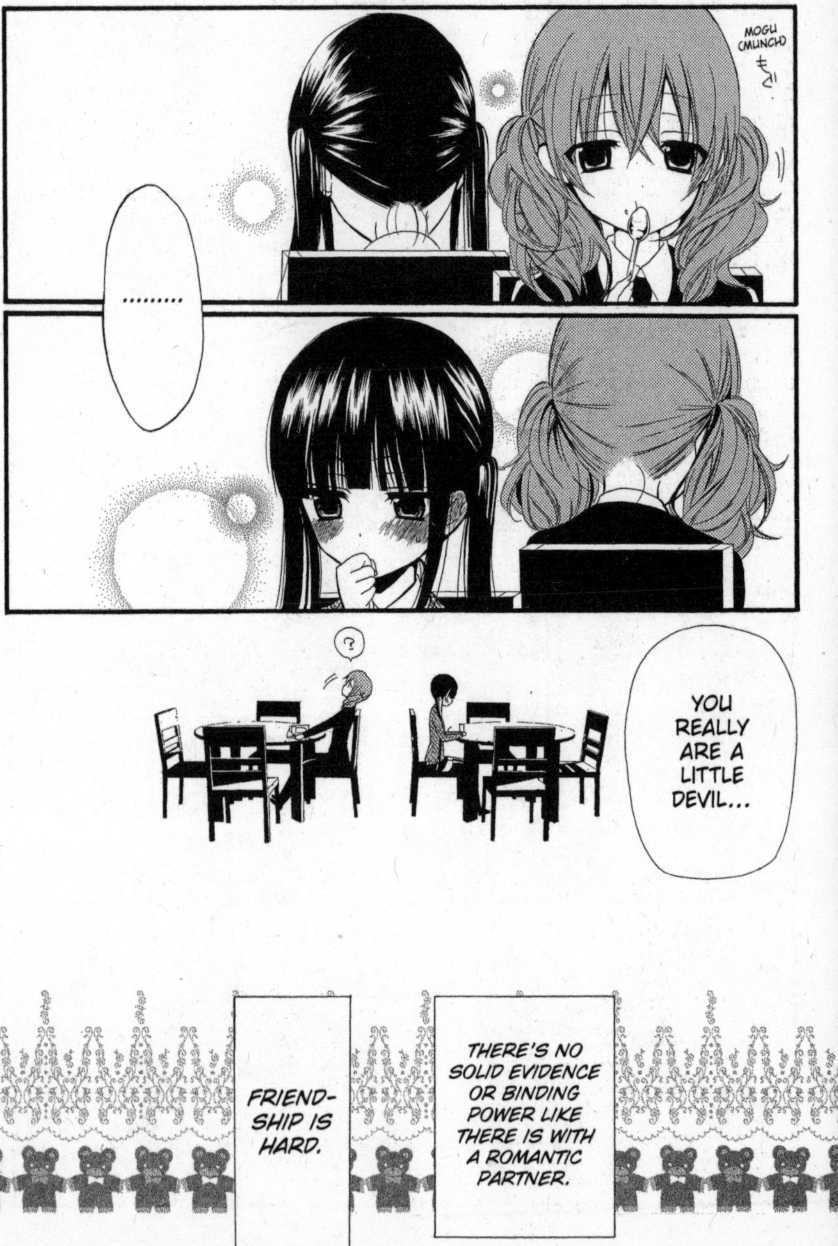
MOGU (MUNCH)
.........
YOU REALLY ARE A LITTLE DEVIL...
?
THERE'S NO SOLID EVIDENCE OR BINDING POWER LIKE THERE IS WITH A ROMANTIC PARTNER.
FRIEND-SHIP IS HARD.

# THE MYSTERIOUS COMMANDS, CONT.

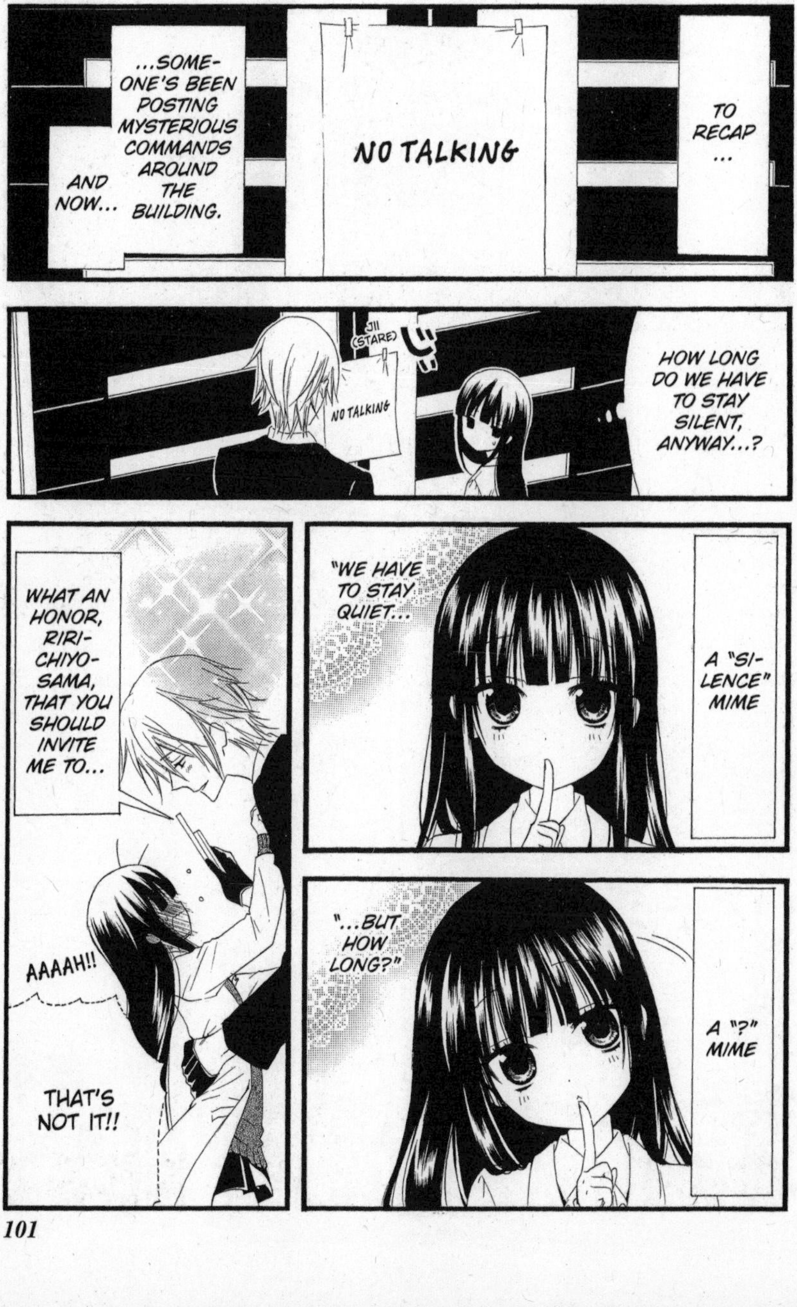
TO RECAP...
...SOMEONE'S BEEN POSTING MYSTERIOUS COMMANDS AROUND THE BUILDING.
AND NOW...
NO TALKING
HOW LONG DO WE HAVE TO STAY SILENT, ANYWAY...?
JII (STARE)
NO TALKING
A "SI-LENCE" MIME
"WE HAVE TO STAY QUIET...
A "?" MIME
"...BUT HOW LONG?"
WHAT AN HONOR, RIRI-CHIYO-SAMA, THAT YOU SHOULD INVITE ME TO...
AAAAH!!
THAT'S NOT IT!!

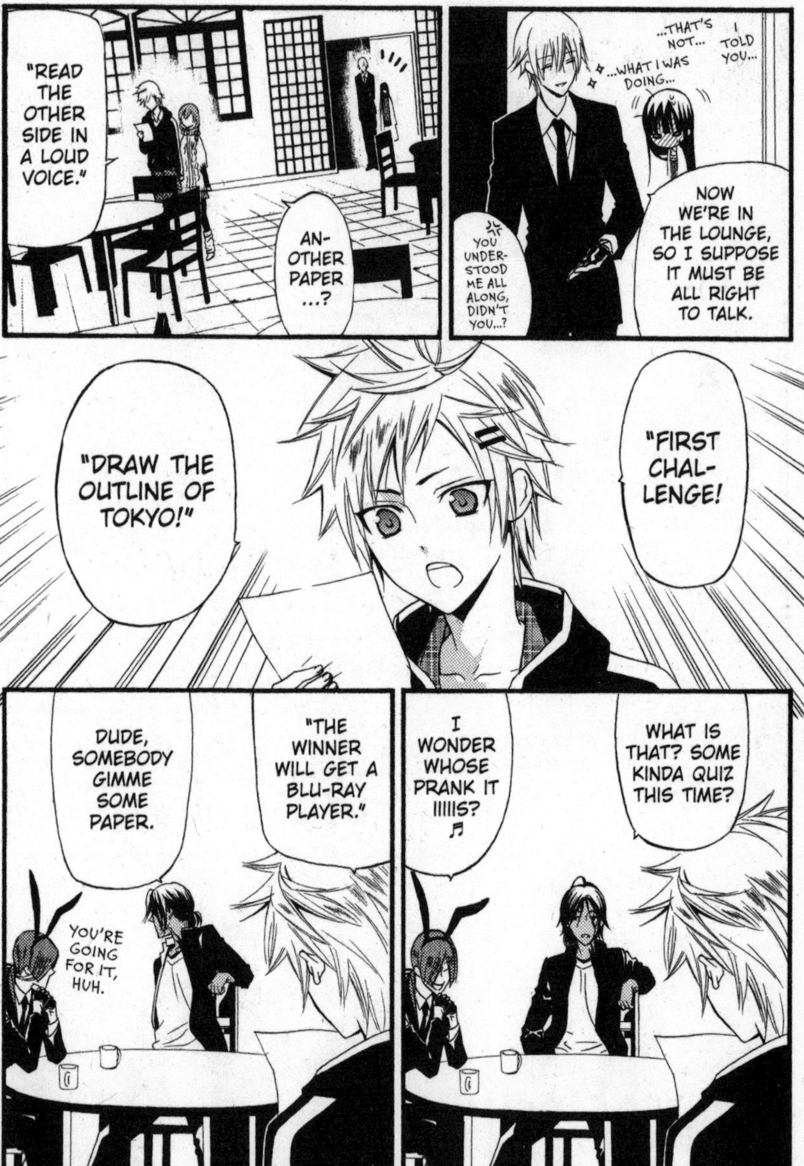
NOW WE'RE IN THE LOUNGE, SO I SUPPOSE IT MUST BE ALL RIGHT TO TALK.
YOU UNDERSTOOD ME ALL ALONG, DIDN'T YOU...?
...THAT'S NOT... ...WHAT I WAS DOING...
I TOLD YOU...
ANOTHER PAPER ...?
"READ THE OTHER SIDE IN A LOUD VOICE."
"FIRST CHALLENGE!
"DRAW THE OUTLINE OF TOKYO!"
WHAT IS THAT? SOME KINDA QUIZ THIS TIME?
I WONDER WHOSE PRANK IT IIIIIS? ♬
"THE WINNER WILL GET A BLU-RAY PLAYER."
DUDE, SOMEBODY GIMME SOME PAPER.
YOU'RE GOING FOR IT, HUH.

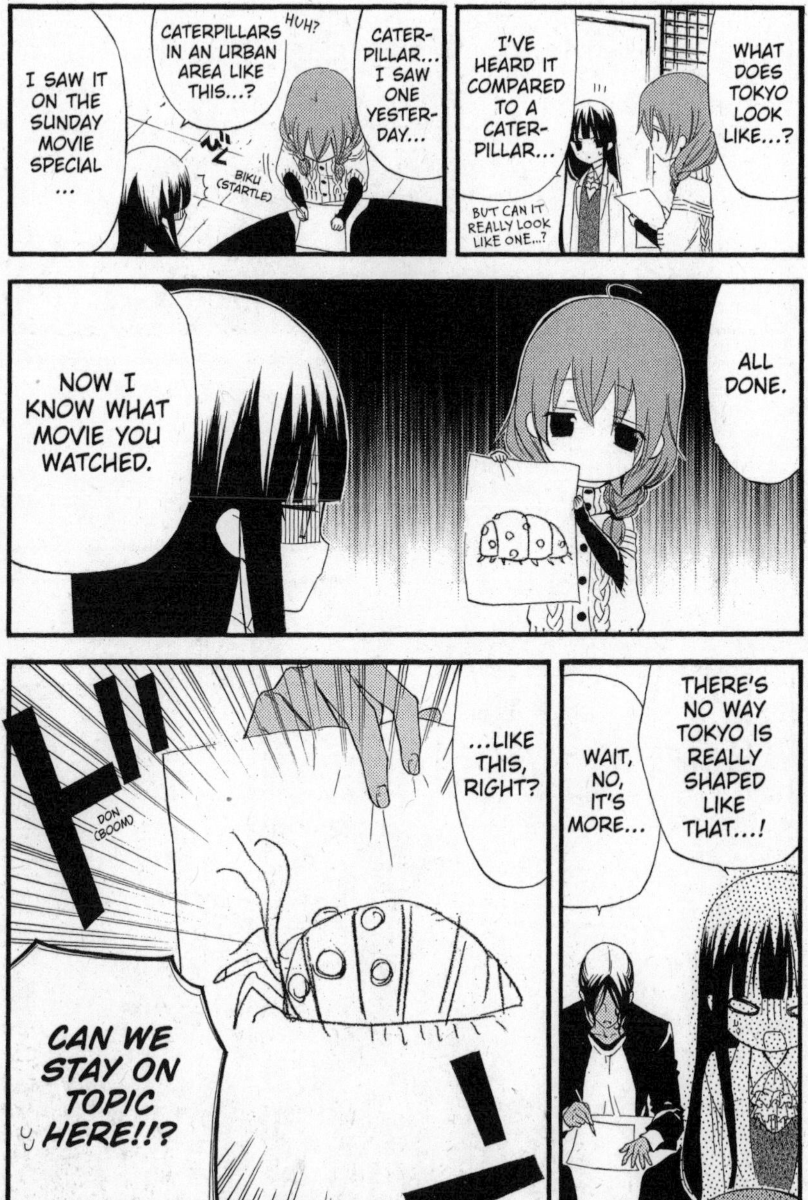
WHAT DOES TOKYO LOOK LIKE...?
I'VE HEARD IT COMPARED TO A CATER-PILLAR...
BUT CAN IT REALLY LOOK LIKE ONE...?
CATER-PILLAR... I SAW ONE YESTER-DAY...
HUH?
CATERPILLARS IN AN URBAN AREA LIKE THIS...?
BIKU (STARTLE)
I SAW IT ON THE SUNDAY MOVIE SPECIAL ...
ALL DONE.
NOW I KNOW WHAT MOVIE YOU WATCHED.
THERE'S NO WAY TOKYO IS REALLY SHAPED LIKE THAT...!
WAIT, NO, IT'S MORE...
...LIKE THIS, RIGHT?
DON (BOOM)
CAN WE STAY ON TOPIC HERE!!?

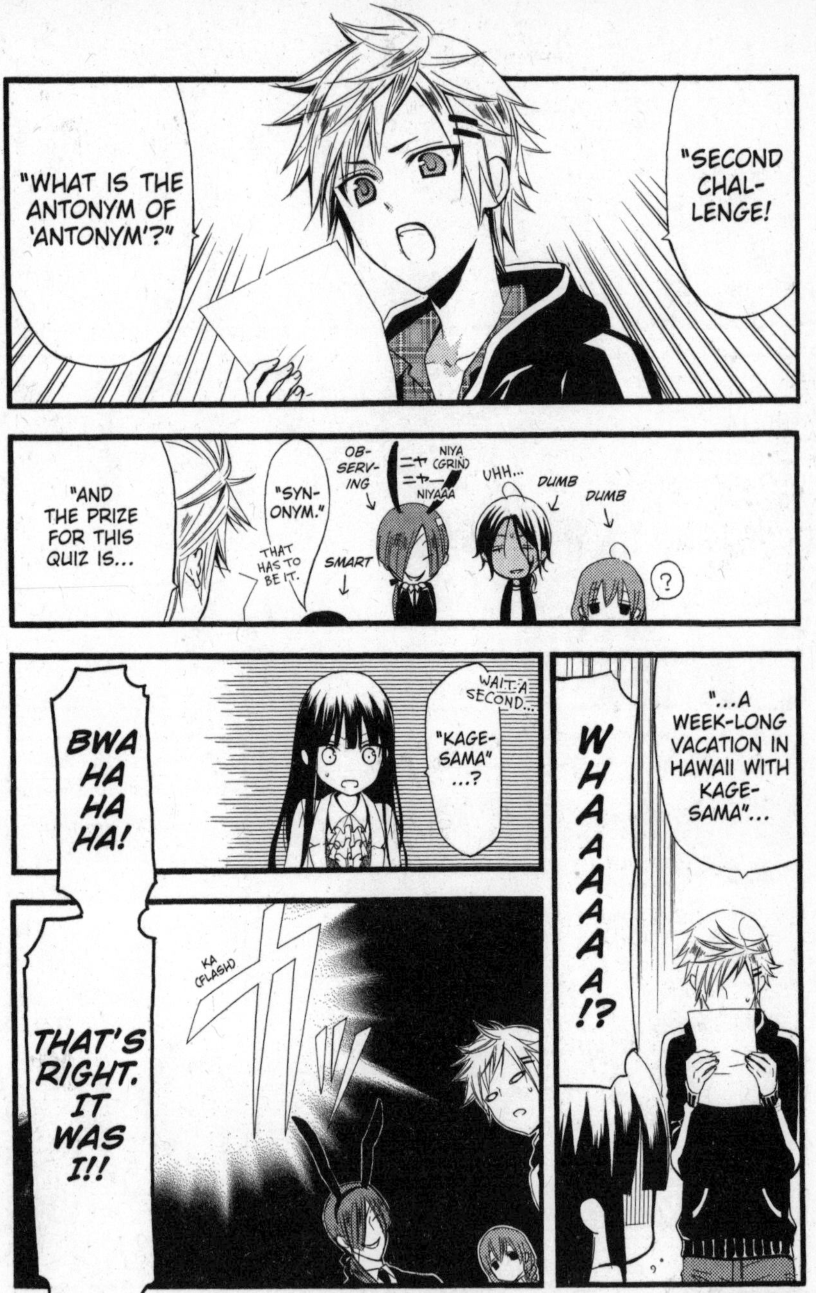
"SECOND CHAL-LENGE!
"WHAT IS THE ANTONYM OF 'ANTONYM'?"
?
DUMB
DUMB
UHH...
NIYA (GRIN)
ニヤ ニヤー
NIYAAA
OB-SERV-ING
SMART
"SYN-ONYM."
THAT HAS TO BE IT.
"AND THE PRIZE FOR THIS QUIZ IS...
"...A WEEK-LONG VACATION IN HAWAII WITH KAGE-SAMA"...
WHAAAAAAA!?
WAIT A SECOND...
"KAGE-SAMA" ...?
BWA HA HA HA!
KA (FLASH)
THAT'S RIGHT. IT WAS I!!

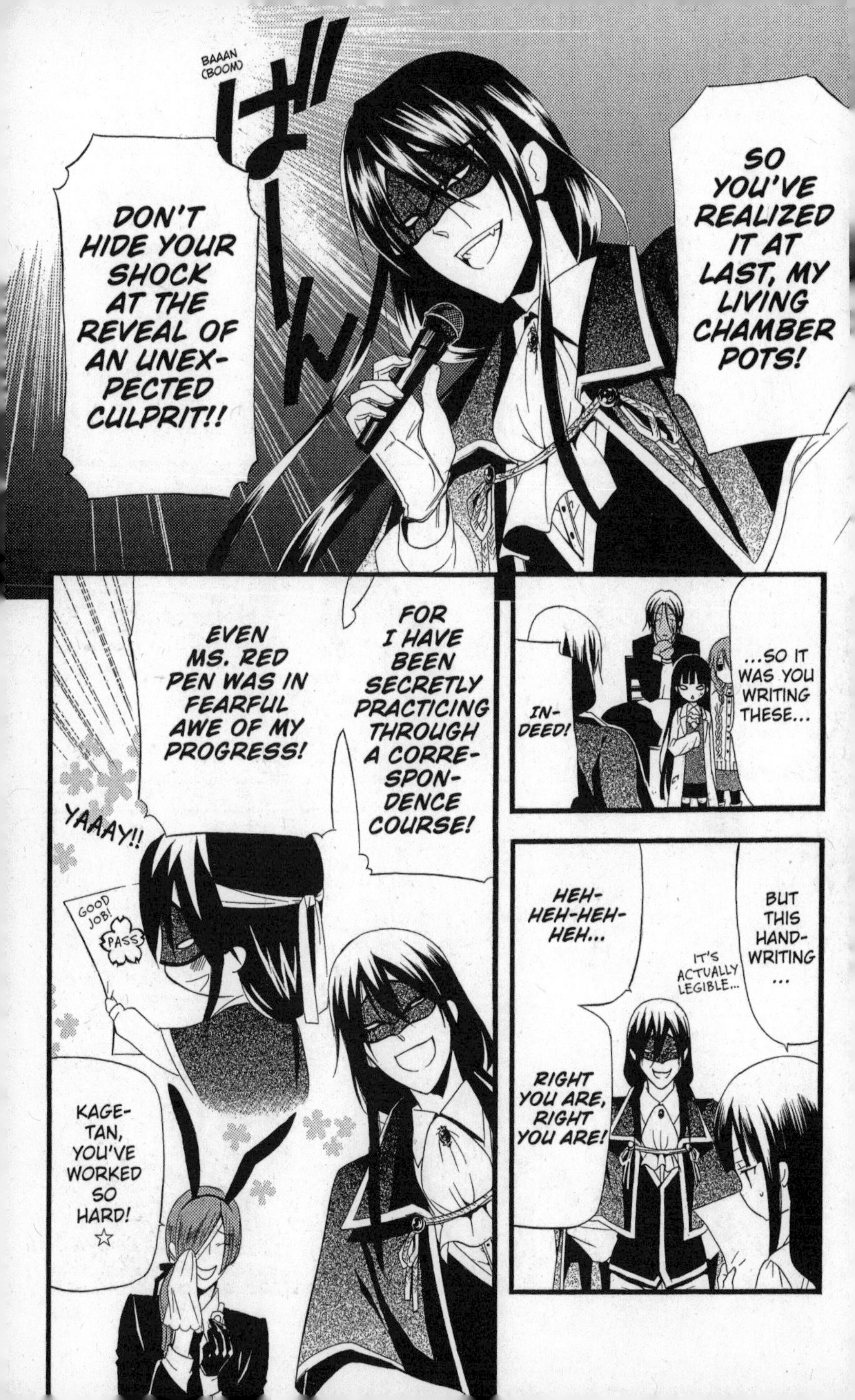
SO YOU'VE REALIZED IT AT LAST, MY LIVING CHAMBER POTS!
BAAAN (BOOM)
DON'T HIDE YOUR SHOCK AT THE REVEAL OF AN UNEX-PECTED CULPRIT!!
...SO IT WAS YOU WRITING THESE...
IN-DEED!
BUT THIS HAND-WRITING ...
IT'S ACTUALLY LEGIBLE...
HEH-HEH-HEH-HEH...
RIGHT YOU ARE, RIGHT YOU ARE!
FOR I HAVE BEEN SECRETLY PRACTICING THROUGH A CORRE-SPON-DENCE COURSE!
EVEN MS. RED PEN WAS IN FEARFUL AWE OF MY PROGRESS!
YAAAY!!
GOOD JOB!
PASS
KAGE-TAN, YOU'VE WORKED SO HARD! ☆

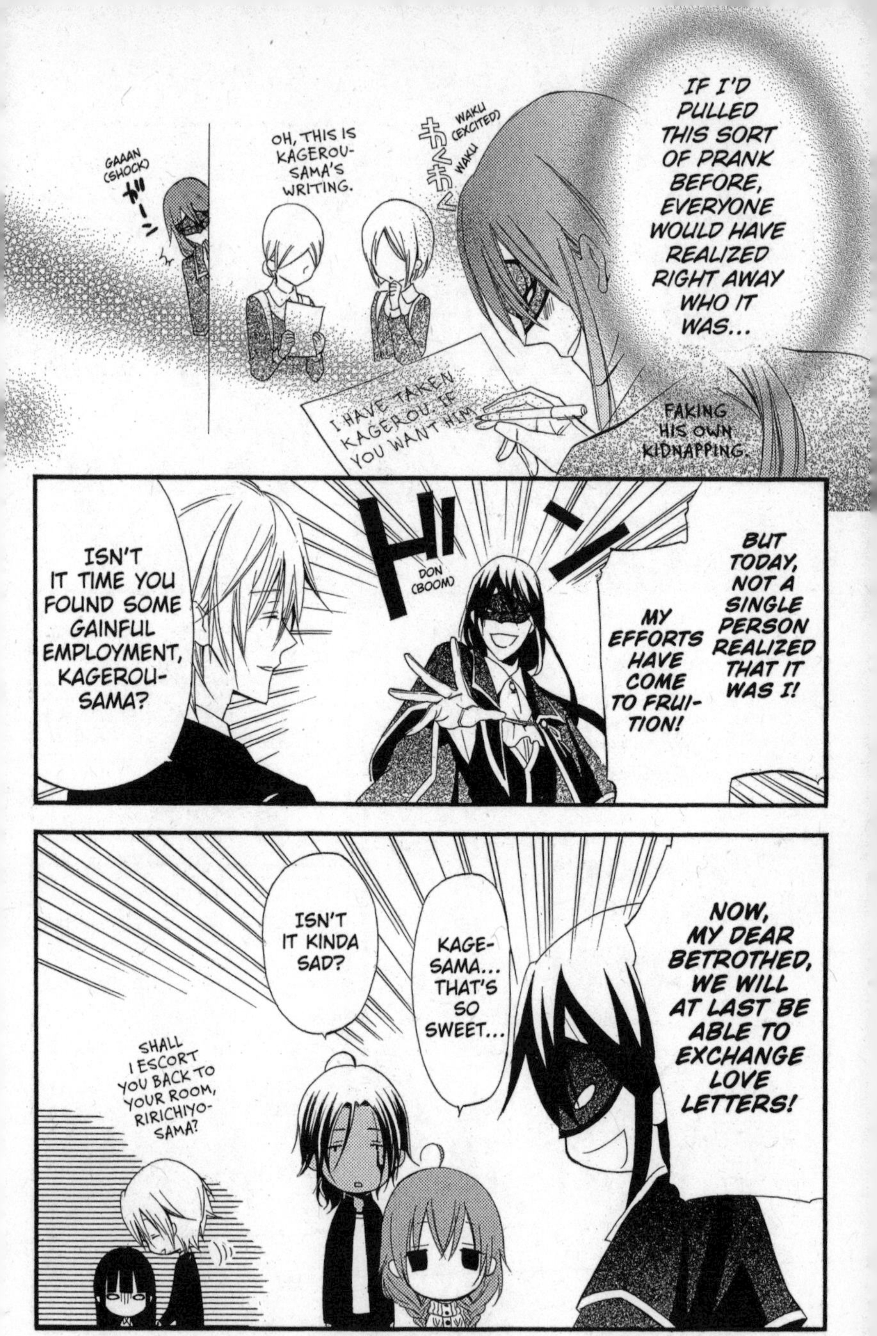

IF I'D PULLED THIS SORT OF PRANK BEFORE, EVERYONE WOULD HAVE REALIZED RIGHT AWAY WHO IT WAS...
FAKING HIS OWN KIDNAPPING.
I HAVE TAKEN KAGEROU. IF YOU WANT HIM
わくわく
WAKU (EXCITED) WAKU
OH, THIS IS KAGEROU-SAMA'S WRITING.
がーん
GAAAN (SHOCK)
BUT TODAY, NOT A SINGLE PERSON REALIZED THAT IT WAS I!
MY EFFORTS HAVE COME TO FRUITION!
DON (BOOM)
ISN'T IT TIME YOU FOUND SOME GAINFUL EMPLOYMENT, KAGEROU-SAMA?
NOW, MY DEAR BETROTHED, WE WILL AT LAST BE ABLE TO EXCHANGE LOVE LETTERS!
KAGE-SAMA... THAT'S SO SWEET...
ISN'T IT KINDA SAD?
SHALL I ESCORT YOU BACK TO YOUR ROOM, RIRICHIYO-SAMA?

# EVENING AT AYAKASHI HALL

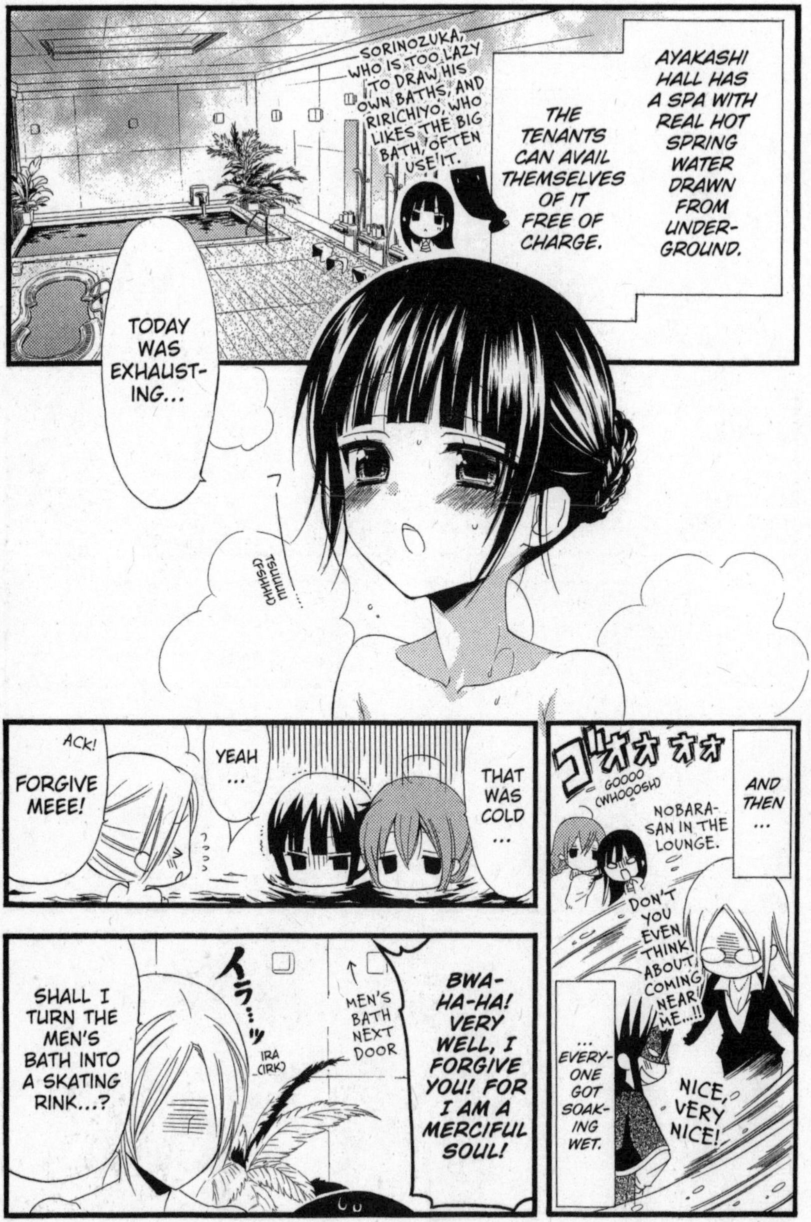
AYAKASHI HALL HAS A SPA WITH REAL HOT SPRING WATER DRAWN FROM UNDER-GROUND.
THE TENANTS CAN AVAIL THEMSELVES OF IT FREE OF CHARGE.
SORINOZUKA, WHO IS TOO LAZY TO DRAW HIS OWN BATHS, AND RIRICHIYO, WHO LIKES THE BIG BATH, OFTEN USE IT.
TODAY WAS EXHAUST-ING...
TSUUUU (PSHHH)
AND THEN...
ゴォオオ オオ
GOOOO (WHOOOSH)
NOBARA-SAN IN THE LOUNGE.
DON'T YOU EVEN THINK ABOUT COMING NEAR ME...!!
NICE, VERY NICE!
...EVERY-ONE GOT SOAK-ING WET.
THAT WAS COLD...
YEAH...
ACK!
FORGIVE MEEE!
BWA-HA-HA! VERY WELL, I FORGIVE YOU! FOR I AM A MERCIFUL SOUL!
MEN'S BATH NEXT DOOR
イラ…ッ
IRA (IRK)
SHALL I TURN THE MEN'S BATH INTO A SKATING RINK...?

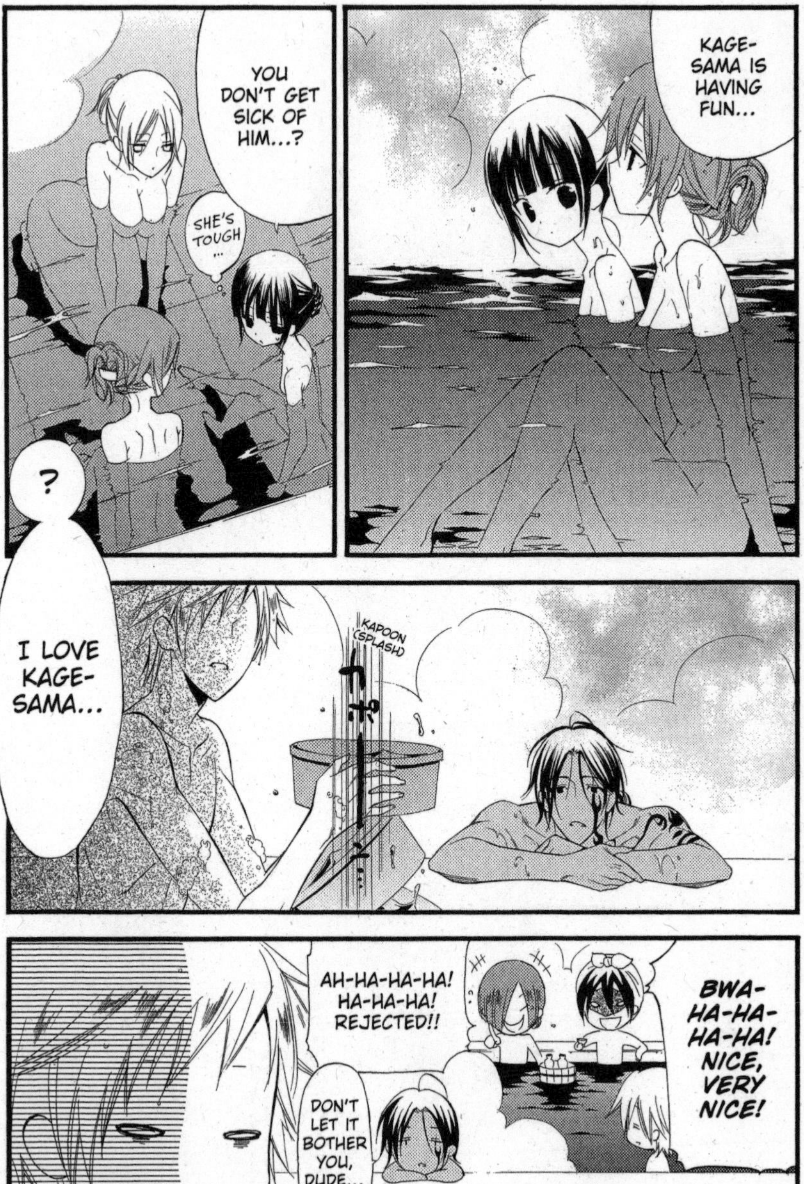

KAGE-SAMA IS HAVING FUN...
YOU DON'T GET SICK OF HIM...?
SHE'S TOUGH...
?
KAPOON (SPLASH)
I LOVE KAGE-SAMA...
BWA-HA-HA-HA-HA! NICE, VERY NICE!
AH-HA-HA-HA! HA-HA-HA! REJECTED!!
DON'T LET IT BOTHER YOU, DUDE...

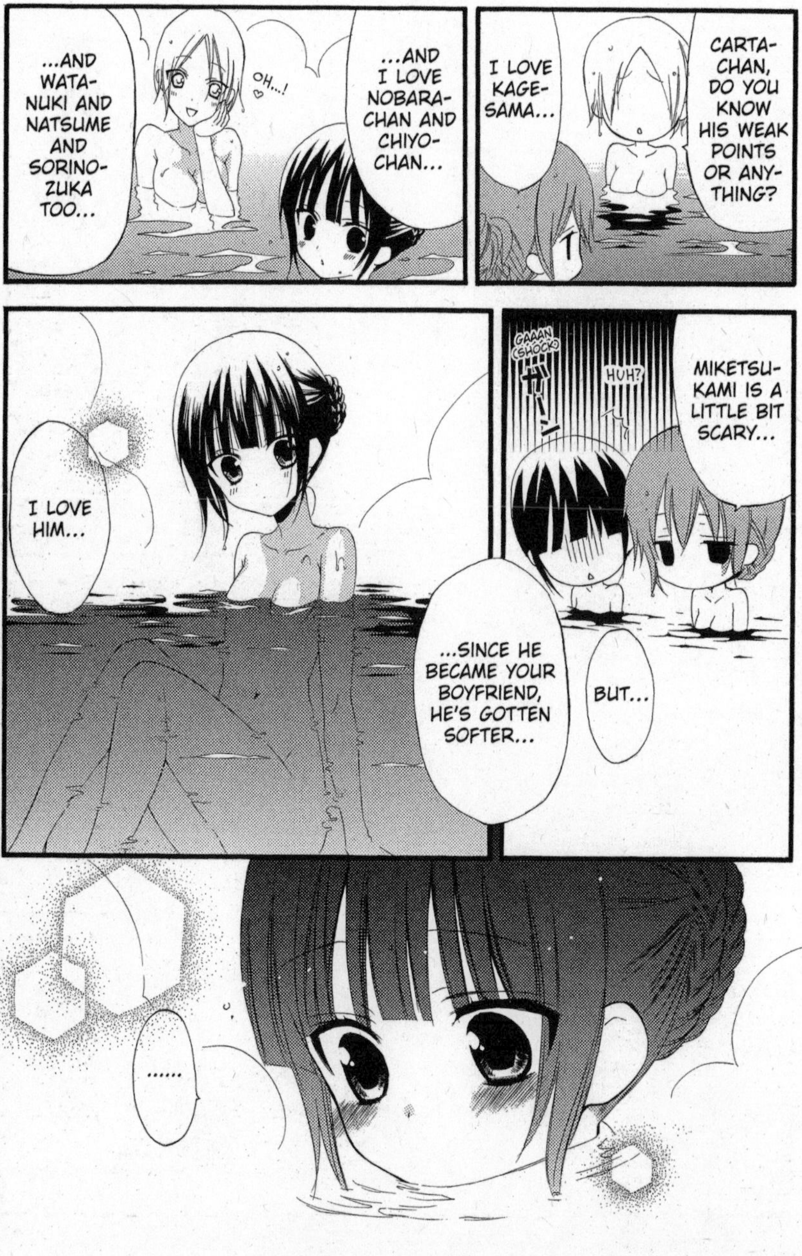
CARTA-CHAN, DO YOU KNOW HIS WEAK POINTS OR ANYTHING?
I LOVE KAGE-SAMA...
...AND I LOVE NOBARA-CHAN AND CHIYO-CHAN...
OH...! ♡
...AND WATA-NUKI AND NATSUME AND SORINO-ZUKA TOO...
MIKETSU-KAMI IS A LITTLE BIT SCARY...
HUH?
GAAAN (SHOCK)
BUT...
...SINCE HE BECAME YOUR BOYFRIEND, HE'S GOTTEN SOFTER...
I LOVE HIM...
......

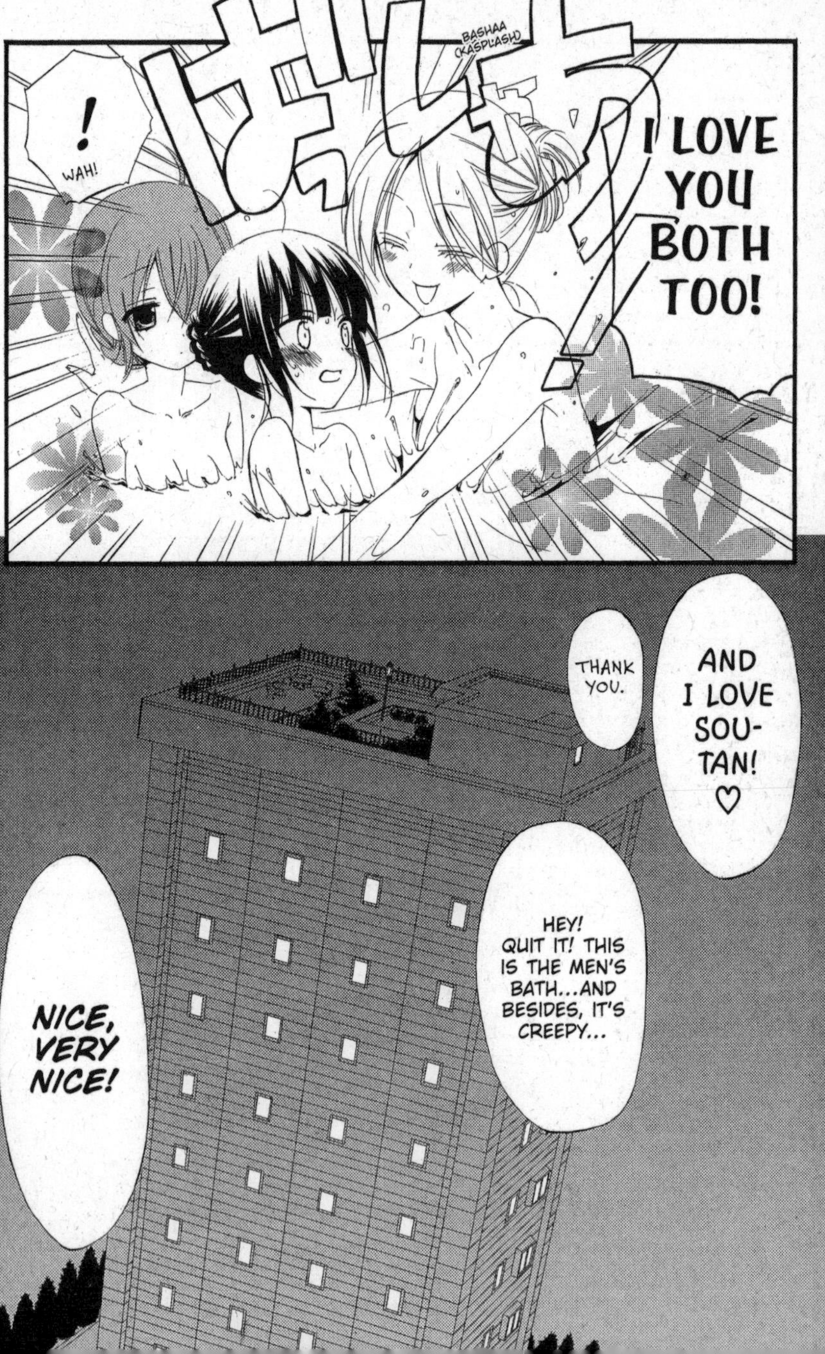
BASHAA (KASPLASH)
I LOVE YOU BOTH TOO!
!
WAH!
AND I LOVE SOU-TAN! ♡
THANK YOU.
HEY! QUIT IT! THIS IS THE MEN'S BATH...AND BESIDES, IT'S CREEPY...
NICE, VERY NICE!

INU×BOKU SS

maison de ayakashi

Welcome to Maison de Ayakashi.
The exclusive Secret Service of
this Mansion guarantees
your mental and physical
safety by providing
superior escorts.

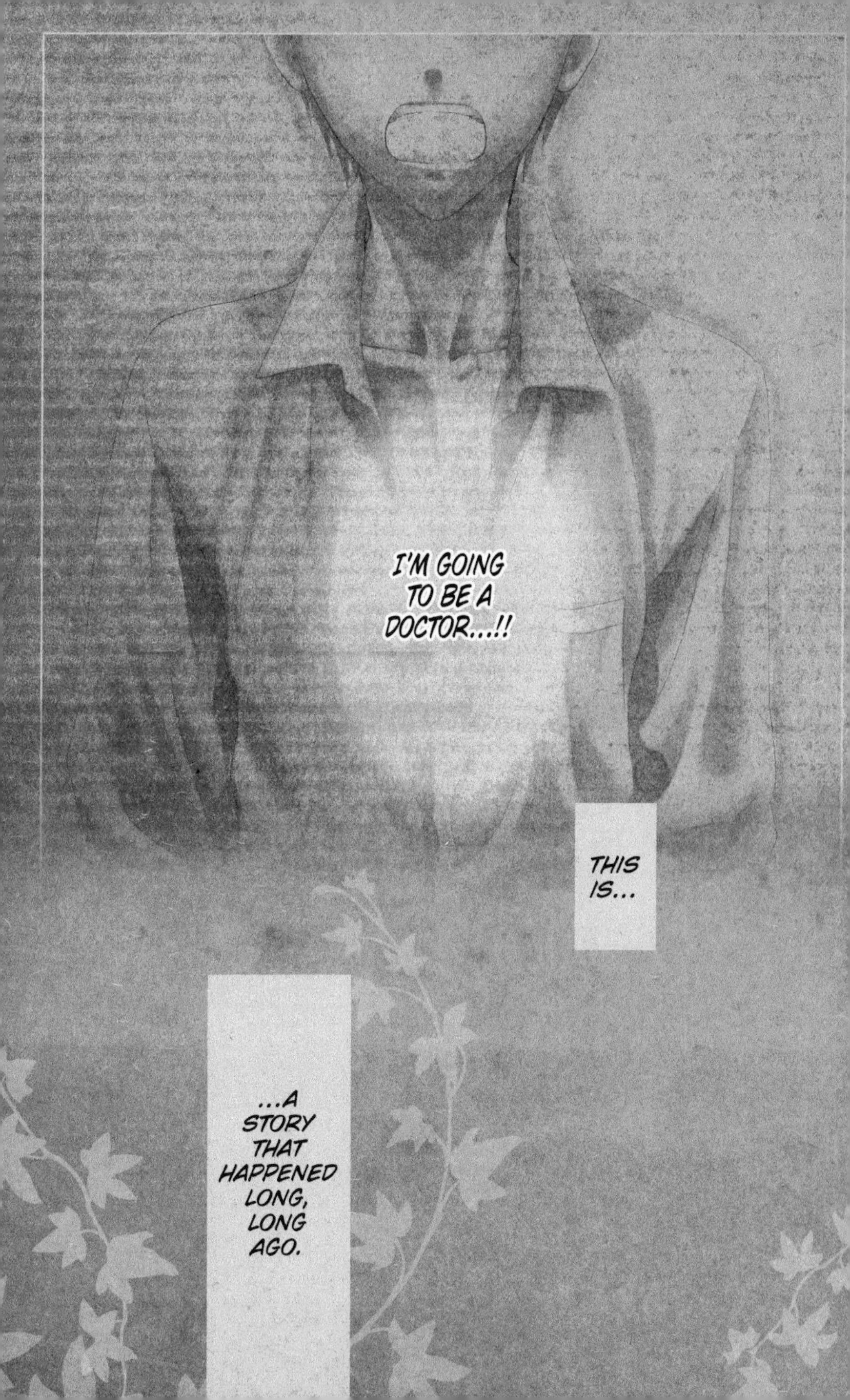
I'M GOING TO BE A DOCTOR...!!
THIS IS...
...A STORY THAT HAPPENED LONG, LONG AGO.

# Chapter 12: The Second Couple

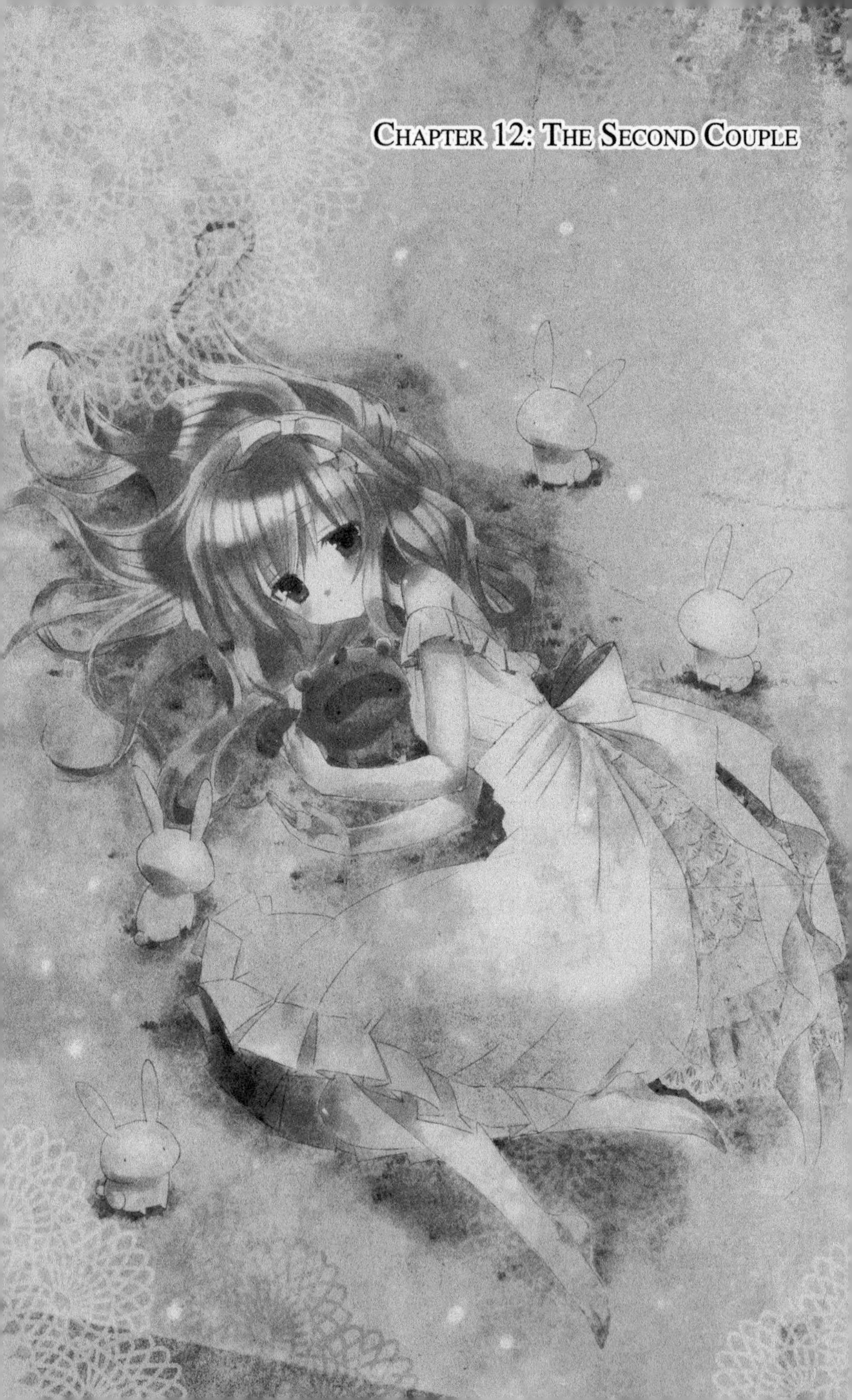

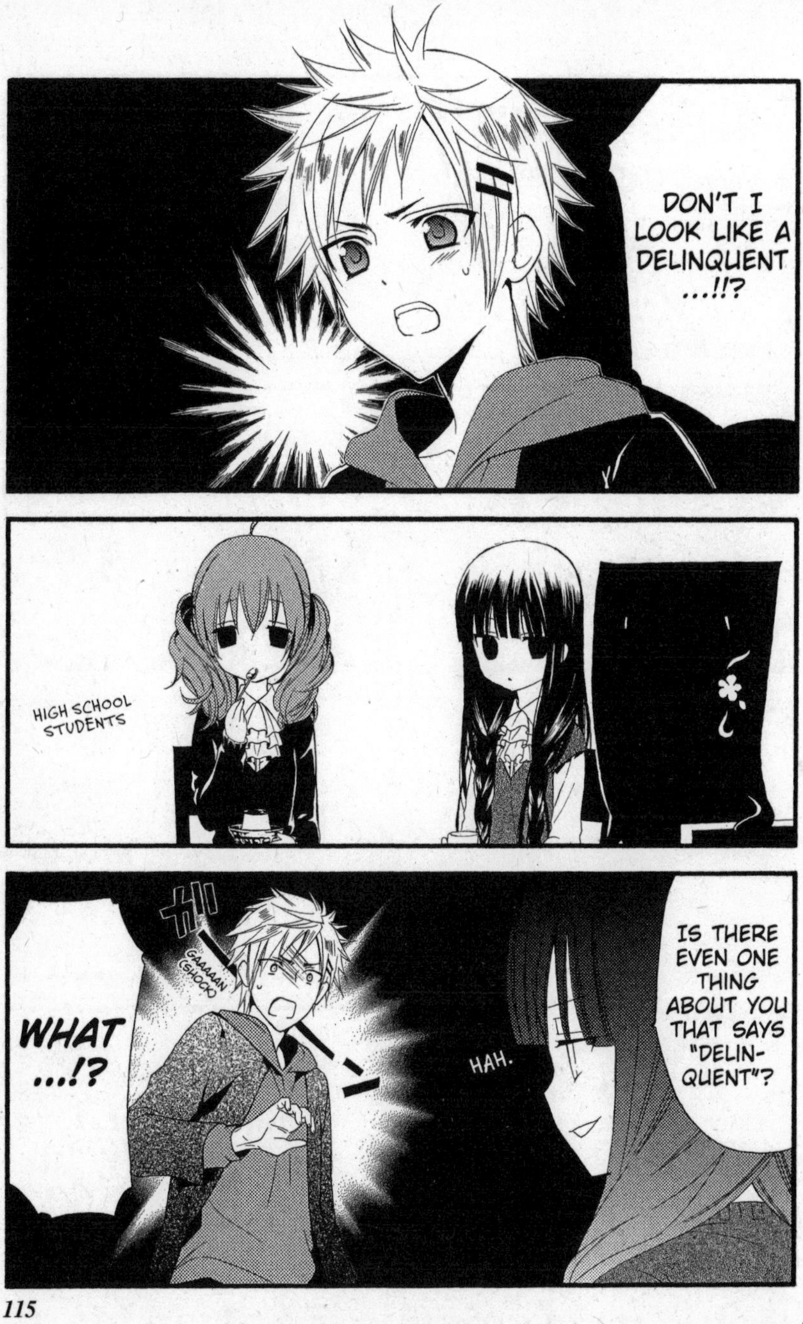
DON'T I LOOK LIKE A DELINQUENT ...!!?
HIGH SCHOOL STUDENTS
IS THERE EVEN ONE THING ABOUT YOU THAT SAYS "DELIN-QUENT"?
HAH.
GAAAAAN (SHOCK)
WHAT ...!?

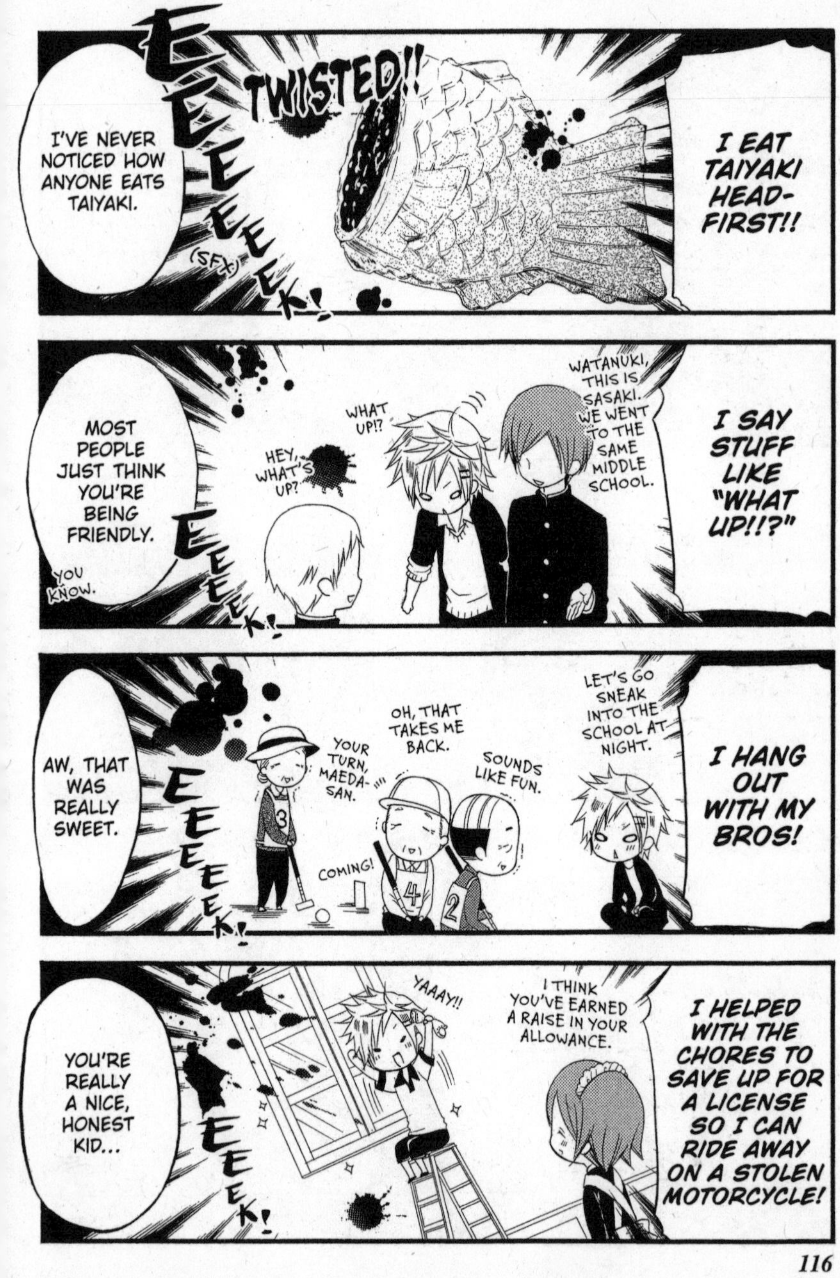
I EAT TAIYAKI HEAD-FIRST!!
TWISTED!!
EEEEEEEK!
(SFX)
I'VE NEVER NOTICED HOW ANYONE EATS TAIYAKI.
I SAY STUFF LIKE "WHAT UP!!?"
WATANUKI, THIS IS SASAKI. WE WENT TO THE SAME MIDDLE SCHOOL.
WHAT UP!?
HEY, WHAT'S UP?
EEEEEK!
MOST PEOPLE JUST THINK YOU'RE BEING FRIENDLY.
YOU KNOW.
I HANG OUT WITH MY BROS!
LET'S GO SNEAK INTO THE SCHOOL AT NIGHT.
SOUNDS LIKE FUN.
OH, THAT TAKES ME BACK.
YOUR TURN, MAEDA-SAN.
COMING!
EEEEEEK!
AW, THAT WAS REALLY SWEET.
I HELPED WITH THE CHORES TO SAVE UP FOR A LICENSE SO I CAN RIDE AWAY ON A STOLEN MOTORCYCLE!
I THINK YOU'VE EARNED A RAISE IN YOUR ALLOWANCE.
YAAAY!!
EEEEEK!
YOU'RE REALLY A NICE, HONEST KID...

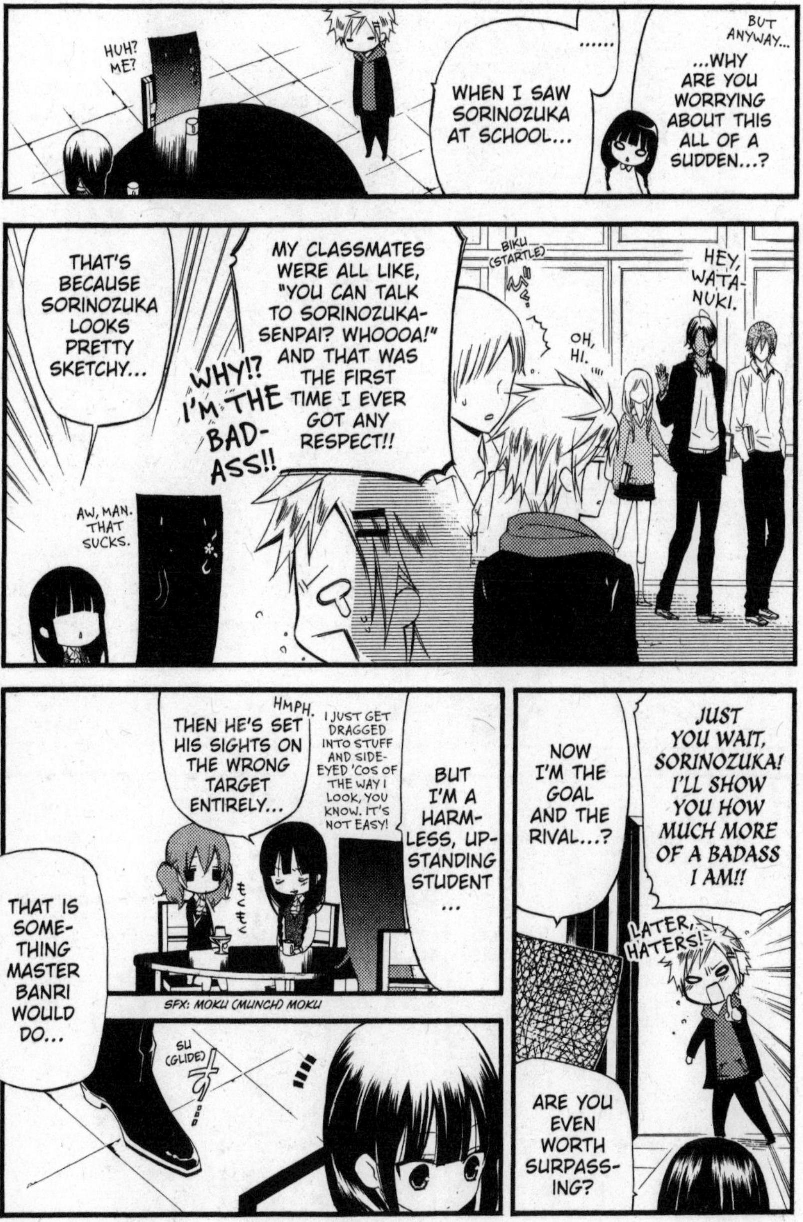
BUT ANYWAY...
...WHY ARE YOU WORRYING ABOUT THIS ALL OF A SUDDEN...?
......
WHEN I SAW SORINOZUKA AT SCHOOL...
HUH? ME?
HEY, WATA-NUKI.
BIKU (STARTLE)
OH, HI.
MY CLASSMATES WERE ALL LIKE, "YOU CAN TALK TO SORINOZUKA-SENPAI? WHOOOA!" AND THAT WAS THE FIRST TIME I EVER GOT ANY RESPECT!!
WHY!? I'M THE BAD-ASS!!
THAT'S BECAUSE SORINOZUKA LOOKS PRETTY SKETCHY...
AW, MAN. THAT SUCKS.
JUST YOU WAIT, SORINOZUKA! I'LL SHOW YOU HOW MUCH MORE OF A BADASS I AM!!
NOW I'M THE GOAL AND THE RIVAL...?
LATER, HATERS!
ARE YOU EVEN WORTH SURPASS-ING?
BUT I'M A HARM-LESS, UP-STANDING STUDENT...
I JUST GET DRAGGED INTO STUFF AND SIDE-EYED 'COS OF THE WAY I LOOK, YOU KNOW. IT'S NOT EASY!
HMPH.
THEN HE'S SET HIS SIGHTS ON THE WRONG TARGET ENTIRELY...
SFX: MOKU (MUNCH) MOKU
THAT IS SOME-THING MASTER BANRI WOULD DO...
SU (GLIDE)

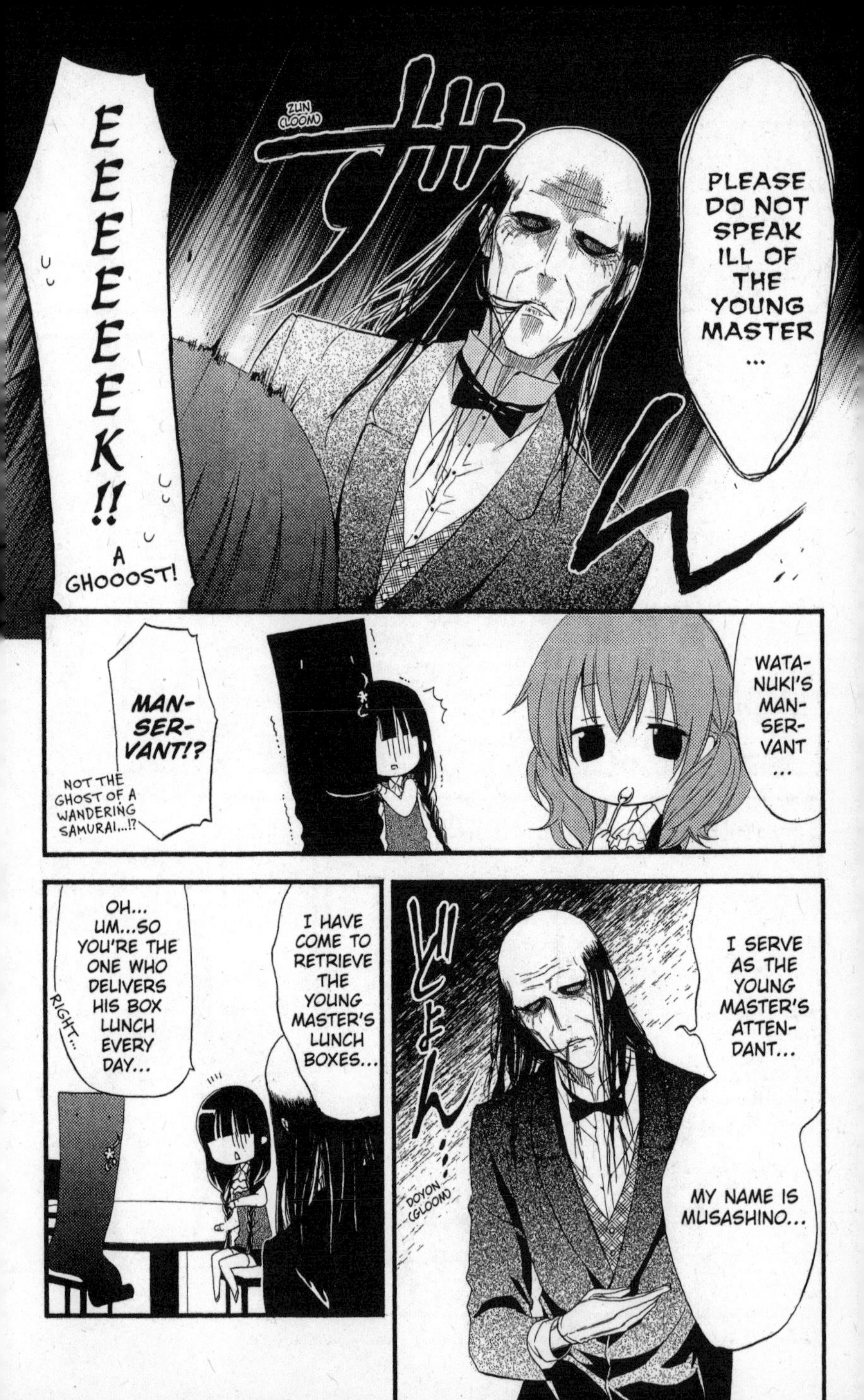
PLEASE DO NOT SPEAK ILL OF THE YOUNG MASTER ...
ZUN (GLOOM)
EEEEEEEK!!
A GHOOOST!
WATA-NUKI'S MAN-SER-VANT ...
MAN-SER-VANT!?
NOT THE GHOST OF A WANDERING SAMURAI...!?
I SERVE AS THE YOUNG MASTER'S ATTEN-DANT...
MY NAME IS MUSASHINO...
DOYON (GLOOM)
I HAVE COME TO RETRIEVE THE YOUNG MASTER'S LUNCH BOXES...
OH... UM...SO YOU'RE THE ONE WHO DELIVERS HIS BOX LUNCH EVERY DAY...
RIGHT...

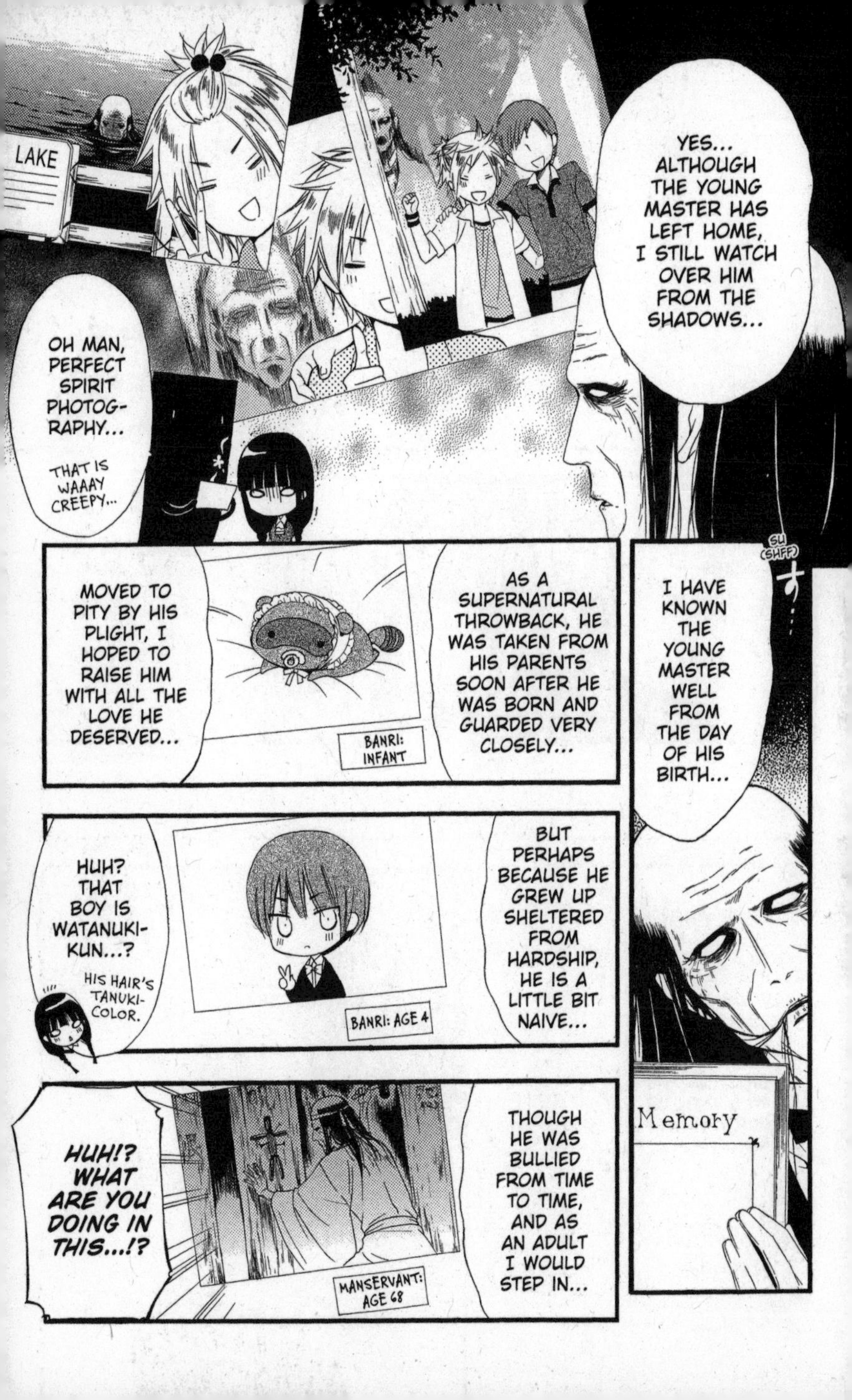
YES... ALTHOUGH THE YOUNG MASTER HAS LEFT HOME, I STILL WATCH OVER HIM FROM THE SHADOWS...
LAKE
OH MAN, PERFECT SPIRIT PHOTOG-RAPHY...
THAT IS WAAAY CREEPY...
SU (SHFF)
I HAVE KNOWN THE YOUNG MASTER WELL FROM THE DAY OF HIS BIRTH...
Memory
AS A SUPERNATURAL THROWBACK, HE WAS TAKEN FROM HIS PARENTS SOON AFTER HE WAS BORN AND GUARDED VERY CLOSELY...
BANRI: INFANT
MOVED TO PITY BY HIS PLIGHT, I HOPED TO RAISE HIM WITH ALL THE LOVE HE DESERVED...
BUT PERHAPS BECAUSE HE GREW UP SHELTERED FROM HARDSHIP, HE IS A LITTLE BIT NAIVE...
BANRI: AGE 4
HUH? THAT BOY IS WATANUKI-KUN...?
HIS HAIR'S TANUKI-COLOR.
THOUGH HE WAS BULLIED FROM TIME TO TIME, AND AS AN ADULT I WOULD STEP IN...
MANSERVANT: AGE 68
HUH!? WHAT ARE YOU DOING IN THIS...!?

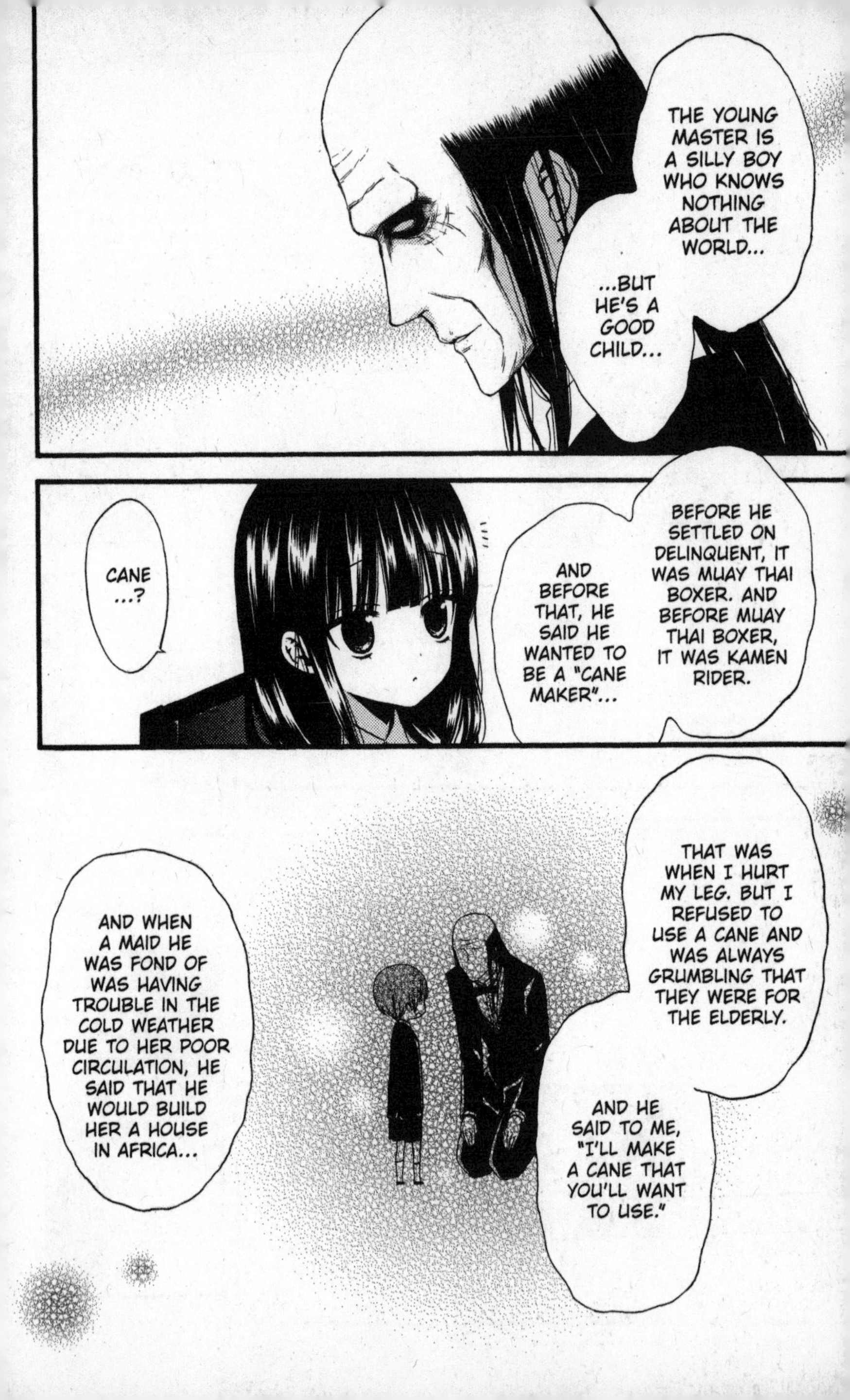
THE YOUNG MASTER IS A SILLY BOY WHO KNOWS NOTHING ABOUT THE WORLD...
...BUT HE'S A GOOD CHILD...
BEFORE HE SETTLED ON DELINQUENT, IT WAS MUAY THAI BOXER. AND BEFORE MUAY THAI BOXER, IT WAS KAMEN RIDER.
AND BEFORE THAT, HE SAID HE WANTED TO BE A "CANE MAKER"...
CANE ...?
THAT WAS WHEN I HURT MY LEG. BUT I REFUSED TO USE A CANE AND WAS ALWAYS GRUMBLING THAT THEY WERE FOR THE ELDERLY.
AND HE SAID TO ME, "I'LL MAKE A CANE THAT YOU'LL WANT TO USE."
AND WHEN A MAID HE WAS FOND OF WAS HAVING TROUBLE IN THE COLD WEATHER DUE TO HER POOR CIRCULATION, HE SAID THAT HE WOULD BUILD HER A HOUSE IN AFRICA...

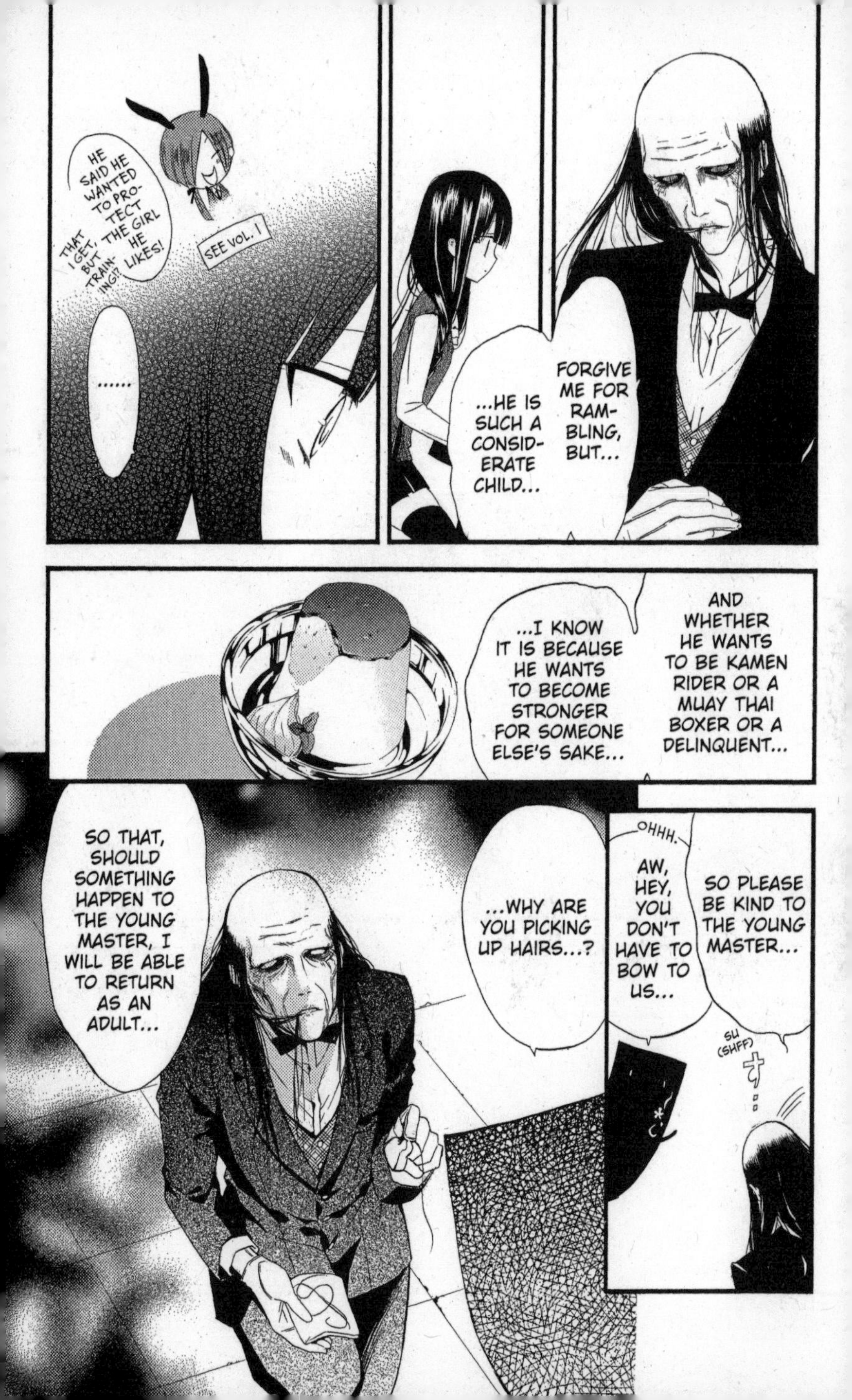
FORGIVE ME FOR RAMBLING, BUT...
...HE IS SUCH A CONSIDERATE CHILD...
HE SAID HE WANTED TO PROTECT THE GIRL HE LIKES!
THAT I GET, BUT TRAINING!?
SEE VOL. 1
......
AND WHETHER HE WANTS TO BE KAMEN RIDER OR A MUAY THAI BOXER OR A DELINQUENT...
...I KNOW IT IS BECAUSE HE WANTS TO BECOME STRONGER FOR SOMEONE ELSE'S SAKE...
SO PLEASE BE KIND TO THE YOUNG MASTER...
SU (SHFF)
す
OHHH.
AW, HEY, YOU DON'T HAVE TO BOW TO US...
...WHY ARE YOU PICKING UP HAIRS...?
SO THAT, SHOULD SOMETHING HAPPEN TO THE YOUNG MASTER, I WILL BE ABLE TO RETURN AS AN ADULT...

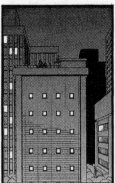

WHAT'S
THEIR
PROBLEM!?

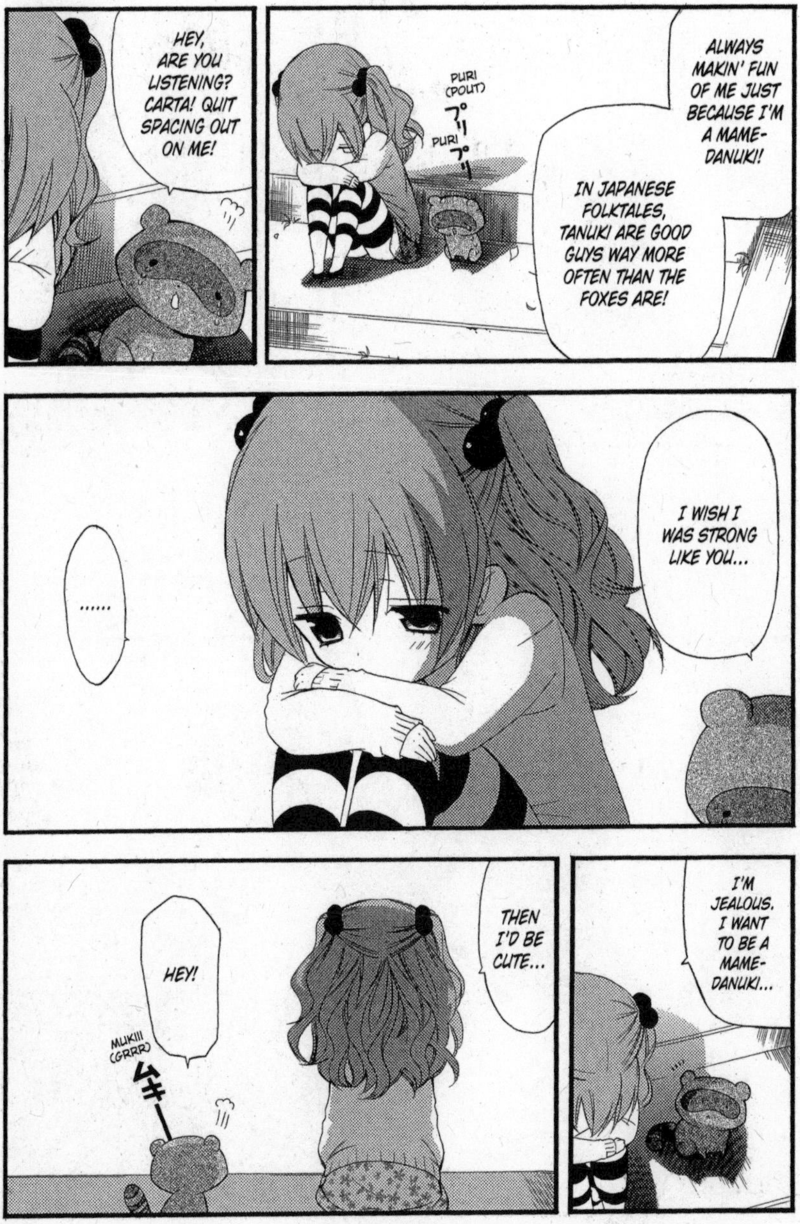
ALWAYS MAKIN' FUN OF ME JUST BECAUSE I'M A MAME-DANUKI!
IN JAPANESE FOLKTALES, TANUKI ARE GOOD GUYS WAY MORE OFTEN THAN THE FOXES ARE!
PURI (POUT)
プリ
PURI
プリ
HEY, ARE YOU LISTENING? CARTA! QUIT SPACING OUT ON ME!
I WISH I WAS STRONG LIKE YOU...
......
I'M JEALOUS. I WANT TO BE A MAME-DANUKI...
THEN I'D BE CUTE...
HEY!
MUKIII (GRRR)
ムキー

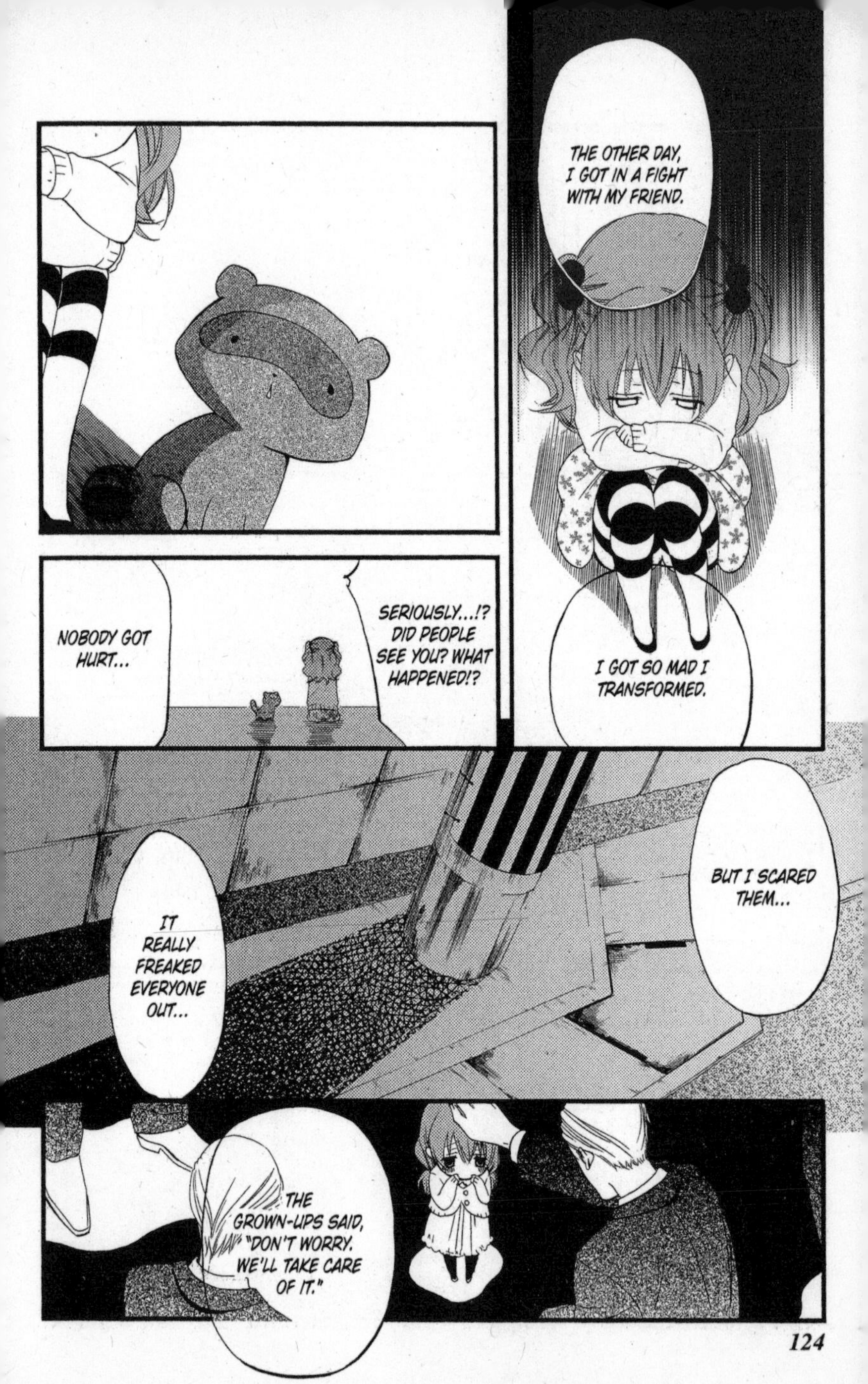
THE OTHER DAY, I GOT IN A FIGHT WITH MY FRIEND.
I GOT SO MAD I TRANSFORMED.
SERIOUSLY...!? DID PEOPLE SEE YOU? WHAT HAPPENED!?
NOBODY GOT HURT...
BUT I SCARED THEM...
IT REALLY FREAKED EVERYONE OUT...
THE GROWN-UPS SAID, "DON'T WORRY. WE'LL TAKE CARE OF IT."

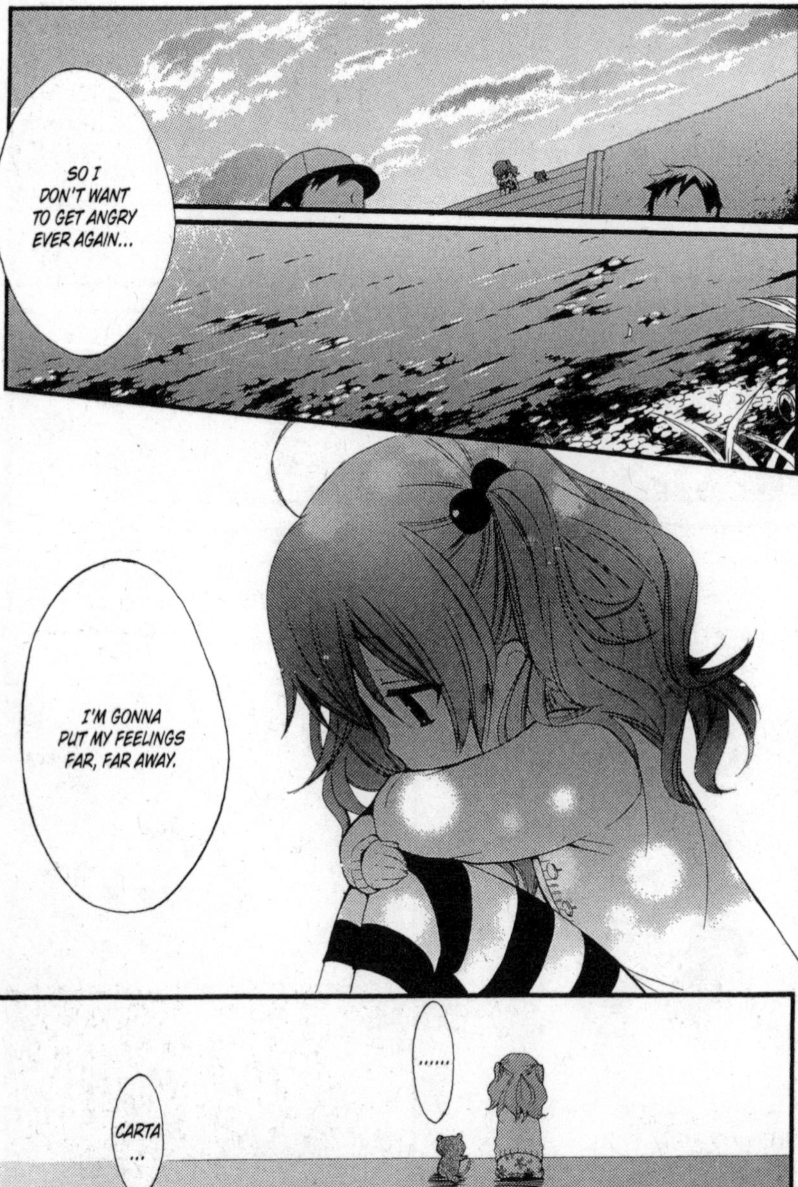
SO I DON'T WANT TO GET ANGRY EVER AGAIN...
I'M GONNA PUT MY FEELINGS FAR, FAR AWAY.
......
CARTA ...

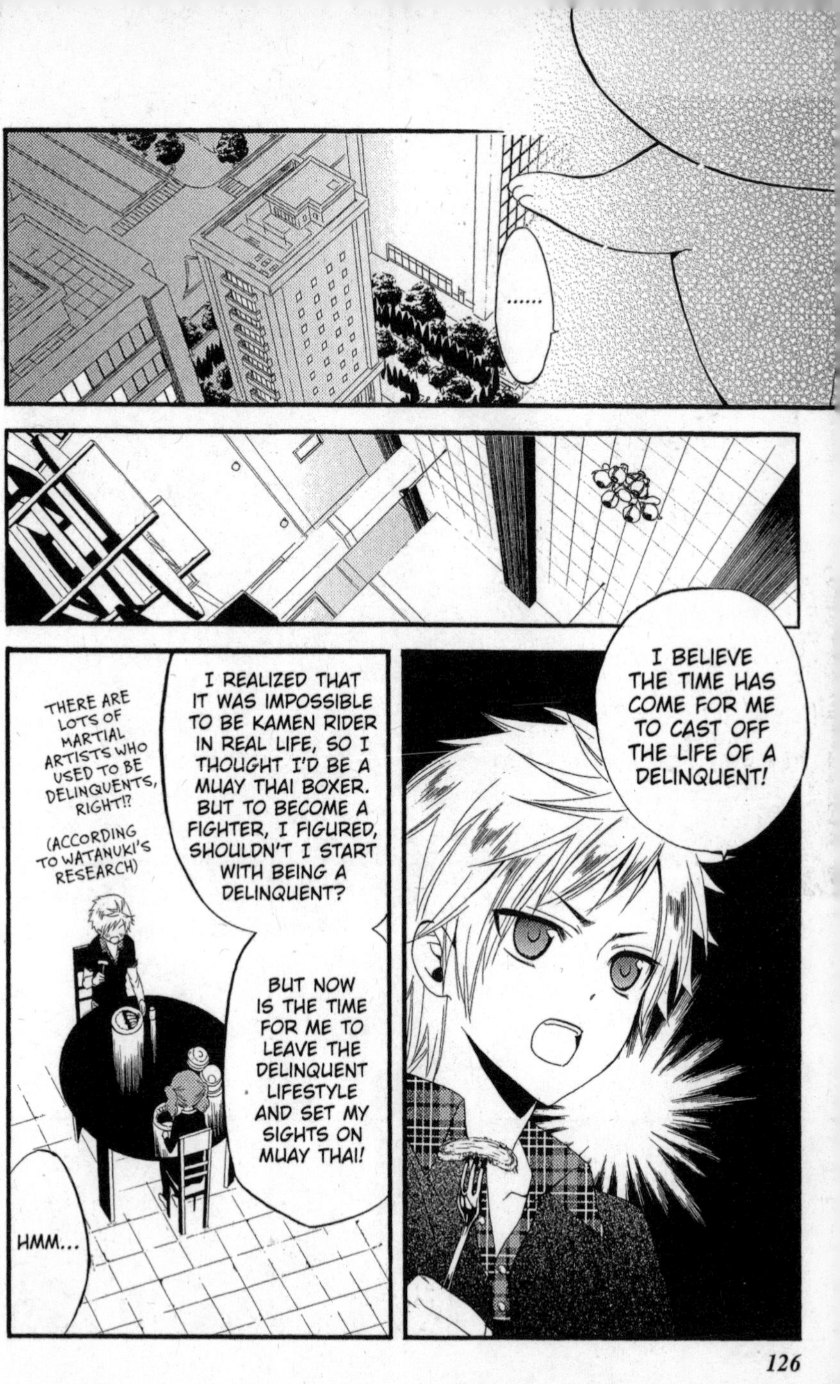
......
I BELIEVE THE TIME HAS COME FOR ME TO CAST OFF THE LIFE OF A DELINQUENT!
I REALIZED THAT IT WAS IMPOSSIBLE TO BE KAMEN RIDER IN REAL LIFE, SO I THOUGHT I'D BE A MUAY THAI BOXER. BUT TO BECOME A FIGHTER, I FIGURED, SHOULDN'T I START WITH BEING A DELINQUENT?
THERE ARE LOTS OF MARTIAL ARTISTS WHO USED TO BE DELINQUENTS, RIGHT!?
(ACCORDING TO WATANUKI'S RESEARCH)
BUT NOW IS THE TIME FOR ME TO LEAVE THE DELINQUENT LIFESTYLE AND SET MY SIGHTS ON MUAY THAI!
HMM...

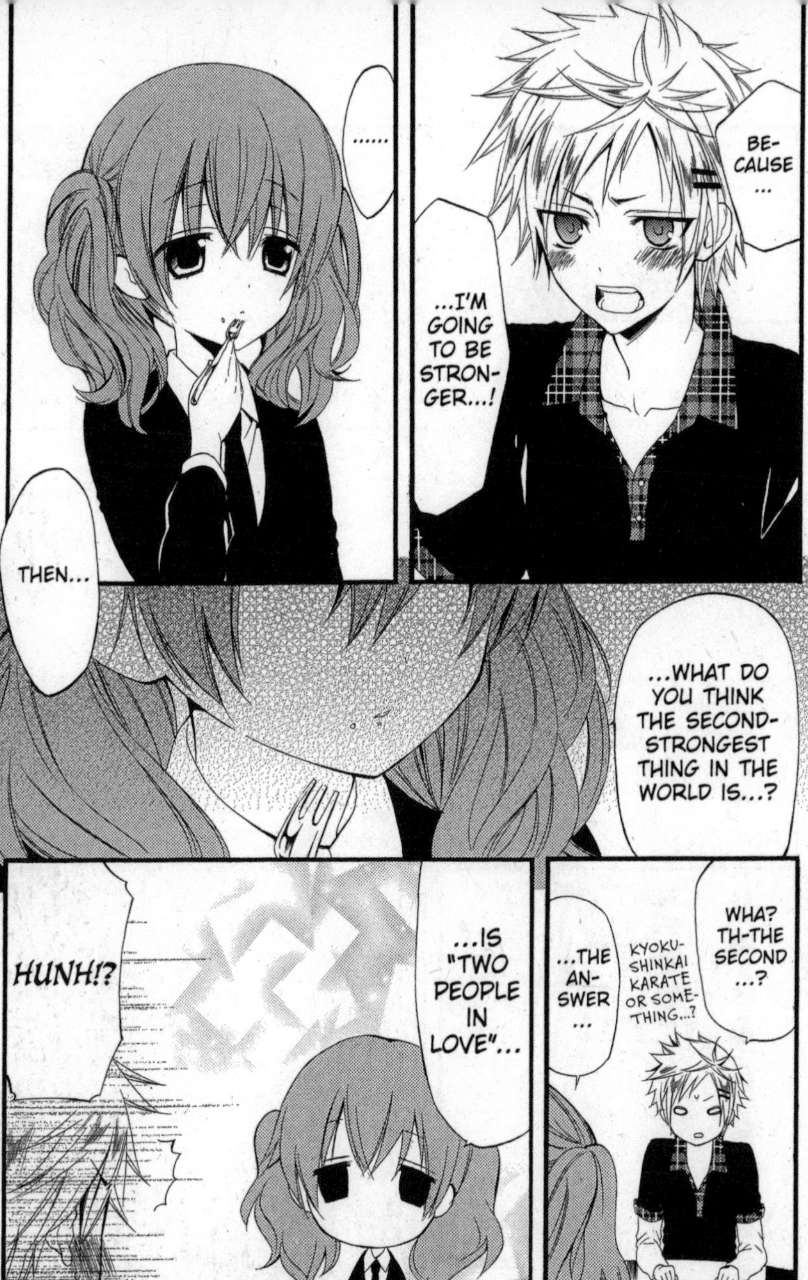
BE-CAUSE ...
...I'M GOING TO BE STRONGER...!
......
THEN...
...WHAT DO YOU THINK THE SECOND-STRONGEST THING IN THE WORLD IS...?
WHA? TH-THE SECOND ...?
KYOKU-SHINKAI KARATE OR SOME-THING...?
...THE AN-SWER ...
...IS "TWO PEOPLE IN LOVE"...
HUNH!?
HOW POETIC!!

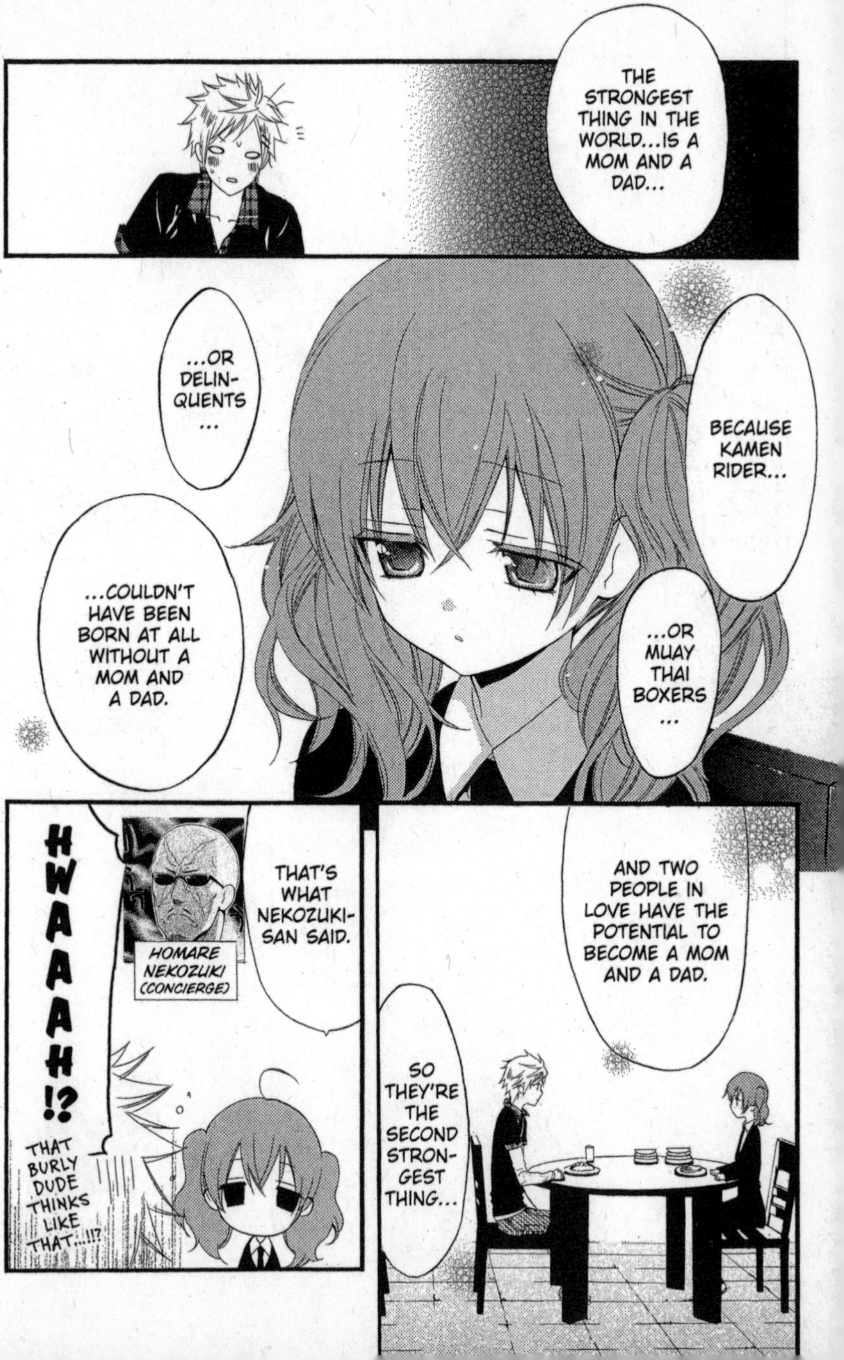

THE STRONGEST THING IN THE WORLD...IS A MOM AND A DAD...
BECAUSE KAMEN RIDER...
...OR DELIN- QUENTS ...
...OR MUAY THAI BOXERS ...
...COULDN'T HAVE BEEN BORN AT ALL WITHOUT A MOM AND A DAD.
AND TWO PEOPLE IN LOVE HAVE THE POTENTIAL TO BECOME A MOM AND A DAD.
SO THEY'RE THE SECOND STRON- GEST THING...
THAT'S WHAT NEKOZUKI- SAN SAID.
HOMARE NEKOZUKI (CONCIERGE)
HWAAAAH!?
THAT BURLY DUDE THINKS LIKE THAT...!!?

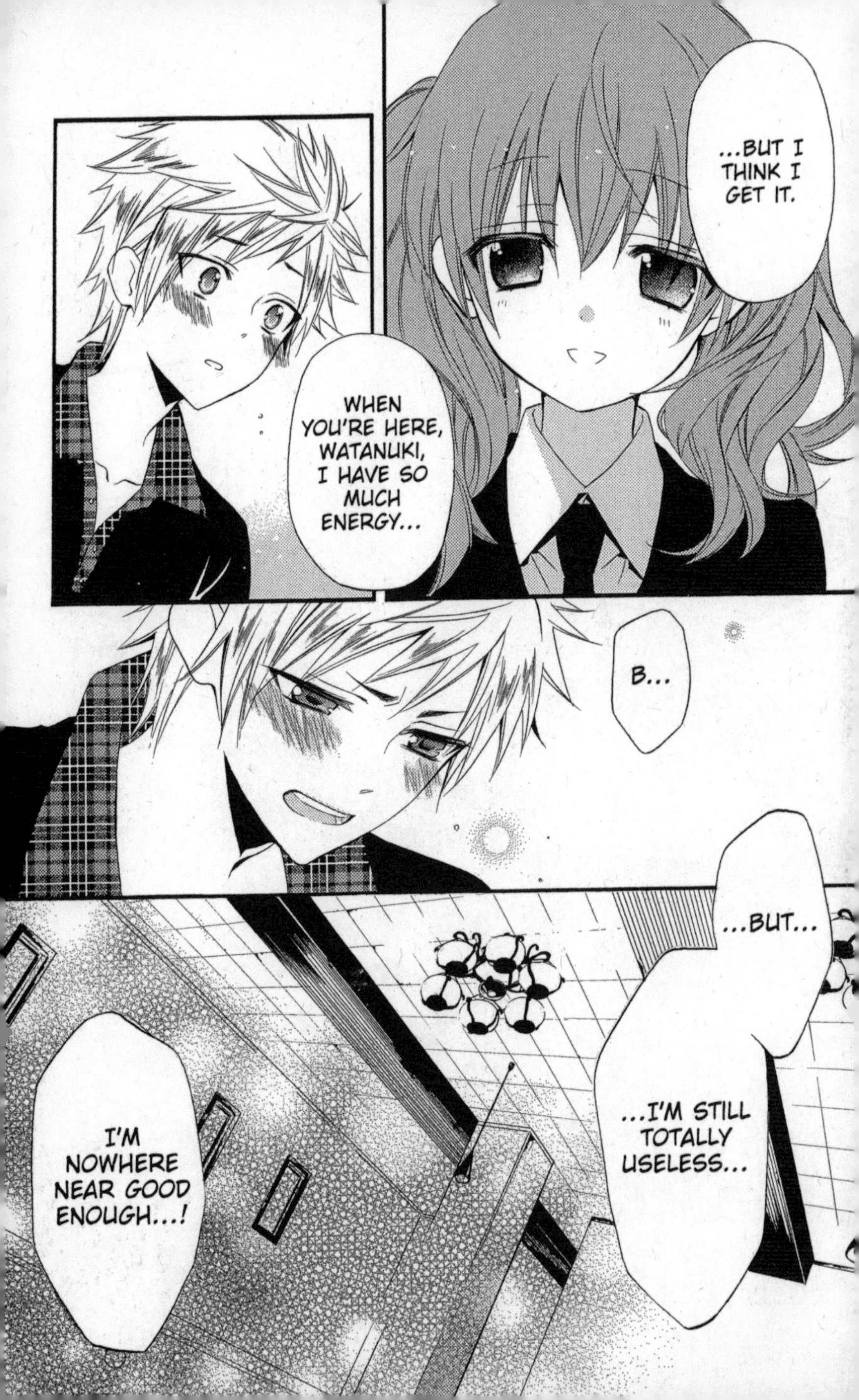
...BUT I THINK I GET IT.
WHEN YOU'RE HERE, WATANUKI, I HAVE SO MUCH ENERGY...
B...
...BUT...
...I'M STILL TOTALLY USELESS...
I'M NOWHERE NEAR GOOD ENOUGH...!

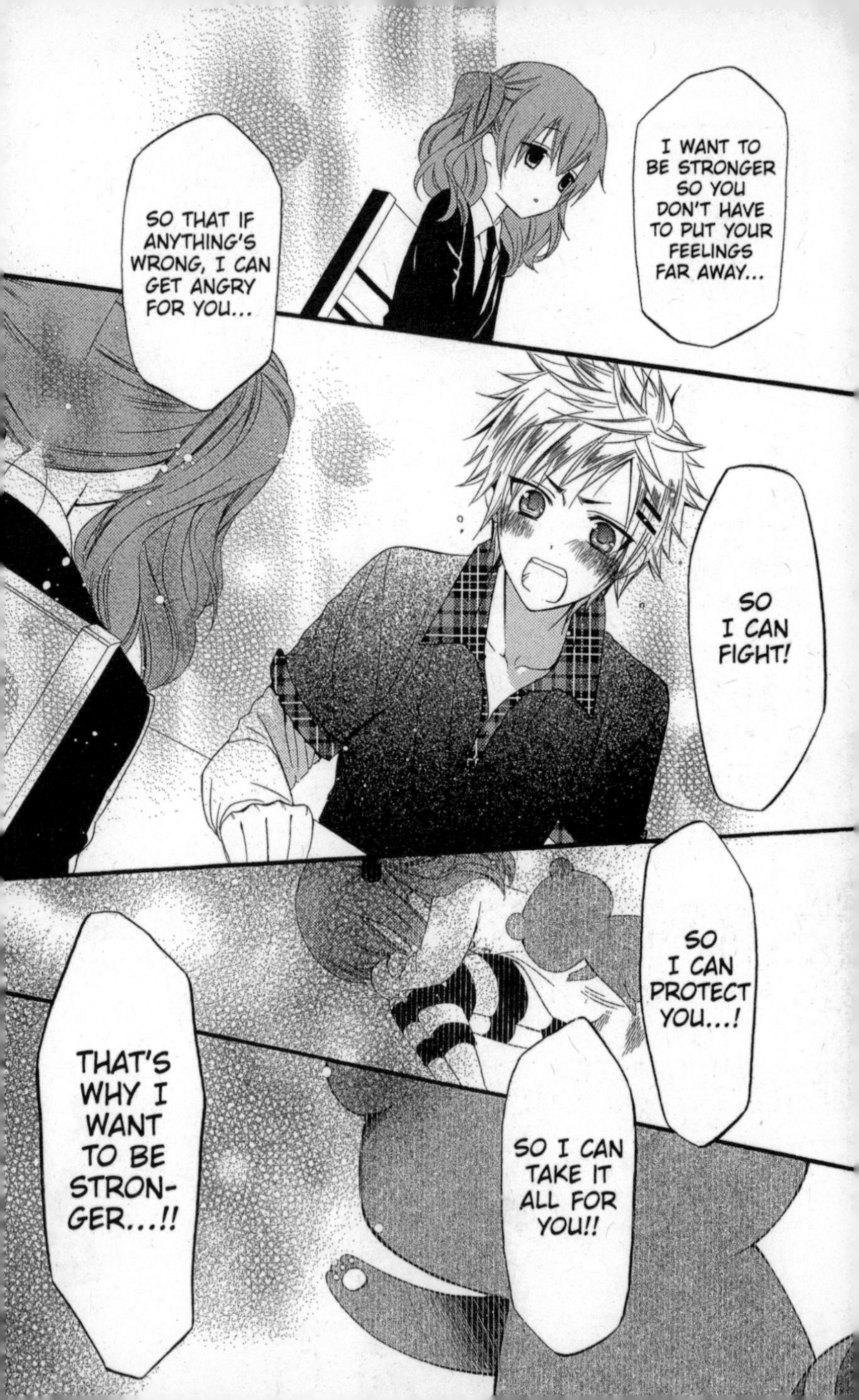
I WANT TO BE STRONGER SO YOU DON'T HAVE TO PUT YOUR FEELINGS FAR AWAY...
SO THAT IF ANYTHING'S WRONG, I CAN GET ANGRY FOR YOU...
SO I CAN FIGHT!
SO I CAN PROTECT YOU...!
SO I CAN TAKE IT ALL FOR YOU!!
THAT'S WHY I WANT TO BE STRON-GER...!!

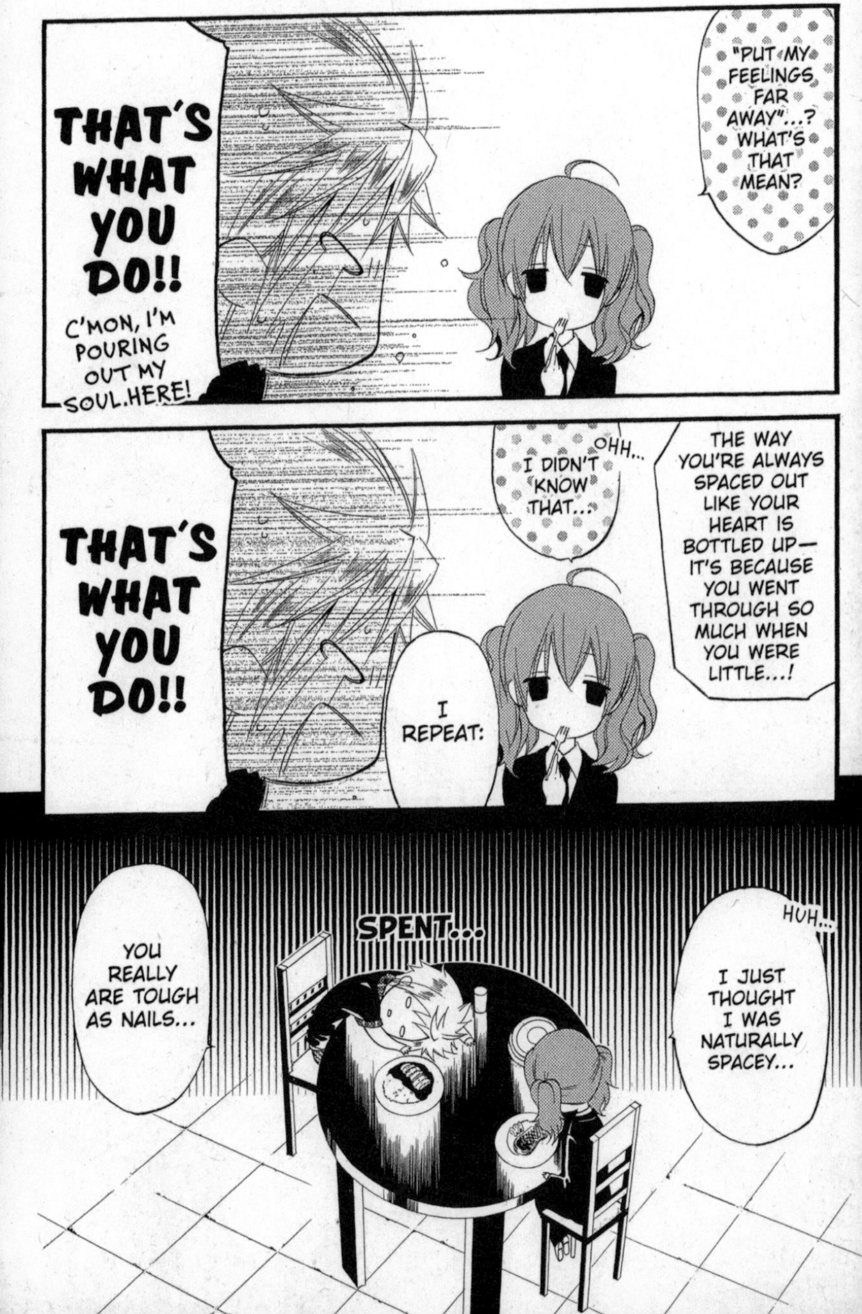
"PUT MY FEELINGS FAR AWAY"...? WHAT'S THAT MEAN?
THAT'S WHAT YOU DO!!
C'MON, I'M POURING OUT MY SOUL HERE!
THE WAY YOU'RE ALWAYS SPACED OUT LIKE YOUR HEART IS BOTTLED UP—IT'S BECAUSE YOU WENT THROUGH SO MUCH WHEN YOU WERE LITTLE...!
OHH... I DIDN'T KNOW THAT...
I REPEAT:
THAT'S WHAT YOU DO!!
HUH... I JUST THOUGHT I WAS NATURALLY SPACEY...
SPENT...
YOU REALLY ARE TOUGH AS NAILS...

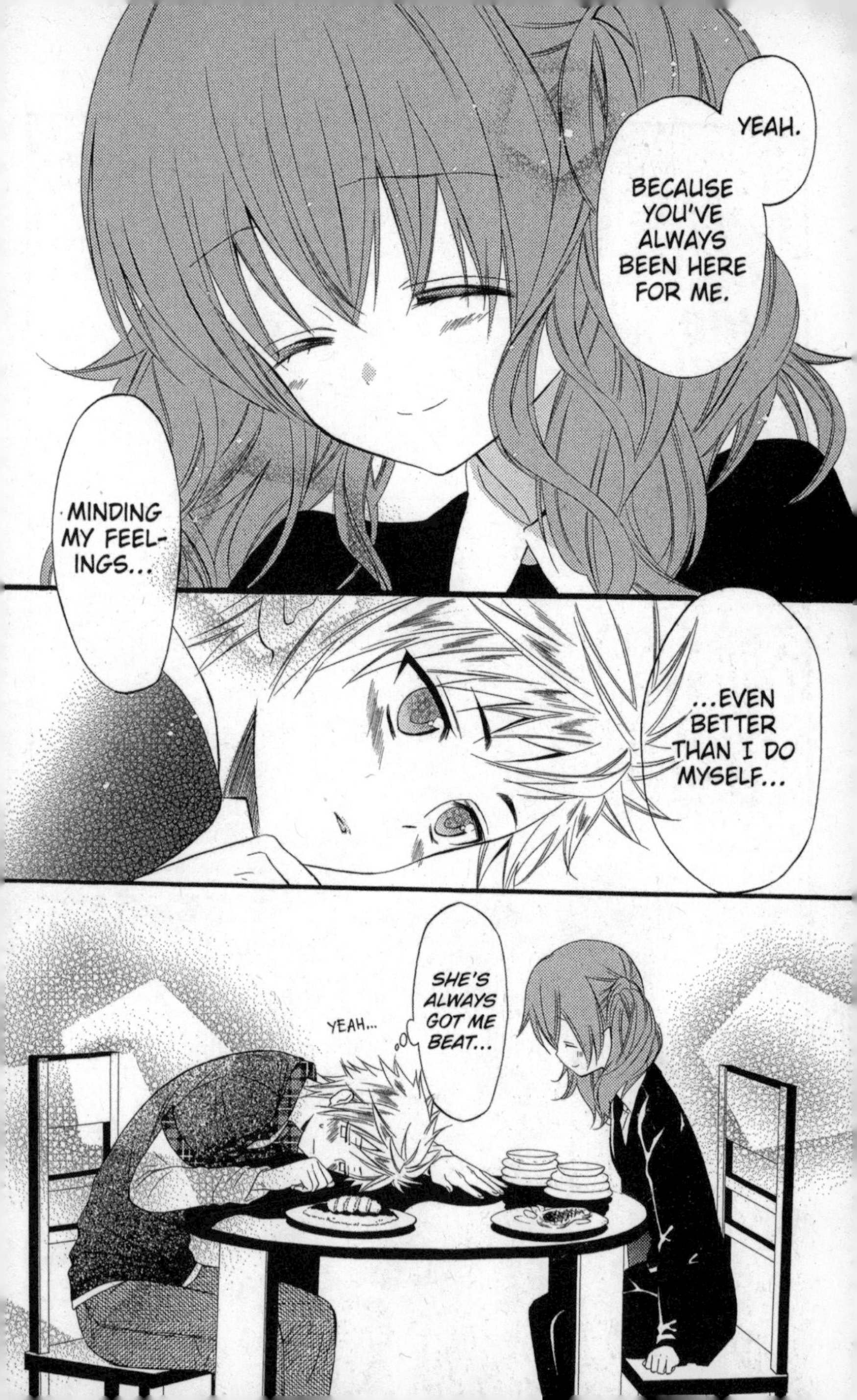
YEAH.
BECAUSE YOU'VE ALWAYS BEEN HERE FOR ME.
MINDING MY FEEL-INGS...
...EVEN BETTER THAN I DO MYSELF...
SHE'S ALWAYS GOT ME BEAT...
YEAH...

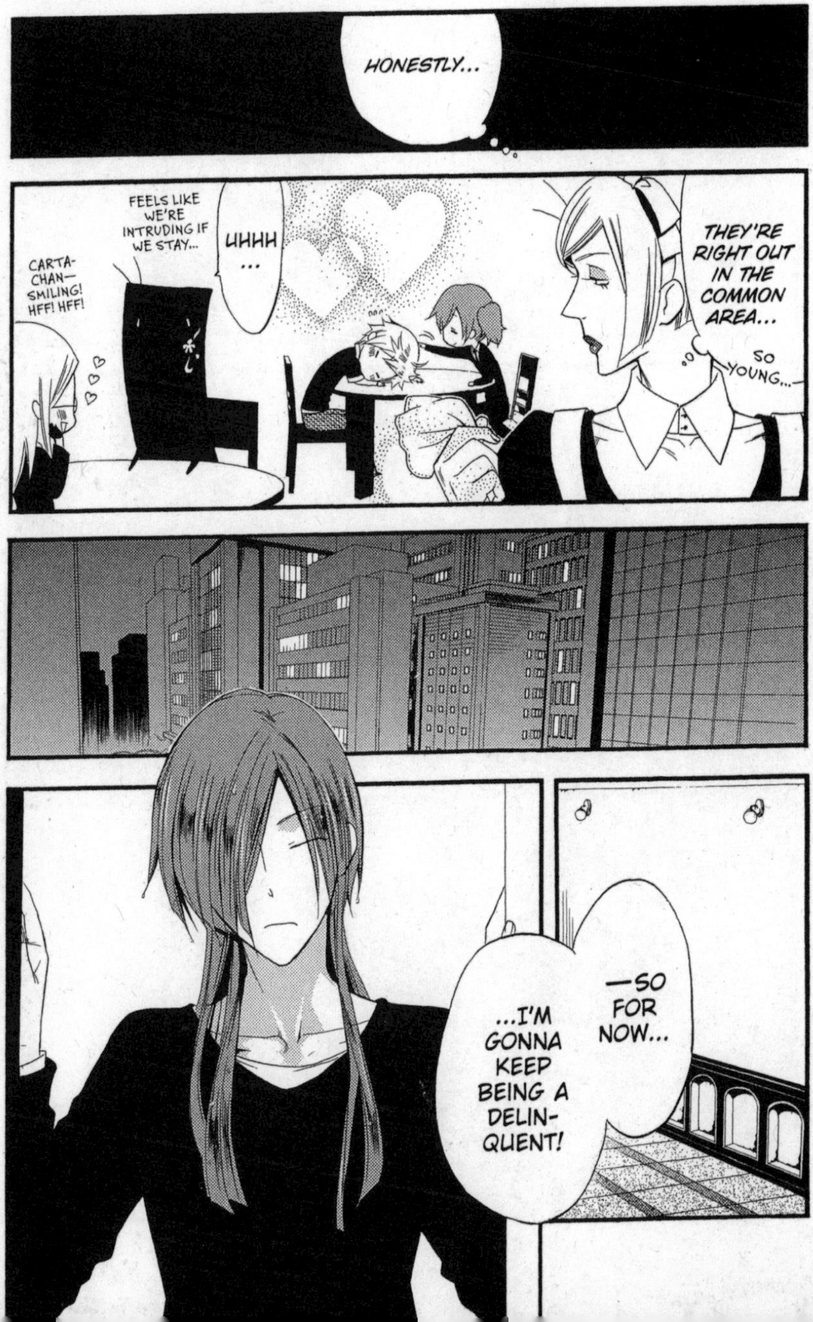
HONESTLY...
THEY'RE RIGHT OUT IN THE COMMON AREA...
SO YOUNG...
UHHH ...
FEELS LIKE WE'RE INTRUDING IF WE STAY...
CARTA-CHAN—SMILING! HFF! HFF!
—SO FOR NOW...
...I'M GONNA KEEP BEING A DELIN-QUENT!

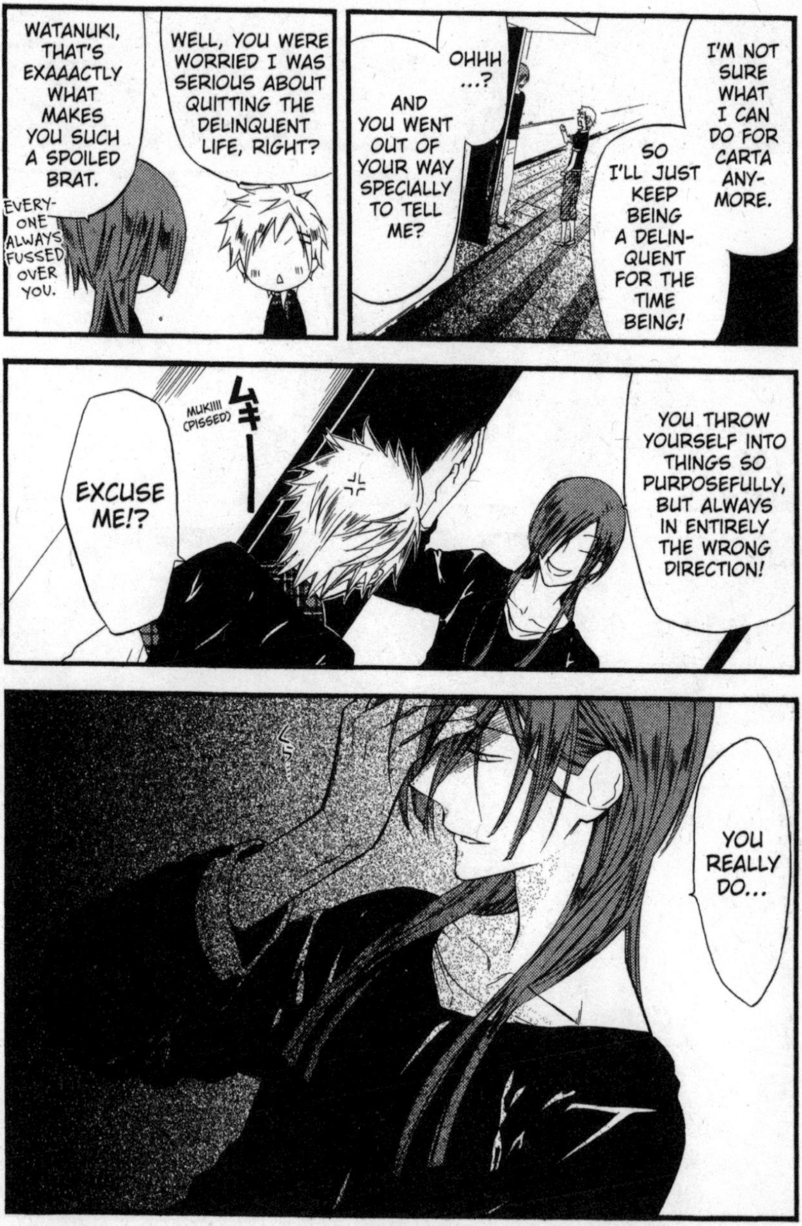
I'M NOT SURE WHAT I CAN DO FOR CARTA ANYMORE.
SO I'LL JUST KEEP BEING A DELINQUENT FOR THE TIME BEING!
OHHH ...?
AND YOU WENT OUT OF YOUR WAY SPECIALLY TO TELL ME?
WELL, YOU WERE WORRIED I WAS SERIOUS ABOUT QUITTING THE DELINQUENT LIFE, RIGHT?
WATANUKI, THAT'S EXAAACTLY WHAT MAKES YOU SUCH A SPOILED BRAT.
EVERYONE ALWAYS FUSSED OVER YOU.
YOU THROW YOURSELF INTO THINGS SO PURPOSEFULLY, BUT ALWAYS IN ENTIRELY THE WRONG DIRECTION!
ムキー
MUKIIII (PISSED)
EXCUSE ME!?
YOU REALLY DO...

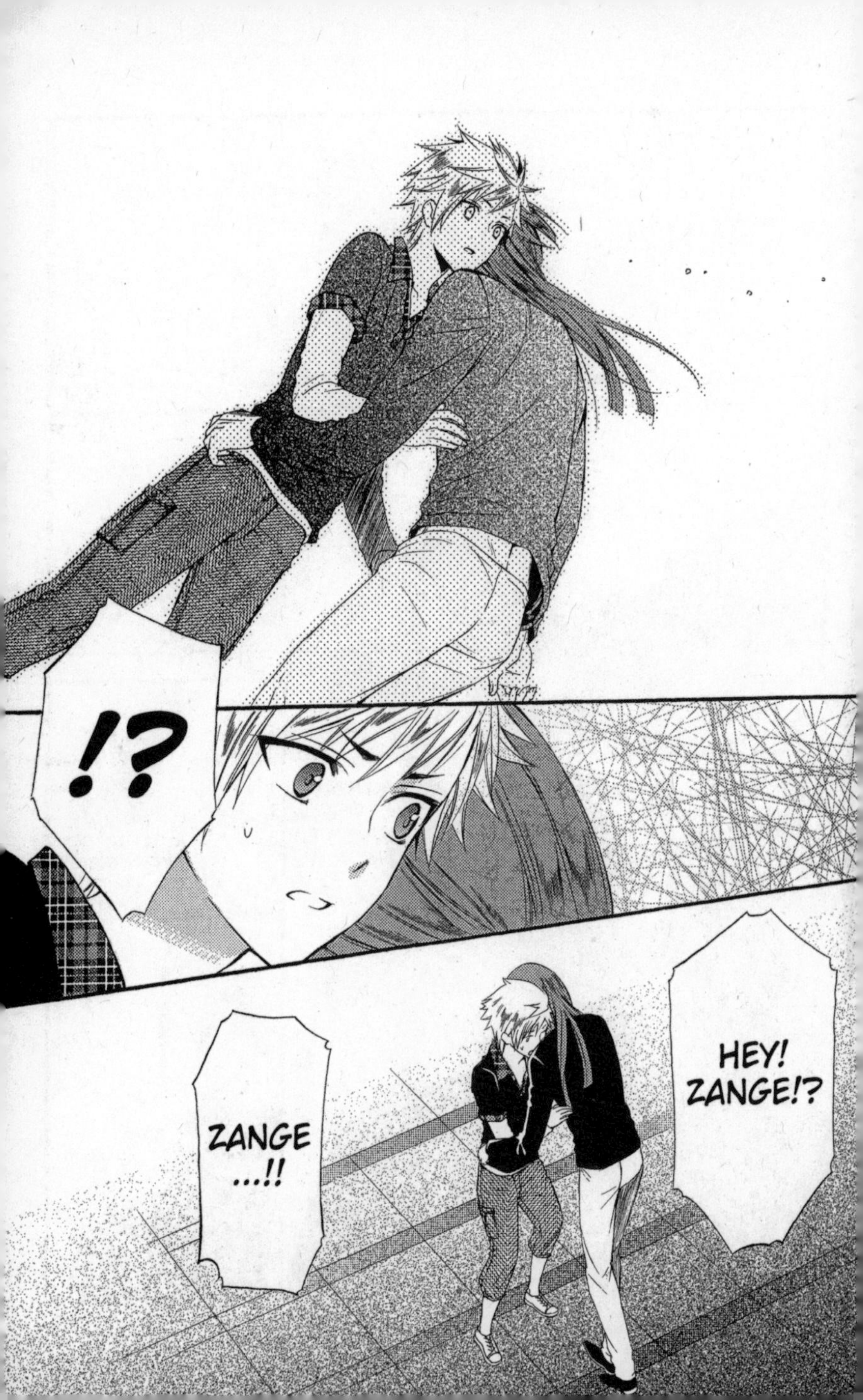
!?
HEY! ZANGE!?
ZANGE ...!!

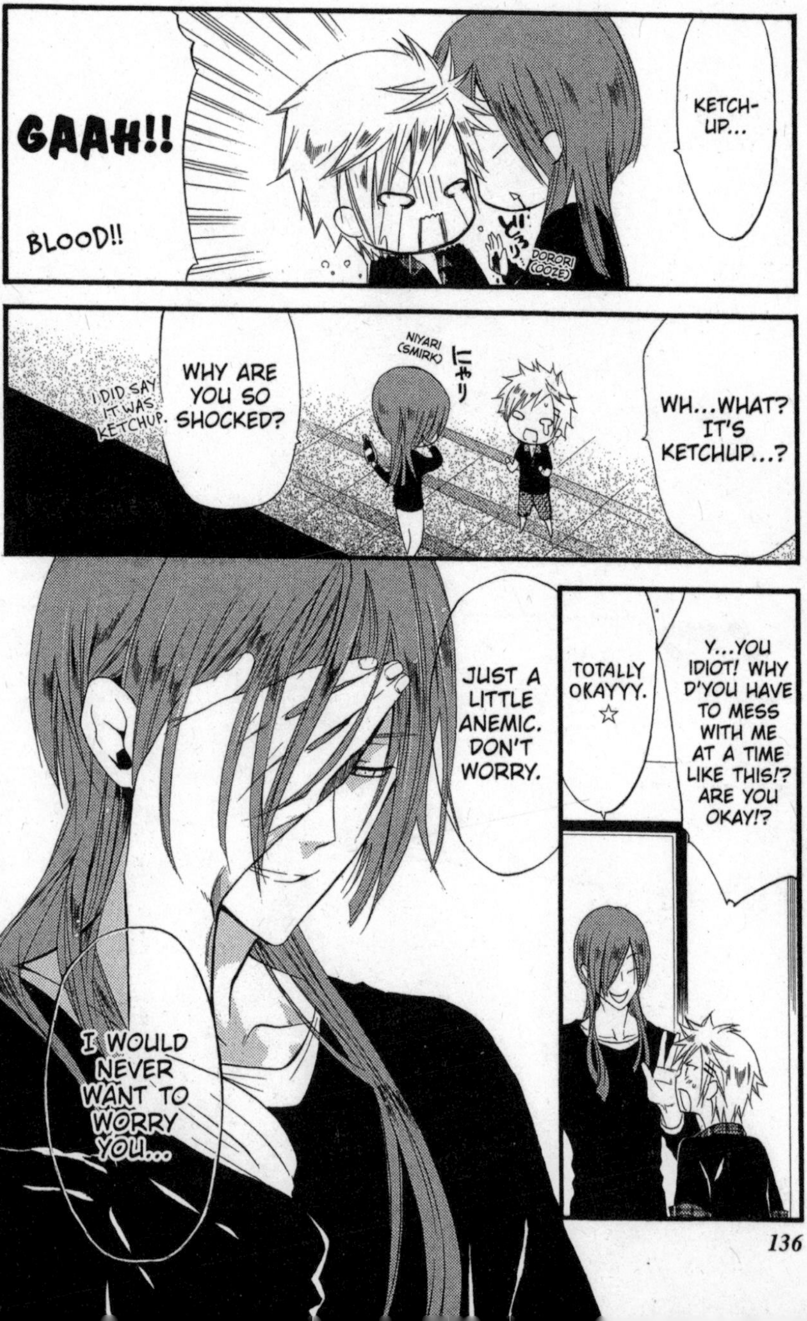
KETCH-UP...
DORORI (OOZE)
どろり
GAAH!!
BLOOD!!
WH...WHAT? IT'S KETCHUP...?
NIYARI (SMIRK)
にやり
WHY ARE YOU SO SHOCKED?
I DID SAY IT WAS KETCHUP.
Y...YOU IDIOT! WHY D'YOU HAVE TO MESS WITH ME AT A TIME LIKE THIS!? ARE YOU OKAY!?
TOTALLY OKAYYY. ☆
JUST A LITTLE ANEMIC. DON'T WORRY.
I WOULD NEVER WANT TO WORRY YOU...

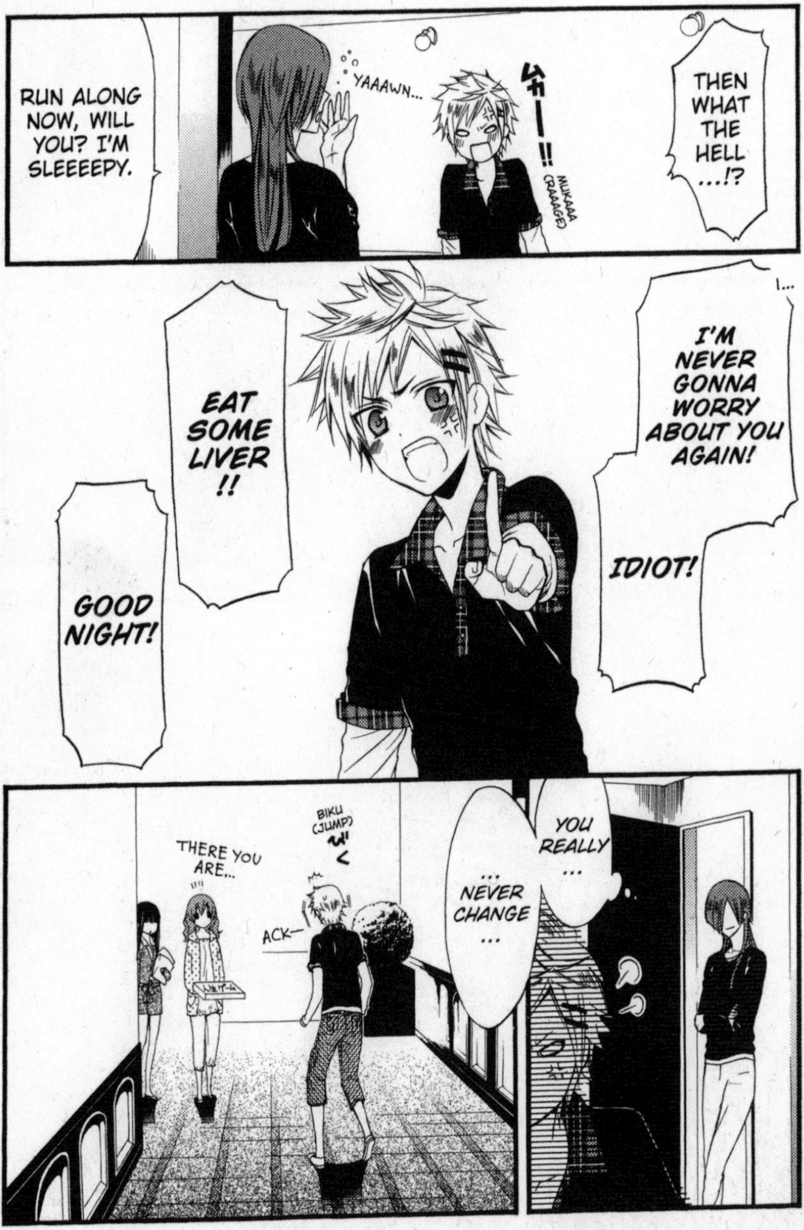
THEN WHAT THE HELL ...!?
ムカー!!
MUKAAA (RAAAGE)
YAAAWN...
RUN ALONG NOW, WILL YOU? I'M SLEEEEPY.
I...
I'M NEVER GONNA WORRY ABOUT YOU AGAIN!
IDIOT!
EAT SOME LIVER !!
GOOD NIGHT!
YOU REALLY ...
... NEVER CHANGE ...
BIKU (JUMP)
THERE YOU ARE...
ACK—

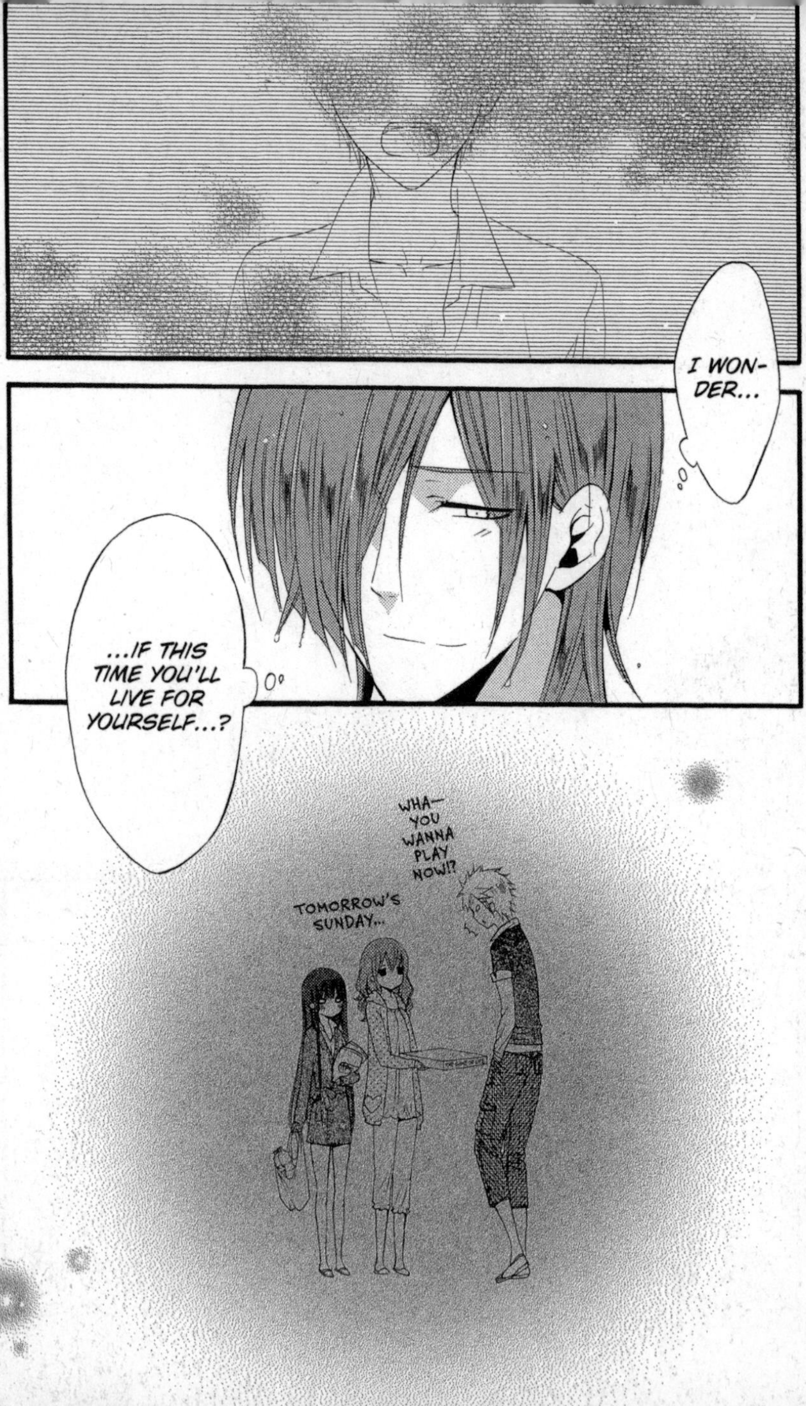
I WON-DER...
...IF THIS TIME YOU'LL LIVE FOR YOURSELF...?
WHA— YOU WANNA PLAY NOW!?
TOMORROW'S SUNDAY...

INU×BOKU SS

maison de ayakashi

Welcome to Maison de Ayakashi.
The exclusive Secret Service of
this Mansion guarantees
your mental and physical
safety by providing
superior escorts.

# Chapter 13: Until the Spring

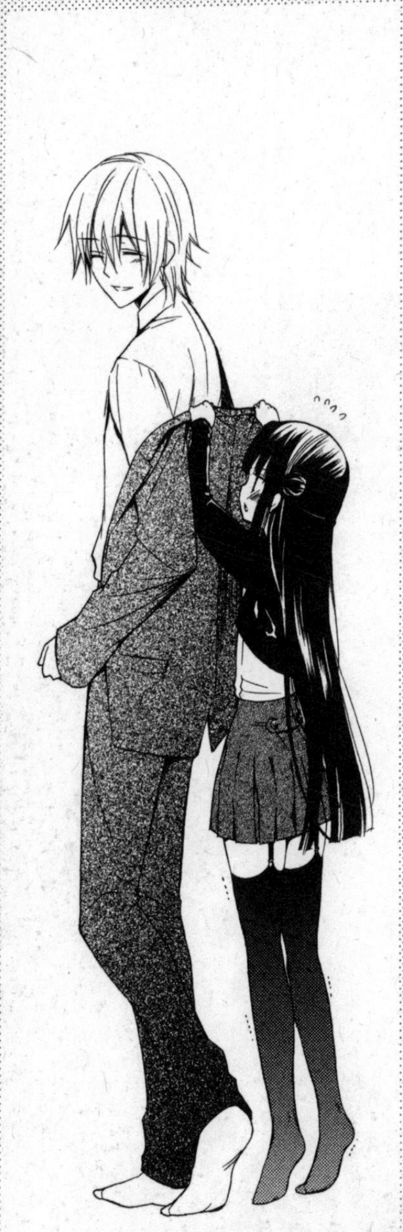

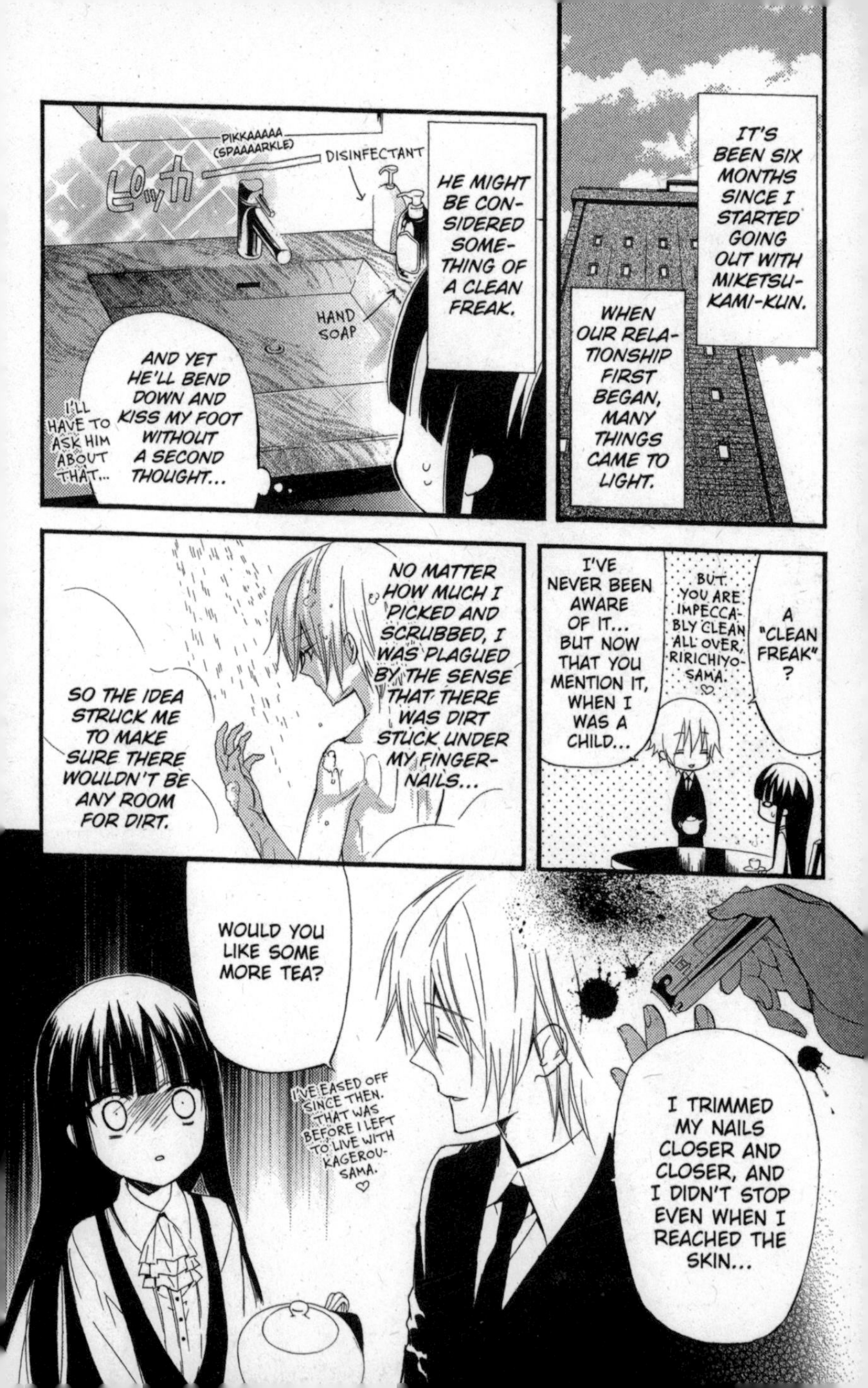
IT'S BEEN SIX MONTHS SINCE I STARTED GOING OUT WITH MIKETSUKAMI-KUN.
WHEN OUR RELATIONSHIP FIRST BEGAN, MANY THINGS CAME TO LIGHT.
HE MIGHT BE CONSIDERED SOMETHING OF A CLEAN FREAK.
DISINFECTANT
PIKKAAAAA (SPAAAARKLE)
HAND SOAP
AND YET HE'LL BEND DOWN AND KISS MY FOOT WITHOUT A SECOND THOUGHT...
I'LL HAVE TO ASK HIM ABOUT THAT...
A "CLEAN FREAK"?
BUT YOU ARE IMPECCABLY CLEAN ALL OVER, RIRICHIYO-SAMA ♡.
I'VE NEVER BEEN AWARE OF IT... BUT NOW THAT YOU MENTION IT, WHEN I WAS A CHILD...
NO MATTER HOW MUCH I PICKED AND SCRUBBED, I WAS PLAGUED BY THE SENSE THAT THERE WAS DIRT STUCK UNDER MY FINGERNAILS...
SO THE IDEA STRUCK ME TO MAKE SURE THERE WOULDN'T BE ANY ROOM FOR DIRT.
I TRIMMED MY NAILS CLOSER AND CLOSER, AND I DIDN'T STOP EVEN WHEN I REACHED THE SKIN...
WOULD YOU LIKE SOME MORE TEA?
I'VE EASED OFF SINCE THEN. THAT WAS BEFORE I LEFT TO LIVE WITH KAGEROU-SAMA. ♡

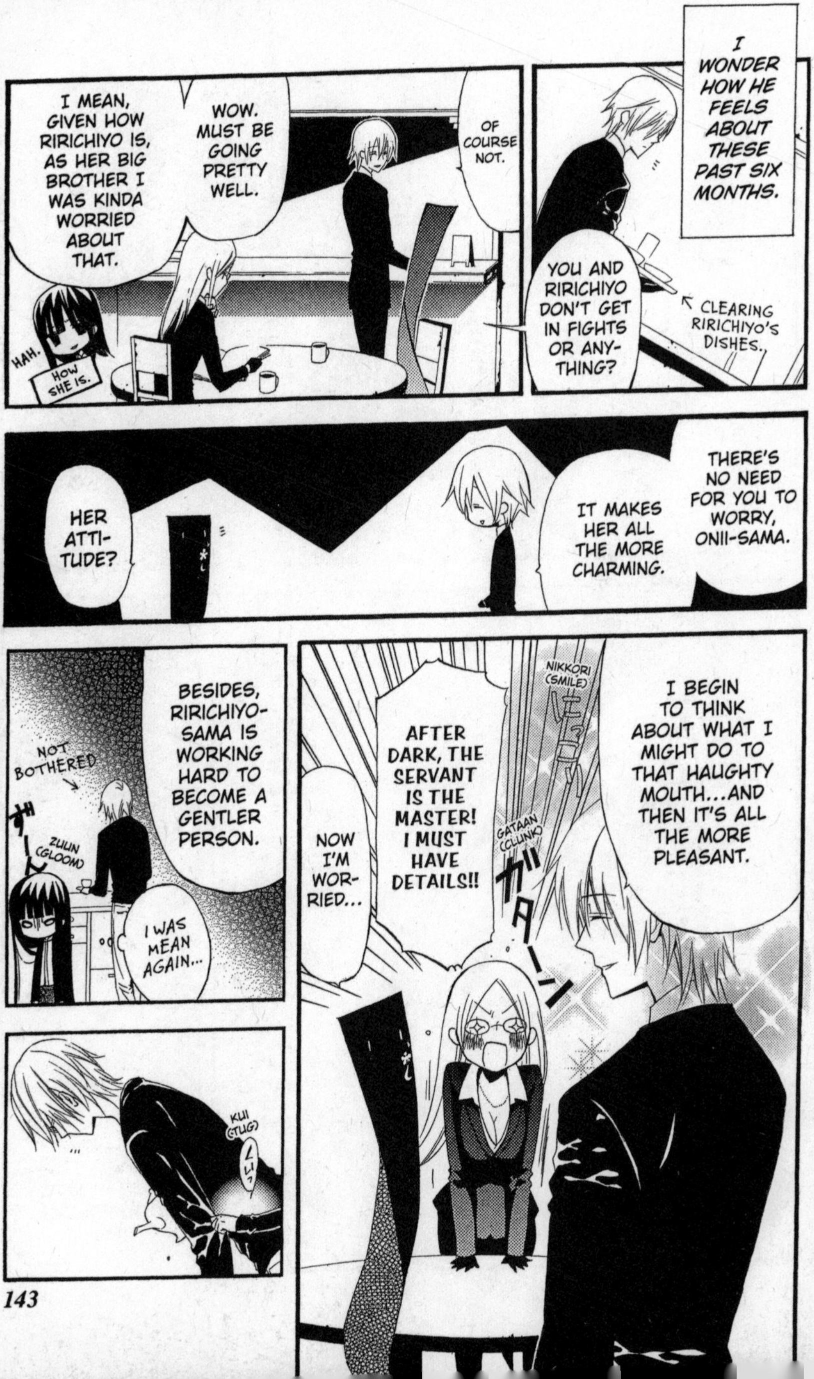
I WONDER HOW HE FEELS ABOUT THESE PAST SIX MONTHS.
YOU AND RIRICHIYO DON'T GET IN FIGHTS OR ANY-THING?
CLEARING RIRICHIYO's DISHES.
OF COURSE NOT.
WOW. MUST BE GOING PRETTY WELL.
I MEAN, GIVEN HOW RIRICHIYO IS, AS HER BIG BROTHER I WAS KINDA WORRIED ABOUT THAT.
HAH.
HOW SHE IS.
THERE'S NO NEED FOR YOU TO WORRY, ONII-SAMA.
IT MAKES HER ALL THE MORE CHARMING.
HER ATTI-TUDE?
I BEGIN TO THINK ABOUT WHAT I MIGHT DO TO THAT HAUGHTY MOUTH...AND THEN IT'S ALL THE MORE PLEASANT.
NIKKORI (SMILE)
GATAAN (CLUNK)
AFTER DARK, THE SERVANT IS THE MASTER! I MUST HAVE DETAILS!!
NOW I'M WOR-RIED...
BESIDES, RIRICHIYO-SAMA IS WORKING HARD TO BECOME A GENTLER PERSON.
NOT BOTHERED
ZUUN (GLOOM)
I WAS MEAN AGAIN...
KUI (TUG)

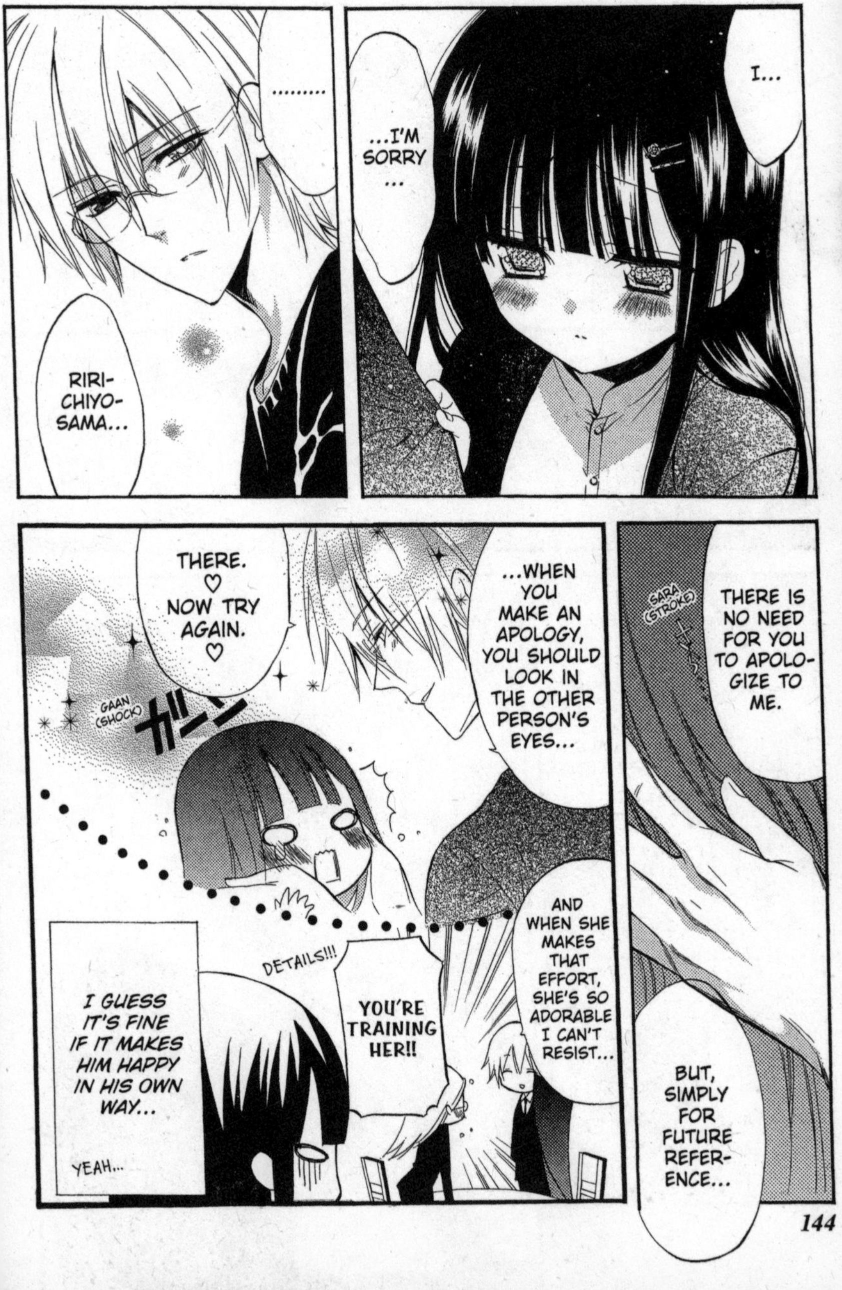
I...
...I'M SORRY ...
..........
RIRI-CHIYO-SAMA...
SARA (STROKE)
THERE IS NO NEED FOR YOU TO APOLOGIZE TO ME.
BUT, SIMPLY FOR FUTURE REFERENCE...
...WHEN YOU MAKE AN APOLOGY, YOU SHOULD LOOK IN THE OTHER PERSON'S EYES...
THERE. ♡ NOW TRY AGAIN. ♡
GAAN (SHOCK)
ガーン
AND WHEN SHE MAKES THAT EFFORT, SHE'S SO ADORABLE I CAN'T RESIST...
DETAILS!!!
YOU'RE TRAINING HER!!
I GUESS IT'S FINE IF IT MAKES HIM HAPPY IN HIS OWN WAY...
YEAH...

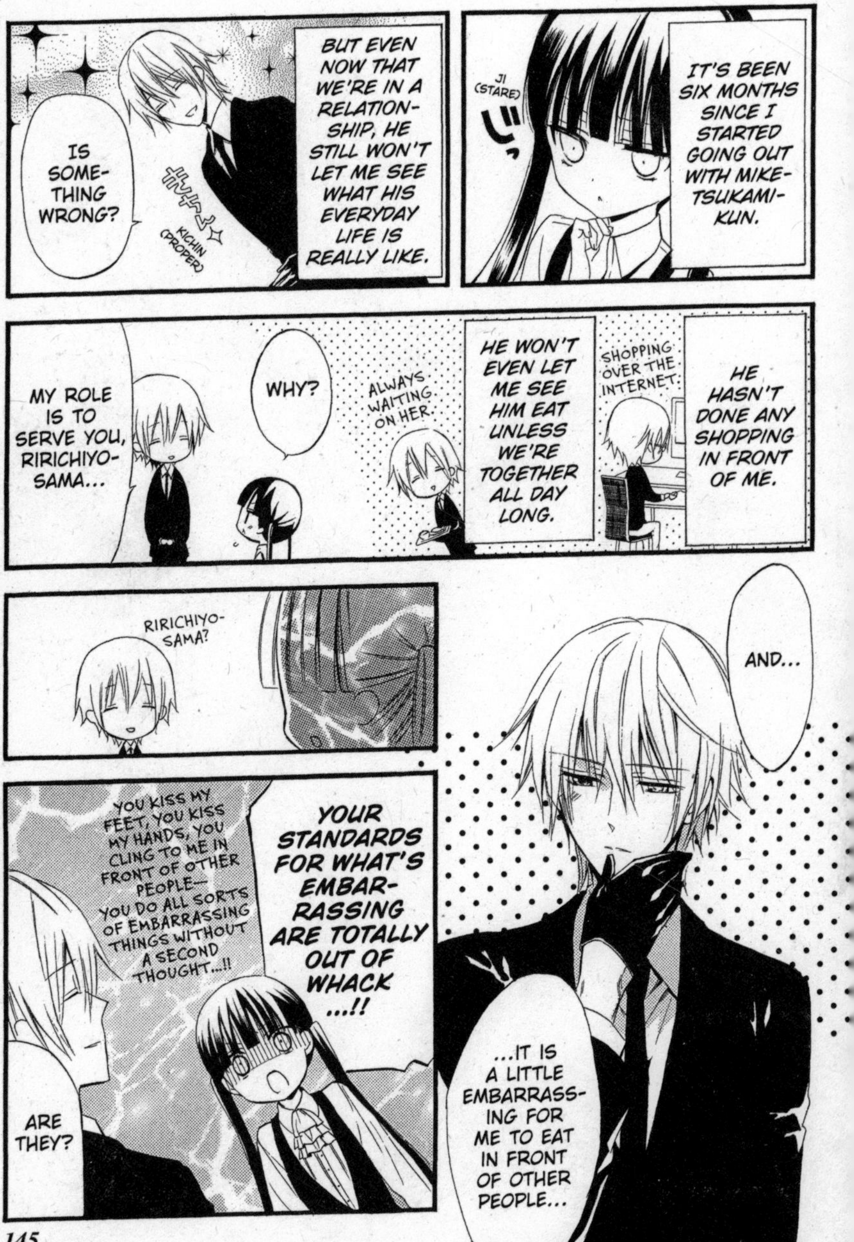
IT'S BEEN SIX MONTHS SINCE I STARTED GOING OUT WITH MIKETSUKAMI-KUN.
JI (STARE)
BUT EVEN NOW THAT WE'RE IN A RELATIONSHIP, HE STILL WON'T LET ME SEE WHAT HIS EVERYDAY LIFE IS REALLY LIKE.
KICHIN (PROPER)
IS SOMETHING WRONG?
HE HASN'T DONE ANY SHOPPING IN FRONT OF ME.
SHOPPING OVER THE INTERNET.
HE WON'T EVEN LET ME SEE HIM EAT UNLESS WE'RE TOGETHER ALL DAY LONG.
ALWAYS WAITING ON HER.
WHY?
MY ROLE IS TO SERVE YOU, RIRICHIYO-SAMA...
AND...
...IT IS A LITTLE EMBARRASSING FOR ME TO EAT IN FRONT OF OTHER PEOPLE...
RIRICHIYO-SAMA?
YOUR STANDARDS FOR WHAT'S EMBARRASSING ARE TOTALLY OUT OF WHACK...!!
YOU KISS MY FEET, YOU KISS MY HANDS, YOU CLING TO ME IN FRONT OF OTHER PEOPLE— YOU DO ALL SORTS OF EMBARRASSING THINGS WITHOUT A SECOND THOUGHT...!!
ARE THEY?

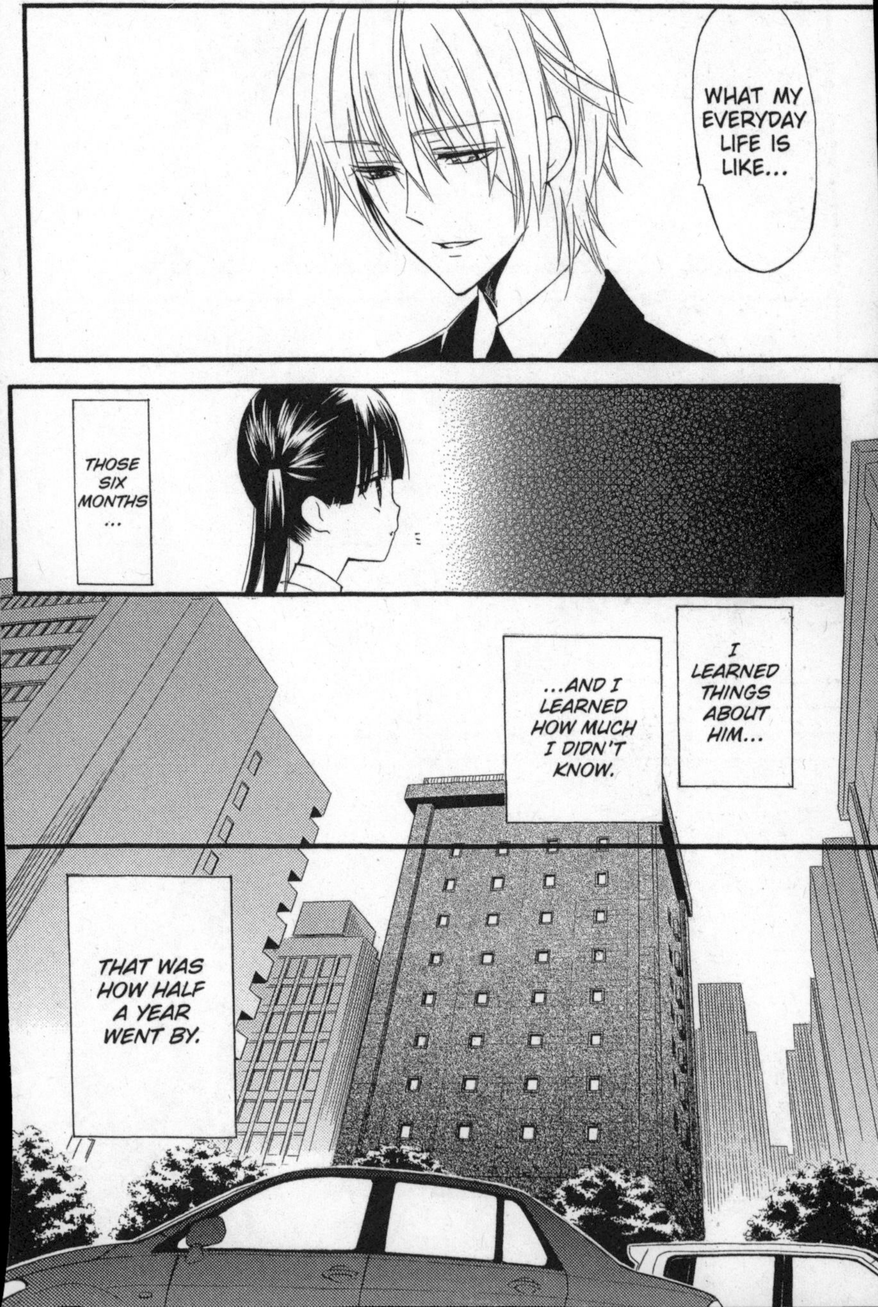
WHAT MY EVERYDAY LIFE IS LIKE...
THOSE SIX MONTHS...
I LEARNED THINGS ABOUT HIM...
...AND I LEARNED HOW MUCH I DIDN'T KNOW.
THAT WAS HOW HALF A YEAR WENT BY.

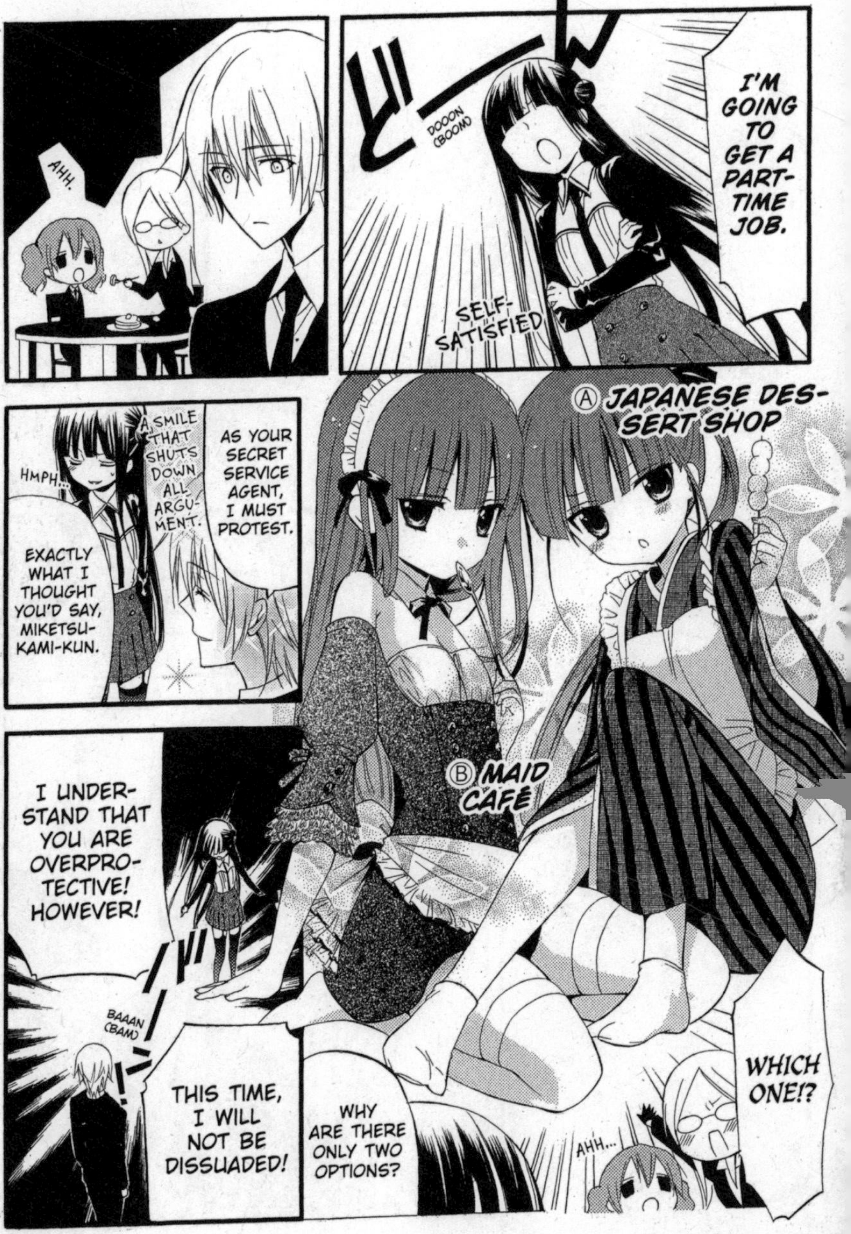
I'M GOING TO GET A PART-TIME JOB.
DOOON (BOOM)
SELF-SATISFIED
AHH.
Ⓐ JAPANESE DES-SERT SHOP
Ⓑ MAID CAFÉ
AS YOUR SECRET SERVICE AGENT, I MUST PROTEST.
A SMILE THAT SHUTS DOWN ALL ARGU-MENT.
HMPH...
EXACTLY WHAT I THOUGHT YOU'D SAY, MIKETSU-KAMI-KUN.
I UNDER-STAND THAT YOU ARE OVERPRO-TECTIVE! HOWEVER!
WHICH ONE!?
AHH...
WHY ARE THERE ONLY TWO OPTIONS?
THIS TIME, I WILL NOT BE DISSUADED!
BAAAN (BAM)

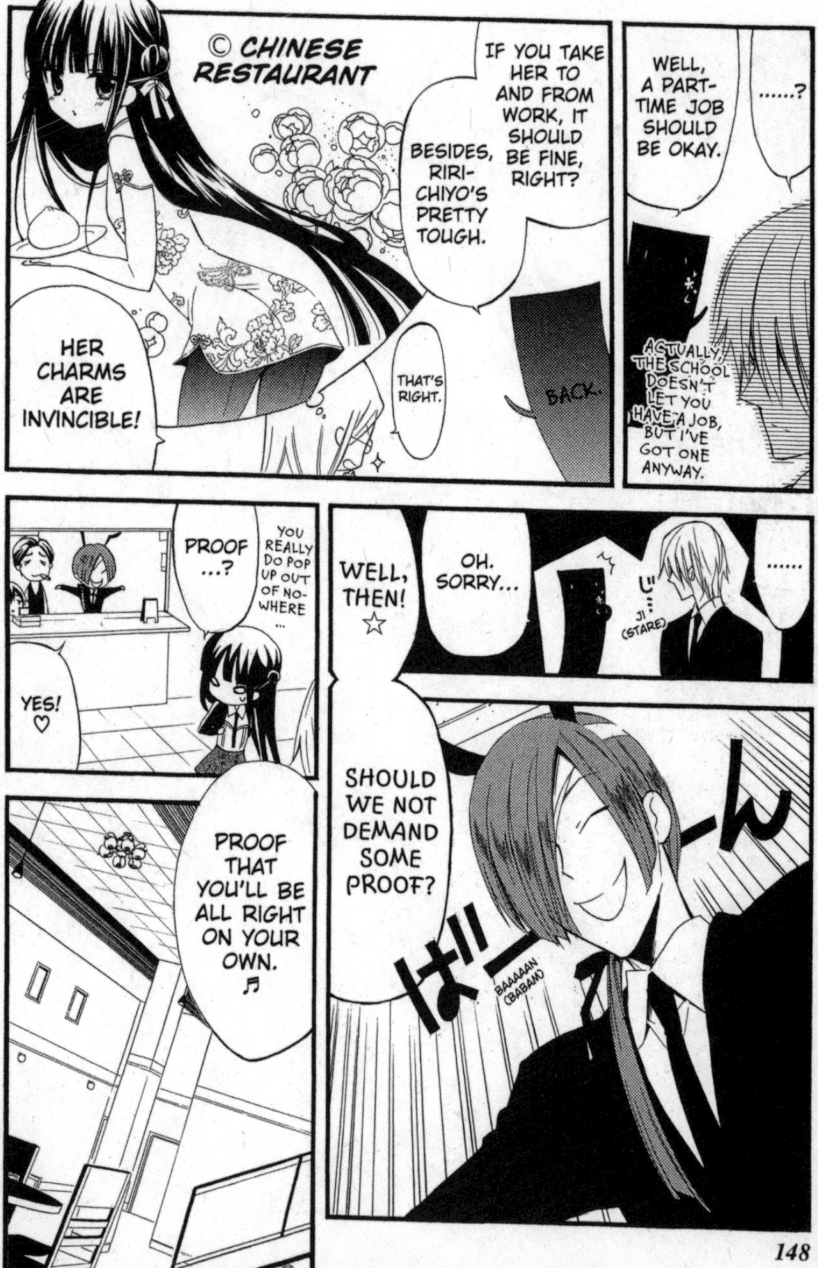
WELL, A PART-TIME JOB SHOULD BE OKAY.
......?
ACTUALLY, THE SCHOOL DOESN'T LET YOU HAVE A JOB, BUT I'VE GOT ONE ANYWAY.
IF YOU TAKE HER TO AND FROM WORK, IT SHOULD BE FINE, RIGHT?
BESIDES, RIRI-CHIYO'S PRETTY TOUGH.
© CHINESE RESTAURANT
BACK.
THAT'S RIGHT.
HER CHARMS ARE INVINCIBLE!
......
じ
JI (STARE)
OH. SORRY...
WELL, THEN! ☆
SHOULD WE NOT DEMAND SOME PROOF?
ばーーん
BAAAAAN (BABAM)
YOU REALLY DO POP UP OUT OF NO-WHERE...
PROOF...?
YES! ♡
PROOF THAT YOU'LL BE ALL RIGHT ON YOUR OWN. ♬

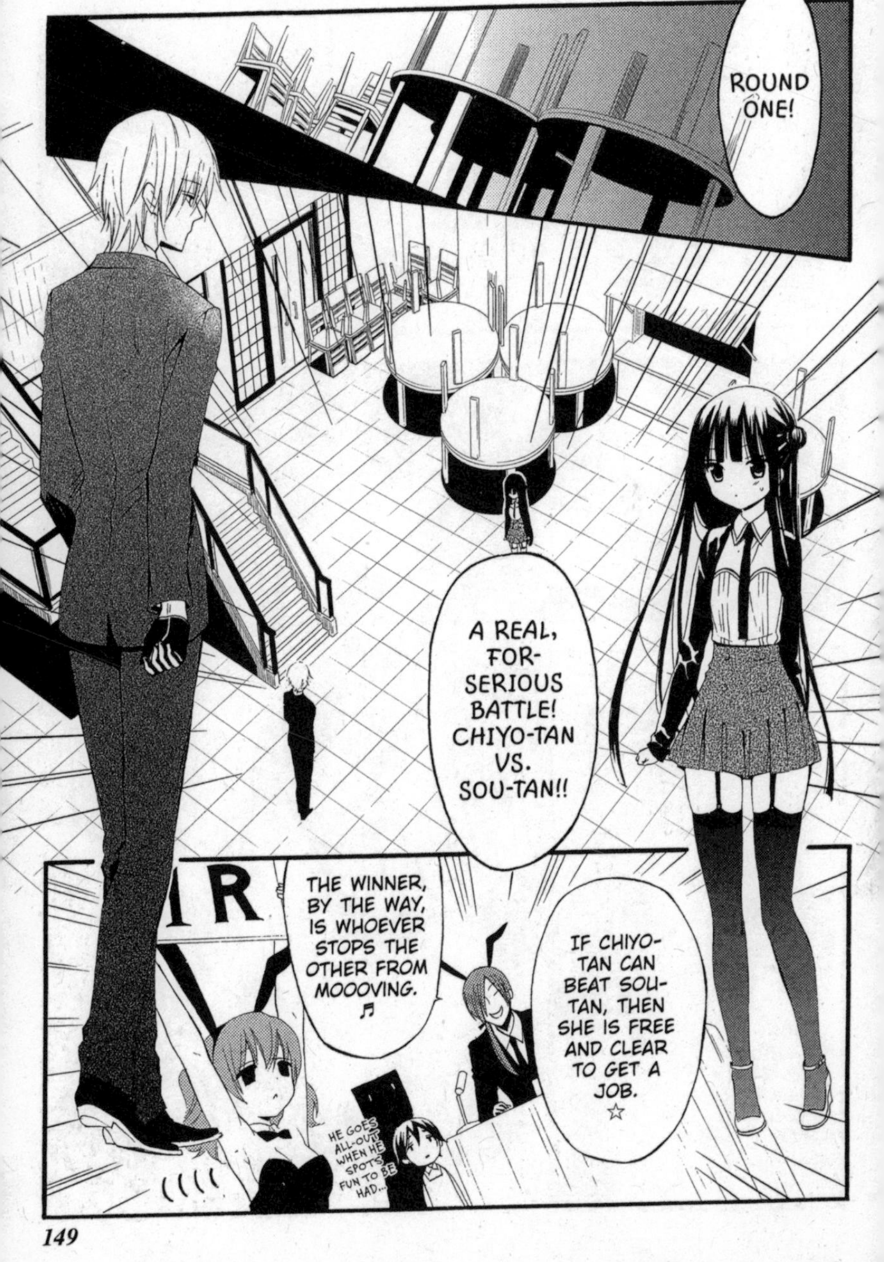
ROUND ONE!
A REAL, FOR-SERIOUS BATTLE! CHIYO-TAN VS. SOU-TAN!!
IF CHIYO-TAN CAN BEAT SOU-TAN, THEN SHE IS FREE AND CLEAR TO GET A JOB. ☆
THE WINNER, BY THE WAY, IS WHOEVER STOPS THE OTHER FROM MOOOVING. ♬
HE GOES ALL-OUT WHEN HE SPOTS FUN TO BE HAD...

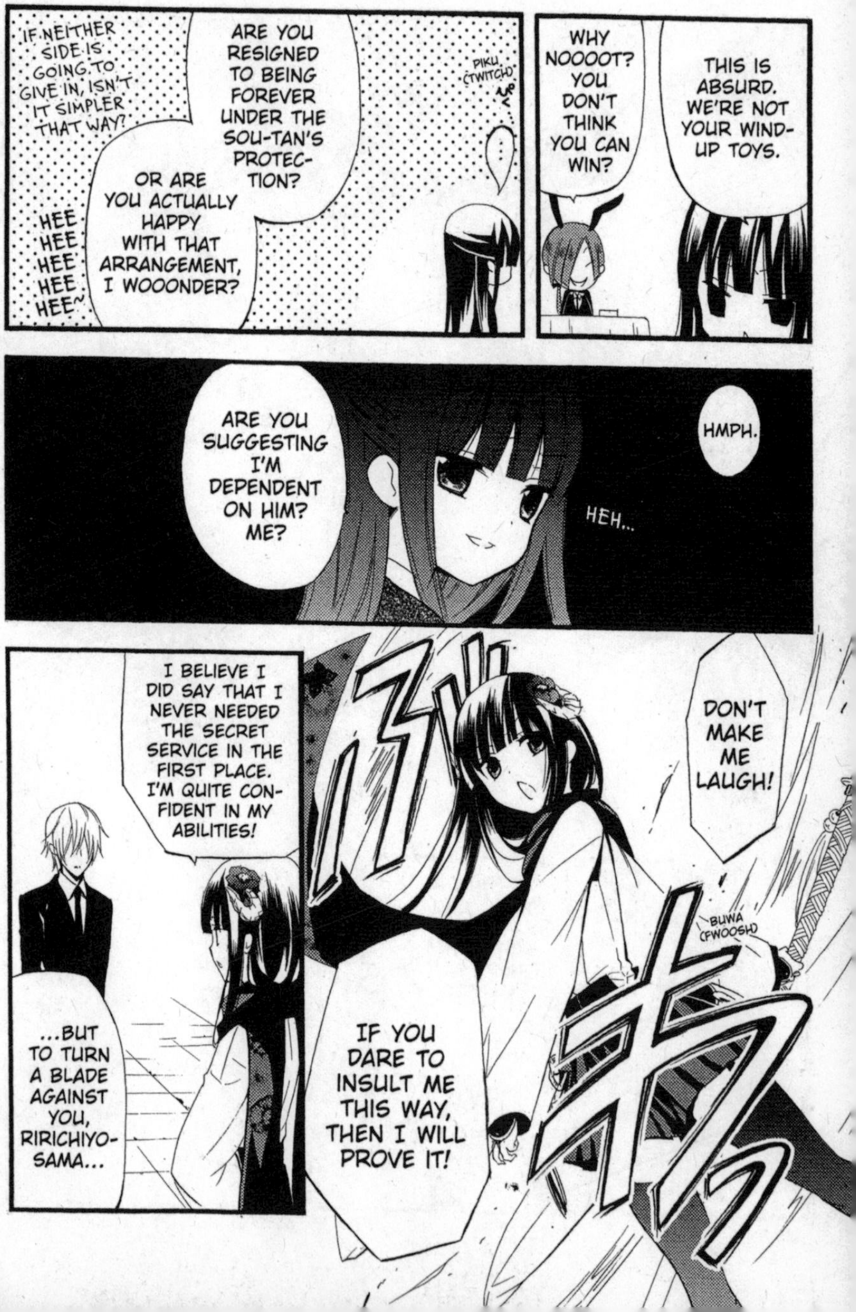
THIS IS ABSURD. WE'RE NOT YOUR WIND-UP TOYS.
WHY NOOOOT? YOU DON'T THINK YOU CAN WIN?
PIKU (TWITCH)
...
ARE YOU RESIGNED TO BEING FOREVER UNDER THE SOU-TAN'S PROTECTION?
IF NEITHER SIDE IS GOING TO GIVE IN, ISN'T IT SIMPLER THAT WAY?
OR ARE YOU ACTUALLY HAPPY WITH THAT ARRANGEMENT, I WOOONDER?
HEE HEE HEE HEE HEE~
HMPH.
HEH...
ARE YOU SUGGESTING I'M DEPENDENT ON HIM? ME?
DON'T MAKE ME LAUGH!
BUWA (FWOOSH)
IF YOU DARE TO INSULT ME THIS WAY, THEN I WILL PROVE IT!
I BELIEVE I DID SAY THAT I NEVER NEEDED THE SECRET SERVICE IN THE FIRST PLACE. I'M QUITE CONFIDENT IN MY ABILITIES!
...BUT TO TURN A BLADE AGAINST YOU, RIRICHIYO-SAMA...

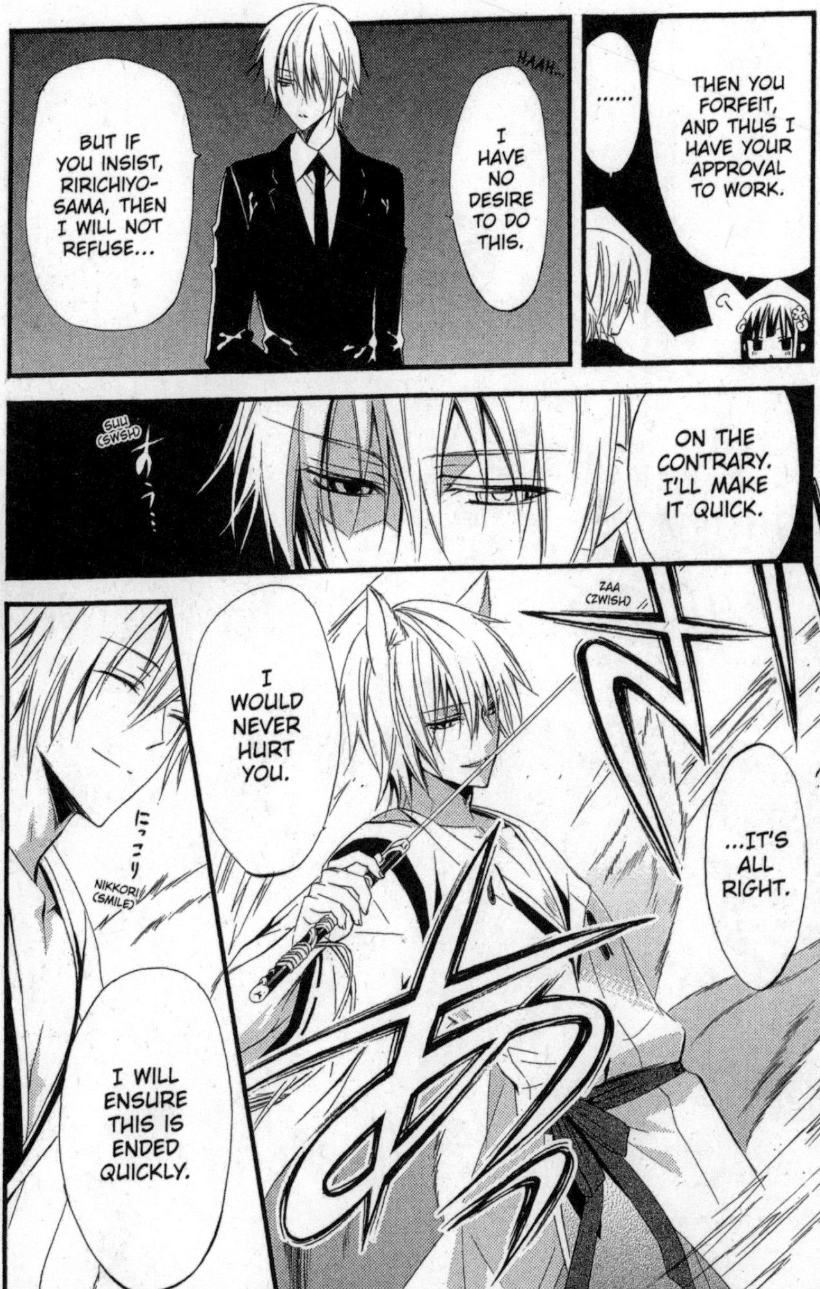
THEN YOU FORFEIT, AND THUS I HAVE YOUR APPROVAL TO WORK.
......
HAAH...
I HAVE NO DESIRE TO DO THIS.
BUT IF YOU INSIST, RIRICHIYO-SAMA, THEN I WILL NOT REFUSE...
ON THE CONTRARY. I'LL MAKE IT QUICK.
SUU (SWSH)
ZAA (ZWISH)
...IT'S ALL RIGHT.
I WOULD NEVER HURT YOU.
にっこり
NIKKORI (SMILE)
I WILL ENSURE THIS IS ENDED QUICKLY.

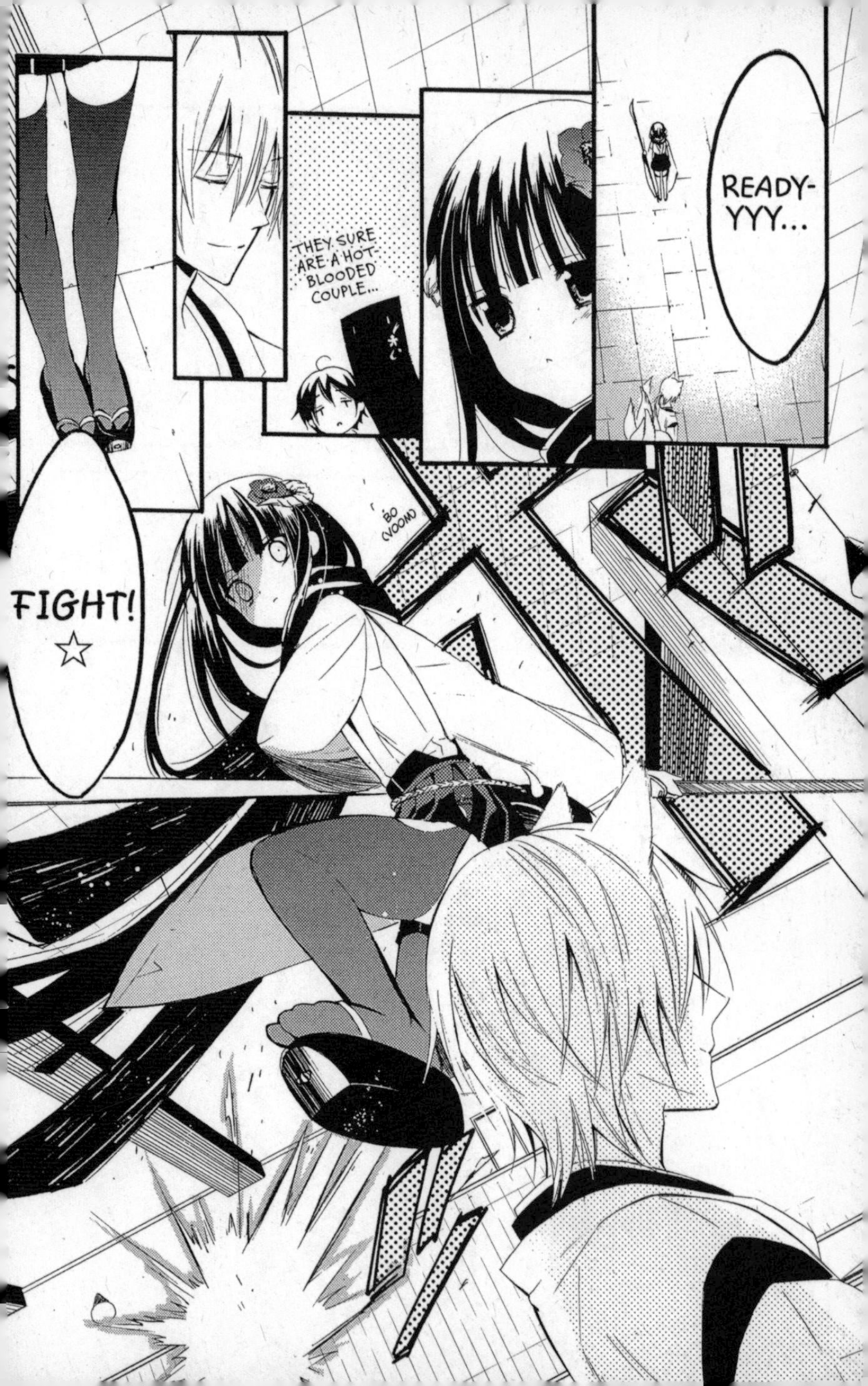

READY-YYY...
THEY SURE ARE A HOT-BLOODED COUPLE...
BO (VOOM)
FIGHT! ☆

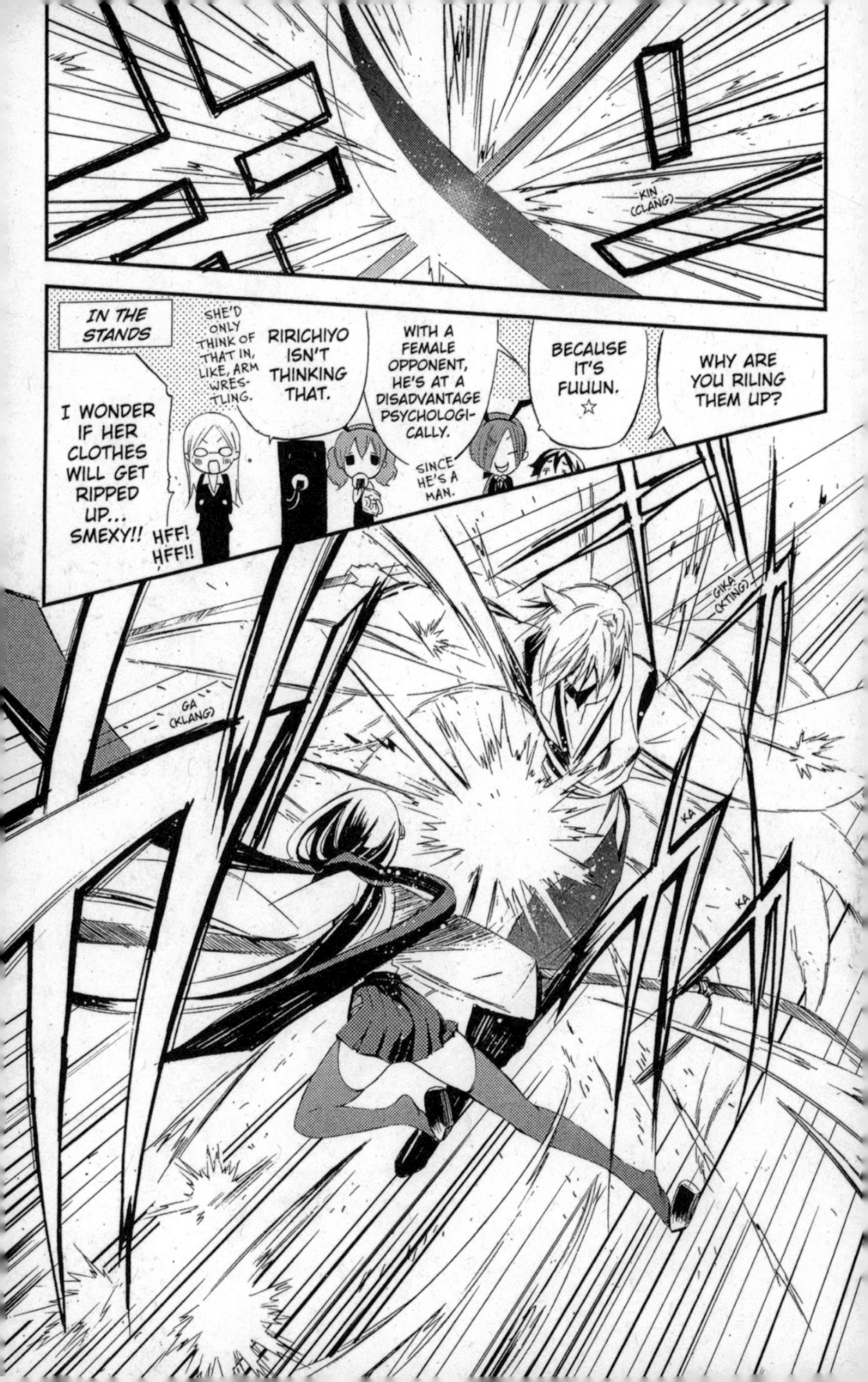
KIN (CLANG)
IN THE STANDS
WHY ARE YOU RILING THEM UP?
BECAUSE IT'S FUUUN. ☆
WITH A FEMALE OPPONENT, HE'S AT A DISADVANTAGE PSYCHOLOGICALLY.
SINCE HE'S A MAN.
RIRICHIYO ISN'T THINKING THAT.
SHE'D ONLY THINK OF THAT IN, LIKE, ARM WRES-TLING.
I WONDER IF HER CLOTHES WILL GET RIPPED UP... SMEXY!!
HFF! HFF!!
GIKA (KTING)
KA
KA
GA (KLANG)

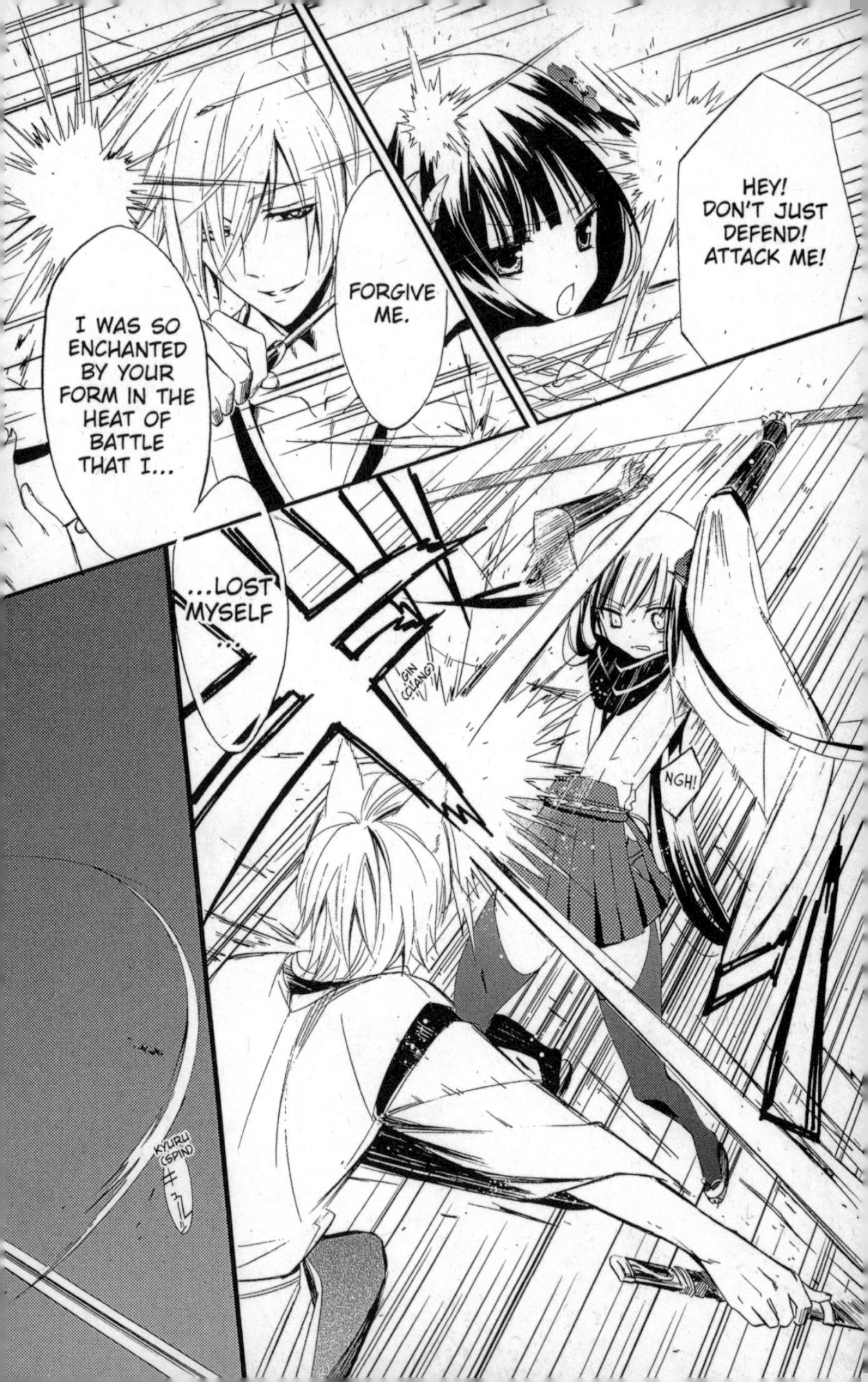
HEY! DON'T JUST DEFEND! ATTACK ME!
FORGIVE ME.
I WAS SO ENCHANTED BY YOUR FORM IN THE HEAT OF BATTLE THAT I...
...LOST MYSELF...
NGH!
GIN (CLANG)
KYURU (SPIN)

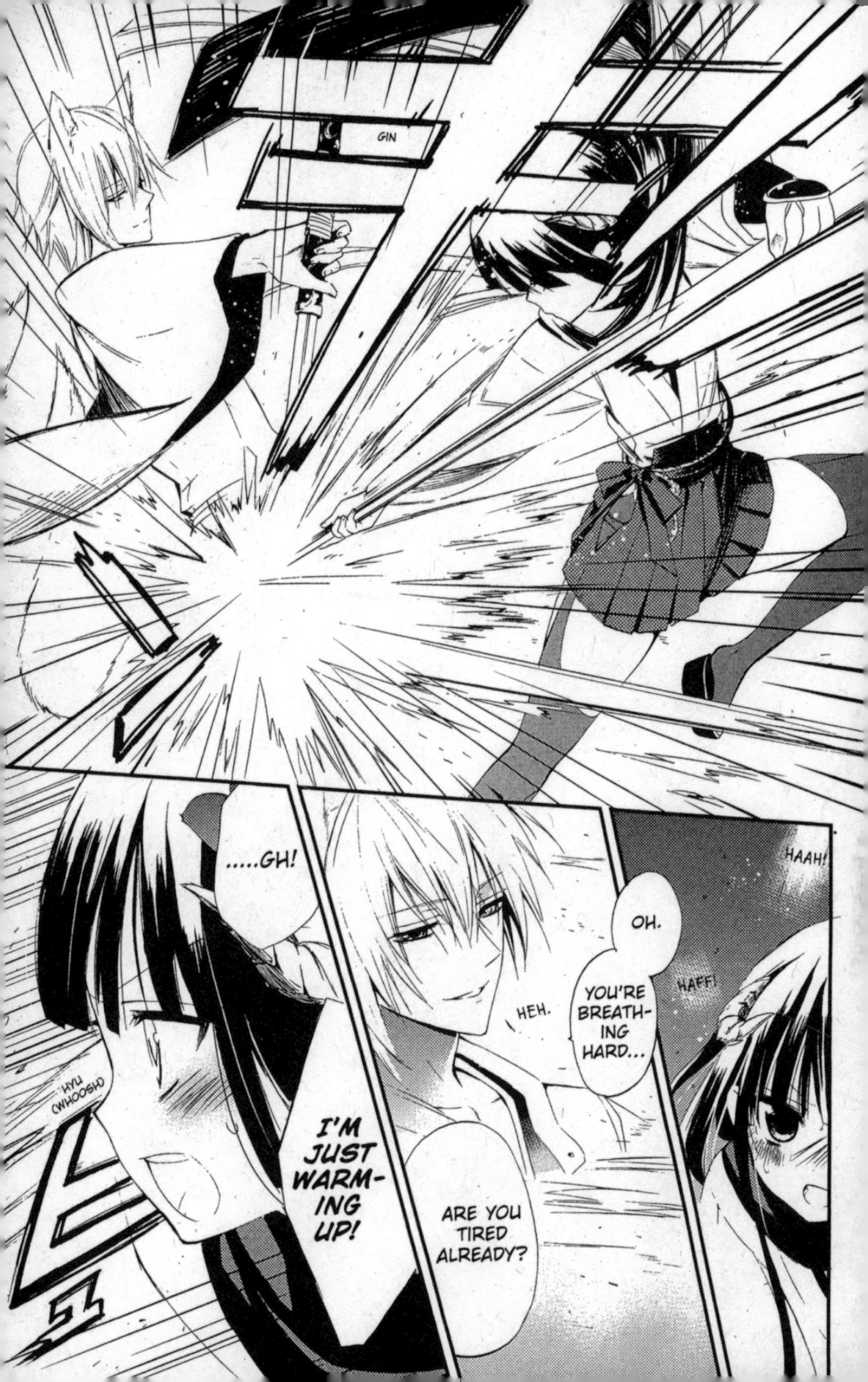
GIN
HAAH!
HAFF!
OH.
YOU'RE BREATH-ING HARD...
HEH.
ARE YOU TIRED ALREADY?
.....GH!
I'M JUST WARM-ING UP!
HYU (WHOOSH)

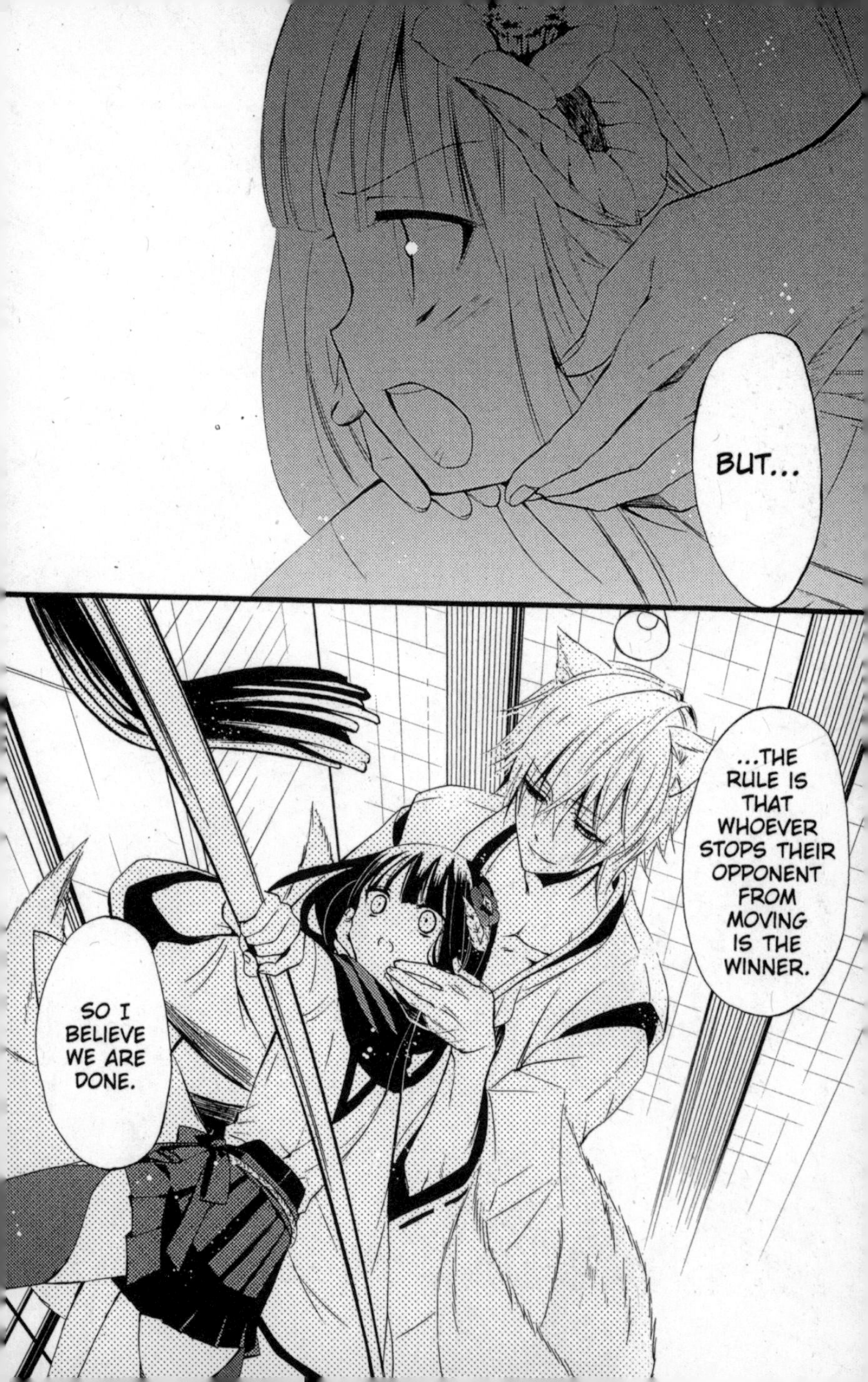
BUT...
...THE RULE IS THAT WHOEVER STOPS THEIR OPPONENT FROM MOVING IS THE WINNER.
SO I BELIEVE WE ARE DONE.

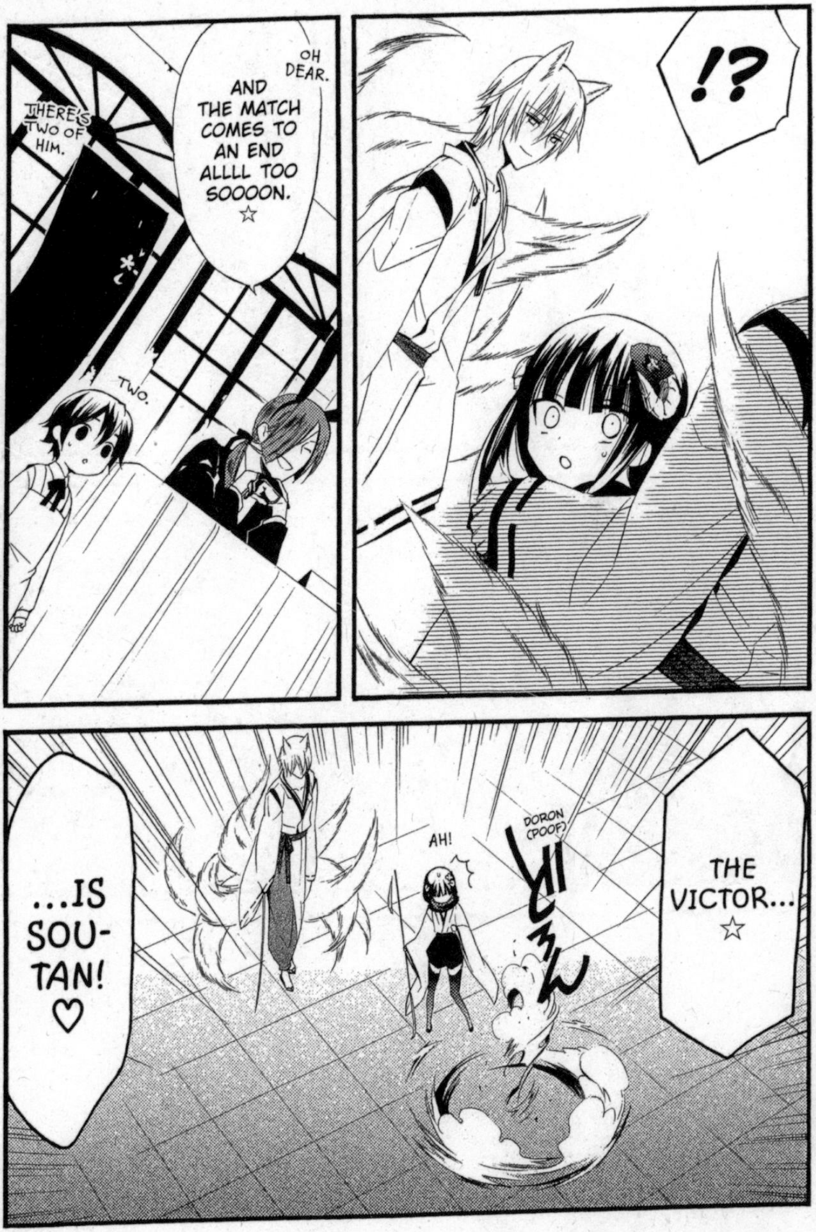

!?
OH DEAR.
AND THE MATCH COMES TO AN END ALLLL TOO SOOOON. ☆
THERE'S TWO OF HIM.
TWO.
THE VICTOR... ☆
DORON (POOF)
AH!
...IS SOU-TAN! ♡

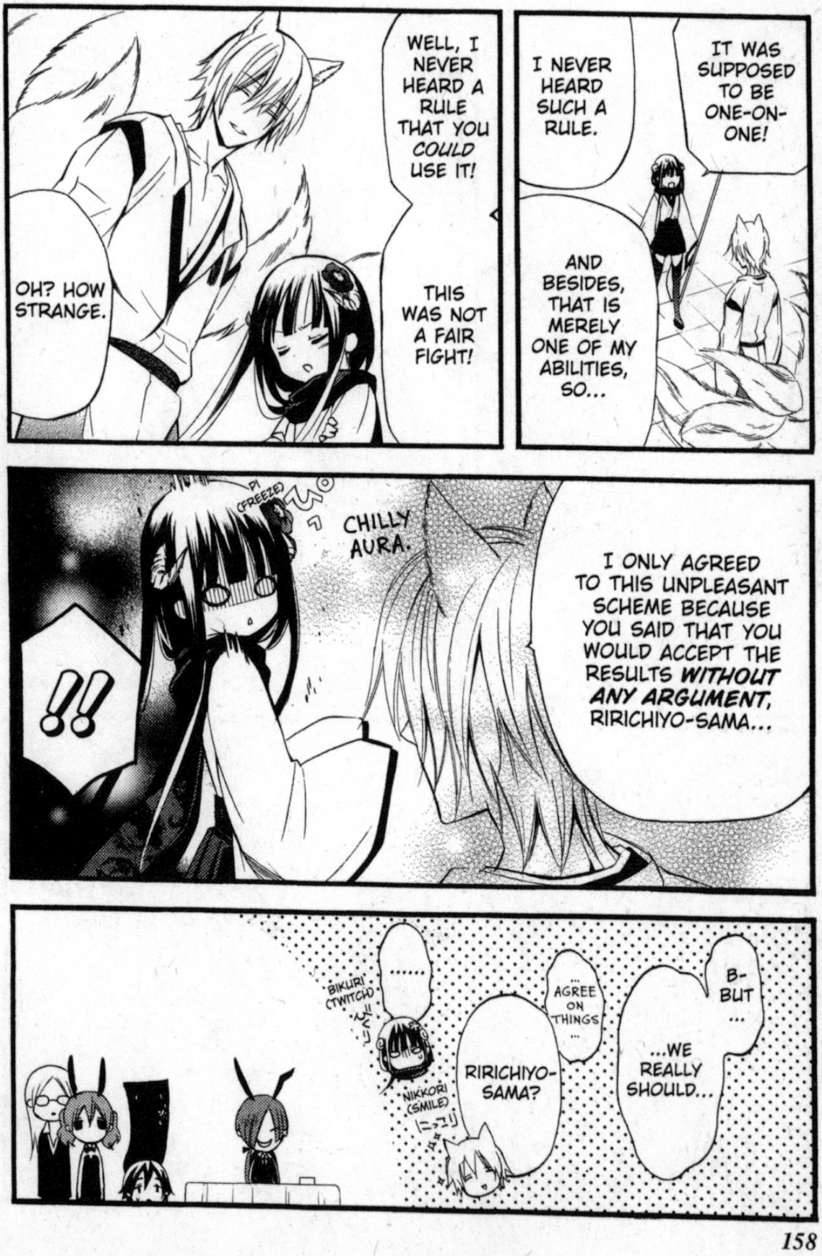
IT WAS SUPPOSED TO BE ONE-ON-ONE!
I NEVER HEARD SUCH A RULE.
AND BESIDES, THAT IS MERELY ONE OF MY ABILITIES, SO...
WELL, I NEVER HEARD A RULE THAT YOU *COULD* USE IT!
THIS WAS NOT A FAIR FIGHT!
OH? HOW STRANGE.
I ONLY AGREED TO THIS UNPLEASANT SCHEME BECAUSE YOU SAID THAT YOU WOULD ACCEPT THE RESULTS ***WITHOUT ANY ARGUMENT***, RIRICHIYO-SAMA...
CHILLY AURA.
PI (FREEZE)
!!
B-BUT...
...WE REALLY SHOULD...
...AGREE ON THINGS...
RIRICHIYO-SAMA?
NIKKORI (SMILE)
BIKURI (TWITCH)
......

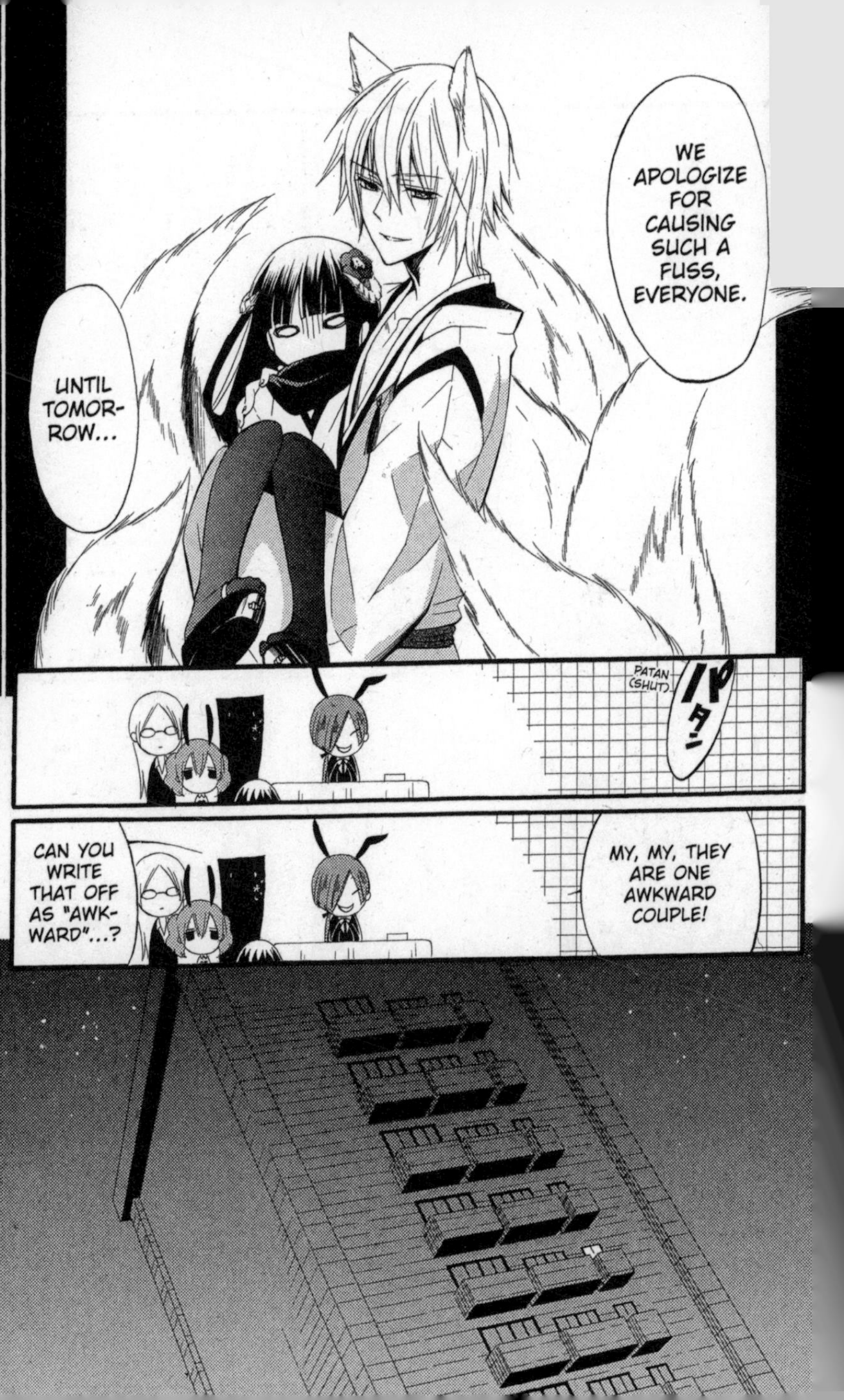
WE APOLOGIZE FOR CAUSING SUCH A FUSS, EVERYONE.
UNTIL TOMOR-ROW...
パタン
PATAN (SHUT)
MY, MY, THEY ARE ONE AWKWARD COUPLE!
CAN YOU WRITE THAT OFF AS "AWK-WARD"...?

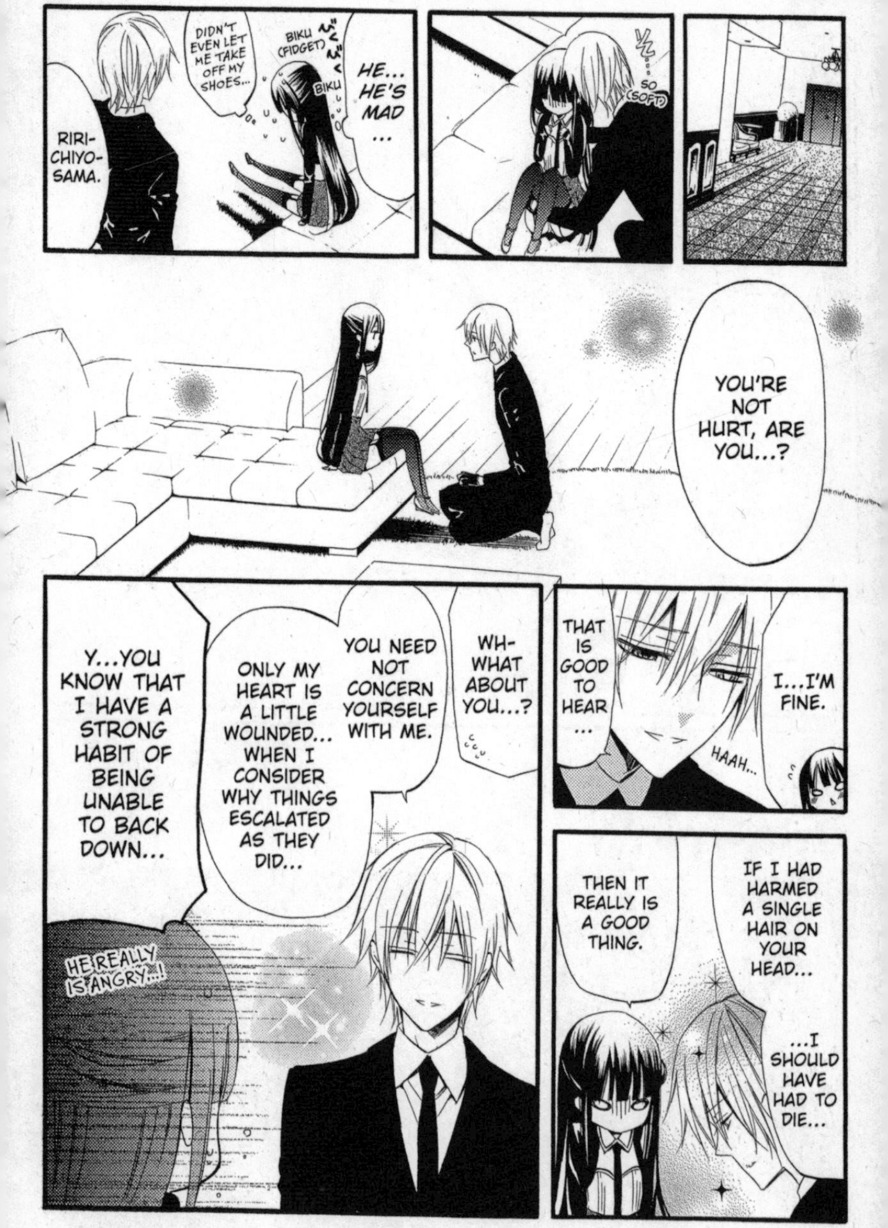
SO (SOFT)
HE... HE'S MAD...
BIKU (FIDGET)
BIKU
DIDN'T EVEN LET ME TAKE OFF MY SHOES...
RIRI-CHIYO-SAMA.
YOU'RE NOT HURT, ARE YOU...?
I...I'M FINE.
HAAH...
THAT IS GOOD TO HEAR...
IF I HAD HARMED A SINGLE HAIR ON YOUR HEAD...
...I SHOULD HAVE HAD TO DIE...
THEN IT REALLY IS A GOOD THING.
WH-WHAT ABOUT YOU...?
YOU NEED NOT CONCERN YOURSELF WITH ME.
ONLY MY HEART IS A LITTLE WOUNDED... WHEN I CONSIDER WHY THINGS ESCALATED AS THEY DID...
Y...YOU KNOW THAT I HAVE A STRONG HABIT OF BEING UNABLE TO BACK DOWN...
HE REALLY IS ANGRY...!

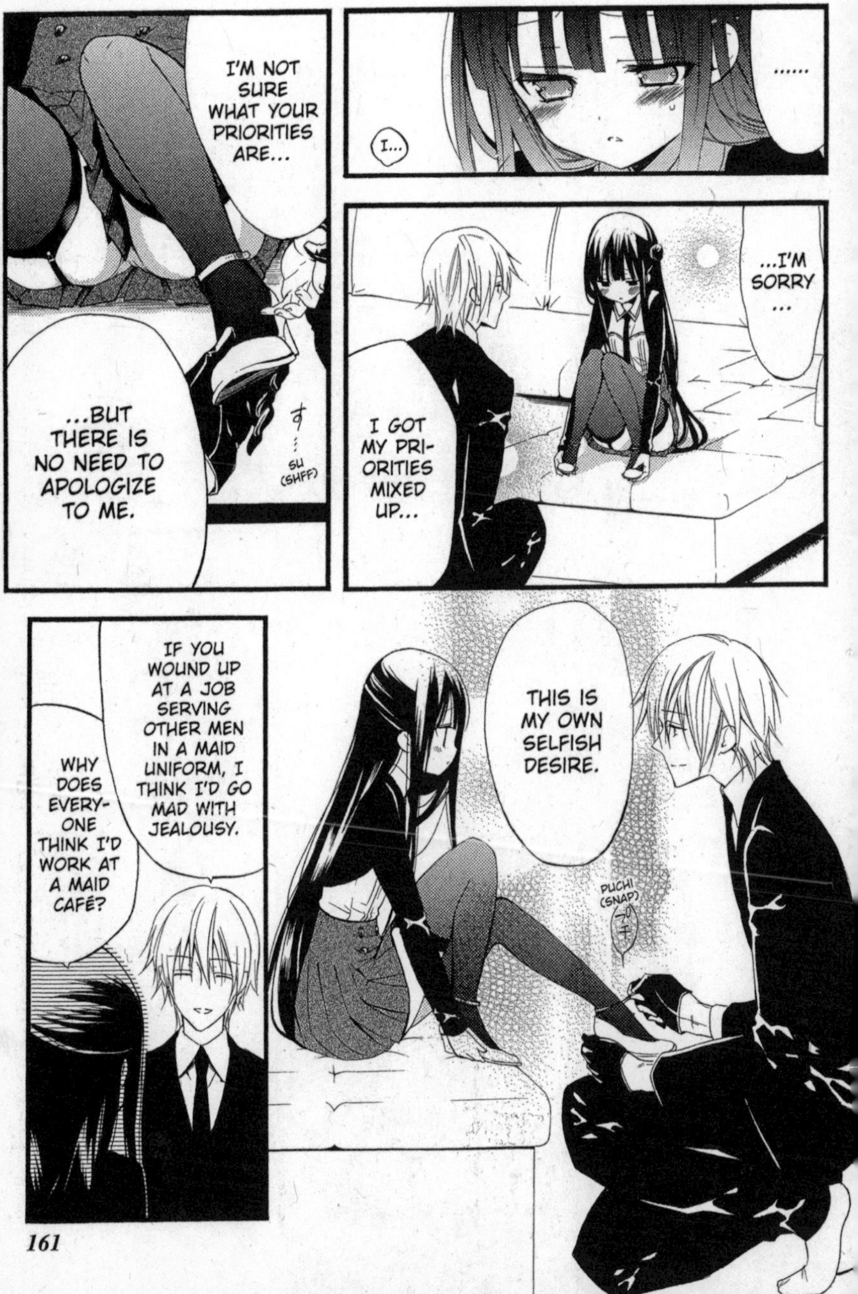
......
I...
...I'M SORRY...
I GOT MY PRIORITIES MIXED UP...
I'M NOT SURE WHAT YOUR PRIORITIES ARE...
す…
SU (SHFF)
...BUT THERE IS NO NEED TO APOLOGIZE TO ME.
THIS IS MY OWN SELFISH DESIRE.
PUCHI (SNAP)
IF YOU WOUND UP AT A JOB SERVING OTHER MEN IN A MAID UNIFORM, I THINK I'D GO MAD WITH JEALOUSY.
WHY DOES EVERYONE THINK I'D WORK AT A MAID CAFÉ?

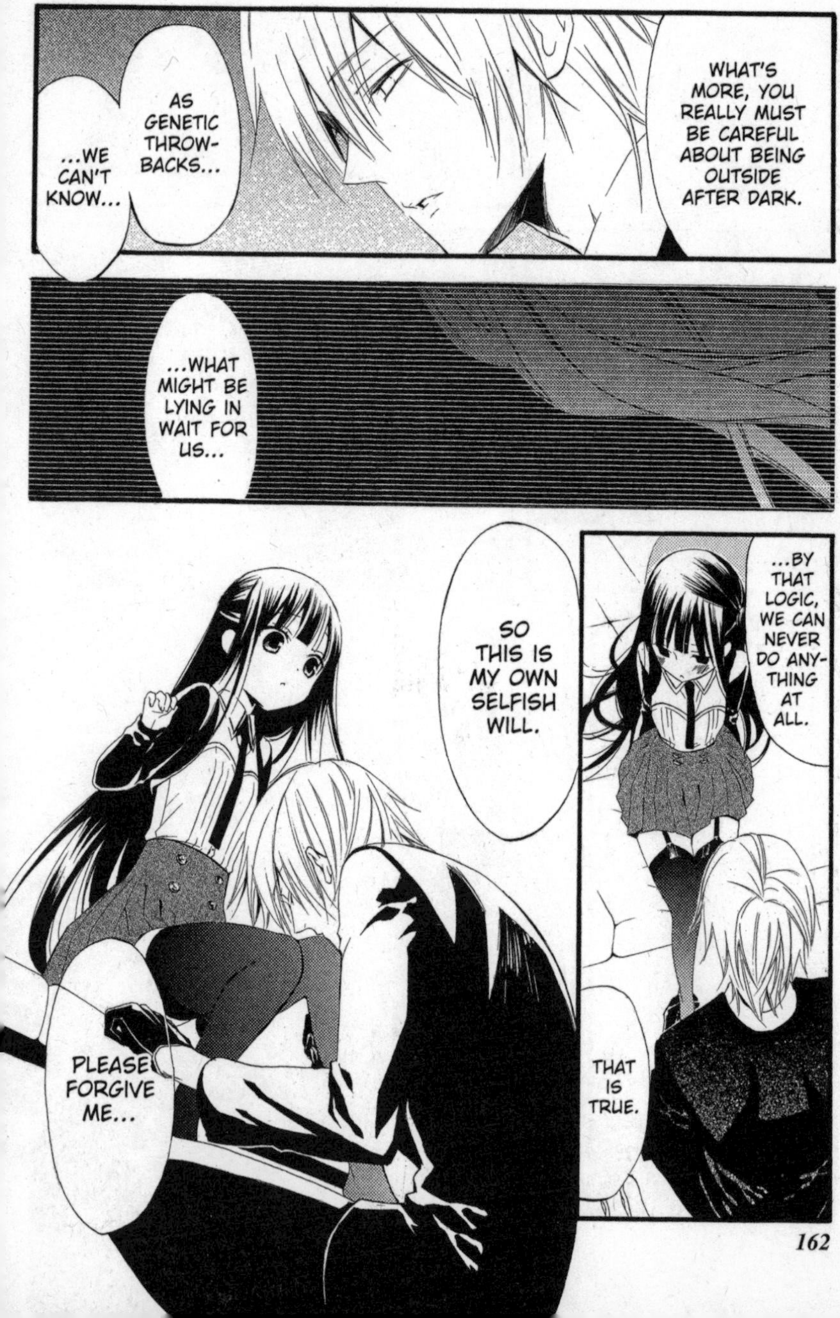
WHAT'S MORE, YOU REALLY MUST BE CAREFUL ABOUT BEING OUTSIDE AFTER DARK.
AS GENETIC THROW-BACKS...
...WE CAN'T KNOW...
...WHAT MIGHT BE LYING IN WAIT FOR US...
...BY THAT LOGIC, WE CAN NEVER DO ANY-THING AT ALL.
THAT IS TRUE.
SO THIS IS MY OWN SELFISH WILL.
PLEASE FORGIVE ME...

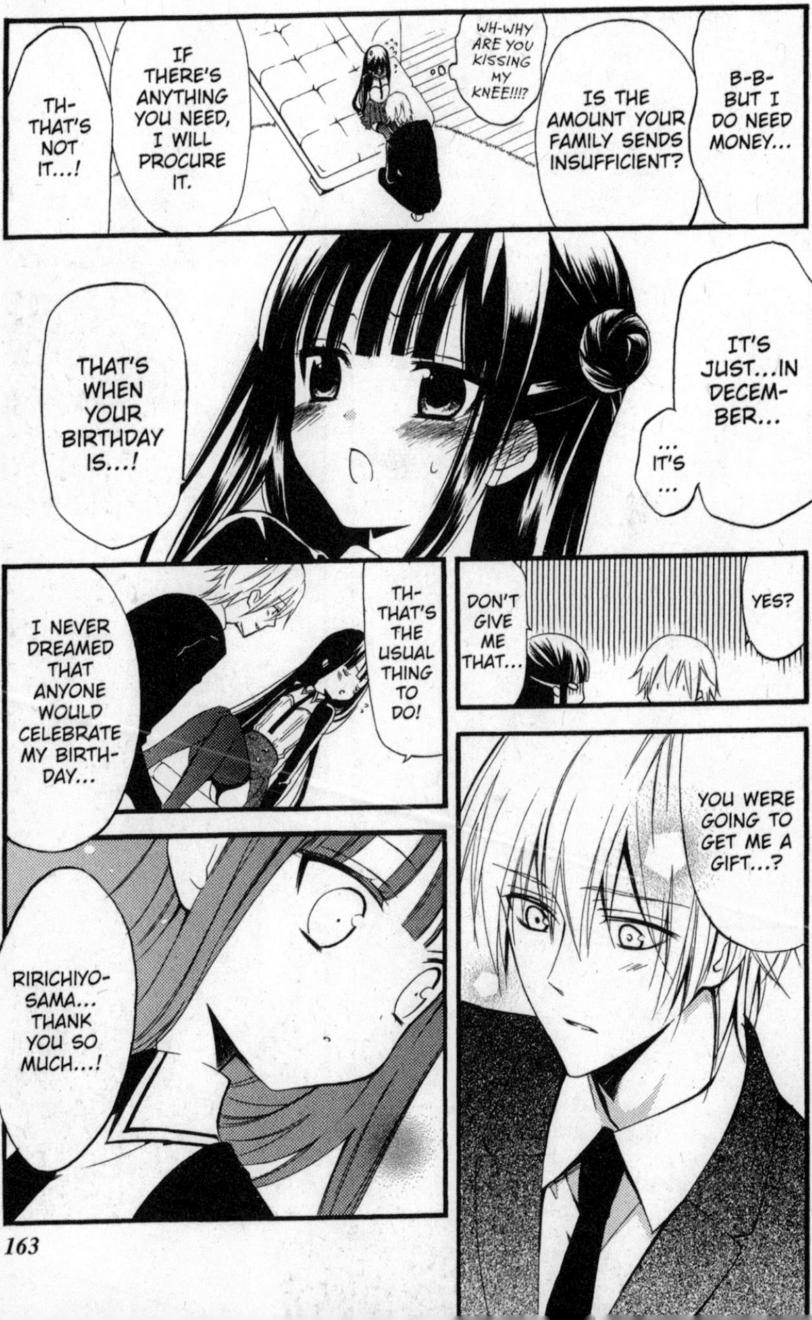
B-B-BUT I DO NEED MONEY...
IS THE AMOUNT YOUR FAMILY SENDS INSUFFICIENT?
WH-WHY ARE YOU KISSING MY KNEE!!!?
IF THERE'S ANYTHING YOU NEED, I WILL PROCURE IT.
TH-THAT'S NOT IT...!
IT'S JUST...IN DECEMBER...
...IT'S...
THAT'S WHEN YOUR BIRTHDAY IS...!
YES?
DON'T GIVE ME THAT...
YOU WERE GOING TO GET ME A GIFT...?
TH-THAT'S THE USUAL THING TO DO!
I NEVER DREAMED THAT ANYONE WOULD CELEBRATE MY BIRTHDAY...
RIRICHIYO-SAMA... THANK YOU SO MUCH...!

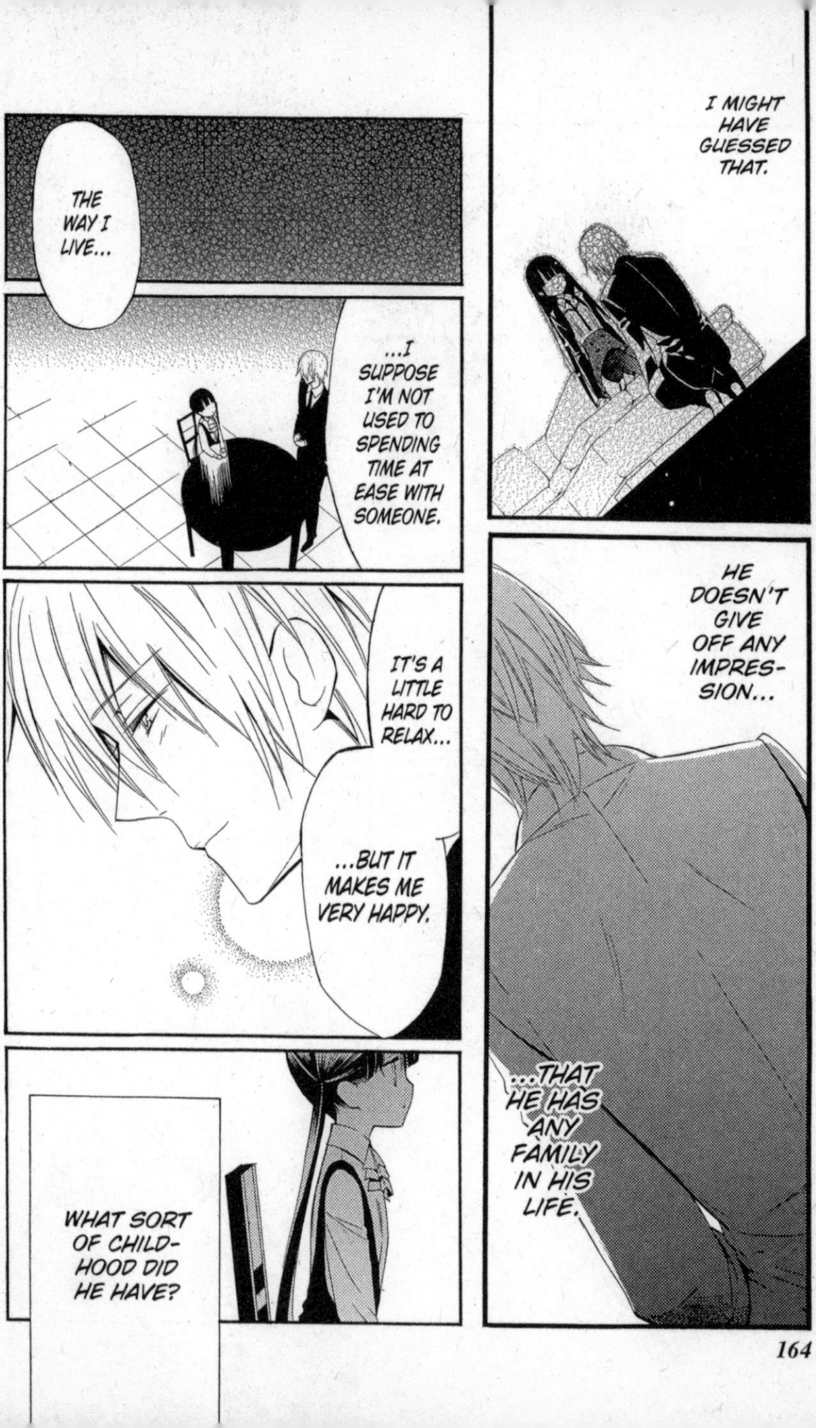
I MIGHT HAVE GUESSED THAT.
THE WAY I LIVE...
...I SUPPOSE I'M NOT USED TO SPENDING TIME AT EASE WITH SOMEONE.
HE DOESN'T GIVE OFF ANY IMPRESSION...
...THAT HE HAS ANY FAMILY IN HIS LIFE.
IT'S A LITTLE HARD TO RELAX...
...BUT IT MAKES ME VERY HAPPY.
WHAT SORT OF CHILDHOOD DID HE HAVE?

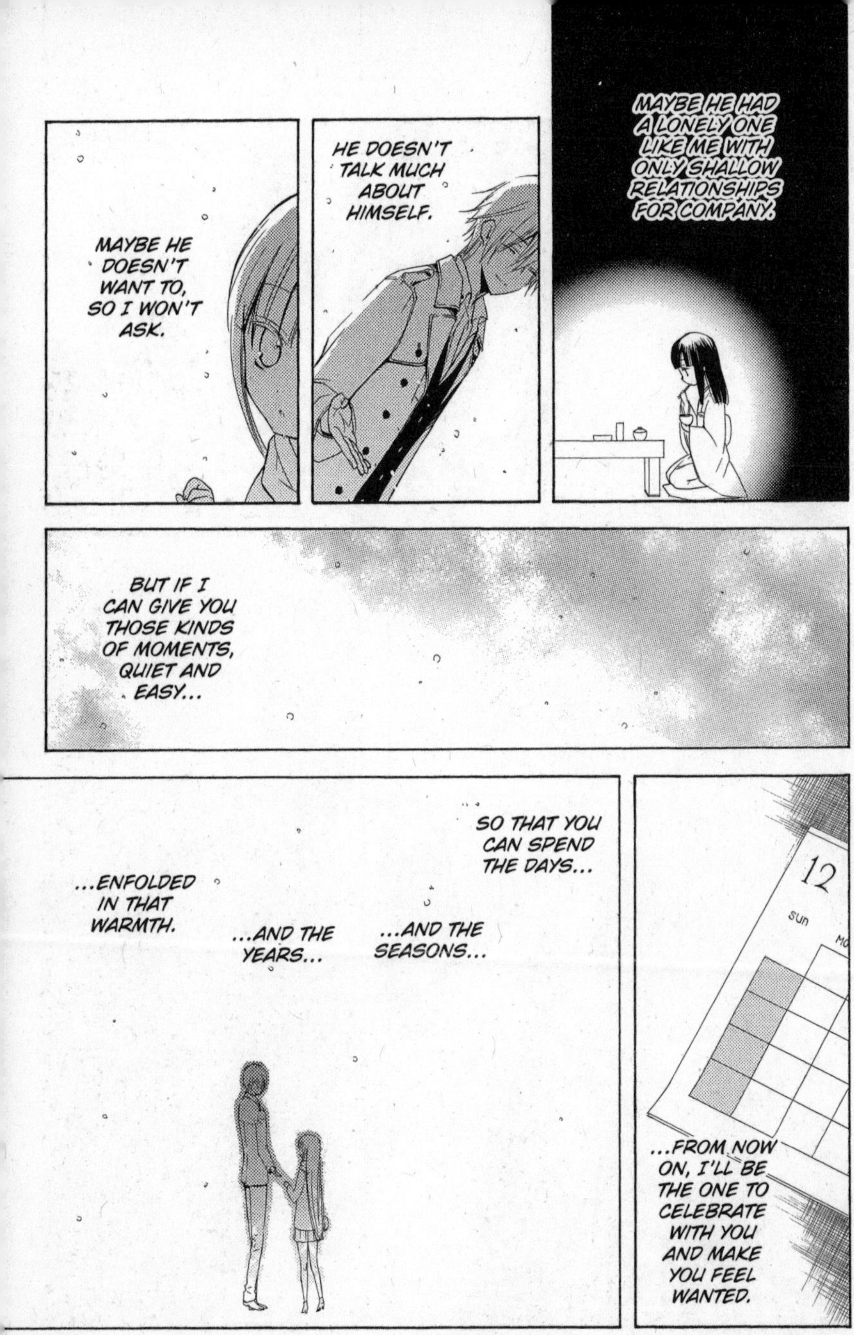
MAYBE HE HAD A LONELY ONE LIKE ME WITH ONLY SHALLOW RELATIONSHIPS FOR COMPANY.
HE DOESN'T TALK MUCH ABOUT HIMSELF.
MAYBE HE DOESN'T WANT TO, SO I WON'T ASK.
BUT IF I CAN GIVE YOU THOSE KINDS OF MOMENTS, QUIET AND EASY...
12
SUN
...FROM NOW ON, I'LL BE THE ONE TO CELEBRATE WITH YOU AND MAKE YOU FEEL WANTED.
SO THAT YOU CAN SPEND THE DAYS...
...AND THE SEASONS...
...AND THE YEARS...
...ENFOLDED IN THAT WARMTH.

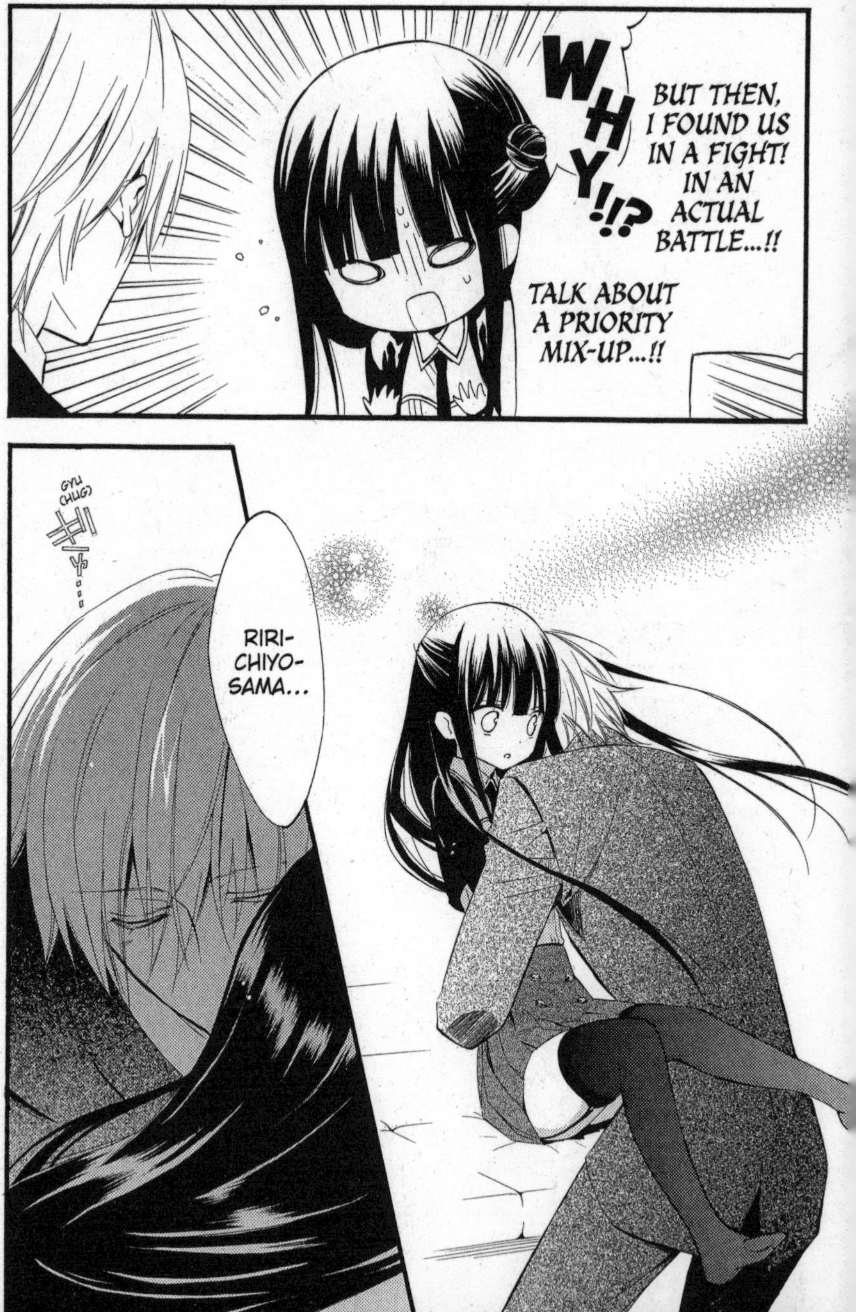
BUT THEN, I FOUND US IN A FIGHT! IN AN ACTUAL BATTLE...!!
WHY!!?
TALK ABOUT A PRIORITY MIX-UP...!!
GYU (HUG)
RIRI-CHIYO-SAMA...

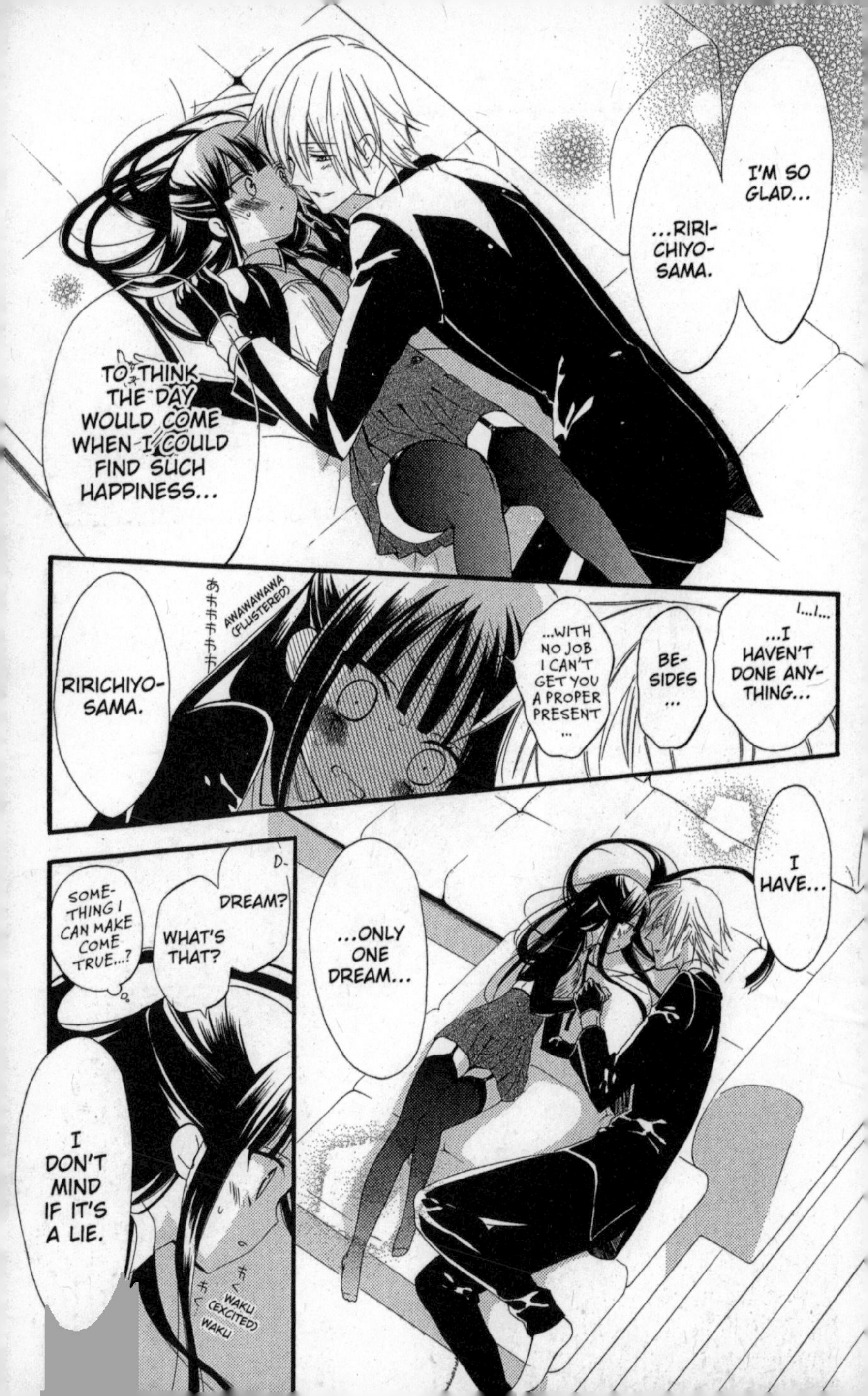
I'M SO GLAD...
...RIRI-CHIYO-SAMA.
TO THINK THE DAY WOULD COME WHEN I COULD FIND SUCH HAPPINESS...
I...I...
...I HAVEN'T DONE ANYTHING...
BE-SIDES...
...WITH NO JOB I CAN'T GET YOU A PROPER PRESENT...
あわわわわ
AWAWAWAWA (FLUSTERED)
RIRICHIYO-SAMA.
I HAVE...
...ONLY ONE DREAM...
D-
DREAM?
WHAT'S THAT?
SOMETHING I CAN MAKE COME TRUE...?
I DON'T MIND IF IT'S A LIE.
わくわく
WAKU (EXCITED) WAKU

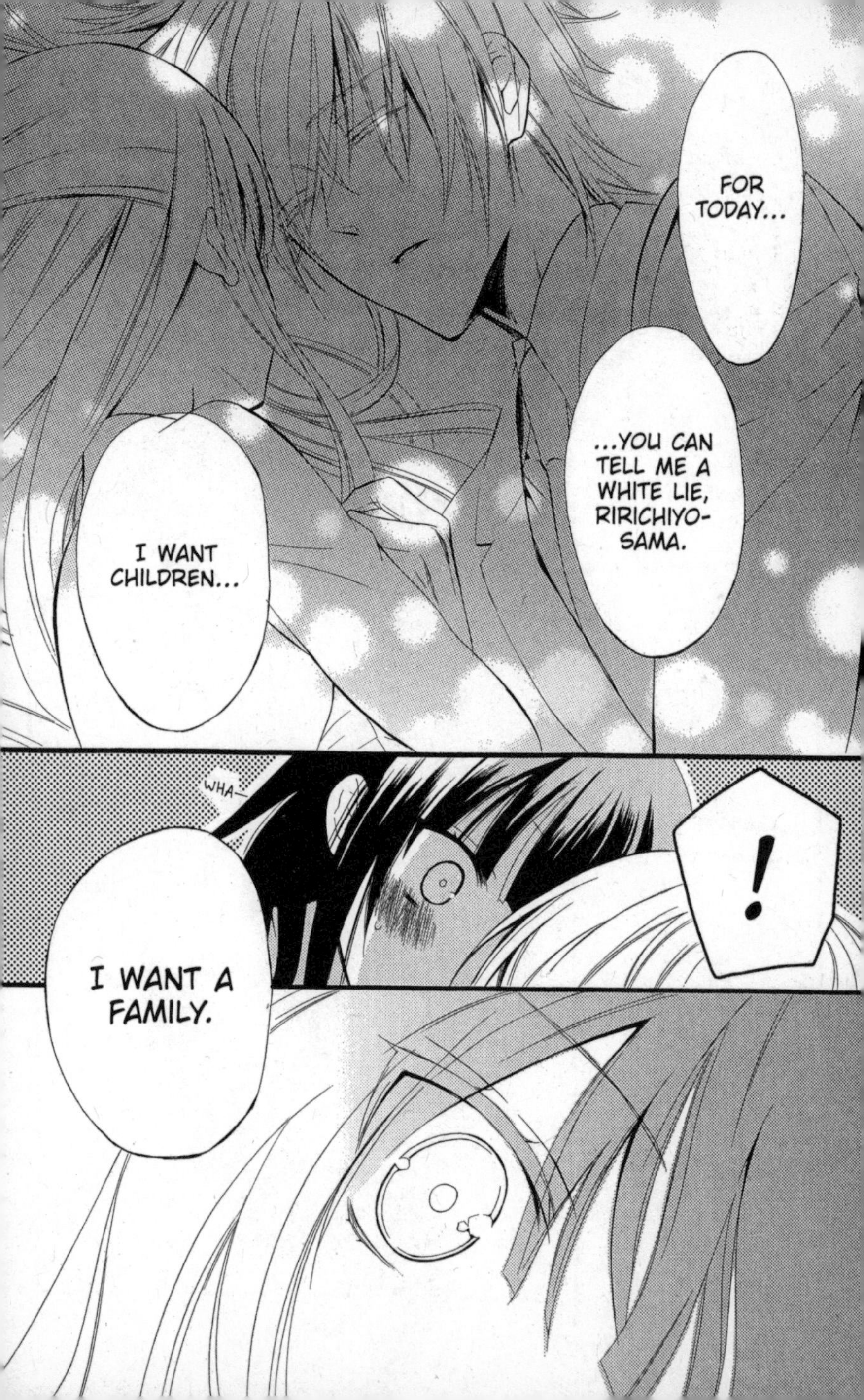
FOR TODAY...
...YOU CAN TELL ME A WHITE LIE, RIRICHIYO-SAMA.
I WANT CHILDREN...
!
WHA—
I WANT A FAMILY.

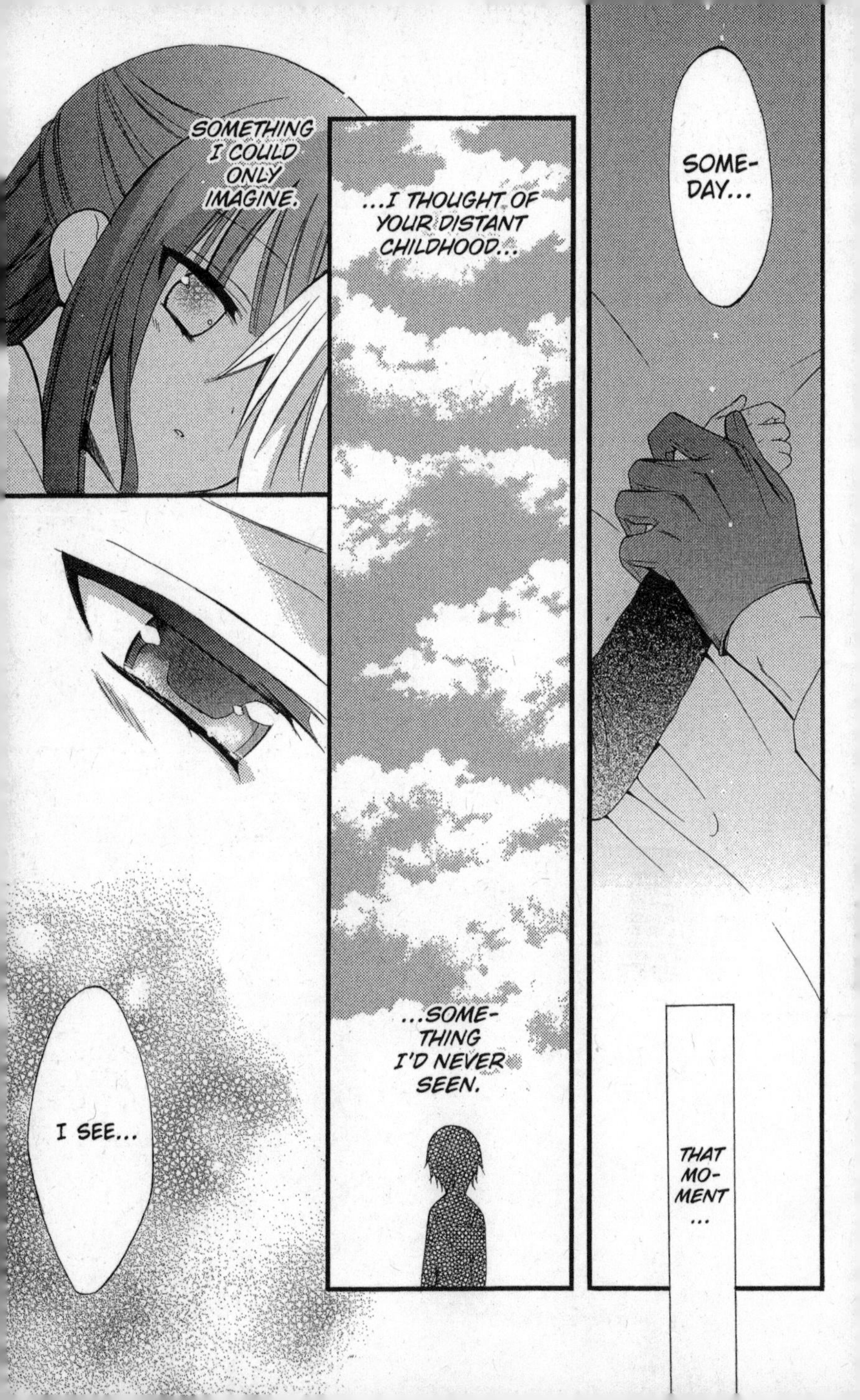
SOME-DAY...
THAT MO-MENT...
...I THOUGHT OF YOUR DISTANT CHILDHOOD...
...SOME-THING I'D NEVER SEEN.
SOMETHING I COULD ONLY IMAGINE.
I SEE...

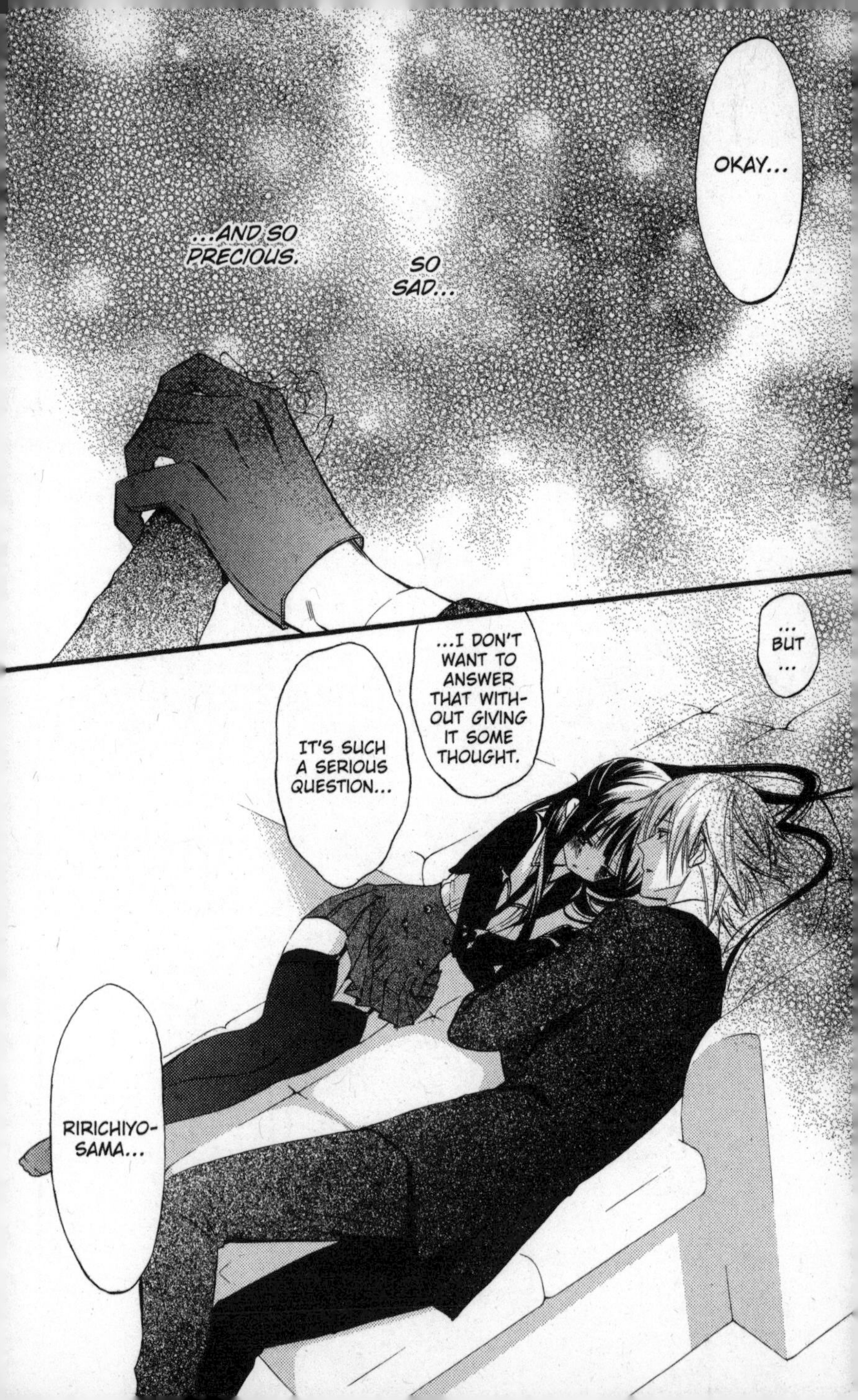
OKAY...
SO SAD...
...AND SO PRECIOUS.
...BUT...
...I DON'T WANT TO ANSWER THAT WITH-OUT GIVING IT SOME THOUGHT.
IT'S SUCH A SERIOUS QUESTION...
RIRICHIYO-SAMA...

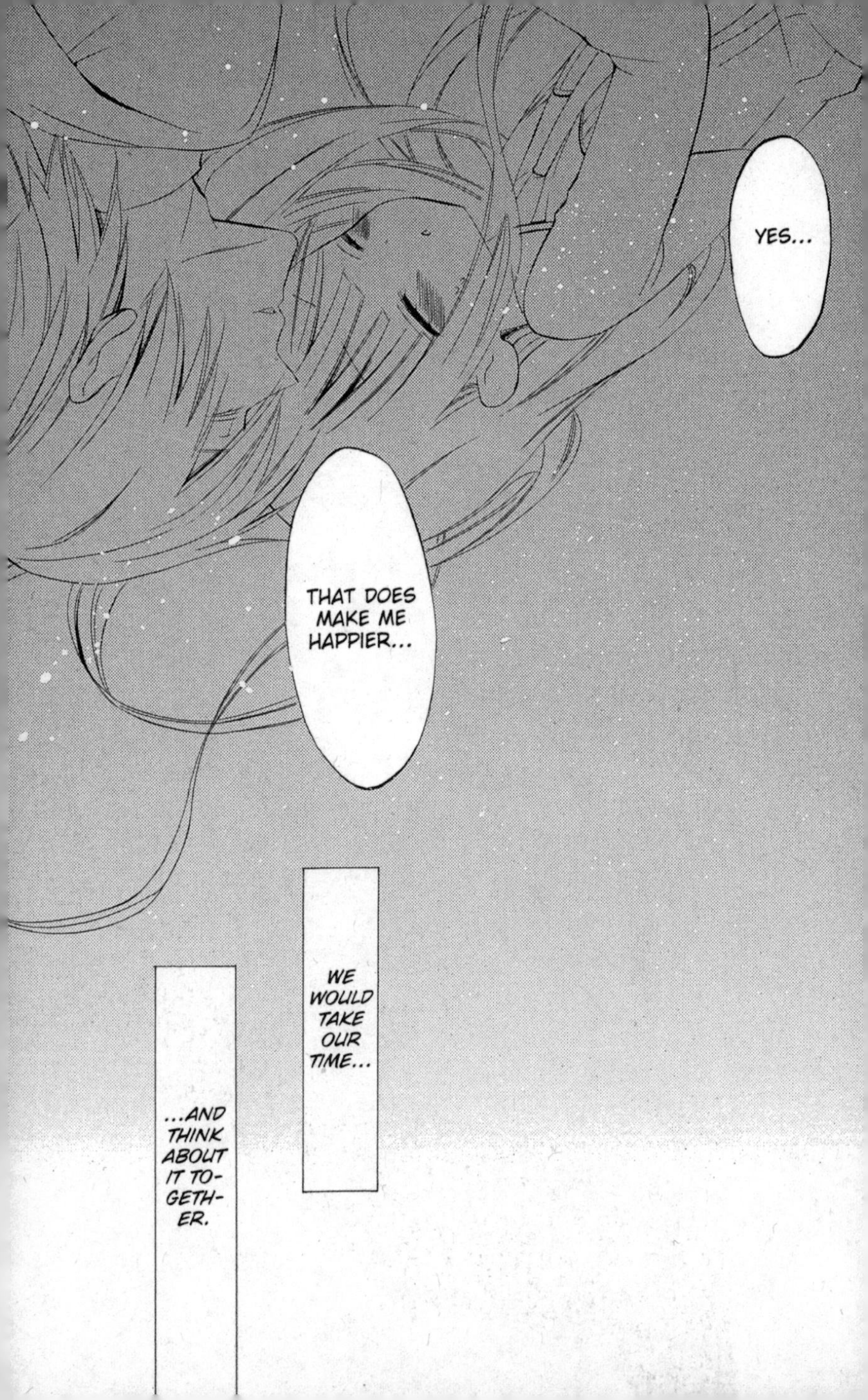
YES...
THAT DOES MAKE ME HAPPIER...
WE WOULD TAKE OUR TIME...
...AND THINK ABOUT IT TO-GETH-ER.

# THAT'S WHAT I THOUGHT THEN...

# ...WITHOUT ANY IDEA THAT NEXT SPRING WOULD BE UPON US SO SOON.

INU✕BOKU SS

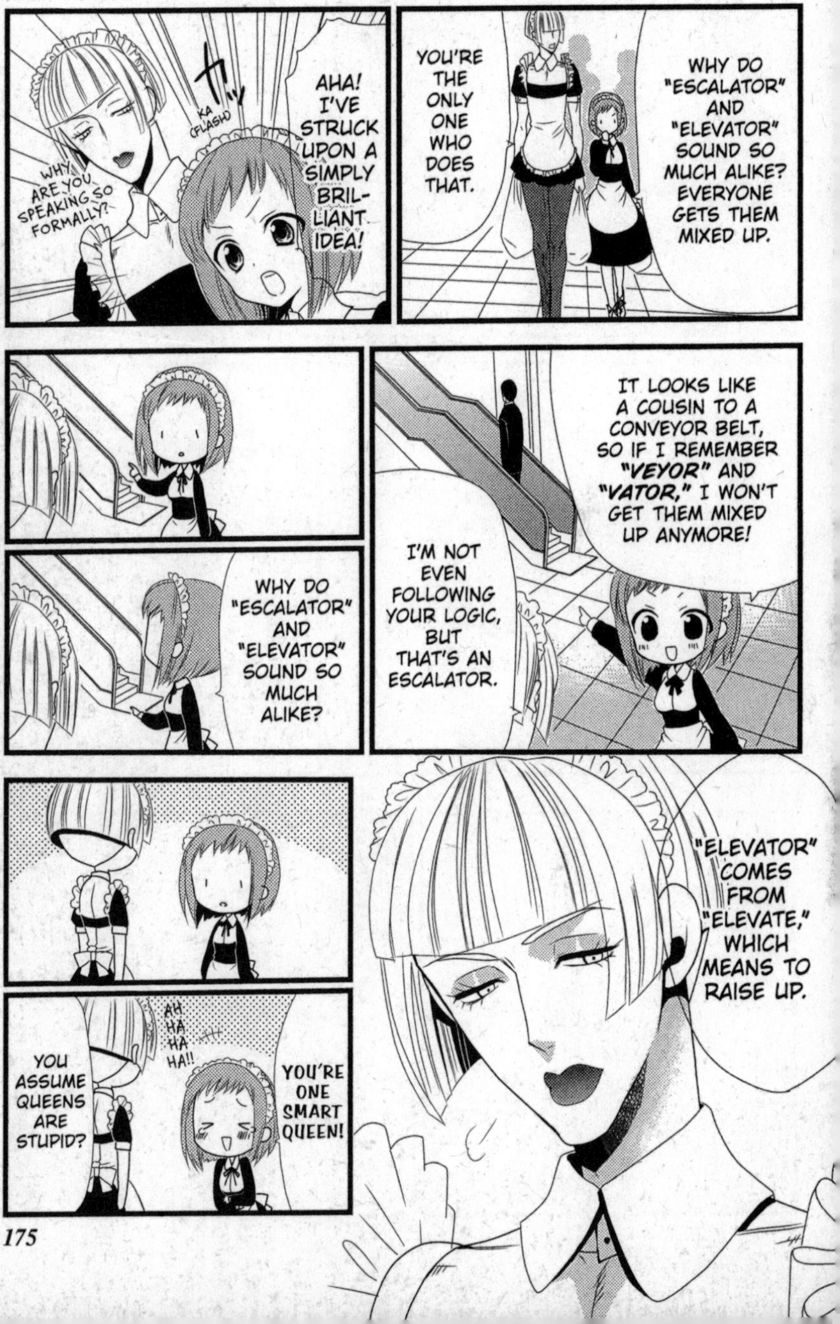
WHY DO "ESCALATOR" AND "ELEVATOR" SOUND SO MUCH ALIKE? EVERYONE GETS THEM MIXED UP.
YOU'RE THE ONLY ONE WHO DOES THAT.
KA (FLASH)
AHA! I'VE STRUCK UPON A SIMPLY BRIL-LIANT IDEA!
WHY ARE YOU SPEAKING SO FORMALLY?
IT LOOKS LIKE A COUSIN TO A CONVEYOR BELT, SO IF I REMEMBER "VEYOR" AND "VATOR," I WON'T GET THEM MIXED UP ANYMORE!
I'M NOT EVEN FOLLOWING YOUR LOGIC, BUT THAT'S AN ESCALATOR.
WHY DO "ESCALATOR" AND "ELEVATOR" SOUND SO MUCH ALIKE?
"ELEVATOR" COMES FROM "ELEVATE," WHICH MEANS TO RAISE UP.
YOU'RE ONE SMART QUEEN!
AH HA HA HA!!
YOU ASSUME QUEENS ARE STUPID?

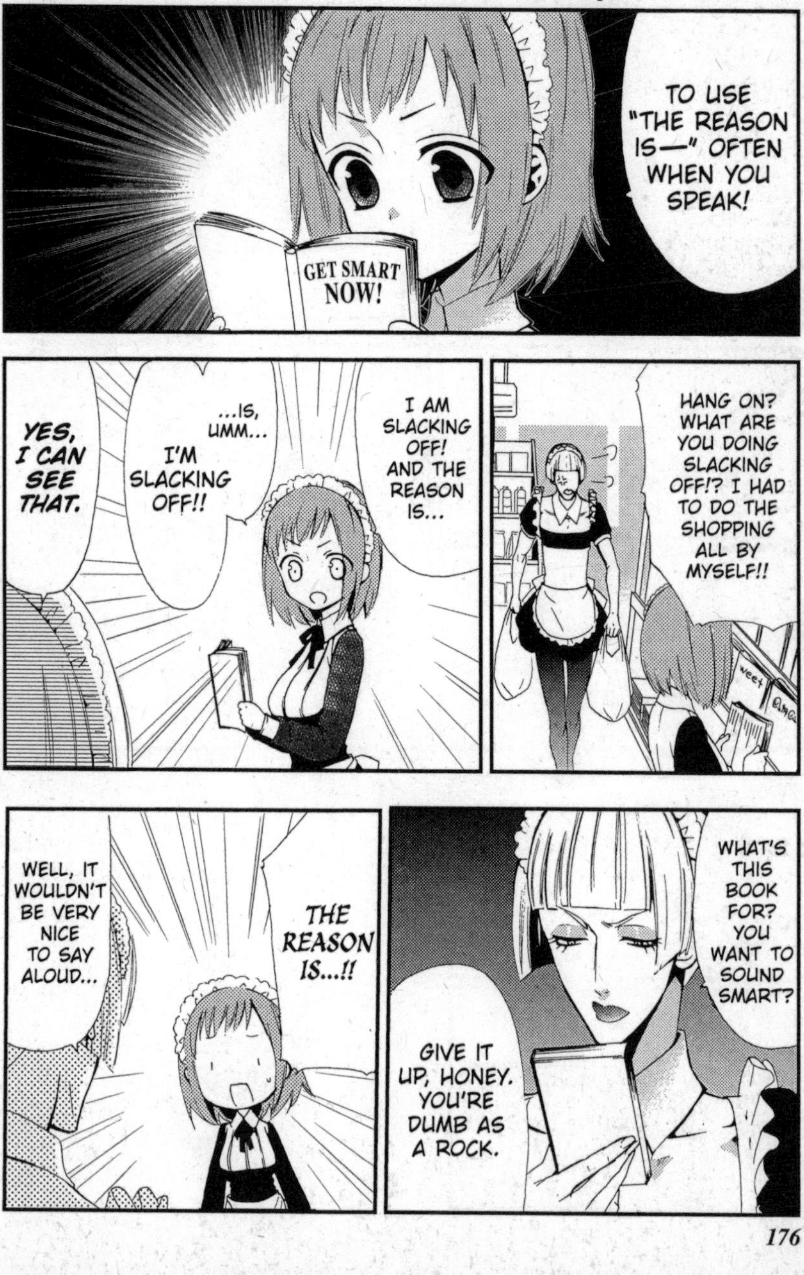
TO USE "THE REASON IS—" OFTEN WHEN YOU SPEAK!
GET SMART NOW!
HANG ON? WHAT ARE YOU DOING SLACKING OFF!? I HAD TO DO THE SHOPPING ALL BY MYSELF!!
I AM SLACKING OFF! AND THE REASON IS...
...IS, UMM... I'M SLACKING OFF!!
YES, I CAN SEE THAT.
WHAT'S THIS BOOK FOR? YOU WANT TO SOUND SMART?
GIVE IT UP, HONEY. YOU'RE DUMB AS A ROCK.
THE REASON IS...!!
WELL, IT WOULDN'T BE VERY NICE TO SAY ALOUD...

**INTRO**

HELLO, AND THANK YOU FOR PICKING UP THE THIRD VOLUME OF *INUBOKU*. I'M THE CREATOR, FUJIWARA, AND I CAN'T SLEEP AT NIGHT BECAUSE I WORRY THAT PEOPLE MUST BE GETTING SICK OF THIS SERIES EVEN THOUGH IT'S ONLY THE THIRD VOLUME!

**ANEC-DOTE**

BUT WHAT STICKS OUT MOST IN MY MIND FROM VOLUME THREE, I THINK, IS THE THING WITH THE PRAYING MANTIS. EDITING THE PHOTO OF MY OWN HAND HOLDING UP THAT POOR BUG WAS A PRETTY INDESCRIBABLE FEELING...MY EDITOR, WHO GOT THE MATERIALS TOGETHER, SEEMED TO BE OVERCOME WITH THAT FEELING TOO. IT WAS QUITE THE EXPERIENCE.

AND RIRICHIYO AND SOUSHI START GOING OUT IN THIS VOLUME. I GET ASKED A LOT HOW FAR THEY'RE ACTUALLY GOING, BUT I'M LEAVING THAT UP TO YOUR IMAGINATION... IF I MAY SAY JUST ONE THING, THOUGH—SOUSHI IS AN EXTREME SORT OF PERSON. (LOL)

THANK YOU FOR READING THIS FAR! THE STORY IS REALLY GOING TO TAKE OFF IN VOLUME FOUR, SO BE SURE TO PICK IT UP! I'LL BE THRILLED IF YOU DO!

special thanks

| | |
|---|---|
| MY EDITOR | MY MOM |
| REI-CHAN | YAMAMOTO-SENSEI |
| MY DEAR TEPPEI | MY DEAR JET |
| MY DEAR SUMIDA | and you... ♡ |

**CLOS-ING**

maison de ayakashi

Welcome to Maison de Ayakashi.
The exclusive Secret Service of
this Mansion guarantees
your mental and physical
safely by providing
superior escorts.

# SHE LIKES CUTE THINGS

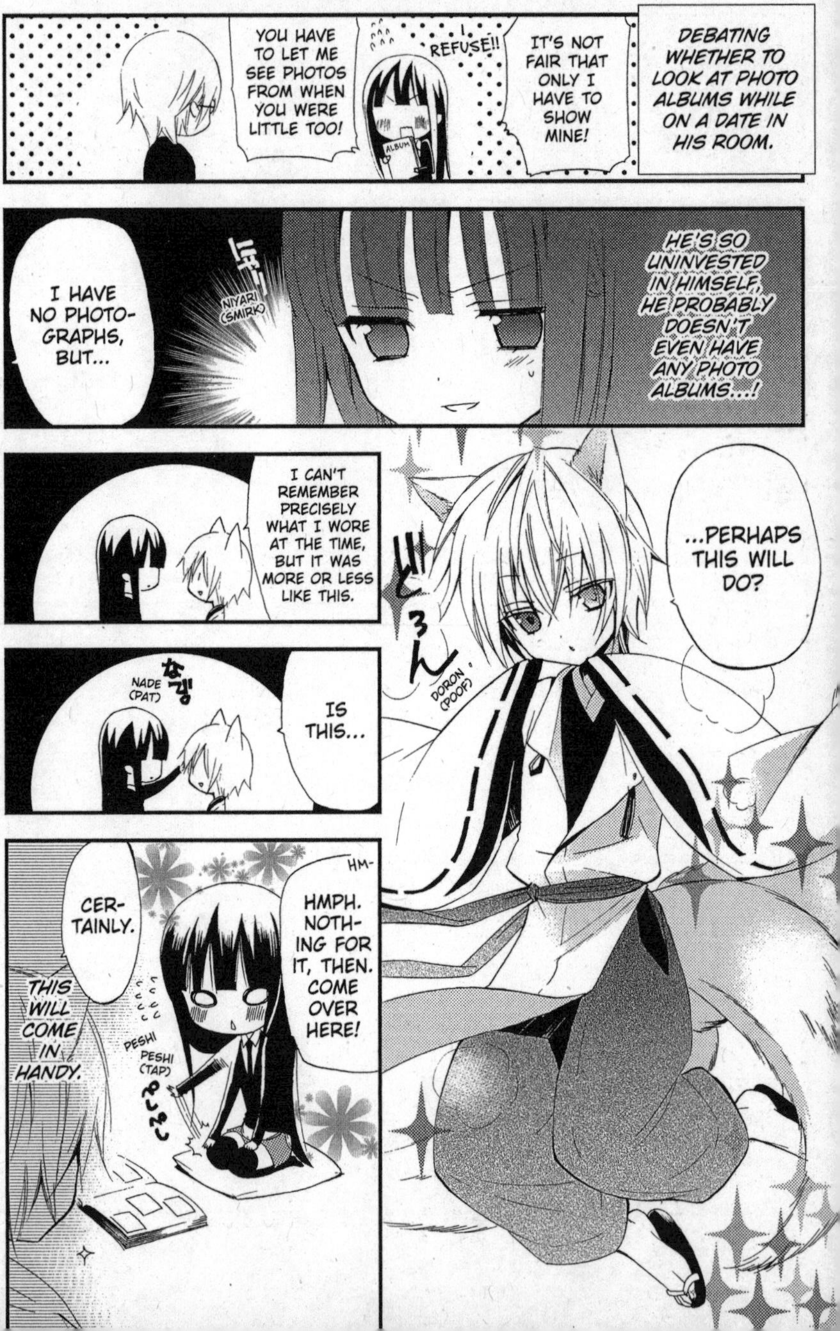
DEBATING WHETHER TO LOOK AT PHOTO ALBUMS WHILE ON A DATE IN HIS ROOM.
IT'S NOT FAIR THAT ONLY I HAVE TO SHOW MINE!
I REFUSE!!
YOU HAVE TO LET ME SEE PHOTOS FROM WHEN YOU WERE LITTLE TOO!
ALBUM
HE'S SO UNINVESTED IN HIMSELF, HE PROBABLY DOESN'T EVEN HAVE ANY PHOTO ALBUMS...!
NIYARI (SMIRK)
I HAVE NO PHOTO-GRAPHS, BUT...
...PERHAPS THIS WILL DO?
DORON (POOF)
I CAN'T REMEMBER PRECISELY WHAT I WORE AT THE TIME, BUT IT WAS MORE OR LESS LIKE THIS.
IS THIS...
NADE (PAT)
HM-HMPH. NOTH-ING FOR IT, THEN. COME OVER HERE!
CER-TAINLY.
PESHI PESHI (TAP)
THIS WILL COME IN HANDY.

## CONVERSATIONS IN THE BATH FROM CHAPTER 11

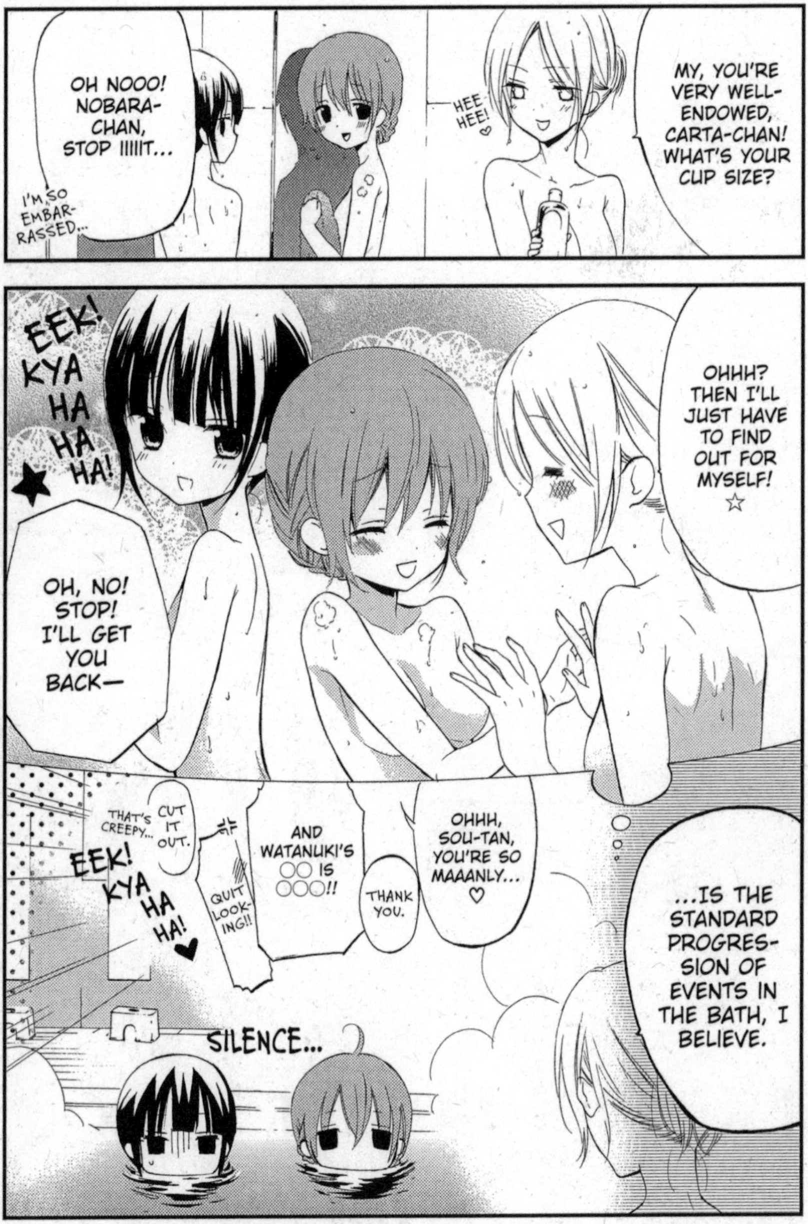
MY, YOU'RE VERY WELL-ENDOWED, CARTA-CHAN! WHAT'S YOUR CUP SIZE?
HEE HEE! ♡
OH NOOO! NOBARA-CHAN, STOP IIIIIT...
I'M SO EMBARRASSED...
OHHH? THEN I'LL JUST HAVE TO FIND OUT FOR MYSELF! ☆
OH, NO! STOP! I'LL GET YOU BACK—
EEK! KYA HA HA HA!
...IS THE STANDARD PROGRESSION OF EVENTS IN THE BATH, I BELIEVE.
OHHH, SOU-TAN, YOU'RE SO MAAANLY... ♡
THANK YOU.
AND WATANUKI'S ○○ IS ○○○!!
QUIT LOOKING!!
CUT IT OUT.
THAT'S CREEPY...
EEK! KYA HA HA HA! ♥
SILENCE...

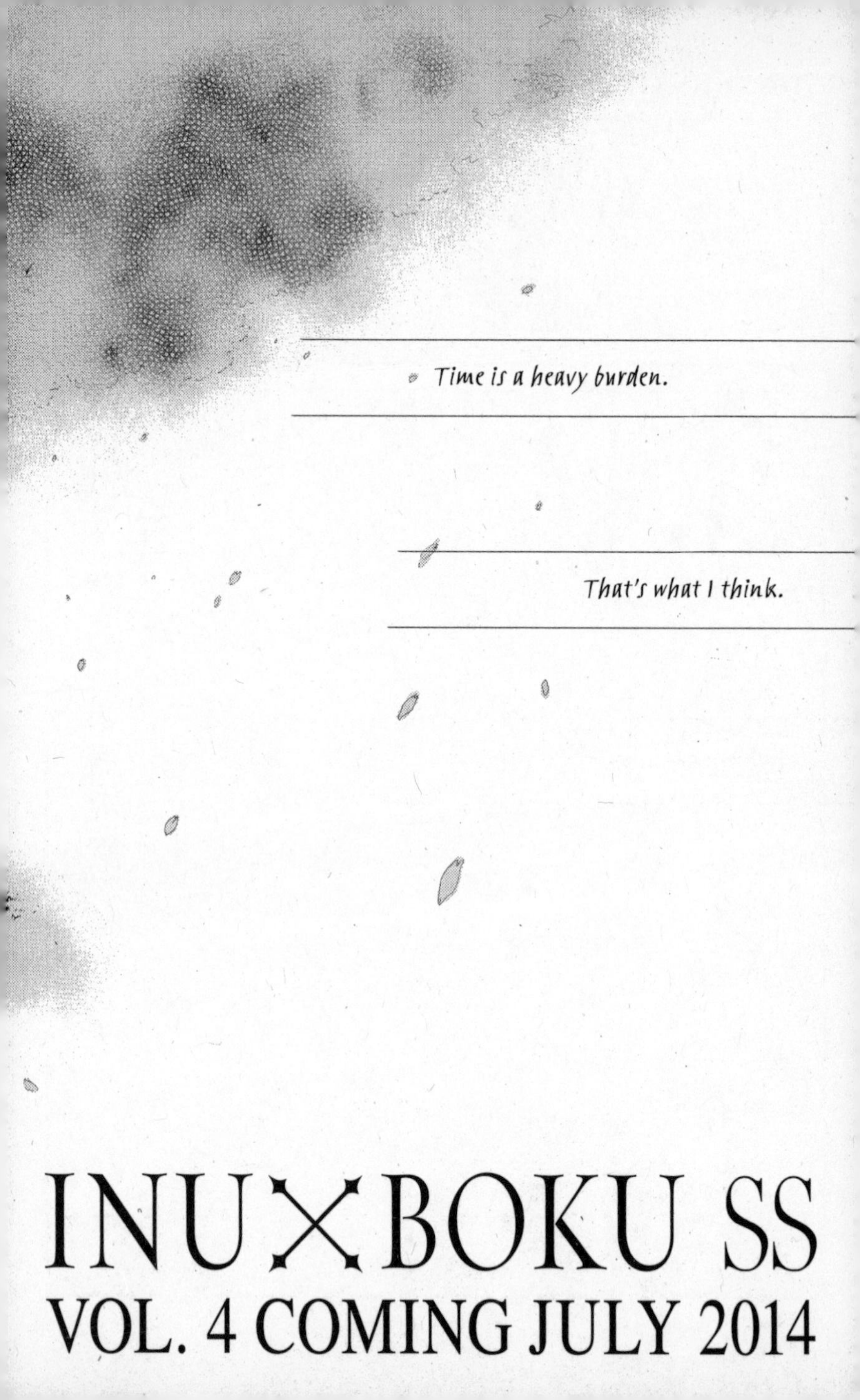
Time is a heavy burden.
That's what I think.
INU×BOKU SS
VOL. 4 COMING JULY 2014

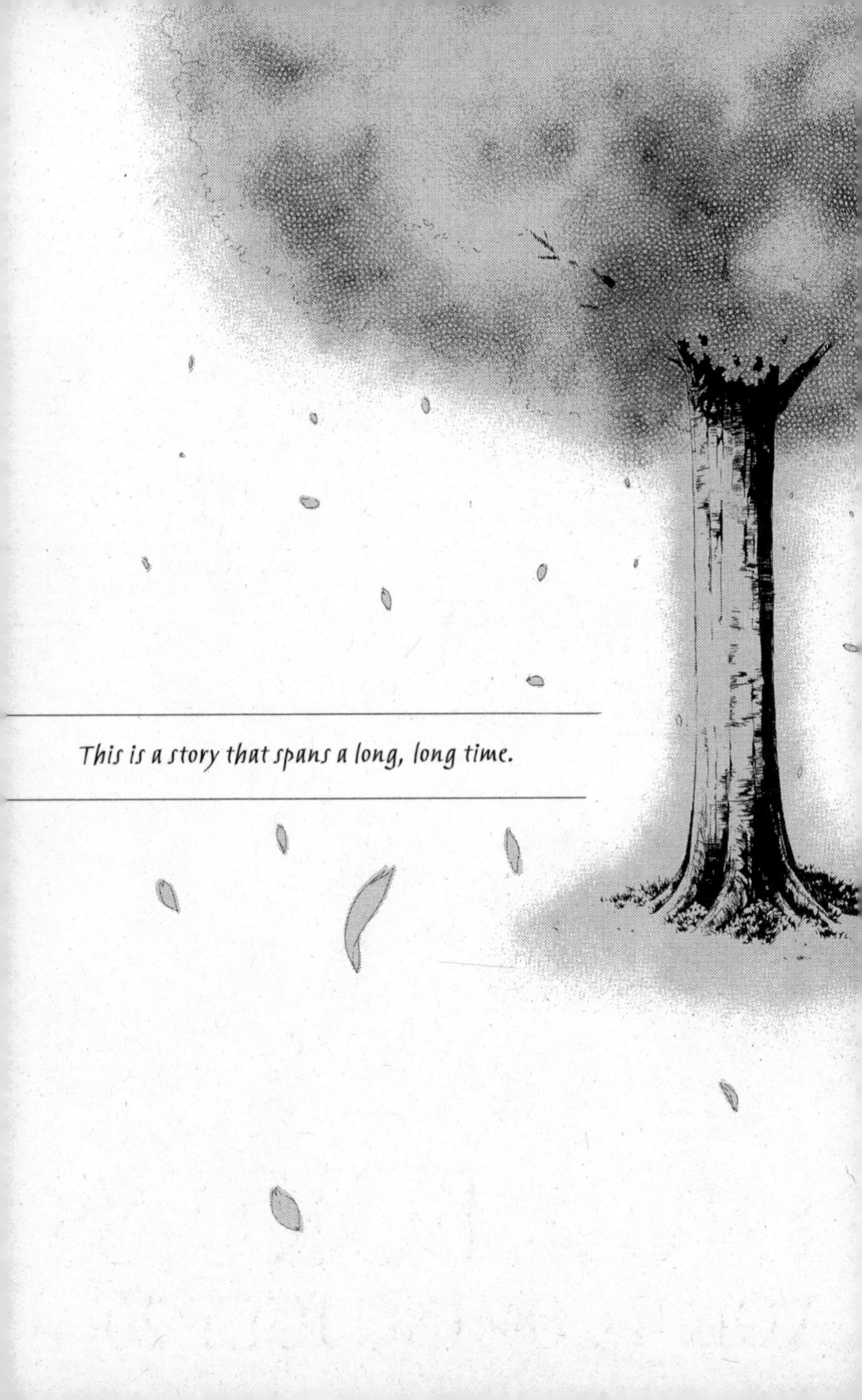
This is a story that spans a long, long time.

# TRANSLATION NOTES

**COMMON HONORIFICS**

**no honorific:** Indicates familiarity or closeness; if used without permission or reason, addressing someone in this manner would be an insult.

**-san:** The Japanese equivalent of Mr./Mrs./Miss. If a situation calls for politeness, this is the fail-safe honorific.

**-sama:** Conveys great respect; may also indicate that the social status of the speaker is lower than that of the addressee.

**-kun:** Used most often when referring to boys, this indicates affection or familiarity. Occasionally used by older men among their peers, but it may also be used by anyone referring to a person of lower standing.

**-chan, -tan:** An affectionate honorific indicating familiarity used mostly in reference to girls; also used in reference to cute persons or animals of either gender.

Used throughout the original text, *youkai* and *ayakashi* are umbrella terms for ghosts, monsters, haunted objects, mythical animals, and all sorts of uncanny things from Japanese folklore.

**PAGE 116**

*Taiyaki* is a fish-shaped pastry made of pancake batter filled with sweet red bean paste. Maybe it would look gory if you bit the head off, but whatever part you eat first, it's pretty tasty.

**PAGE 120**

**Kamen Rider** is a long-running TV and movie franchise that debuted in 1971. The protagonist is a grasshopper-like costumed hero who fights supervillains. *Tokusatsu* entertainment like the Kamen Rider series refers to live-action productions that make liberal use of special effects. One of the most popular *tokusatsu* series in the U.S. is the Power Rangers series.

INU×BOKU SS

# To become the ultimate weapon, one boy must eat the souls of 99 humans...

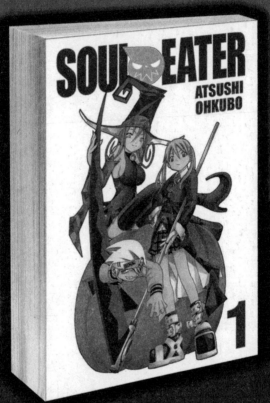

## ...and one witch.

Maka is a scythe meister, working to perfect her demon scythe until it is good enough to become Death's Weapon—the weapon used by Shinigami-sama, the spirit of Death himself. And if that isn't strange enough, her scythe also has the power to change form—into a human-looking boy!

The Phantomhive family has a butler who's almost too good to be true...

...or maybe he's just too good to be human.

# Black Butler

## YANA TOBOSO

**VOLUMES 1-16 IN STORES NOW!**

Yen Press

www.yenpress.com

BLACK BUTLER © Yana Toboso / SQUARE ENIX
Yen Press is an imprint of Hachette Book Group.

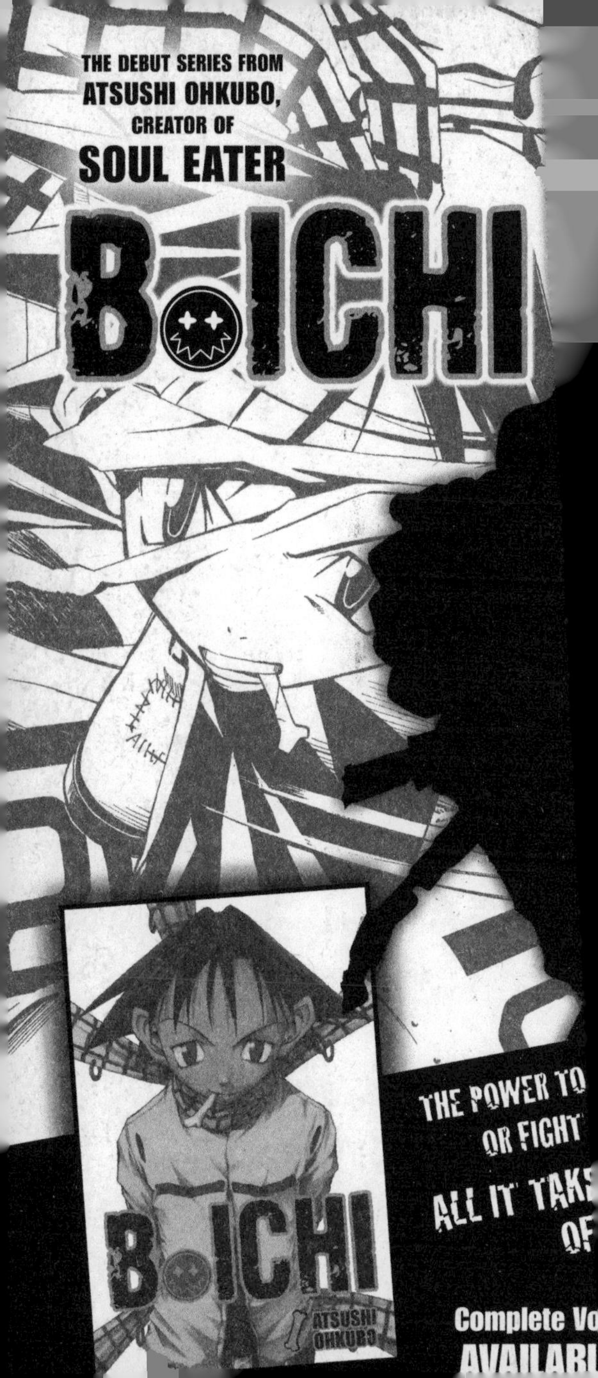
THE DEBUT SERIES FROM
ATSUSHI OHKUBO,
CREATOR OF
SOUL EATER
B●ICHI
THE POWER TO
OR FIGHT
ALL IT TAK
OF
B●ICHI
ATSUSHI
OHKUBO
Complete Vo
AVAILABL

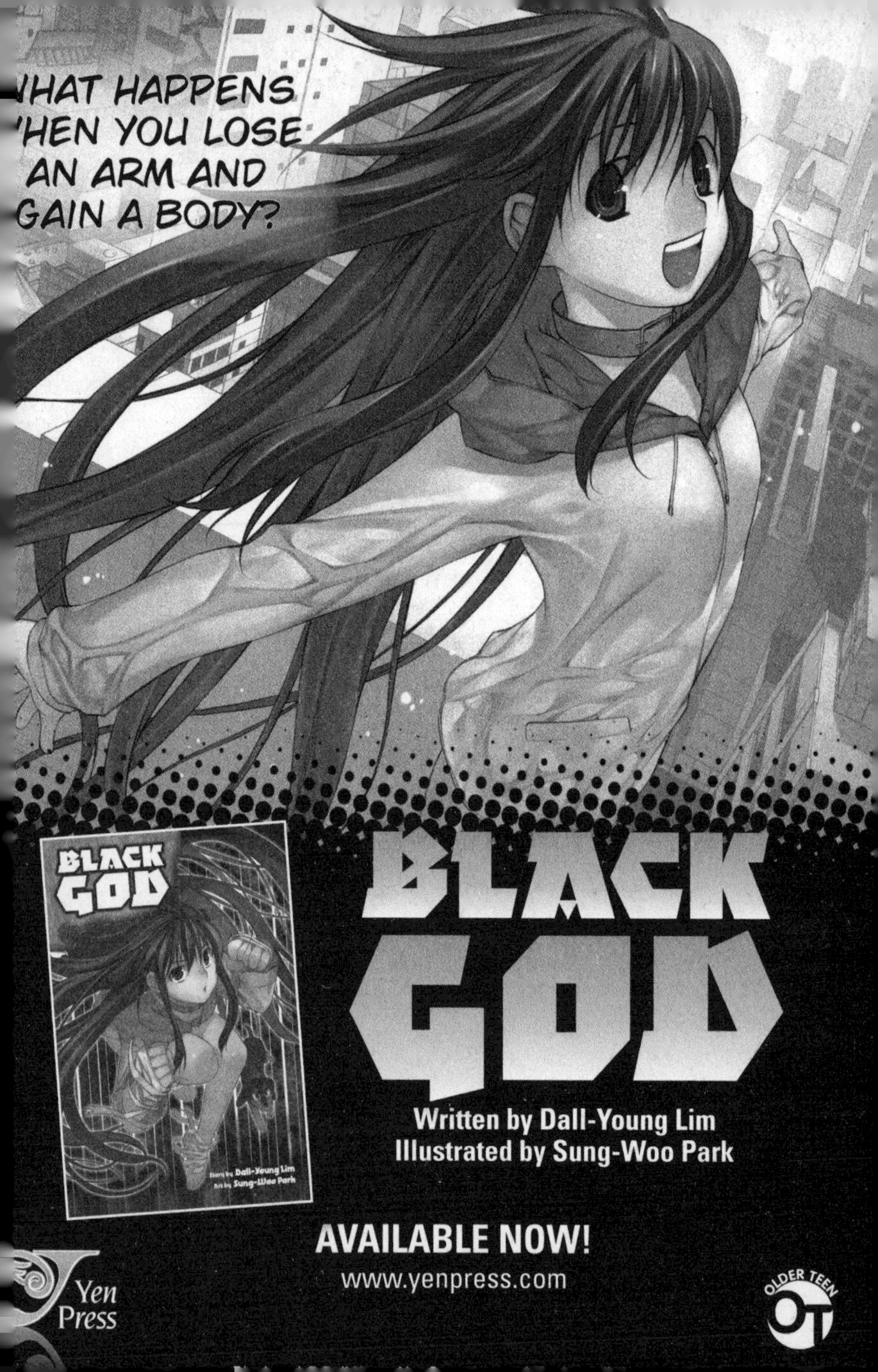

HAT HAPPENS
HEN YOU LOSE
AN ARM AND
GAIN A BODY?
BLACK GOD
Story by Dall-Young Lim
Art by Sung-Woo Park
BLACK GOD
Written by Dall-Young Lim
Illustrated by Sung-Woo Park
AVAILABLE NOW!
www.yenpress.com
Yen Press
OLDER TEEN
OT

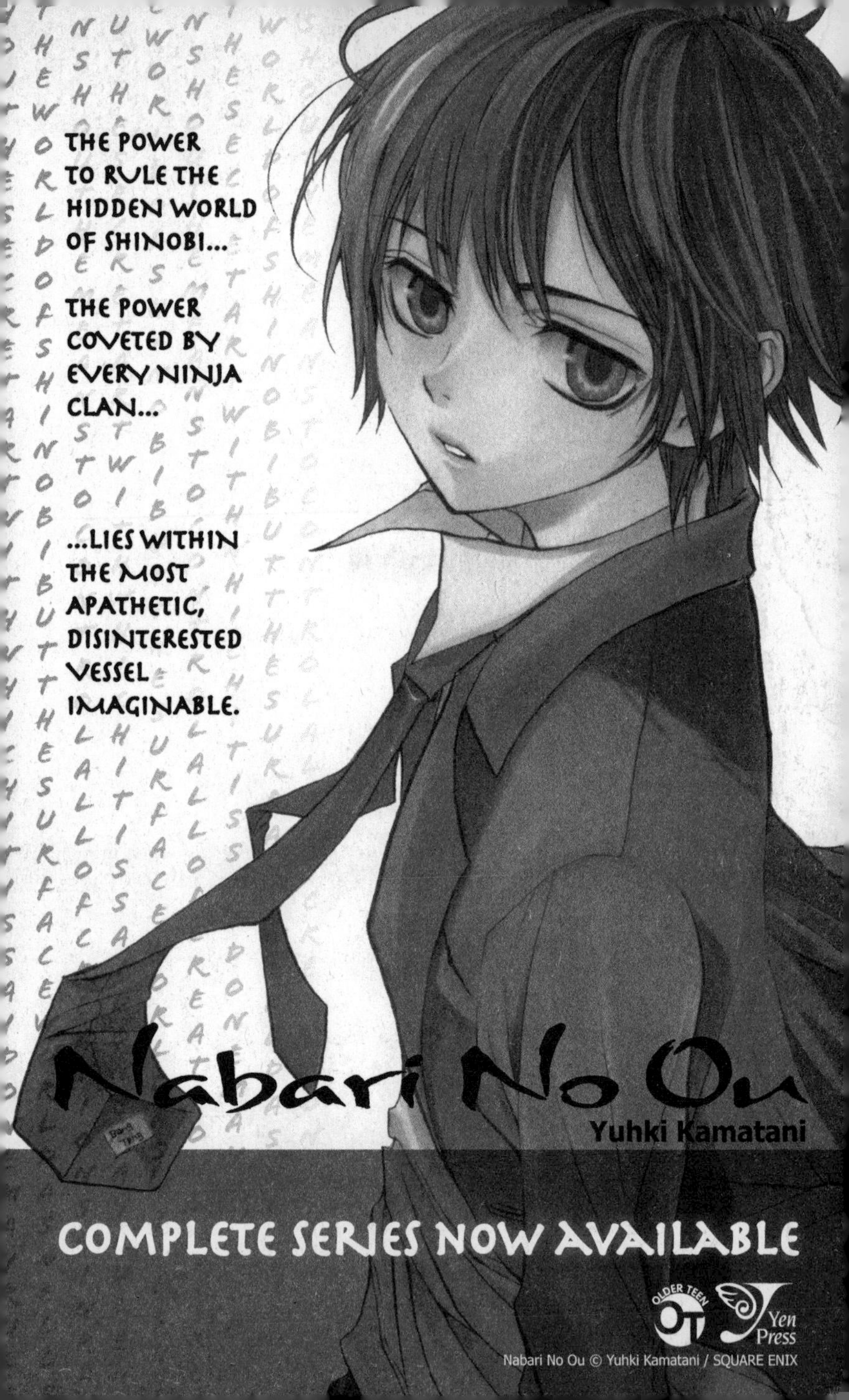
THE POWER TO RULE THE HIDDEN WORLD OF SHINOBI...
THE POWER COVETED BY EVERY NINJA CLAN...
...LIES WITHIN THE MOST APATHETIC, DISINTERESTED VESSEL IMAGINABLE.
Nabari No Ou
Yuhki Kamatani
COMPLETE SERIES NOW AVAILABLE
OLDER TEEN OT
Yen Press
Nabari No Ou © Yuhki Kamatani / SQUARE ENIX

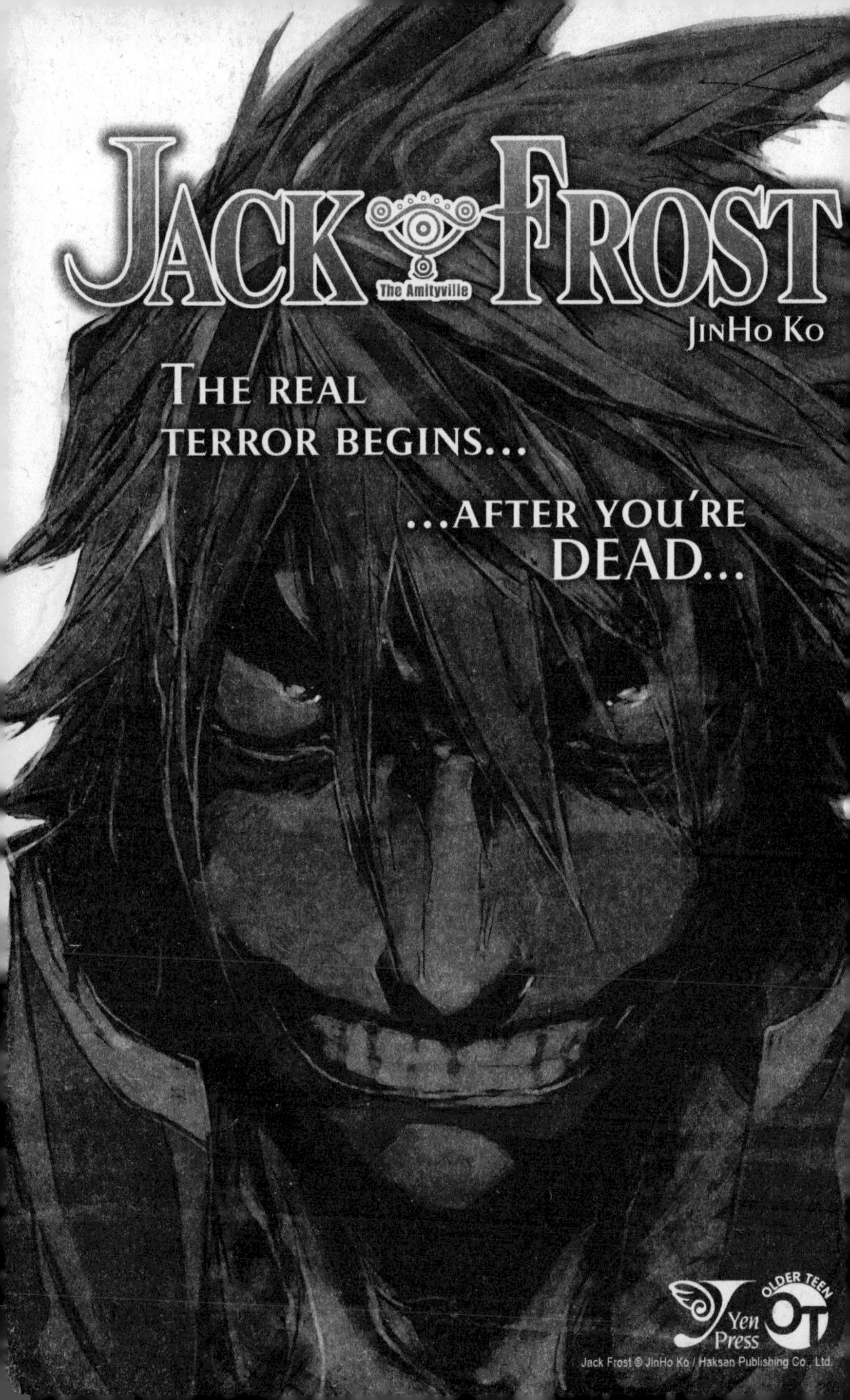
JACK FROST
The Amityville
JINHO KO
THE REAL TERROR BEGINS...
...AFTER YOU'RE DEAD...
Yen Press
OLDER TEEN
OT
Jack Frost © JinHo Ko / Haksan Publishing Co., Ltd.

# INU X BOKU SS ❸

## COCOA FUJIWARA

**Translation: Melissa Tanaka • Lettering: Abigail Blackman**

This book is a work of fiction. Names, characters, places, and incidents are the product of the author's imagination or are used fictitiously. Any resemblance to actual events, locales, or persons, living or dead, is coincidental.

INUBOKU SECRET SERVICE Vol. 3 © 2010 Cocoa Fujiwara / SQUARE ENIX CO., LTD. First published in Japan in 2010 by SQUARE ENIX CO., LTD. English translation rights arranged with SQUARE ENIX CO., LTD. and Hachette Book Group through Tuttle-Mori Agency, Inc., Tokyo.

Translation © 2014 by SQUARE ENIX CO., LTD.

Yen Press
Hachette Book Group
237 Park Avenue, New York, NY 10017

www.HachetteBookGroup.com
www.YenPress.com

Yen Press is an imprint of Hachette Book Group, Inc. The Yen Press name and logo are trademarks of Hachette Book Group, Inc.

First Yen Press Edition: April 2014

ISBN: 978-0-316-32209-6

10  9  8  7  6  5  4  3  2  1

BVG

Printed in the United States of America